Early Images of the Americas

EARLY IMAGES
OF THE
AMERICAS

Transfer and Invention

Edited by

Jerry M. Williams
& Robert E. Lewis

THE UNIVERSITY OF ARIZONA PRESS
Tucson & London

The University of Arizona Press
Copyright © 1993
The Arizona Board of Regents
All rights reserved
∞ This book is printed on acid-free, archival-quality
paper.
Manufactured in the United States of America

98 97 96 95 94 93   6 5 4 3 2 1

Library of Congress Cataloging-in-Publication Data
Early images of the Americas : transfer and invention /
    edited by Jerry M. Williams and Robert E. Lewis.
        p.   cm.
    Includes index.
    ISBN 0-8165-1184-5 (acid-free paper)
    1. Latin America—Civilization—16th century.
2. Latin America—Description and travel. 3. Indians—
First contact with Europeans. 4. America—Relations—
Europe. 5. Europe—Relations—America. I. Williams,
Jerry M., 1952– .II. Lewis, Robert Earl, 1946–
    F1411.E27   1993
    980'.013—dc20   92-36116
                                                    CIP

British Cataloguing-in-Publication Data
A catalogue record for this book is available from the
British Library.

An earlier version of Chapter 5 originally appeared in
the *William and Mary Quarterly*, 3d ser., 49 (1992):
183–209.

Thanks to Martín and Camilo Lewis-González for
understanding the demands made on their father's time and
attention by this project.   REL

To Sallie B. Smith, for the song in her voice . . .
and to the childhood and future of Corey, Damon, and
Sean.   JMW

Contents

Contributors

MAUREEN AHERN is Professor of Spanish at Ohio State University in Columbus. She published "The Certification of Cibola in the 'Relación de Fray Marcos de Niza'" in *Dispositio* (1989). Another study on "The Articulation of Alterity on the Northern Frontier" in Fernando de Alarcón's account of his navigation of the Colorado River is forthcoming in a collection of studies in honor of Lewis Hanke. She is currently completing a book on narratives of first contact on the northern frontiers of New Spain from 1527 to 1583. Professor Ahern also published *A Rosario Castellanos Reader* (1988).

SANTA ARIAS is Visiting Assistant Professor of Spanish at Wake Forest University. She has published several articles on Bartolomé de Las Casas, including "La *Historia de las Indias* de Bartolomé de las Casas: Estrategias de poder y de persuasión" in *Confluencia* (1991) and "Autoescritura y autoridad de la escritura de la historia de Bartolomé de las Casas" in *Semiosis* (1992). She is also author of "Escribiendo el suroeste: Relaciones poéticas y políticas de exploración" forthcoming in *Texto Crítico*. Currently her research focuses on Latin American colonial history of the sixteenth century and Cuban and Puerto Rican literature in the United States.

ANGEL DELGADO-GÓMEZ is Associate Professor of Spanish Literature at the University of Notre Dame. He is the author of several articles on Golden-Age Spanish literature and historiography, and a critical edition of the Hernando Cortés *Cartas de relación* (in press). Professor Delgado-Gómez was a National Endowment for the Humanities Fellow at the John Carter Brown Library in Providence, Rhode Island, in 1986.

MARGARET S. DILKE is the author of articles on education, geography, and the environment. With O.A.W. Dilke, she has published essays on geography and the history of cartography. She was joint editor of *Dunbartonshire* in The Third Statistical Account of Scotland (1958); editor of *Field Studies for Schools*, vols. 1–2 (1965); and joint editor of *Experiments in the Teaching of Geography* (1981).

OSWALD A. W. DILKE is Professor of Latin (Emeritus) at the University of Leeds. He has published editions of Statius, Horace, and Lucan and wrote *The Roman Land Surveyors* (1971; Italian trans. 1979), *The Ancient Romans: How They Lived and Worked* (1974), *Roman Books and Their Impact* (1977), and *Greek and Roman Maps* (1985). He contributed to J. B. Harley and D. Woodward's *The History of Cartography*, vol. 1 (1987), and *Mathematics and Measurement* in the series Reading the Past (British Museum Publications, 1987; German trans. 1991). He has also published articles on Latin and on ancient surveying as well as on ancient geography and cartography (many jointly with Margaret S. Dilke).

HARRY KELSEY is Mead Fellow at the Huntington Library in San Marino, California. He is the author of *Juan Rodríguez Cabrillo* (1986), a biography of the sixteenth-century explorer of the California coast. He was recently awarded the Orden de Isabel la Católica by the King of Spain, Juan Carlos I.

ROBERT E. LEWIS is Assistant Professor of Spanish and Latin American Literature at Louisiana State University. He is the author of articles on Bartolomé de Las Casas, Alvar Núñez Cabeza de Vaca, Francisco López de Gómara, and Bernal Díaz del Castillo, which have appeared in the *Revista de Indias*, the *Revista Iberoamericana*, and in published collections of essays on Latin American literature. His article "Los *Naufragios* de Alvar Núñez: Historia y ficción" is being republished in a collection of studies on Núñez (in press).

STEPHANIE MERRIM is Professor of Hispanic Studies at Brown University. She has written many articles on sixteenth-, seventeenth-, and twentieth-century Latin American topics. She is also the author of *Logos and the Word* (1983). Most recently, she edited and contributed to *Feminist Perspectives* on *Sor Juana Inés de la Cruz* (1991). A long-standing focus of her research is the early historiography of the New World, and her articles on the subject have appeared in *Dispositio, Revista Iberoamericana, Modern Language Notes,* and the *Revista de Estudios Hispánicos.*

KATHLEEN ANN MYERS is Associate Professor of Spanish at Indiana University in Bloomington. Professor Myers has published articles on Gonzalo Fernández de Oviedo and Sor Juana Inés de la Cruz in *Hispania,* the *Michigan Quarterly Review,* and the *Revista Canadiense de Estudios Hispánicos,* and has contributed essays to books on women writers, specifically the writings of nuns in colonial Latin America. She is the author of *Word from New Spain: The Spiritual Autobiography of María de San Joseph (1656–1719)* (1992). Currently she is working on a monograph on Fernández de Oviedo.

MICHAEL PALENCIA-ROTH is Professor of Comparative Literature, Criticism and Interpretive Theory, and Latin American Studies, and is Director of the Program in Comparative Literature, at the University of Illinois. His publications include *Perspectives on Faust* (1983), *Gabriel García Márquez: La línea, el círculo y las metamorfosis del mito* (1984), and *Myth and the Modern Novel* (1987). He has also written essays on Germanic subjects, English literature, Latin American literature, and comparative civilizational topics. He recently served as the president of the International Society for the Comparative Study of Civilizations.

CAROLYN PRAGER is Dean of the College of Arts and Sciences at Franklin University. Her most recent publications include "'Blak as a bla mon': Reflections Upon a Medieval English Image of the Non-European" in *Studies in Medieval and Renaissance Teaching,* and "The Problem of Slavery" in *The Custom of the Country.* She is currently working on a full-length study of the relationships among gender, race, and slavery in English Renaissance drama.

JOSÉ RABASA is Assistant Professor of Spanish at the University of Maryland at College Park. He has published articles in *Cultural Critique, Hispanic Issues, Dispositio,* and *Poetics Today.* The topics of his writings range from the rhetoric of cartography in Mercator's *Atlas* to the culture of conquest in Alvar Núñez's *Naufragios* and *Comentarios.* He is the author of *Inventing America: Spanish Historiography and the Formation of Eurocentrism* (1993) and is completing a book-length study of the colonization and written accounts of Florida and New Mexico, *Representing Violence on the Northern Frontier: Sixteenth-Century Cíbola and Florida.*

ANTONIO RODRÍGUEZ-BUCKINGHAM is Professor of Library Science at
the University of Southern Mississippi. He is the author of a number of
articles on early typography and problems related to the semiotics of
book illustration and image transfer in sixteenth-century Mexican and
Peruvian imprints. He has been a visiting professor at various universities, including the University of Puerto Rico in 1990. He spent the summer of 1991 at the Escuela de Estudios Hispano-Americanos in Seville,
with a grant from the National Endowment for the Humanities and
Ohio State University.

PATRICIA SEED teaches in the Department of History at Rice University. She
is the author of *To Love, Honor, and Obey in Colonial Mexico: Conflicts Over
Marriage Choice, 1573–1821* (1988), which won the 1989 Bolton Prize, and
has published articles on colonial and postcolonial discourse in the *Latin
American Research Review* and on poststructuralism in postcolonial history
in the *Maryland Historian*. Professor Seed's essay in this collection originally appeared in the *William and Mary Quarterly* in 1992. It is part of a
comparative history of European expansion entitled *The Politics and Ceremony of European Expansion in the Americas*.

JERRY M. WILLIAMS is Associate Professor of Spanish and Latin American
Studies at West Chester University in Pennsylvania. Professor Williams
is the author of *El teatro del México colonial: Época misionera* (1992) and *Censorship and Art in Pre-Enlightenment Lima: Pedro de Peralta Barnuevo's 'Diálogo de
los muertos: La causa académica'* (in press). He has published essays on colonial historiography, Latin American theatre, the early history of science, religious iconography, and censorship in journals such as *Chasqui,
Brasil/Brazil*, the *Luso-Brazilian Review*, the *Revista Canadiense de Estudios Hispánicos, Hispanófila*, the *Revista de Estudios Hispánicos*, and *La Palabra y el Hombre*.

Preface

Beyond Columbus and the physical encounter, conquest, and colonization of Hispanic America lies an intellectual and religious movement that embraces vast and challenging bodies of new knowledge in branches of science, theology, historiography, ethnography, and literature. The approach to decoding the significance of the New World invokes the use of fundamentals to be found in these disciplines. In this volume the notion of a transatlantic encounter (rather than discovery) and of the transfer and exchange of materials, ideas, and customs is examined using the theories of cultural criticism and their attempt to define the correspondence between literature and history.

The geographical presence of a continent previously unknown to Europeans and the resulting doubling of the circumference of the world stimulated Old World thinking and sensibilities, pitting them against New World realities and phenomena. Unsettling questions continue to occasion uneven considerations regarding new images of humankind and nature, the ethics of conquest and enslavement, theological inquiries, and practical and theoretical aspects of evangelization.

We believe there is a need for a volume that brings together research efforts that represent unique approaches to the literary and historical legacy of colonial Latin America. Traditional scholarship has favored discipline-specific articles and monographs that study only isolated aspects of the colonial ethos. *Early Images of the Americas* is therefore a way of engaging in dialogue with contributors about the diversity of the colonial world and the best critical methods for its study. The purpose of this collection is to present to both specialists

and nonspecialists an overview of the complexities that govern diverse manifestations of sixteenth-century Hispanic-American letters. The editors seek to
appeal to a broad-based audience by limiting the focus primarily—though not
exclusively—to an examination of the sixteenth century. These essays are
from American and European researchers who represent diverse fields of
specialization and whose works offer perspectives that enrich and reevaluate
the canon. All the contributions provide an interdisciplinary focus and cross-
reference distinct bodies of knowledge.

The essays in Part I challenge the legitimacy and efficacy of utopian and
barbaric icons of indigenous cultures that have traditionally encouraged writers to describe the New World in negative terms. The ethical and moral di-
lemmas brought on by the first century of contact were rooted in changing
perceptions of the Native Americans, particularly among missionaries, and
in juridical responses of the Church and the State to New World practices
among the natives. This also made possible the sociopolitical reworking of
traditional European valuations of peoples such as Africans, Moors, and Turks
who were at odds with Christian sensibility. The commonly held notion of
the Indian as noble savage is challenged by Angel Delgado-Gómez's analysis
of reports representative of the first thirty years of the encounter. Far from
depicting an idealized and prejudiced image, early writers showed evidence
of realism and independence of thought. The force exerted by Europe's obsession with cannibalism is examined by Michael Palencia-Roth through cultural perceptions and definitions that have influenced the historical record.
Palencia-Roth deciphers iconographic and cartographic aspects of anthropophagi in a refutation of present and past assessments. José Rabasa appraises
missionary writings spanning the first hundred years of Spanish colonization
in Mexico and sees them as constituting the basis for forming judgments regarding the practice, nature, and efficacy of conversion; various conceptualizations of indigenous religious beliefs; and patterns in the transformation of
native cultures. For Carolyn Prager, the sixteenth-century English literature of
conquest and "discovery" reconfigures the image of the African, amplifying
older chromatic or metaphoric valuations with newer economic and political
ones. In the initial quest for empire in America, the English transferred and
invented the image of the African destined for the Americas within the seemingly incompatible constructs of ally and slave.

Historical and literary invention as essential components of the cross-
cultural transfer of authority lies at the heart of the essays in Part II. These
essays argue for the centrality of language as a cultural tool for rewriting the

history of the New World and for promoting alternative views of both the colonizers and the colonized. The fundamental issue is that of the relationship between writing and the major undertaking of nascent sixteenth-century empires: colonization and its attendant consequences. While the conquest of the New World was often physically established by military means or by occupation, the authority for these actions was substantiated by the skillful use of language in written texts. By contrasting two highly divergent enactments of imperial authority—taking possession and reading texts—Patricia Seed adjudges cultural differences between England and Spain in their respective means of claiming possession and securing political authority over colonial territories. In the early historiography of the New World, topics, motifs, and formulas pass from text to text and change meaning according to the context in which they are used. Stephanie Merrim studies the textual family of writings of the first fifty years, with Columbus's diary as the prototype for the demythifying chronicles of Bartolomé de Las Casas. The juridical and theological arguments Las Casas used to subvert satanic and conflicting descriptions found in official histories was an inventive frame for describing the superior moral position of the Indian. This process, as related by Santa Arias, is understood as demarginalizing the native Americans and delegitimating the official negative stereotype for Renaissance readers.

The symbolic dimensions of the representation of New World realities during the first half of the sixteenth century are addressed in Part III. Deciphering the communicative role of visual illustrations in colonial historiography and the ways in which symbolic objects become bridges for cultural mediation or catalysts for cultural collision in the American context is crucial to comprehending the transfer of information from one context to another. To this end, Kathleen Myers discusses the verbal and iconographic modes of representation employed by Spain's first official chronicler of the New World, Gonzalo Fernández de Oviedo, to convey information about American phenomena. Through the illustrative drawings in his history, Oviedo emphasized the basis of his criterion for the representation of history as the primacy of sight and experience. In response to the Myers essay, Maureen Ahern shows that, in the two earliest reports of European and Amerindian contacts beyond the northernmost frontiers of New Spain, cultural interactions were carried out through the appropriation of ritual signs. A discursive reading of the production and reception of these signs in the two reports demonstrates how crucial a role the semiosis of cross-cultural communication played in determining paradigms of cultural contacts in the region.

Europe's geographical confrontation with the changing boundaries of science are reevaluated in light of the transfer and invention of cosmographic and cartographic knowledge in initial reports about America. In Part IV, further European scientific developments and new sources for the construction of books and maps are discussed along with the changes they suggest for later theoretical models. Data gleaned from experiments indicate how, in the process of applying them, European knowledge was transformed; how Old World notions evolved in response to New World empiricism; and how revisions of scientific language and traditions were gradually received.

Harry Kelsey's contribution to this volume concerns the sources of information and methods used in map construction, together with how map legends recorded significant events in the course of exploring the American coasts. Kelsey demonstrates that the Sancho Gutiérrez planisphere reflects the cartographic views of Spanish pilots and cosmographers of the mid sixteenth century.

The Ptolemaic model, argue Oswald A. W. Dilke and Margaret Dilke, established a scientific basis for the development of American cartography and exploration, one that was not rendered outmoded as a result of the age of discovery. Coordinates compiled by Ptolemy thirteen centuries before were the point of departure for many changes, and the Dilkes examine them in relation to later theoretical models. The science of bookmaking and printing in America, in the estimation of Antonio Rodríguez-Buckingham, reveals books that are a conflation of both worlds. He argues for a greater incidence of informational transfer between Europe and Mexico in the art of printing than was previously assumed for the period. An analysis of the decorative initial letters adorning a sample of English and Mexican books proves that many of their motifs are similar. Other observations of early book technology, made with the help of modern computers and documentary evidence, strongly suggest the need to reevaluate commonly held views about the early history of the book industry in the New World and the technological and intellectual relations between sixteenth-century America and Europe.

Each essay in this volume thus serves as an introduction to a polemical aspect of the history of the New World and prepares readers for more advanced studies, which is reinforced by detailed bibliographic information. English translations are provided for most quotations from foreign languages, and in most instances, excerpts in the foreign language remain faithful in orthography to the original source cited.

The editors have attempted to address the issue of exclusionary language, particularly the use of the terms *Amerindian* and *Native American* versus *Indian*. The latter is applied within the context of sixteenth-century historical-literary discourse and is in keeping with the form and dialogue of early chronicles; the former terms are employed in full deference to contemporary political and cultural discourse. In assessing the impact of encounter, we also address the role played by language (written, oral, signed, and iconographic) and the debate it has continued to inspire. Terms such as *encounter* and *contact* are favored in this volume over *discovery*, a word that betrays a Eurocentric perspective and the critical appreciations associated with it to the exclusion of Native American points of view.

In the initial and final stages of the project, we were encouraged by helpful informative exchanges from several colleagues, particularly Robert R. Bensen, George Cunningham, Walter Mignolo, and Stanko Vranich. Others who contributed in meaningful ways to the project include Felix Bolaños, Francisco Javier Cevallos, Audrey Duckett, Carlton Goodwin, Vilma Manzotti, Margaret Parker, Angela Robledo, Enrique Sacerio-Garí, C. Christopher Soufas, Karen Stolley, and Daniel Torres. We acknowledge with gratitude David Prout's careful reading of the manuscript in draft form.

We are grateful to the following institutions for their support in the form of financial assistance, research grants, and travel opportunities: the Graduate Research Council of Louisiana State University, the National Endowment for the Humanities, the Fulbright-Hays Commission, the Newberry Library Columbian Quincentennial Fellowship program, the Pennsylvania State System of Higher Education, the University of Illinois/University of Chicago Joint Center for Latin American Studies, the University of Pittsburgh Research Fellowship program in Latin American Studies, the West Chester University Dean of the College of Arts and Sciences Support and Development Awards program, and the West Chester University Research and Publications Committee.

In particular, we wish to acknowledge various staff members of the John Carter Brown Library, the Louisiana State University libraries, the Newberry Library, the University of Chicago, the University of Pennsylvania, and West Chester University for their research assistance. We are especially thankful to Susan Danforth of the John Carter Brown Library and David Buisseret of the Newberry Library for their counsel.

Joanne O'Hare of the University of Arizona Press has been a patient and helpful editor whose direction and support we relied on during times of uncertainty. Her commitment to this book was encouraging to us at every stage of its development. Likewise, it has been a rewarding experience for us to work with Alan M. Schroder, our manuscript editor, whose critical eye and thoroughness helped shape the final version.

Special thanks to Patricia Mason-Browne for her years of inspiration and Emma Walton for her ability to nurture. We also thank Munish Agarwal and Chris Williams for research assistance; John Fleury and Todd McKay for photographic assistance; and the many colleagues and contributors whose interest made this collaborative venture possible.

Introduction

America as a catalogue of marvels is an image that abounds in the early literature of the sixteenth century. Elements of surprise, mystery, and speculation constituted the foundation for describing natural phenomena by using elaborate narrative techniques. The task the first reporters of the new landscape encountered was to find adequate modes of representing the New World and validating for the reader the authenticity of their relations. This they achieved by offering varying degrees of proof, including sketches.

For historians, the answer to unraveling the marvels of the Atlantic was to be found in the reorganization of European knowledge and culture and its ability to assimilate a new reference (America), one that held the potential for detaching signs from their meaning (see Ahern's and Myers's essays in this volume), of influencing the rectification of the readers' relationship with their global index of truths as determined by the challenges to be found in the New World. Significantly, in the pre-Enlightenment world, metaphor was fundamental to understanding the order of things, that is, the prevailing system of resemblances. How chroniclers described things reflected how they thought and saw the world about them; in many cases, terminological poverty and conceptual lacunae forced them to examine things from an unaccustomed perspective.

Chroniclers and narrators of the period can be divided into two groups. The first is composed of the original authors (like Columbus, Vespucci, and Cortés), who as eyewitnesses provided firsthand accounts of the events they recorded. The second group is composed of the copyists or interpreters (like

Peter Martyr and Francisco López de Gómara), who saw the New World more through reconstructive imagination than through direct contact with the land. The body of writings (letters, relations, diaries, histories, treatises, commentaries, and so on) produced by these chroniclers, together with the corpus of juridical and legislative writings generated by the Church and the state, opened a dialogue between textual and discursive formations.

The Columbian exchange transcends the mere transfer of plants and animals, a fact that can be amply demonstrated by examining selected components of the New World enterprise that reflect the constant interplay between that transfer and the creation of ideas, institutions, and sensibilities in a colonial setting.

The history of religious instruction in America commences with Pope Leo X's bull of 5 April 1521 consenting to Cortés's appeal for missionaries. In 1524, just five years after his entrance into Mexico City, Cortés welcomed the "first twelve apostles," the Friars Minor of the Franciscan order, who laid the foundation for evangelization on a collective and individual basis. In this they were aided by the Dominicans (who arrived in 1526), the Augustinians (in 1533), and lastly the Jesuits (in 1572). Numerous schools, colleges, and universities predate the arrival of the Jesuits and their focus on scholastic theology and philosophy over basic literacy. As a cornerstone of the desired Christian republic in America, religious education stressed the need to comprehend and build upon the existing native educational methods while preserving, where possible, indigenous customs deemed not prejudicial to the Christian faith (Mignolo 1989b). Within the confines of native villages and church schools, the religious produced an Amerindian literature of *sermonarios*, *confesionarios*, dictionaries, illustrated catechisms, and grammars, as well as plays, paintings, drawings, and other works of art. The result was the adaptation or marriage of aspects of European and Native American pedagogy into an "audiovisual campaign" of instruction that included refashioning indigenous hieroglyphics to achieve Christian symbolism (Williams 1990). The specifics of how to attend doctrinally to the spiritual welfare of the indigenous peoples were outlined in the Laws of Burgos of 1513.

From the very inauguration of their missions, the religious orders met personal and cultural demands that varied in the degree of their severity. Insufficient linguistic training and limited field experience impeded meaningful communication, for there existed many autonomous nations and diverse tongues and dialects throughout the extension of the new territories. Unsettling conflicts in the ideological and material framework of the two cultures paved the way, alternately, for constructive and destructive phases of Christianization in the face of inquisitorial orthodoxy. Shortages of basic supplies and volunteers made the unequal distribution of resources and personnel more acute, a situation that was exacerbated by inexact planning. Organized resistance from natives and, in particular, hostility from resident Spaniards were underestimated by authorities and often aggravated tensions. Examples of misunderstandings precipitated by zealousness and cultural anomalies are amply recorded in early narratives (see Rabasa's essay in this volume).

Although the rational capacity of the Indians to receive the Christian faith was morally and politically settled in the bull *Sublimis Deus* issued by Pope Paul III in 1537, the chronicles nonetheless offer abundant testimony to pro-testations lodged by Spaniards who felt that the Church, in offering asylum and social and instructional programs, infringed on their rights (assumed or granted) to govern the Indians. Only danger to society and to the faith, it was felt, could result from offering higher education to inferior beings who were by nature incapable of salvation. This body of testimony also relates how the Indians struggled to identify with the spiritual essence of the teachings and how they were often moved to devotion by pageantry designed to overwhelm their senses.

In contrast to the disordered state of politics, religion, and culture in Eu-rope, there existed an impressionable Indian populace whose spiritual devel-opment, though wanting and at odds with Spanish Christianity, could be cor-rected. Columbus's exploratory voyage was commissioned, he wrote, "after Your Highnesses had made an end of the war with the Moors who reigned in Europe and had brought that war to a conclusion in the very great city of Granada . . . [and] after having driven out all the Jews from your realms and dominions" ("después de Vuestras Altezas haber dado fin a la guerra de los moros que reinaban en Europa, y haber acabado la guerra en la muy grande ciudad de Granada . . . [y] después de haber echado fuera todos los judíos de todos vuestros reinos y señoríos"; Columbus 1971, 15–16). The Crown's recent campaign against the infidel found a logical extension in America through Columbus. Firsthand knowledge of, and contact with, the conven-tions of non-Christian peoples—Africans, Jews, Moors, Orientals, Moriscos, Turks—served many chroniclers as the basis for launching observations and conjectures about the Indians which were based on limited experience (see Prager's essay in this volume). Various depictions of the New World offered a conflation of utopian and barbarian icons of indigenous cultures. A thematic overview of the early accounts underscores the fact that the distinguishing attributes of European civilization were patently absent in America. After a mere glance the natives were defined as naked, cannibalistic, licentious, and bestial. The initial impressions Columbus and other commentators registered rounded out this view of the indigenous peoples as lawless, bibulous, innocent, self-indulgent, and spiritually misguided people who enjoyed neither private property nor metallurgy for the construction of weapons. Within this oxymoronic notion of a "wild humanity" (White 1978, 193) was the promotion of a marked differentness that resulted in a vagueness about the Indians' humanity and made possible the dual presentation of the native populace as a savage yet redeemable race (see Delgado-Gómez's essay in this volume).

With the models of paradise and the Golden Age of antiquity as points of departure for evaluating the providential discoveries, narrators and historians pursued an assimilationist approach to the Indians (Todorov 1984, 43), casting them in the European image by providing them with Christian dress, religion, and customs. The Indians existed in a natural state as if in defiance of the laws of reason and civilization. They were to be tamed with clothing, instructed in the use of arms, taught how to cultivate and build on the land and how to adapt to European customs. Within the framework of "description by deficiency" (Berkhofer 1979, 27), moral judgments and ethnographic particulars are inseparable. Michel de Certeau points to the historian's need to combine empirical data with that received from tradition: "Only an appeal to the senses (hearing, sight, touch, taste) and a link to the body (touched, carved, tested by experience) seem capable of bringing closer together and guaranteeing, in a singular but indisputable fashion, the real" (Certeau 1986, 74). The ideals of Arcadia, the Garden of Eden, medieval Christendom, and classical antiquity collided with the duality of character (civilization versus barbarism) of the newly encountered Atlantic nations and peoples.

Native receptivity to spiritual guidance notwithstanding, there remained one important obstacle that overshadowed even the question of their genealogical separation from the rest of Christendom: linguistic isolation. Although propitious circumstances for advancing the Catholic faith were present because the natives shared common "manners and language" (costumbres y lengua; Columbus 1988, 10–11), Indians' voices within the discourse of encounter were perceived as being imperfect. It was considered a voice of prelinguistic sounds. To be wholly Christian and to gain access to culture, the natives needed both to understand and to be understood. America seduced European thought and sensibility and challenged the very nature of Europe's legacy and relationship to the existing continents. Most tempting was the fact that the New World offered theoretical discourse a forum in which diverse narrative forms could probe each other's boundaries and authority.

Given the changes that cultural encounters imposed on Renaissance historiography, the struggle was as much for adequate words as it was for accuracy and authority. The level of empiricism, of experimental autonomy, that America afforded to a large extent molded the attitude of historians to accommodate the "new sky and new land" (caelum novum et terra nova) of biblical prophecy. It was, after all, López de Gómara, the official biographer of Cortés, who declared, "The greatest event since the creation of the world (excluding the incarnation and death of Him who created it) is the discovery of the Indies" (Elliott 1970, 10).

The colonial enterprise, in its trail of gospel, gold, and glory, paved the way for the outcry against Spanish tyranny. The factors that engendered the cruelties and slaughter of the indigenous populations are as complex as they are numerous, and are riddled with as many complexities as was the court debate that ensued between Bartolomé de Las Casas and Juan Ginés de Sepúlveda in Valladolid in 1550–51 (see, respectively, Arias's and Merrim's essays in this volume). Before the court the two disputants presented theological and juridical arguments to influence the Crown's policies with respect to sovereignty over the Indians. The reasoning of Las Casas opposed the illegality of the empire waging war against its own subjects and included a call for conversion by peaceful means, the abolishment of slavery and mistreatment, and a recognition of the natives' rationality and humanity. Sepúlveda countered the theses of his opponent with equally stirring claims as to why the Indians could be rightfully enslaved by their Christian superiors: according to Aristotelian doctrine, the Indians were barbarians or slaves by nature (servus a natura), inferior beings without rights or honor, by virtue of their depraved habits. Though far from being definitively settled, his polemic netted Las Casas a moral and philosophical victory, for the Council of the Indies drew up ordinances to reflect, in principle, the spirit of his campaign in favor of Native American rights (Friede 1971; Hanke 1944 and [1949] 1965; Llaguno 1963).

Reports of savage practices such as cannibalism and the fear these reports engendered in Europeans were singled out as the principal justification for waging war against Native Americans. In evaluating the subjective reports of commentators, where self-aggrandizement and narrative authority were inseparable in the eyewitness accounts, we uncover a preoccupation with human sacrifice that extends from Columbus's diary entry of 5 December 1492 to Las Casas, from Las Casas to the illustrator Theodore de Bry, and beyond. As a chronicler, Cortés best exemplified the corrective posture colonizers assumed (more often than it was legally granted to them) when they were faced with the evil of cannibalism and native violence (see Palencia-Roth's essay in this volume). As a citizen of the Catholic nation selected by God and the Pope to Christianize the New World and as a representative of the Crown and its mission, Cortés responded to bestiality with savagery and thus set the stage for a theatre of violence on which scenes of cruelty are presented as justifiable. He makes little attempt to address the paradox of condemning the consumption of human flesh while sacrificing human beings at the stake, for the ends of creating a Christian republic were thought to justify the means (Todorov 1984, 179; Williams 1992). After all, with respect to Mexico City, Motolinía and other clerics argued that "God delivered the great city into the hands of His people because of the great sins and abominations committed in it" ("Dios entregó la gran ciudad en las manos de los suyos por los muy grandes pecados y abominables cosas que en ella se cometían"; Motolinía 1973, 152). To Europeans, cannibalism, along with native pagan rituals, provides both a metaphorical and a reality-based justification for imposing their own forms of cruelty and a justification for inculcating values that were perhaps as violent as the military conquests. In America the impulse toward self-importance and excess was left largely unchecked by legal restraints (Slotkin 1973).

Some sixteenth-century Europeans saw the New World as a land of possibility, where new social realities could be created free from the strictures and limitations of the Old World. Thomas More, of course, located his utopia somewhere in America, and in 1516, the same year that More published his famous book Utopia, Bartolomé de Las Casas directed to the king of Spain a curious "brief of appeals" (memorial de remedios) detailing a plan for the creation of Indian communities which bears a striking resemblance to More's description of an ideal society. Nothing came of this plan of Las Casas, but as is well known, More's Utopia was later used as a blueprint by the bishop of Michoacán, Vasco de Quiroga, in his design for Indian communities in Mexico, which were, in fact, brought into being and which lasted for many years. Las Casas, for his part, was not done with social experimentation, as can be seen in his successful missionary work using only peaceful means in the "land of true peace" ("tierra de la vera paz") and in his unsuccessful attempt to create communities where Indians and imported "ennobled" Spanish peasants[1] would intermarry and live together in harmony on the coast of Cumaná (present-day Venezuela). Embedded in these blueprints or inventions for alternative societies is a nostalgic evocation of a utopian ideal that could not be realized in Europe.

The life and works of the Inca Garcilaso de la Vega (1539–1616) are indicative of the new society that Las Casas and company envisioned, for Garcilaso did more to promote an understanding of indigenous cultures than any other writer of his time. Born of an Inca princess, Isabel Yupanqui Ñusta (aka Chimpu Occio) and the noble Garcilaso de la Vega the Elder,[2] he received instruction in his native Quechua and learned Spanish and Latin as part of his standard European education. Later in life, when Garcilaso set about to correct the "fabulous" histories penned by misinformed chroniclers about his native Peru and Cuzco, its former capital—"another Rome" ("otra Roma")– he did so with the power of memory, authoritative oral sources, and a sense of historical mission. His stated aim was to benefit the new Christian republic of which he was a part.[3] His *Comentarios reales de los Incas* (Royal commentaries of the Incas) are of ethnohistorical significance not only because they provide intimate appraisals of native Peruvian culture from the point of view of one of its respected citizens but also because the author provides an invaluable view of the changing nature of New World society. As if in defiance of Spain's time-honored preoccupation with racial purity, or *limpieza de sangre*–where the ancestral presence of Jewish or Moorish blood was tantamount to heresy, hence the term *old Christian* (*cristiano viejo*) as a point of honor and *new Christian* (*cristiano nuevo*) of dishonor—the encounter of cultures had produced human hybrids who needed to be introduced to the rest of humanity: *criollos, mulatos, mestizos, cuatralvos, tresalvos.*[4] For many, Garcilaso incarnated the cultural symbiosis of America's humanity, which was favored by nature, and the best of Europe's humanistic tradition.

One of the "new men" also produced by the encounter was the Native American writer Felipe Guaman Poma de Ayala (ca. 1526 to after 1614), author of *Nueva crónica y buen gobierno* (The New chronicle and good government), a history of Peru that begins before the rise of the Inca empire and continues into the seventeenth century. A descendant both of Inca nobility and of the older Yarovilza Allauca Huanoco lineage, Guaman Poma held a complex but coherent worldview, which Rolena Adorno (1986, 1990) describes as combining elements from both European and Native American cultures. An anticleric, Guaman was nonetheless fervently Christian; anti-Incan, he also opposed European colonialism and favored instead the establishment of an Andean state that would take its place in a universal Christian empire ruled by the Spanish king. To supplement the more than one thousand pages of text in his chronicle, written in Spanish and Quechua, Guaman included some three hundred original drawings, which he skillfully employed to entertain, to teach, and to persuade the reader of the validity of the author's point of view. Both Garcilaso and Guaman Poma were conscious of the need to rewrite history, and in turn they helped to reinvent the image of Native Americans.

It is during the period of conquest and colonization that Spain—never recognized as a leader in scientific research—distinguished itself in the area of the natural sciences through the multifaceted documents, including secondhand accounts, penned by sources ranging from court-appointed historians to conquistadors and from naturalists to missionaries. The methodical questioning and desire for scientific knowledge that America stirred in Europe added to the complexity of the chronicle as both a literary and historical form of documentation and as the foremost repository of early scientific information.

The disputed origins of colonial science begin with Columbus's description of evidence that set in motion the identification and classification of flora and fauna and, by speculation, a reevaluation of cosmographic and hydrographic knowledge (see Kelsey's and the Dilkes' essays in this volume). Contrary to popular belief, Columbus's geodetic theory reasoned that the earth was not spherical but pear-shaped: the earthly paradise was positioned on the stem, whose rise no individual could ascend without express permission from God. That he had discovered Eden was indisputable, "for the situation agrees with the opinion of these holy and wise theologians" ("porque el sitio es conforme a la opinión de estos santos y sanos teólogos"; Columbus 1988, 38).

On the heels of Columbus's interest in indigenous pharmacotherapy, we find experimentation that included the use of simple substances and the invention and employment of formulas for the preparation of compounds. The effects of the indigenous contribution were the gradual incorporation of vegetable remedies into European therapeutics, the widespread use of narcotics and stimulants, the publication of comparative studies of like species of flora and fauna, the rectification of geographic determinations into a coherent and ordered body, and the use of new metal alloys (notably the preference for amalgamation over smelting in Mexico beginning in 1555 for the extraction of silver from its ores by the use of mercury). One of the earliest research institutions was the Colegio de Santa Cruz of Tlatelolco, established in 1536 and dedicated to higher education and the study of native medicine.

In the early sixteenth century, theological inquiries cast an unfavorable light on the budding discipline of science. Theology, the Divine Science, was often reinforced by folklore and common sense, yet the struggle for scientific inquiry born out of America's discovery and its confrontation with European theology opposed a reliance on faith and demanded empirical truth. When theologians and the texts of the ancients failed adequately to answer the questions posed by the New World phenomena, naturalists, botanists, cosmographers, and others stepped in to fill the void. The 1590 *Historia natural y moral de las Indias*, written by the Jesuit priest and orator José de Acosta, serves to illustrate the dilemma.

In the face of the Counter-Reformation and the drive for adherence to orthodoxy in intellectual and religious questions, Acosta set out to reconcile the paradoxes he recognized as a result of pondering the challenging new continent. Against the grain of established traditions of the ancients, he formulated hypotheses concerning (1) the shape of the heavens and the earth, (2) the existence of the antipodes, (3) the habitability of the torrid zones, (4) the ancients' knowledge of the New World, and (5) the settlement of the New World by men and beasts. Like Aristotle, he held that the earth was round, and through careful observation he confirmed the presence of stars that exhibited circular rotations about otherwise fixed points. Yet, swimming against the current of Aristotelianism, he advanced the idea that the shadow of the earth on the moon during an eclipse was round rather than flat or square. Acosta's ultimate achievement was to refute aggressively the apocryphal stories about the settlement of the Indies.[5] If, according to biblical lore, beasts were sheltered in Noah's Ark, what circumstances provided for the existence of certain animals known only in the New World? After the deluge, by what means did they migrate to America? Acosta wrote that "It is certainly a matter that has perplexed me for quite some time" ("Cierto es cuestión que me ha tenido perplejo mucho tiempo"; Acosta [1604] 1940, 202). He realized the improbability of their having reached the New World before the invention of the sophisticated navigational techniques that were just coming into use. Even if it were possible that individuals had in some way crossed to the New World, how was it possible that all the flora and fauna of the Indies differed from that found in Spain?

The core of empirical data gleaned from observation drove Acosta to construct a theory that the New World was not severed and disjoined from the Old World. This notion fell squarely within the metaphysical and philosophical context of science, yet it bordered on upsetting "the vast synthesis, backed by the resources of Church and State, which held that God, people, angels, animals, planets, and elements, all had their place in a world where humankind and earth were at the center, and heaven beyond its circumference" (Kearney 1971, 8). Further, although New World findings may have lessened the reliance on scriptural authority, an evolutionary explanation of the origins of American flora and fauna was out of the question. After all, the argument went, separate creations of the same species in different regions was all part of a divine plan, with the entire vegetable and animal kingdom being no more than four to five days older than humankind (Sauer 1972, 23).

If the Age of Reason could be traced back to a single germ of thought, it might be found in Acosta, who came to know that learning and knowledge are the by-products of the resolution of contradictions. Devout, he desired an answer; resolute, he investigated; perplexed, he questioned. It took only a few questions to sever him from the medieval rationalizations and bind him to seductive Cartesian ideals in the quest for new explanations of God and Scripture.

What these scientists and naturalists lacked in the cultivation of solid theoretical science and discipline was more than balanced by the emphasis they accorded experience and observable facts, which ultimately facilitated a move toward increased experimentalism (Astuto 1959; Leonard 1963). This move toward empiricism occurred in a context in which New World historians witnessed the prohibition, loss, mutilation, and late publication of their texts by censors determined to make them conform to the interests of the Crown. As scientific data became more verifiable and a rational, objective concept of the universe was formed, the concepts of the ancients were refuted, and ecclesiastical authority met its decline while science consolidated itself.

Legislation in America was molded by bureaucratic entanglements and complex political machinery which, when transferred to America, were revised to accommodate changing sociopolitical realities (see Seed's essay in this volume). Spain's rule over its peoples and resources from across the Atlantic was overseen by administrative offices such as the Council of the Indies (established in 1524) and was often undermined by patronage systems (e.g., the encomienda and the repartimiento)[6] that granted authority and Indian labor to colonists. A glimpse at sixteenth-century Mexico reveals that the reins of colonial magistracy rested within the grasp of dissimilar hands: countless missionaries, ten viceroys, six archbishops, six military governors, diverse town councils (cabildos), five ecclesiastical juntas, three religious councils, the Inquisition, and high courts (audiencias), as well as other appointed officials. Conflicting claims and access to privileges, exemptions, titles, and sovereignty plagued efforts at reform. Early references reflect mounting internal tensions within missions and squabbles between competing orders—between friars and prelates, prelates and mayors, and mayors and viceroys, among others—all of whom were vying for power. Examples range from seemingly overlapping local juridical matters involving the interpretation and enforcement of statutes to arenas of practical religious instruction (where clerical sovereignty was thought to be so widespread that it exerted an undue influence on public matters concerning the native populace). The rapid growth of civil and ecclesiastical sumptuary laws during the period typified the proliferating nature of legislative measures and their selective enforcement.

In these areas and others examined by the essays in this collection, the New World beckoned Europeans to experience and comprehend the significance of cultural encounter and transfer. Today, America as a subject that is invented and reinvented[7] poses stimulating questions that continue to occupy the attention of the educated public, as this volume attests.

NOTES

1. Las Casas's plan for enticing ordinary Castilian peasants to Cumaná included obtaining for them the right to wear a habit that would approximate in severity those worn by the prestigious military orders (Santiago, Calatrava, and Alcántara). The legend surrounding these so-called "brown-habited knights" (*caballeros pardos*) is the subject of Marcel Bataillon's revealing essay, "Cheminement d'une légende: Les 'caballeros pardos' de Las Casas" ([1952] 1966). Social experimentation with Indians in the New World is the subject of Lewis Hanke's essay "El despertar de la conciencia en América" (1963).

2. Sebastián Garcilaso de la Vega (1495–1559) served in Mexico with Cortés before accompanying Pedro de Alvarado to Peru.

3. In his prologue, Garcilaso stressed, with respect to "the same historians who treated [the history of the Incas] wholly or in part, that it is not my intention to contradict them but rather serve them as an explanatory note and gloss [and] to serve the Christian republic" ("los mismos historiadores que tocaron en parte o en todo, que mi intención no es contradecirles, sino servirles de comento y glosa . . . servir a la república cristiana"; Avalle-Arce 1970, 37–38). In addition to *La Florida del Inca* (1605), based on the exploration of Hernando de Soto in Florida, and the *Comentarios reales* (1609), whose second part was published posthumously under the title of *Historia general del Perú* (1617), Garcilaso prepared a skillful translation from Italian to Spanish of Leon Hebreo's *Dialoghi d'amore* (1590). See *Obras completas del Inca Garcilaso de la Vega*, edited by P. Carmelo Sáenz de Santa María, 4 vols. (Madrid: Atlas, 1960), and Margarita Zamora's *Language, Authority and the Indigenous History in the 'Comentarios Reales' of the Incas* (Cambridge: Cambridge University Press, 1988).

4. Garcilaso referred with pride to the Spaniards and blacks as "the best

thing that has happened to these Indies" ("lo mejor de lo que ha pasado a estas Indias"; Avalle-Arce 1970, 255) because from their union were born *criollos* (the offspring of Spanish parents), *mulatos* (the offspring of Indian and Negro parents), and *mestizos* (the offspring of Spanish and Indian parents). *Cuatralvos* were the children of Spanish and mestizo parentage (one-quarter Indian and three-quarters Spanish), and *tresalvos* were the progeny of mestizo and Indian parents (three-quarters Indian, one-quarter Spanish). Garcilaso defended his criollo heritage with tenacity: "I openly call myself [criollo] and I honor myself with it" ("Me lo llamo yo a boca llena y me honro con él"; Avalle-Arce 1970, 256).

5. The Amerindians' system of writing did not permit Europeans to glean from documents the disputed origins of New World inhabitants. Gonzalo Fernández de Oviedo was among the first chroniclers to claim that the Indians had descended from the lost Ten Tribes of Israel (Hanke 1949, 6; Pagden 1982, 156, 230). This argument was vigorously challenged by Acosta ([1604] 1940, bk. 1, chap. 23, pp. 60–62), yet it continued to find acceptance in the histories of respected writers such as Toribio Motolinía (1973, 8) and Gerónimo de Mendieta (1971, 539–40, 558). Another contested claim was that the Indies were part of the Hesperides (Las Casas 1957, 1:57–66).

6. Under the encomienda, colonizers were granted allotments of Indians whom they were to be responsible for Christianizing and protecting in exchange for tribute and labor. The *repartimiento* was more complex in that it involved the assignment—or conscription—of Indians and/or land to settlers, and it could be expanded to include the forced sale of merchandise to Indians.

7. The invention and reinvention of America was addressed in a seminal study by Edmundo O'Gorman (1951). Walter Mignolo has registered his discomfort with designations such as Latin America or the New World: "The first should refer to the colonial situation rather than to a 'new' continent. Colonial situations, such as the one initiated by Columbus's voyages, have generated a 'New World' in the sense that [they] confronted people from 'Two Old Worlds' " (1989a, 337).

BIBLIOGRAPHY

Acosta, José de. [1604] 1940. *Historia natural y moral de las Indias*. Ed. Edmundo O'Gorman. Mexico City: Fondo de Cultura Económica.

————. [1604] 1970. *The Natural and Moral History of the Indies.* Ed. Clements R. Markham. 2 vols. New York: Burt Franklin.

Adorno, Rolena. 1986. *Guaman Poma: Writing and Resistance in Colonial Perú.* Austin: University of Texas Press.

————. 1990. Iconos de persuasión: La predicación y la política en el Perú colonial. In *La iconografía política en el Nuevo Mundo,* ed. Mercedes López-Baralt, 27–49. Río Piedras: Editorial de la Universidad de Puerto Rico.

Astuto, Philip L. 1959. Scientific Expeditions and Colonial Hispanic America. *Thought Patterns* 6: 1–27.

Avalle-Arce, Juan Bautista. 1970. *El Inca Garcilaso en sus 'Comentarios.'* Madrid: Gredos.

Bataillon, Marcel. [1952] 1966. Cheminement d'une légende: Les 'caballeros pardos' de Las Casas. *Symposium* [Syracuse University] 6: 1–21. Reprinted in *Etudes sur Bartolomé de Las Casas réunies avec la collaboration de Raymond Marcus,* ed. Marcel Bataillon, 115–36. Paris: Centre de Recherches de l'Institut d'Etudes Hispaniques, 1966.

Berkhofer, Robert E., Jr. 1979. *The White Man's Indian: Images of the American Indian from Columbus to the Present.* New York: Vintage Books.

Certeau, Michel de. 1986. *Heterologies: Discourse on the Other.* Trans. Brian Massumi. Minneapolis: University of Minnesota Press.

Columbus, Christopher. 1971. *Los cuatro viajes del Almirante y su testamento.* Ed. Ignacio B. Anzóategui. 5th ed. Madrid: Espasa-Calpe.

————. 1988. *The Four Voyages of Columbus.* Ed. Cecil Jane. New York: Dover.

Cortés, Hernán. 1971. *Cartas de relación.* Ed. Manuel Alcalá. Mexico City: Porrúa.

————. 1929. *Five Letters of Cortés to the Emperor, 1519–26.* Trans. J. Bayard Morris. New York: R. M. McBride and Co.

Elliott, John. H. 1970. *The Old World and the New, 1492–1650.* London: Cambridge University Press.

Friede, Juan, and Benjamin Keen. 1971. *Bartolomé de las Casas in History.* De Kalb: Northern Illinois University Press.

Guaman Poma de Ayala, Felipe. 1987. *Primer nueva cronica i buen gobierno.* Ed. John V. Murra, Rolena Adorno, and Jorge L. Urioste. 3 vols. Madrid: Crónicas de America.

Hanke, Lewis. 1944. More Heat and Some Light on the Spanish Struggle for Justice in the Conquest of America. *Hispanic American Historical Review* 44: 293–340.

————. 1949. *Aristotle and the American Indians: A Study in Race Prejudice in the Modern World*. Philadelphia: University of Pennsylvania Press.

————. 1963. El despertar de la conciencia en América. *Cuadernos Americanos* 4:184–202.

Kearney, Charles. 1971. *Science and Change, 1500–1700*. New York: McGraw-Hill.

Las Casas, Bartolomé de. 1957. Historia de las Indias. In *Obras escogidas de Fray Bartolomé de las Casas*, ed. Juan Pérez de Tudela and E nilio López Oto, vol. 1. Madrid: Biblioteca de Autores Españoles.

Leonard, Irving L. 1963. Science, Technology. and Hispanic America. *Michigan Quarterly Review* 2:237–45.

Llaguno, José A. 1963. *La personalidad jurídica del indio y el Tercer Concilio provincial mexicano (1585)*. Mexico City: Porrúa.

Mendieta, Geronimo de. [1596] 1971. *Historia eclesiástica indiana*. Mexico City: Porrúa. Facsimile of 1870 edition.

Mignolo, Walter. 1989a. Afterword: From Colonial Discourse to Colonial Semiosis. *Dispositio* 14:333–37.

————. 1989b. Literacy and Colonization: The New World Experience. In *1492–1992: Re/Discovering Colonial Writing*, ed. René Jara and Nicholas Spadaccini. Hispanic Issues series, 4:51–96. Minneapolis: Prisma Institute.

Motolinía, Toribio de. 1973. *Historia de los indios de la Nueva España*. Ed. Edmundo O'Gorman. Mexico City: Porrúa.

————. 1950. *History of the Indians of New Spain*. Trans. and ed. Elizabeth Andros Foster. New York: Cortes Society.

Pagden, Anthony. 1982. *The Fall of Natural Man: The American Indian and the Origins of Comparative Ethnology*. Cambridge: Cambridge University Press.

O'Gorman, Edmundo. 1951. *La idea del descubrimiento de América*. Mexico City: Universidad Nacional Autónoma de México, Centro de Estudios Filosóficos.

Sauer, Jonathan D. 1976. Changing Perceptions and Exploitation of New World Plants in Europe, 1492–1800. In *First Images of America*, ed. Fredi Chiappelli, 2:813–32. Berkeley: University of California Press.

Slotkin, Richard. 1973. *Regeneration Through Violence: The Mythology of the American Frontier, 1600–1860*. Middletown, Conn.: Wesleyan University Press.

Todorov, Tzvetan. 1984. *The Conquest of America: The Question of the Other*. Trans. Richard Howard. New York: Harper & Row.

White, Hayden. 1978. *Tropics of Discourse: Essays in Cultural Criticism*. Baltimore: John Hopkins University Press.

Williams, Jerry M. 1990. El arte dramático y la iconografía en la trayectoria misionera del siglo XVI. *La Palabra y el Hombre* 76:94–124.

———. 1992. Framing Colonial Discourse: The Textual Battlefield of Religion and Violence. *Hispanic Journal* 13:7–26.

I Cultural Spaces

The Earliest European Views of the New World Natives

Angel Delgado-Gómez

The French historian Jules Michelet made the often-quoted remark that the sixteenth century did more for the discovery of mankind and the discovery of the world than all the former centuries combined. John H. Elliott rightly points out that by the "discovery of mankind" Michelet naturally meant the Europeans' discovery of themselves as both physical organisms and moral beings (Elliott 1989, 42). The close relation between both kinds of discovery is undeniable. It is true that the philosophical and medical dimensions of human life had been explored since classical antiquity. Yet a new dimension of life, that of human behavior and its relation with the environment, reached hitherto unknown proportions as a result of the great geographical discoveries of the sixteenth century.

To be sure, the insatiable thirst for geographical knowledge was also extended to regions that were already part of the known world. The most notable of these was Turkey, but this was clearly the result of political factors—the Ottoman empire had become a direct military threat to the Christian nations of western Europe after gaining domination of the eastern states. It is also true, however, that finding a New World, more than any other event, brought about a challenge of unparalleled proportions to the notions held by the inhabitants of the Old. Travels in Africa and Asia could indeed shake many long-established ideas and images about those lands, but at least their existence had long been part of the body of geographical knowledge established by the Greeks and Romans. This was not the case with the islands Columbus found, for which no verifiable reference could be obtained.

The discovery of new lands therefore brought encounters with peoples vastly different from what Europeans had seen, read about, or even imagined. This is particularly true of the earliest reports of the New World, those written during the first thirty years of discovery. The natives of the New World were indeed new people to the Europeans, and this meant that the first chroniclers had to produce a new frame of reference to describe them, that is, a new mental perspective to perceive the new kind of people. It has been widely assumed that this challenge proved too difficult for the unprepared adventurers who observed the Indians for the first time. Thus, having been badly misguided by their preconceptions and prejudices, they easily succumbed to associating the islanders with a mixture of biblical inhabitants of paradise and the lost Golden Age described in Greek mythology. The result was the creation of a new myth that would persist in various forms in Western thought, culminating in the popular eighteenth-century notion of the noble savage (Brandon 1986, 147–68).

Arguably, the central idea among the beliefs about the noble savage is the lack of a concept of private property. This is a classical theme that reappeared in the Renaissance with the discovery of the New World and later in the writings of Rousseau, Proudhon, and Marx. It is closely linked to a new notion of liberty: The noble savage lives in a brotherly environment devoid of authority. He knows no rulers, and society is therefore classless. All other elements in the idea of the noble savage, such as extraordinary friendliness and hospitality, pacifism, and mutual caring, are natural consequences of these two notions. One might also add the lack of religion, that is, the absence of beliefs manifested by practices organized by a clergy, a most significant issue during the Reformation.[1]

Greatly distorted or idealized images of the Indians would seem to have been almost inevitable among the first reporters of the New World. Contacts with the inhabitants of the Caribbean islands were limited to a few brief encounters, in which the language barrier proved a formidable obstacle to any real communication.[2] In view of this, it is remarkable that contacts between Spaniards and Taino Indians were not marked by the typical mutual mistrust. The Spaniards could only attempt to describe the life of the Indians while they were in contact with the intruders, whose presence no doubt altered their normal lives. Inevitably, because they lacked the opportunity for prolonged observation, much of what the early explorers could produce was a description of the Indians' external aspect and behavior.[3]

One could also argue that another important political factor helped the portrayal of the Indians as paradisiacal human beings: The Europeans were participants in a national enterprise of discovery and colonization, and by depicting the Indians as primitive and friendly pagans, they were reaffirming both the necessity of the domination—the conquest was soon characterized as a missionary enterprise—and the willingness of the islanders to be subdued. A careful examination of the earliest literature of discovery, however, suggests that far from depicting a commonly naive, highly idealized, and prejudiced image of the native Indians, the early writers generally showed a remarkable sense of realism and independence of thought. The purpose of this essay is to show how, with one important exception, none of these writers embraced the notion of the noble savage.

The first account of the New World Indians is that of Columbus himself. He summarized his thoughts on the islanders in his famous letter to Luis de Santángel (1493), in which he announced the news of his recent discoveries of previously unknown Asian islands. The tone of the letter is necessarily euphoric. Having failed to find any evidence of material riches that would justify his adventure, the Admiral of the Ocean Sea was prone to exaggerating the beauty of both the natural and the human landscape of the islands. Yet, all things considered, one cannot but marvel at the restraint and caution he showed in describing the Indians.[4] First of all, he negates any notion of uniformity among them by drawing a sharp distinction between the Indians of Hispaniola and the Caribs. The latter, he writes, are ferocious cannibals who, well-equipped with bows and darts, mercilessly raid the other islands (Columbus 1892, 9). Their victims on Hispaniola, on the other hand, are timid, affable people who welcomed the Spaniards with utmost generosity. A striking characteristic of their physical aspect is their nakedness (4–5). To the prevailing European mentality, the fact that all the men and many of the women walked about completely naked without experiencing any shame could easily be linked to customs in the biblical paradise. But Columbus establishes no such link.

On the key question of private property, Columbus adopted an exemplary restraint even though he clearly saw no division of property in the European manner. "I was not able to find out surely whether they have individual property, for I saw that one man had the duty of distributing to the others, especially refreshments, food and things of that kind" (Columbus 1892, 9). It is also relevant to point out that when trying to prove the natives' "excellent and acute understanding," the Admiral refers to their seafaring skills and huge canoes, which he describes in detail. The purpose of traveling is "to perform their trading and carry on commerce among them" (7), thereby assuming a considerable degree of economic activity. As for authority, Columbus explicitly describes the *cacique* on Hispaniola as the "king of this island." That he is unequivocally someone of a different rank is further underlined in Columbus's discussion of marriage practices. Again, with characteristic caution he writes that "as I have understood, each man is content with only one wife, except the princes or kings, who are permitted to have twenty" (9). Only on the question of pacifism does Columbus seem to associate himself with the idea of a people incapable of aggression. Nevertheless, his assertion that the Indians of Hispaniola have no weapons is contradicted by another statement describing a rudimentary sword they evidently used in self-defense (5). Rather than a lack of violence, then, Columbus seems to stress the primitiveness of their military capability, which is no match for the superior tactics and weaponry of the Caribs.

Columbus's ideas quickly became well known as editions of the letter multiplied. Unfortunately, his long and detailed *diario*, containing his daily thoughts and actions during the sea journey, remained unknown to most of his contemporaries, having come to us only recently in the extracted version of Father Bartolomé de Las Casas. A reading of the diario confirms the notions expressed in the Letter. Columbus carefully notes the clear differences between the groups, communities, or "cities" he sees. Thus we learn that there is a certain place in Cuba that he calls the Río de Mares whose inhabitants seem the closest to noble savages. He writes, "they are very gentle and do not know what evil is; nor do they kill others, nor steal; and they are without weapons and so timid. . . . [T]hese people have no religious beliefs, nor are they idolaters" (1989, 143). However, this is just a small community that he encountered only briefly, and all these characteristics are in sharp contrast to the dominant features of other islanders, like those of Fernandina, who "appear somewhat more civilized and given to commerce and more astute. . . . [T]hey know better how to bargain payment than the others did" (89). At the top of his hierarchy are the Indians of Hispaniola, whom Columbus thinks are "more handsome and of better quality than any of the others" (225). Indeed, he named the island Hispaniola not only because he saw a similarity between it and certain regions in Spain but also because of the clear superiority of its people. He repeatedly points out that they are "as white as any in Spain" (225, 233) and calls them "plump and brave and not weak like the others [I] had found before" (234). The differences even extend to their language, for although he cannot understand them, he notices that they have a "very sweet speech." The Admiral even dares to note that they are "without false religion," a rather odd statement that is open to interpretation.

Regarding authority, a central point of this study, Columbus offers a more

elaborate description of political structure. He marvels at the pomp and ceremony extended toward one of the "kings" of the island who is carried about
on a litter, all of which, the Admiral says, "would have seemed well to Your
Highness, even though everyone went about naked" (241). It is precisely the
marvelous way in which these lords, whom he correctly notes are referred to
as caciques (271), exercise their authority that persuades Columbus that the
caciques are unquestionably superior and more civilized—that is to say, more
prone to assimilating European ways—than the other islanders. Accordingly,
he makes a pact with Guacanagari, whom he identifies as the cacique who
rules over five other kings, agreeing to build a Spanish fortress that would be
the first European settlement in the New World.

Columbus published no other writing about his expeditions, and the logs
of his subsequent three Atlantic crossings have been lost. The private documents that have been preserved lead us to believe that if Columbus had at
one point a faint temptation to find a group of noble savages, this illusion,
which he had already dismissed in the Letter and the diario, became impossible after the Indian rebellion that wiped out the ill-fated first colony. Columbus could no longer believe that the Indians were naturally peaceful people,
unable to take up arms against an enemy. The tragic events were recorded by
Doctor Alvarez Chanca, the official physician of the second expedition. His
report is incomplete and was not published during his lifetime, and therefore
it exerted no influence on his contemporaries. Professor Gerbi claims that
Chanca's attitude toward the New World shows a sharp contrast between his
enthusiastic admiration for the landscape and a negative, almost scornful view
of the Indians (1985, 23–26). It is true that Chanca expresses a prejudiced
dissatisfaction with what he calls the laughable aspect of the Indians on Hispaniola because of their haircuts and the way they painted themselves
(Chanca, 66) or their unhealthy living conditions. But he also acknowledges
his admiration for their food. Although he condemns their habit of eating
worms (66), he praises their ajes, or yams, as very nourishing (65–66) and
writes of their tools "such as hatchets and axes, made of stone, so handsome
and so fashioned, that it is marvelous how they are able to make them without
iron" (65). He also corrects Columbus's former impression about religion,
expressing with neutral objectivity that the idols found in many huts clearly
prove they are idolaters.

Chanca makes no observation about property ownership, but from the
way he describes his inquiry into the killing of the first settlers, it is evident
that he, along with Columbus, has no doubts about the absolute power the
cacique Guacanagari exerts over his subjects. Chanca discovered that the cause

of the political trouble on the island lay in the rivalry between the three main caciques of Hispaniola, as Guacamari, the ally of the Admiral, was in competition with the chiefs named Caonabá and Mayrené for control of the island. This picture of constant clashes between lords certainly resembles the power struggles of European monarchs more than it does the paradisiacal life of the noble savage.

Chanca's report is also important because it is the first to describe actual contact with the Caribs of Guadeloupe, of whom Columbus had written only by hearsay. Their ferocious resistance to any kind of political accommodation with the Spaniards—unlike the other Indians, these react to all encounters in the most aggressive way—prevents him from being able to observe their daily life. Therefore he can say nothing about their social structure other than that they systematically raid the other islands. Among themselves they seemed to behave harmoniously "as if they were of one family" (31). As for their behavior in war, he notes that women were as adept as men in the use of their bows against the Spaniards. An inspection of an abandoned living site also allowed him to learn more about their cannibalistic practices. They eat only adult males, keeping the females as slaves and raising the young males as castrated servants until they grow up, when they are slaughtered (31). Most important of all, Chanca remarks that the housing, the woven textiles, and "the signs of industry, both of men and women, prove that these people are more civilized than the other islanders" (28).

The second published work on the New World is an epistle written in Latin by the Italian physician Nicolò Scillacio, also known as Nicolaus Scyllacio ([1494] 1859). He was a learned man who never set foot in the New World. The only sources of his information were the oral reports of two sailors who participated in Columbus's second voyage. Scillacio makes the customary distinction between Caribs and peaceful Indians. His description of the Caribs offers fewer details than Chanca's, and he says nothing about the way their society is structured. Scillacio, however, can be credited with two major novelties. He was the first to attempt a systematic relation between the newly discovered islands and the classical world. His goal is, of course, to prove that the New World was known by the Greeks and the Romans, and this leads to his making rather colorful remarks. When describing canoes, for example, the erudite doctor reminds us that "Virgil calls such boates *lintres*" ([1494] 1859, 37). This tendency is responsible for his second achievement, a major distortion in depicting the life of the Indians. Scillacio's purpose of associating the Indians with the happy people of the Golden Age leads him to idealize them in an extreme way, and any recognition of the power of the caciques is rejected in favor of rapturous praise of this profit-free society. "The disposition of this people is placable," he writes. "All things are held in common; there is not even a suspicion of avarice. This is mine, that is thine, the cause of so many crimes, is unknown among them. There is no desire for what belongs to another, no lust of possession; envy is completely banished. They live in great harmony and in the exercise of mutual kindness. They are equally distinguished for good faith and reverential respect" (85). This is indeed the first example of writing on the noble savage, and it is clearly the product of a humanist whose enthusiasm for the New World compels him to describe the Indians whom he had not seen in a most positive light. Thus the painting of their bodies, an object of Chanca's derision, is reported by Scillacio to be a cosmetic protector of their bodies' symmetry and beauty (87). Certain elements of his description can only be attributed to his imagination. For example, he had no way of knowing that the Indians "live to an advanced age" (87) other than by taking the idea from the Golden Age model he is so closely following.

A different image of the people of the New World is provided by Michele da Cuneo in a private report on Columbus's second voyage, in which he participated. Cuneo was not a humanist, but as a member of a noble Savonese family he must have received a good education, for his Italian is elegantly spiced with Latin expressions. He certainly was a keen observer, able to summarize the salient characteristics of both the physical environment and the human settlements he observed (Gerbi 1985, 31). Unlike Scillacio and Peter Martyr but very much in line with Chanca, Cuneo maintains an objective neutrality throughout his report. He is the first to describe the religious practices of the cannibals, of which the most important is the figure of a silent priest dressed in white who without speaking conveyed the impression that he held a meaningful degree of authority over the community (Cuneo 1966, 65). Cuneo is also the first to give an extensive account of the unusual sexual habits of the cannibals, namely, their indiscriminate promiscuity and their widespread practice of homosexuality (65), two features that would be repeated ad nauseam by writers who came after him. Cuneo makes the customary distinction between cannibals and Indians (*Camballi e Indiani*), but he points out some characteristics common to both groups. Contradicting Scillacio's bold assessment, he prudently says that in his opinion all must die at a young age, for "we have not seen anyone who in our judgment looks more than fifty years old" (Cuneo 1966, 65). Of special interest to us are his remarks about the differences between the common people and the caciques, which Cuneo seems to imply existed in both groups, although most authors attribute them only to the Indians. The people sleep on the ground "like beasts," while the caciques sleep in hammocks and are treated with the utmost respect and ceremony. For example, when they get together for dinner, they all wait to eat until the cacique has finished (66).

Cuneo's report unfortunately remained a private document, and thus his balanced view of the natives had no influence among his contemporaries. A completely different fate was awarded the equally private letters of another sailor, Amerigo Vespucci. Both the man and his writings quickly became well known throughout Europe in a controversy that has not diminished even today. Our concern is with his view of the New World natives, so we shall avoid the critical dispute over the number and nature of his travels across the Ocean Sea.[5] As for his writings, he is traditionally credited as the author of three letters to Lorenzo di Pier Francesco de' Medici, the first sent from Seville in 1500, the second from Cape Verde in 1501, and the third from Lisbon in 1502 (see Vespucci 1985). As a result of the voluminous research of Alberto Magnaghi (1926), a fourth letter, dated in August 1504 and entitled Mundus Novus, and another letter, sent to Pier Soderini in 1504 and entitled Quatuor navigationes, are now almost unanimously considered to be contemporary forgeries. Vespucci's defenders may have thought that the controversy concerning these letters would disappear, since most of it centered around the last two, in which errors and contradictions abound. So, despite the fact that the great fame of Vespucci in his time is due solely to the enormous popularity of these two writings—the first three letters were not published until much later—a number of scholars still have a high opinion of him. Arciniegas calls him "a cultivated man, trained in the best school of humanism" (1986, x), and Roberto Levillier, his most ardent defender in modern times, tries to validate Vespucci's claim to being a cosmographer (Vespucci 1951, 28), a claim categorically denied by others, such as Olschki (1941) and more recently Sierra (1968), whose book is a painstaking refutation of Levillier's claims.

There seems to be much more agreement about Vespucci's reputation as an able ethnographer. Olschki, who deems Vespucci's cosmography "sheer nonsense," thinks that the value of his writings lies in his accounts of the manners and customs of the natives of South America and its adjacent islands (1941, 643). Mario Pozzi, his recent editor, credits him with a solid view of reality and a disposition toward scientific accuracy (1984, 17). Morison, who has a low opinion of Vespucci's false claims concerning nonexistent voyages, still holds that he was "one of the few to observe carefully the human beings he encountered" (1974, 284), an opinion shared by Gerbi, who thinks the three authentic letters provide the "first coherent and deliberate description of the physical nature and inhabitants" of the Brazilian and Venezuelan coasts (1985, 36).

In his first letter, Vespucci starts by describing the cannibals of an island that he typically fails to identify or locate properly, since he customarily omits the latitude and the longitude of the places he describes. He mentions some of the features we have seen in other writings, such as the natives' beautiful physiques, complete nakedness, canoe raids to other islands in search of human flesh, and skill in the use of the bow (Pohl 1944, 82). Together with these familiar characteristics, we notice some important oversights and some errors. Vespucci is the only author who does not describe a canoe and the paddles used to propel it. He also says that they generally do not eat the flesh of the females "except those they possess as slaves" (82), a statement contradicted by the other authors, who state that the cannibals never eat female flesh, using the captured women exclusively as slaves and concubines. These would amount to minor omissions, but his report of the encounter between the cannibals and the Spaniards has other problematic elements. Vespucci says that "we had dealings with [the cannibals], and they conducted us to one of their villages. They gave us breakfast and everything we asked of them, but they gave more through fear than affection. And after we had stopped with them all one day, we returned to the ships, remaining friendly with them" (1985, 82). Vespucci claims that the first reaction of the cannibals was to flee due to fear. Yet he himself calls them people of great courage, as do other authors, who unanimously insist on the bellicose nature of the cannibals, who invariably responded to the presence of any intruders with a fierce attack. No other author refers to a friendly encounter with the cannibals, especially due to their fear of the Spaniards. The other authors include no such remarks precisely because they never witnessed such an encounter. Yet Vespucci's way of describing things is typically vague and uninformative. What does he mean when he refers to dealing with them? Was it the whole community or just some old people, male, female, perhaps a cacique? He also seems to have had no problem with the language, a common cause of frustration since Columbus's first voyage. And what were they served for breakfast, since according to him the only food they consume is human flesh? It is also surprising that no mention is made of the physical aspect of the town, its dwellings or surroundings.

The tone of what follows the first encounter is equally vague, fragmentary, and contradictory and cannot be taken at face value. Some of it is clearly absurd. When navigating along the same island, Vespucci notes, the expedition encountered very friendly people from large villages who gave the Spaniards "a very good breakfast of their native dishes" (82). This would seem to imply that these natives were not cannibals but pacific Indians. Such a conclusion, however, would contradict all those authors, including Vespucci himself, who affirm that the two groups do not share the same islands—hence the cannibals' seafaring enterprises. If this island is an exception, then it would be highly improbable that the peaceful Indians' reaction would have been to wait for the intruders "loaded with provisions," for their only experience with foreigners had been with the feared cannibals raiding their villages. Or perhaps they were also cannibals, in which case the friendly reception with a great breakfast—hopefully devoid of human flesh—is all the more improbable.

Yet that is exactly what happened in the next place they anchored, which was, as usual, another large village whose enormous population welcomed the sailors "with great display of affection" and treated them to the customary feast. This time we know that it consisted of wine made of fruit and many other unknown fruits of exquisite taste and aroma (83). The largesse of the Indians did not stop there, however; the Spaniards were presented with some small pearls and eleven large ones. Not satisfied with that, the Indians tell the Spaniards that "if we would wait several days they would go fishing and bring us many [pearls]. Not caring to delay, we departed with many parrots of various colors and with good friendly feeling" (83). Historical records indicate that every expedition that we know of changed course when there was even the most remote possibility of finding gold or precious stones, which, after all, was the yet-unfulfilled purpose of all these navigations. Did Vespucci really think anyone would believe that the sailors happily let an opportunity pass by in which they were being offered banquets and in which their hosts would soon make them wealthy? Certainly they were not in a hurry, and for them not to investigate this matter was not only unthinkable but tantamount to treason to the interests of the Crown! It is passages like this that prove Vespucci's account has little connection with reality, and not just in matters concerning the New World natives.

In this latter category, however, things get worse as the account progresses along what Vespucci believes is the main coast of eastern Asia. Each day, he says, they discover "an endless number of people with various languages" (Pohl 1944, 83). Then they encounter hostile tribes with whom they engage in heroic battles in which the Spaniards "often fought with an endless number of men and always defeated them" (84). We are astonished to learn at the end of Vespucci's letter that the outcome of this thirteen-month voyage, after these and later fierce battles, was the loss of only two Spaniards!

Our astonishment is even greater upon learning of the expedition's encounter with giants. This famous episode, which occurs on yet another un-named and undescribed island, is such an outrageous product of Vespucci's fantasy that even his admirers concede that the story is indeed "picturesque and unlikely" (Gerbi 1985, 43). Vespucci claims to have run into seven women "taller than every one of us by a span and a half" (Pohl 1944, 85), one of whom is their chief. These women are later visited by thirty-six giant men "of such lofty stature that each of them was taller when upon his knees than I was when standing erect." They are heavily armed, but the encounter pro-ceeds "without controversy" and the scouts return to the ships unharmed. What must we make of this nonsense? One could argue that this episode is similar to references to Amazons and other mythological beings, but there is a notable difference. Columbus mentions that he heard the Indians talk about women living on an island without the presence of men, but he never went as far as to claim to have actually paid them a visit.

The voyage progresses to the north with the modest discovery of "more than a thousand islands" invariably inhabited by "many naked people timid and of small intellect" (87). This, we read, is the last stretch of the voyage, and by now we are no longer surprised to see a complete lack of specific geo-graphical or even incidental information. After almost a year of supposed sea-faring, the reader has not been provided with the name of any island or ca-cique, nor has the text described any specific natural phenomenon, animal, or plant, nor any human product or custom. We have no hint about how the native societies are governed or organized (there is no mention of the exis-tence of caciques), how they sleep or what they eat (no mention of ham-mocks or the cazabe [cassava]), or how they fight or simply behave in everyday life. Finally, it must be said that Vespucci's disinformation is also linguistic, for while boasting of having heard more than forty different languages (86), he is the sole traveler among the group considered here who fails to mention a single native term or name.

This omission comes as no surprise, for what are we to expect of a letter about an expedition whose content reveals not a word about its purpose and financing, the names of the captain and pilots, or the number of hands and ships? Vespucci's discourse is nothing more than a careful composition con-sisting of vague generalities and gross exaggerations sprinkled with improb-able and impossible facts. He includes all this while frequently reminding the reader that he is withholding information "in order not to be prolix" or "for the pen" (88), implying that in due course he will write extensively on the matter, which of course he never did. All things considered, Vespucci's first letter is not simply the weakest of all the writings considered thus far; it is an

entirely different kind of text. Gerbi tries to blame the unlikeliness of the
episode of the giants on malarial fever suffered by Vespucci upon his return.
Perhaps so, but I would favor attributing the whole letter to a fever of the
poetic kind. Vespucci has the dubious honor of being the first author to use
the New World as the basis for a work of fiction.

Vespucci's other writing about the New World natives is his third letter.
This letter is also a report about a recently finished voyage to the New World
on behalf of the king of Portugal. Again, no date of departure or number of
ships is given, nor does he mention the names of the captain or any of the
sailors. He makes no reference to his role in the expedition but does say that
their sole purpose was to make discoveries, not to search the land or look for
profits (Pohl 1944, 135). The expedition sailed some eight hundred leagues
along "a new land," a surprising statement since he must have been aware
that it was the same land he had visited two years before. Vespucci then goes
on to describe the nature and the people of this unnamed land, and here our
surprise turns to astonishment, for when he refers to the inhabitants of this
land he writes about only one group of people. It is hard to believe that he
encountered only this group along four hundred leagues (which is at least
1,200 miles), yet no mention is made of any other tribe along the same coast
seen in this or a former trip. Vespucci claims he spent twenty-seven days
among these natives "to understand their conduct and customs" (132), but
he does not explain how this stay was arranged with the natives or what the
other sailors did meanwhile, since they were not supposed to search the land.
We assume from what he says that the natives gave him—and by extension
all the Europeans traveling with him—a most friendly welcome, but this behavior would be contrary to the norm among the cannibals. In 1555, Vice
Admiral Durand de Villegagnon, influenced by Vespucci, tried to establish the
first French colony in Brazil. His dream quickly turned sour. In a long letter,
Villegagnon explains how he had hoped to find a paradise, but all he saw was
a wasteland without a single roof or dwelling. As for the natives, they were
ferocious and wild, devoid of any religion, beasts that just looked like humans
(Arciniegas 1986, 111).

Vespucci then proceeds with his ethnographic report. It is, of course, impossible for us to determine if it is based partially or entirely on his own
observation, but what follows is a curious mixture of the two kinds of natives
we know by other authors, the good Indians and the fierce cannibals. This is
the first description of a people who live in perfect harmony with nature,
entirely without religion, private property, laws, king, authority, or the administration of justice (Pohl 1944, 132). Unlike his former letter, though, this one

contains a few specifics about the community and its way of life. Most of the customs were well known by the time the letter was written, such as the use of hammocks or the habit of eating while squatting on the ground (133). His new information is typically marred by gross exaggeration, such as the reference to "habitations which are two hundred and twenty paces long and thirty wide" (133) or the man whom he judged to be 132 years old (134). As for cannibalism, the only specific information provided concerns a tribal diabolical frenzy in which the whole community eats a mother and her children who had been killed in certain ceremonies. This sounds strange in view of what we know about other cannibals eating only adult males. Vespucci also contradicts his own former statement about their not having any religion, for this "frenzy" is described as a ritualistic killing that obviously implies some religious practice.

Judging from his two attempts to interpret tribal behavior, we cannot expect much of Vespucci the ethnographer. The first is his explanation of marriage customs, which is never clear. "They mate with whom they desire and without much ceremony," he says. The category of people "whom they desire" is later restricted to unmarried virgins, who by virtue of being seduced or violated—Vespucci uses both terms—then become married to a male. This male can accumulate a number of wives, and Vespucci supports this point by telling us of a man he knew "who had ten women. He was jealous of them, and if it happened that one of them was guilty, he punished her and sent her away" (133). Vespucci does not seem to realize the enormous inconsistencies of such statements. How can we reconcile this with his unqualified general statement that "there is no administration of justice, which is unnecessary to them, because in their code no one rules" (132)? Perhaps Vespucci was referring to the absence of any sort of public justice in the Western way. Still, the presence of jealousy among the tribesmen implies the existence of a strong social code by which both men and women must abide, a fact proven by the guilt and its specific punishment for a woman who breaks it. His second reflection concerns his puzzlement about the common practice of war among these natives, as he claims that there is neither a lust for riches nor a desire to rule, and these he takes to be the causes of war and disorder. So his explanation is purportedly drawn from the natives themselves (how did he achieve this level of communication in three weeks?), who told him that their only motivation is the mindless continuation of an ancient practice established by their forefathers. Vespucci's vague explanation pales in comparison with the one advanced by Columbus, Chanca, and Cuneo, which attributes the raids on islands to the double purpose of obtaining male flesh and female slaves.

We must, then, conclude that Vespucci's third letter does not contain the minimum requirements for credibility, which the other authors studied here easily meet. First, Vespucci is very vague about the location, the name, and the configuration of the place described. Second, his account makes no mention of the circumstances surrounding his long encounter, that is, the reaction of natives and Europeans to each other's presence, a particularly important fact since he calls the cannibals warlike and cruel people (134). His description seems to imply that the presence of him and his men among the natives had passed unnoticed. Third, no linguistic evidence of the native speech is given, not even a personal name or the term for an object or custom. And fourth, inconsistencies, exaggerations, and vague statements are so prevalent that the result is an incoherent picture of a contradictory or undefined social environment. Indeed, a close comparison of this letter with the much derided *Mundus Novus* reveals that, as far as information about the New World natives is concerned, there is no substantial difference between the two writings.[6] Other than the incorporation of the episode of the giants from the first letter into the *Mundus Novus* and the addition of some explicit details of its own about the sexual practices of the cannibals, the *Mundus Novus* is basically a re-writing of the third letter that turns the same impossible mixture of pacific Indians and warlike cannibals into a community of noble savages.

The destiny of the works discussed here does not match their merits. Ironically, the only work among them that was to achieve an immediate and lasting popularity was the *Mundus Novus*, by far the least entitled to glory.[7] Its crafted idealism prevailed over the much more realistic and singular depictions of the other texts, and thanks to its colorful writing, it was guaranteed a pervasive influence, particularly in France. There it not only inspired the writings of Montaigne about the cannibals but it was undoubtedly also a key element in promoting the French attempts to establish colonies in Brazil based on the assumption that this land was both a natural and a human paradise.[8] Curiously, it was also in France where two centuries later the concept of the noble savage was developed by philosophers like Rousseau (Brandon 1986, 109–12).

Vespucci is therefore an exception. The other authors studied here generally did a remarkable job of describing entirely unfamiliar people in the most objective way that could be expected of them. All the authors showed genuine interest and respect for the natives. The infrequent instances in which their writings reveal a condescending or derogatory perception are balanced by the more numerous cases of sincere praise. The common denominator of all the writings considered here is their authors' belief that the natives were unquestionably part of a common humanity. As such, their writings are a vivid attempt to express a coherent way of living within the realm of the humanly familiar, therefore balancing the strange and exotic elements of the Indians— their naked primitiveness, either pacific or bellicose, or their lack of private property in the way Europeans understood it—with the common features typical of universal human behavior, above all the existence of a social structure based on a monarchical hierarchy. The attempt itself must be considered no small achievement.

NOTES

1. See Fairchild 1928; Bernheimer 1952; and Combee and Plax 1973.

2. Urs Bitterli points out that after long experience with this type of encounter, it was common for eighteenth-century European explorers and unfamiliar tribes to act with such extreme caution that many avoided mutual contact (1982, 90–94). In view of this, it is remarkable that contacts between Spaniards and Taino Indians were not marked by the typical mutual mistrust.

3. A notable exception is Fray Ramón Pané's *Relación acerca de las antigüedades de los indios*. Pané's report, completed around 1498, resulted from a prolonged stay in Hispaniola, during which Pané carefully studied the language and customs of the Taino Indians. Although brief, his report has rightly been termed the first anthropological study of the New World. An excellent Spanish edition is Pané [ca. 1498] 1974. An English translation can be found in Bourne 1906.

4. Olschki 1941, 639. Elliott points out that passages showing a remarkable amount of realistic observation alternate with others heavily influenced by the European imagination (1970, 19). Gerbi (1985, 12) correctly stresses the importance of Columbus's psychological reactions to both nature and events as a key factor in these differences. This is particularly true in the *diario*, written on the spot under every imaginable mood from depression to enthusiasm.

5. A good summary of the controversy is found in Morison 1974.

6. For a history of the problem, see Pozzi (1984, 21–27, 34–36), and especially Formisano's introduction to his edition of Vespucci's writings (Vespucci 1985). The question regarding authorship of *Mundus Novus* has not been satisfactorily resolved. As noted above, it is unclear why some obscure author should rework Vespucci's Soderini letter. It is startling that Vespucci did not

disassociate himself from a small work that had become so popular by his death in 1512 (Morison 1974, 309). Giuseppe Caraci has suggested that his motive was financial, as a large number of copies were expected to be sold (1964, 16).

7. Between the years 1492 and 1521 the popularity of Vespucci's published writings was even greater than Columbus's, especially in France (Hirsh 1976).

8. For the influence of Vespucci on Montaigne, see Arciniegas 1986, 106–10. For Montaigne's ideas on the Amerindians, see Conley 1989. The French attempts to colonize Brazil were enhanced by the persecution of the Huguenots, who for the first time thought of the New World as a promised land free of religious persecution and therefore tended to idealize the paradisiacal condition of America. See Dickason 1984 and Frank Lestringant 1980.

BIBLIOGRAPHY

Arciniegas, Germán. 1955. *Amerigo and the New World: The Life and Times of Amerigo Vespucci.* Trans. Harriet de Onís. New York: Knopf.

———. 1986. *America in Europe: A History of the New World in Reverse.* Trans. Gabriela Arciniegas and R. Victoria Arana. New York: Harcourt Brace Jovanovich.

Bernheimer, R. 1952. *Wild Men in the Middle Ages.* Cambridge, Mass.: Harvard University Press.

Bitterli, Urs. 1982. *Los "salvages" y los "civilizados": El encuentro de Europa y Ultramar.* Trans. Pablo Sorozábal. Mexico City: Fondo de Cultura Económica.

Bourne, Edward Gaylor. 1906. Columbus, Ramón Pané and the Beginnings of American Anthropology. *Proceedings of the American Antiquarian Society,* new ser., 17:310–84.

Brandon, William. 1986. *New Worlds for Old: Reports from the New World and Their Effect on the Development of Social Thought in Europe, 1500–1800.* Athens: Ohio University Press.

Caraci, Giuseppe. 1964. The Vespuccian Problem: What Point Have They Reached? *Imago Mundi* 18:12–23.

Chanca, Diego Alvarez. Letter. In *Four Voyages to the New World: Letters and Selected Documents,* by Christopher Columbus, trans. and ed. R. H. Major, 18–68. New York: Corinth Books, 1961.

Chiappelli, Fredi, et al., eds. 1976. *First Images of America: The Impact of the New World on the Old.* 2 vols. Los Angeles: University of California Press.

Columbus, Christopher. 1892. *The Letter of Columbus on the Discovery of America*. Ed. Wilberforce Eames. New York: De Vinne Press.

———. 1989. *The "Diario" of Christopher Columbus's First Voyage to America, 1492–93*. Trans. Oliver Dunn and James E. Kelly. Norman: University of Oklahoma Press.

Combee, Jerry, and Martin Plax. 1973. Rousseau's Noble Savage and European Self-consciousness. *Modern Age* 17:173–82.

Conley, Tom. 1989. Montaigne and the Indies. In *1492–1992: Re/Discovering Colonial Writing*, ed. René Jara and Nicholas Spadaccini, 225–62. Hispanic Issues series, 4. Minneapolis: Prisma Institute.

Cuneo, Michele de. 1966. De Novitatibus insularum occeani Hesperii repertarum a Don Christoforo Colombo Genuensi. In *Colombo, Vespucci, Verrazzano: Prime relazioni di navegatori italiani sulla scoperta dell America*, ed. L. Firpo, 47–75. Turin: Unione Tipografico Editrice.

Dickason, Olive Patricia. 1984. *The Myth of the Savage and the Beginnings of French Colonialism in the Americas*. Edmonton: University of Alberta.

Elliott, John H. 1970. *The Old World and the New, 1492–1560*. Cambridge: Cambridge University Press.

———. 1989. The Discovery of America and the Discovery of Man. In *Spain and Its World, 1500–1700*. New Haven: Yale University Press.

Fairchild, Hoxie Neale. 1928. *The Noble Savage: A Study in Romantic Naturalism*. New York: Columbia University Press.

Gerbi, Antonello. 1985. *Nature in the New World: From Chistopher Columbus to Gonzalo Fernández de Oviedo*. Trans. Jeremy Moyle. Pittsburgh: University of Pittsburgh Press.

Granzotto, Gianni. 1989. *Christopher Columbus*. Trans. Stephen Sartarelli. New York: Doubleday.

Hirsh, Rudolf. 1976. Printed Reports on the Early Discoveries and Their Reception. In *First Images of America: The Impact of the New World on the Old*, ed. Fredi Chiappelli et al., 1:537–60. Los Angeles: University of California Press.

Lestringant, Frank. 1980. Calvinistes et cannibales. *Bulletin de la Societé du Protestantisme Français* 126:9–26.

Magnaghi, Alberto. 1926. *Amerigo Vespucci: Studio critico con speziale riguardo ad una valutazione delle fonti*. Rome: Fratelli Treves.

Morison, Samuel Eliot. 1974. *The European Discovery of America*. Vol. 2: *The Southern Voyages*. New York: Oxford University Press.

Olschki, Leonardo. 1941. What Columbus Saw. *Proceedings of the American Philosophical Association* 84:633–59.

Pané, Fray Ramón. [ca. 1498] 1974. *Relación acerca de las antigüedades de los indios.* Ed. Juan José Arrom. Mexico City: Siglo Veintiuno.

Pohl, Frederick J. 1944. *Amerigo Vespucci: Pilot Major.* New York: Columbia University Press. Includes the text of Vespucci's *Letters.*

Pozzi, Mario. 1984. *Il Mondo Nuovo di Amerigo Vespucci.* Milan: Serra e Riva.

Scyllacio, Nicolaus. [1494] 1859. *De insulis meridiani atque indici maris nuper inventis.* Latin text, with English translation by John Mulligan. New York. First published in Pavia or Milan.

Sierra, Vicente D. 1968. *Amerigo Vespucci: El enigma de la historia de América.* Madrid: Editora Nacional.

Vespucci, Amerigo. 1916. *Mundus Novus.* Trans. George Tyler Northup. Princeton, N.J.: Princeton University Press.

———. 1951. *El nuevo mundo: Cartas relativas a sus viajes y descubrimientos.* Texts in Italian, Spanish, and English. Introduction by Roberto Levillier. Buenos Aires: Nova.

———. 1985. *Lettere di viaggio.* Ed. Luciano Formisano. Milan: Mondadori.

2

The Cannibal Law of 1503

Michael Palencia-Roth

Who was the New Man encountered by Columbus and those who followed him?[1] And what was the New World? During the quincentennary of the discovery of the Americas, these are two of the most basic and significant questions that may be posed today.[2] They are not new questions, but the answers to them are not as obvious or as simple as they may first appear. Over the centuries the questions have been asked—and answered—in various ways in Europe, North America, and Latin America. From the perspective of North America in the late twentieth century, we tend to forget just how those questions were framed—we tend even to forget that they were asked—in the one hundred or so years of New World history preceding Jamestown and Plymouth Rock. Those many years of European activity in the New World, especially in what is now called Latin America, created a cultural image that had profound effects on European thought in the sixteenth century as well as later.

In any intercultural encounter, the way people are viewed has a great deal to do with the way they are treated. Cultural perceptions and assumptions result in policies that, in turn, reinforce those perceptions. This essay explores a particular series of intercultural encounters and cultural perceptions that were partly responsible for the European obsession with cannibalism in the sixteenth century, an obsession largely overlooked today in the historical record[3] and generally glossed over in historical reconstructions of the discovery, conquest, and colonization of the New World.[4]

Some may doubt that cannibalism existed at all in the New World. The most strident of these anticannibalists, anthropologist W. Arens, asserts in *The Man-Eating Myth* (1979) that cannibalism never existed anywhere in the world at any time and that the sources of such reports are all moot.[5] Where, asks Arens in a tactic reminiscent of those used by revisionist Holocaust historians, are the survivors of cannibal feasts? Where are the eyewitness accounts? Where are the man-eaters themselves? Since Arens discredits all accounts for one reason or another, and since he refuses to believe anyone who claims to have been an eyewitness, he can easily maintain his position, though it has been persuasively refuted by a number of scholars, from Donald W. Forsyth (1983) to Marshall Sahlins (1985). Forsyth (1983: 147–78), for instance, documents the existence of cannibalism in colonial Brazil, disproving Arens along the way.

It is true that *some* statements about the existence of cannibalism were lies, but it does not follow that *all* of them were. Some of the fabrications and exaggerations, however, were very important because, as shown later in this essay, they affected the course of history. In a sense, what matters most to the present argument are the *attributions*, whether true or untrue, of cannibalism to this or that people. In the fifteenth and sixteenth centuries, these attributions—the equivalent of cultural perceptions and definitions—brought with them significant consequences, which this essay and some of my other works on the subject explore (see Palencia-Roth 1985: 1–27; Palencia-Roth 1989: 123–37; and forthcoming).

On 30 October 1503, eleven years after Columbus landed on what has been identified as Watling's Island, Queen Isabella signed into law in the city of Segovia a document that seemed to give at least preliminary answers to questions about the New World and the New Man. In succeeding years this document became increasingly important, for both practical and symbolic reasons. I call it the "cannibal law of 1503," and although it was not the only cannibal law (Konetzke discusses a very similar one that was signed in 1511 [1953–62, 1:31–33] and reconfirmed in 1533 [1:45–46]), it was the first such law in New World history. In fact, as far as I have been able to determine, it was the first such law anywhere. This extraordinary edict, which is approached in this essay from legal, theological, anthropological, and cartographic perspectives, is indispensable for an understanding of the New World in the sixteenth century:

> Queen Isabel etc., to the most illustrious princes Phillip and Juana, archdukes of Austria . . . and to all the councils, mayors, council chair-

men, aldermen, sheriffs, royal judges, and other justices of all the cities
and villages and places belonging to my kingdoms and dominions, to
each one of you health and God's grace. . . . Let it be known that my
Lord the King and I, intending that all people who live and are on the
islands and Terra Firma of the Ocean Sea become Christians and be
converted to our Holy Catholic Faith, have ordered by means of a letter of ours that no person or persons of those who by our command
went to those islands and Terra Firma should dare to apprehend or
capture any person or persons of the Indians of the said islands and
Terra Firma of the said Ocean Sea in order to bring them here to my
kingdoms or in order to take them to any other place, and that no
injury either to their persons or their property be done unto them,
under certain penalties spelled out in our letter, even if the motive be
to help the Indians. This is because some people have brought some
Indians from the said islands, and we decreed that they all be placed at
liberty, and they were; and this being done, and in order to persuade
them to become Christians and live like men of reason, we decreed
that some of our captains should go to the said islands and Terra Firma
of the Ocean Sea, and we sent along with them some religious [men]
in order that they should preach and teach the doctrines of our Holy
Catholic Faith, and in order that they should require it of those who
would be in our service. And on some of the said islands they were
well received and made welcome; [but] on the islands of San Bernardo
and Isla Fuerte, and in the ports of Cartagena and the islands of Bura
there was a people who are said to be cannibals and who never wished
to hear [the men of the Church] nor to receive them; rather they defended themselves against [the priests] with their weapons, and they
resisted them so that [our priests] could neither land nor stay on the
said islands where [the cannibals] live, and during the said resistance
they even killed several Christians; and afterwards they have been engaged continuously in making war against those Indians who are in my
service, and they have been capturing them in order to eat them, as
they do in fact; and I have been informed that, the better to serve God
and for the sake of the peace and security of the people who live on
the islands and on Terra Firma and are in my service, the said cannibals should be punished for the crimes they have committed against
my subjects, it is well that I should decree concerning the matter.

    And I ordered my council to look into the matter and discuss it; my
council did so and—zealously desiring like us that the said cannibals

be converted to our Holy Catholic Faith, as indeed they have been asked [required] to do so many times, and that they be incorporated into the communion of the faithful and abide under our rule, living in security and treating their neighbors on the other islands well, all of which not only have they not wished to do, but also they have sought to defend themselves against indoctrination and against being taught our Holy Catholic Faith, and they have continuously waged war against our subjects and have killed many Christians who had gone to the said islands, and since they are hardened in their evil intentions, eating the said Indians and worshipping idols—agreed that I should rule in this letter concerning the matter, and I think well of the advice.

Therefore, by means of the present [letter] I give the permission and the authority to any and every person under my command who should go to the islands and Terra Firma of the said Ocean Sea that up to the present have been discovered or that will be discovered, that if the said cannibals should resist and not wish to receive and welcome in their lands the captains and peoples who by my command go and make the said voyages, and if [the cannibals] do not wish to listen to them in order to be indoctrinated in the things of our Holy Catholic Faith and enter my service and become subject to me, [then the persons under my command] may and can capture [the cannibals] in order to take them to whichever lands and islands . . . they wish, paying us the share of them that belongs to us, in order that [the cannibals] might be sold and a profit be made without [the seller] incurring any penalty whatsoever, and this is so that, being brought to these parts and being in the service of Christians, [the cannibals] can be more easily converted and attracted to our Holy Catholic Faith. . . . Decreed in the city of Segovia on the thirtieth day of the month of October of the year fifteen hundred and three. [Signed] I, THE QUEEN. I, Gaspar de Gricio, secretary to the Queen, our Ladyship, ordered this to be written according to her command.[6]

Doña Isabel etc. A los Ilmos. Príncipes D. Felipe é Doña Juana, Archiduques de Austria, . . . é á todos los Concejos, Corregidores, Alcaldes, Regidores, Alguaciles, Merinos é otras Justicias é Jueces cualquier de todas las Ciudades é Villas é Logares de los mis Reinos é Señoríos, é á cada uno é cualquier de vos, salud é gracia. Sepades que el Rey mi Señor é Yo con fin que todas las personas que viven y están en las Islas é Tierra-firme del mar Océano fuesen cristianos é se redujesen á nuestra

Santa Fe Católica, hobimos mandado por una nuestra Carta que persona ni personas algunas, de los que por nuestro mandado fuesen á las dichas Islas é Tierra-Firme, no fuesen osadas deprender ni cautivar nin alguna persona nin personas de los indios de las dichas Islas é Tierra-firme de dicho mar Océano para los traer á estos mis Reinos nin para los llevar á otras partes algunas nin les ficiesen otro ningun mal ni daño en sus personas ni en sus bienes, so ciertas penas en la dicha nuestra Carta contenidas, y aun por les facer merced, porque algunas personas habian traido de las dichas Islas algunos de los dichos Indios, los mandamos tomar é les mandamos poner, é fueron puestos en toda libertad; y despues de todo esto fecho, por les mas convencer é animar á que fuesen cristianos porque viviesen como hombres razonables, hobimos mandado que algunos nuestros Capitanes fuesen á las dichas Islas é Tierra-firme del dicho mar Océano, é enviamos con ellos algunos Religiosos que les predicasen é dotrinasen en las cosas de nuestra Santa Fe Católica, é para que los requiriesen que estobiesen en nuestro servicio; é como quier que en algunas de las dichas Islas fueron bien rescibidos é acogidos, en las islas de San Bernardo é Isla fuerte, é en los puertos de Cartagena, y en las islas de Bura, donde estaba una gente que se dice Caníbales, nunca los quisieron oir nin acoger, antes se defendieron dellos con sus armas, é les resistieron que non pudiesen entrar ni estar en las dichas Islas donde ellos estan, y aun en la dicha resistencia mataron algunos Cristianos, é despues acá han estado é estan á mi servicio é pertinacia faciendo guerra á los Indios que estan á mi servicio, é prendiéndolos para los comer como de fecho los comen; y como Yo he sido informada que para lo que conviene á servicio de Dios é mio, é á la paz é sosiego de las gentes que viven en las Islas é Tierra-firme que estan á mi servicio, é los dichos Caníbales sean castigados por los delitos que han cometido contra mis súbditos, conviene que yo mandase proveer sobre ello: é Yo mandé á los de mi Consejo que lo viesen á platicasen; é por ellos visto, acatando como Nos con zelo que los dichos Caníbales fuesen reducidos á nuestra Santa Fe Católica, han sido requeridos muchas veces que fuesen Cristianos é se convirtiesen, y estoviesen encorporados en la comunion de los fieles é so nuestra obediencia, é viviesen seguramente, é tratasen bien á los otros sus vecinos de las otras Islas, los cuales non solamente non lo han querido facer, como dicho es, mas antes han buscado é buscan de se defender para no ser dotrinados nin enseñados en las cosas de nuestra Santa Fe Católica, é continuamente han

fecho guerra a nuestros súbditos, é han muerto muchos Cristianos de
los que han ido á las dichas Islas, é por estar como estan endurecidos
en su mal propósito, idolatrando é comiendo los dichos Indios, fue
acordado que debia mandar dar esta mi Carta en la dicha razon, é Yo
tóvelo por bien; por ende por la presente doy licencia é facultad á todas é cualesquier personas que con mi mandado fueren, así á las Islas
é Tierra-firme del dicho mar Océano que fasta agora estan descubiertas, como á los que fueren á descobrir otras cualesquier Islas é Tierra-
firme, para que si todavia los dichos Caníbales resistieren, é non qui-
sieren rescibir é acoger en sus tierras á los Capitanes é gentes que por
mi mandado fueren á facer los dichos viages, é oirlos para ser dotrinados en las cosas de nuestra Santa Fe Católica, é estar en mi servicio é
so mi obediencia, los puedan cautivar é cautiven para los llevar á las
tierras é Islas donde fueren, . . . pagándonos la parte que dellos nos
pertenesca, é para que los puedan vender é aprovecharse dellos, sin
que por ello cayan nin incurran en pena alguna, porque trayéndose á
estas partes é serviéndose dellos los Cristianos, podrán ser mas ligera-
mente convertidos é atraidos á nuestra Santa Fe Católica. . . . Dada en
la ciudad de Segovia á treinta dias del mes de Octubre de mil é qui-
nientos é tres años. = YO LA REINA. = Yo Gaspar de Gricio, Secretario
de la Reina nuestra Señora, la fice escribir por su mandado. (Navarrete
1945, 478–80)

Like many such sixteenth-century documents—be they "writs" (*provisiones*),
royal decrees (*cédulas reales*), or "licenses" (*permisos*)—the cannibal law is divided rhetorically into the head, the body, and the tail.[7] The head consists of
the greetings; the body, the substance of the law; and the tail, the means of
dissemination and the signatories. The body itself is usually further subdi-
vided into the situation under discussion (both past and present), the reasons
why a legal opinion is desirable, and the opinion or law that is then declared,
together with the penalties for disobedience. In general the cannibal law follows this format.

The body—as usual, the most interesting and relevant part—begins with
the phrase, "Let it be known that my Lord the King and I . . . " First the Crown
reviews the reason for colonizing the New World (Christianization) and the
actions undertaken by its representatives, together with the standards of behavior expected and the penalties incurred for not following the prescribed
course of action. (These penalties, not specified here, had been spelled out in

other documents of the late 1490s and early 1500s.) The assessment of the recent past is followed by a more precise review of the current situation. Recounting the Church's missionary activities, the Crown then goes to the heart of the matter and the reason for the present legislation. To the Crown there are basically two kinds of Indians in the New World: good and bad. The cooperative Indians, identified in other documents as *guatiaos* or *taínos*,[8] have willingly accepted Christianity and are considered loyal subjects. As such, they have the rights of any other subjects, including the right to be protected against the criminal elements in their own society. Here the criminal elements are identified as *caníbales*, and their crime consists in refusing to hear the gospel, in resisting with force the Crown's representatives, in continuing to make war on the Crown's newest subjects, and in eating them, "as they do in fact" (in the words of the edict). Further, despite the best efforts of the Spanish, these caníbales have stubbornly persisted in their criminal ways (to which idolatry is now added), and it is therefore important that the queen pass a law to stop such behavior. Accordingly—and this is the ruling itself—Spaniards are granted the authority (should the caníbales prove uncooperative) to capture, enslave, transport, and sell the man-eating Indians (paying the Crown its percentage, known as the royal fifth), without fear of subsequent penalty. The removal of the penalty is important, for New World slavery had been considered illegal before this moment. This new treatment of cannibal Indians is being officially undertaken—so explains the Crown—in order to implement previously established civilizing and salvational policies.

The reasoning in the body of the cannibal law, though tight, is somewhat circular. The law defines and explains an ideal situation that is said to exist, though not everywhere in the New World. After identifying an exception to the ideal, a problem, the law suggests a solution and corrective measures. These measures are meant to ensure that the ideal situation will be achieved throughout the New World. Caníbales, then, are exceptions to the ideal. They violate the Spanish sense of order, both moral and civil.

Such a summary of the cannibal law, though I think accurate, glosses over much of its historical complexity, a complexity that may be explored through the following kinds of questions: How did the Crown come to hold these principles and to make these distinctions concerning New World people? What was the specific source of this document? What were the law's practical effects, both immediate and long-term? How did it shape the discourse concerning the two questions posed at the very beginning of this essay, namely the identity of the New Man and of the New World?

The history of the presence of cannibals in the New World begins with the discovery of their absence. That is, although Columbus and others had expected to see man-eaters during that first voyage, they did not. In his famous letter to Santángel, written in February 1493 and disseminated in several editions and languages through much of Europe during the 1490s, Columbus found it necessary to admit that "on these islands up to this point I have not found monstrous men, as many had thought; rather, the people are all very handsome" ("en estas islas fasta aquí no he hallado ombres mostrudos, como muchos pensavan, más antes es toda gente de muy lindo acatamiento"; Varela 1982, 144). About ten lines further on, the "monstrous men" (*ombres mostrudos*) are identified as the Indians of an island called Carib who "eat human flesh" ("comen carne umana"; Varela 1982, 144–45). This passing reference to man-eaters conceals what is evident to any reader of Columbus's diary of that first voyage: his obsession with man-eaters, an obsession almost as great as that of finding the kingdom of the Great Khan. The man-eater appears repeatedly, from the first mention on 4 November 1492 to the last on 16 January 1493.[9] In the words of Bartolomé de Las Casas, who transcribed much of the diary and summarized the rest, the entry for 4 November reads in part:

> [The Admiral] understood that far from there one could find men with but a single eye and others with dogs' heads who ate men and that on capturing men they decapitated them, drank their blood, and cut off their sex organs.

> Entendió también [el Almirante] que lexos de allí avía hombres de un ojo, y otros con hoçicos de perros que comían los hombres, y que en tomando uno lo degollavan y le bevían la sangre y le cortavan su natura. (Varela 1982, 51)[10]

Columbus's remarks were influenced by a long descriptive tradition in the West concerning the monstrous Other—the stranger, the barbarian, the marginal person. From Homer to Columbus, and passing through, among others, Herodotus, Aristotle, Ktesias the Knidian, Megasthenes, Strabo, Pomponius Mela, Pliny, Ptolemy, Solinus, Saint Augustine, Isidore of Seville, Rabanus Maurus, Prester John, Marco Polo, John Mandeville, and Pierre d'Ailly, descriptions of human otherness or of monstrous people are more or less rhetorically consistent. The hermeneutical tradition concerning the man-eater, like that concerning monsters in general, usually depended on distance or separation. It was in the places most distant from the traveler's home that monsters were said to be found. Textual evidence of this tendency in Western civilization begins with Homer, especially in the *Odyssey*, a work "composed" during Greece's colonization of the Mediterranean and the Black Sea. In book 9 of the *Odyssey*, Odysseus comes upon (and defeats through cunning) a gigantic and cyclopean man-eater named Polyphemus, and in book 10 he barely escapes with his life from a man-eating people, the Lestrygonians. In other Greek and Roman texts, the country of the man-eaters (who were known as *anthropophagi* or *anthropophagoi* until Columbus disseminated another name for them) was generally located beyond an enormous and forbidding desert or beyond an inhospitable mountain range in a terra incognita rumored to be inhabited by strange people. The sheer distance of Columbus's voyage led him to expect monsters. By journeying to the kingdom of the Great Khan, he had in fact entered the realm of monsters as far as was known in his day. Columbus's remarks therefore make historical sense; they were consistent with current knowledge.

Although no icons of *anthropophagi*—or of other monsters such as *acephali* or *cynocephali*—are known to have survived on early maps from Greece and Rome, certainly the descriptions of these beings by geographers like Pliny—and later, encyclopedists like Solinus or Isidore of Seville—were given their iconographic equivalents by manuscript illustrators and the creators of the great *mappaemundi* of the Middle Ages (see Friedman 1981; Wittkower [1942] 1972, 46–74). Medieval mappaemundi placed monsters at the margins of territories or countries. Europe had no monsters,[11] but distant Scythia did (the influence of Herodotus), as did Africa and India (the influence of Ktesias the Knidian and Megasthenes, among others). Monsters appear at the margins, at the decorative circumferences beyond *terrae* in any way *cognitae*, of the circular maps of Ebstorf, Waldsperger, Beatus, Psalter, Borgia, and Hereford (Harley and Woodward 1987, 331).

But the circumferences were not merely decorative. For example, the periphery of the Ebstorf Map (ca. 1235) contains a panel depicting Gog and Magog, traditionally known as the enemies of the Kingdom of God, a characterization that would find an echo in the sixteenth century. Gog and Magog are here seen—so the Latin legend describes them—as eating human flesh and drinking human blood (see fig. 2.1). Human themselves, at least in appearance, they nonetheless have been exiled to the edges of humanity and geographically marginalized. As I argue in this essay, such a cartographical marginalization foreshadows similar legal and moral practices in the sixteenth century.

Columbus himself did not actually see the monstrous man-eater on his first voyage but only heard descriptions of him. That he could not understand the

FIGURE 2.1. Gog and Magog, from the Ebstorfer World Map, ca. 1235. The original map was destroyed in a bombing raid in 1943. (Rosien 1951, pl. 13; courtesy
the Newberry Library.)

Indians' language does not seem to have prevented him from reporting their
conversations and from identifying man-eaters with the term *caníbales* on
23 November, *canimas* on 26 November, and *caribes* on 26 December. This was
the first time, of course, that the Arawakan words appeared in a European
language. In the entry for 15 January, Columbus, still not having seen a single
man-eater in the New World, concluded that he had to inform Europe about
the "scandal of the Indians" ("del escándalo de los indios"; Varela 1982, 117).
He did so in his letter to Santángel. Rather early on in New World history,
therefore, the pattern of writing about cannibals from scant evidence was established. Yet there is ample precedent for such reporting: Herodotus did the
same in his history, as did each of the authors mentioned above.

Columbus described the Indians he encountered on his first voyage as "good," even "handsome" people. In his letter to Santángel, he wrote that they could easily become Christians, "for they are inclined to serve and to love Your Royal Highnesses and the entire Castilian nation" ("se farán cristianos, [y] que se inclinan al amor e cervicio de Sus Altezas y de toda la nación castellana"; Varela 1982, 142). Slavery, then, was not part of the picture in 1492 and 1493; the social structure envisioned by Columbus was closer to feudalism. The subject of slavery—which would become the main topic of the cannibal law of 1503—entered the picture during the second voyage when, Columbus reported, he and his men actually came upon man-eaters, fought with them, and saved other Indians from being eaten. Addressing the Crown in the "Memorandum to Torres" (Memorial a Torres; Varela 1982, 147–62), a seldom-cited but important document penned in the new colonial city of Isabela on Hispaniola on 30 January 1494, Columbus suggested a policy for dealing with these man-eaters. What was "far from there" during the first voyage was now close by, threateningly so. In this way, the rumors of the first voyage began to be transformed into historical fact.

In the Memorandum to Torres, Columbus spoke not as an explorer but as a colonial administrator (which, in fact, he had become). Torres, the bearer of the memorandum, was to obtain the official reaction to each of the propositions put forward in it. Among them are two about Indians identified simply as caníbales, further explanation and qualification no longer being considered necessary. The first item discusses the lack of translators in the islands and therefore the difficulties that the Spaniards faced in attempting to indoctrinate the Indians in "the Holy Catholic Faith." Columbus sent several cannibals to Castile with Antonio Torres with instructions that they be taught Spanish and return to the Indies as translators. He recommended sending many such Indians to Castile, for once in Spain they would abandon the

> inhuman custom that they have of eating people, and there in Castile, on learning the language, they will more easily be baptized for the good of their souls; and even among those peoples who do not have these [cannibal] customs we will gain a great deal of credit, once it is seen how we capture those who seek to do them harm and who are so frightful that even the name alone causes fear.

> inhumana costumbre que tienen de comer ombres, e allá en Castilla, entendiendo la lengua, muy más presto recibirán el bautismo e farán el provecho de sus almas, e aun entre estos pueblos que no son de

> estas costumbres se ganaría gran crédito por nosotros, viendo que
> aquellos prendésemos e captivásemos de quien ellos suelen resci-
> bir daños e tienen tamaño miedo que del nombre sólo se espantan.
> (Varela 1982, 153)

Already by 1494, then, Europeans divided the Indians into two categories, the good and the bad, and the "good" Indians (that is, the new subjects of the Crown) were considered to be best protected and cared for by capturing and controlling the "bad" Indians. The cannibal law of 1503 makes the same distinction between two kinds of Indians; this item in the memorandum is probably the earliest direct source of this way of thinking.

The Crown responded first by ordering Torres to report to Columbus on how the cannibals were treated in Spain. Then, directly addressing the item, the Crown stated:

> This is very good, and this is how he [Columbus] should proceed, but
> he should try to find out how, if possible, he can convert them [the
> cannibals] to our Holy Catholic Faith *over there*, and he should do the
> same with the Indians of the islands where he is [now] (my emphasis).

> Que está muy bien, y así lo debe hacer, pero que procure allá cómo, si
> se puediere, se reduzgan a nuestra santa fe católica, y asimismo lo pro-
> cure con los de las islas donde está. (Varela 1982, 153).

On the one hand, the Crown agreed with Columbus. On the other, it opposed bringing many Indians to Spain. As a result of this decision, the inhabitants of the New World, rarely seen in Spain up to that point, would remain a rarity. They would exist primarily in the words of letters, travel accounts, testimonials, and reports. Holding the people of the New World at a distance, the Crown would respond to them, therefore, as images created and sustained by writing. In effect, the New World and its people became a "text" to Spain that could be read, edited, and revised. The people tended to become textual abstractions.

The second item dealing with man-eaters in the Memorandum to Torres is just as important as the first:

> Item: you should communicate to Your Highnesses that, considering
> the good of the souls of the said cannibals and even of those [other
> Indians] here, it occurs to me that the more Indians who could be
> taken over there [to Spain], the better, and in this regard Your High-
> nesses could make use of them in the following manner: since, as has

been noted, cattle and beasts of burden are necessary for the sustenance of the people who must live here [that is, Spaniards], and for the
good of all these islands, Your Highnesses could grant a license and
permit a sufficient number of caravels to come here every year, bringing the said cattle and other things necessary to populate the land and
cultivate the soil, and all this at reasonable cost, a cost which could be
covered by [shipping back to Spain] cannibal slaves, a people so fierce,
healthy, well-proportioned, and intelligent that, once rid of that inhu-
manity, they would make better slaves than any others.

Item diréis a Sus Altesas qu'el provecho de las almas de los dicho caníbales, e aun d'estos de acá, ha traído en pensamiento que cuantos más
allá se llevasen sería mejor, e en ello Sus Altesas podrían ser servidos
d'esta manera: que visto cuánto son acá menester los ganados e bestias
de trabajo para el sostenimiento de la gente que acá ha de estar, e bien
de todas estas islas, Sus Altesas podrán dar liçençia e permiso a un nú-
mero de carabelas suficiente que vengan acá cada año, e trayan de los
dichos ganados e otros mantenimientos e cosas de poblar el campo e
aprovechar la tierra, y esto en precios razonables a sus costas de los que
truxieren, las cuales cosas se les podrían pagar en esclavos d'estos caníbales, gente tan fiera e dispuesta e bien proporcionada e de muy bien
entendimiento, los cuales quitados de aquella inhumanidad creemos
que serán mejores que otros ningunos esclavos. (Varela 1982, 154)

Having opened the paragraph with a statement of his concern for the well-
being of the cannibals' souls, Columbus advised the Crown to do everything
necessary for the cannibals' salvation. Mixing in this way theological arguments with economic ones, he arrived at a justification of slavery. He was the
first to do so but not the last.

For its part, the Crown postponed to some future date the issue of enslaving cannibals: "On this matter [as the Crown states in the margins] a decision
is suspended for now until someone else should come from over there and
the Admiral writes what he thinks about it" ("En esto [indican los reyes] se ha
suspendido por agora hasta que venga otro camino de allá y escriba el Almirante lo que en esto le pareciere"; Varela 1982, 154). "For now" cannibalism
in itself was not sufficient justification for enslaving Indians. The way that justification was secured is rather complex, and the path must be reconstructed
from widely scattered documents.

On 12 April 1495, the Crown, not yet having received the Memorandum

to Torres that Columbus wrote in January 1494 but already knowing something about the arrival of the caníbales in Spain, dictated a royal decree to the
bishop of Badajoz, informing him that "concerning that which you have written about the Indians who have arrived in the caravels, it seems to us that they
can be sold better in Andalusia than in any other place; you should proceed
to sell them as you see fit" ("cerca de lo que nos escribisteis de los indios que
vienen en las carabelas, parécenos que se podrán vender allá mejor en esta
Andalucía que en otra parte; debéislo facer vender como mejor os pareciere";
Konetzke 1953–62, 1:2). Even before learning of Columbus's intentions along
these lines, the Crown considered the Indians potential slaves. Four days
later, however, the doubts began. Once again the Crown wrote the bishop of
Badajoz, reminding him of the previous letter but asking now that nothing
further be done concerning the Indians:

> We wish to be advised by scholars, theologians, and canon lawyers if
> these [Indians] can in good conscience be sold as slaves or not, and
> such a matter cannot be decided upon until we see the letters that the
> Admiral has written to us and we know why he is sending us [these
> Indians] as captives, and Torres, who has these letters, still has not sent
> them; therefore, concerning the sales which you might make of these
> Indians, hold the money in trust for a brief time until we can deter-
> mine whether or not we can sell [those Indians].

> Porque nos queríamos informarnos de letrados, teólogos y canonistas
> si con buena conciencia se pueden vender éstos por esclavos o no,
> y esto no se puede facer hasta que veamos las cartas que el Almirante
> nos escriba para saber la causa por qué los envía acá para cautivos, y
> estas cartes tiene Torres que no nos las envió; por ende, en las ventas
> que ficiéredes destos indios sea fiado el dinero dellos por algún breve
> término, porque en este tiempo nosotros sepamos si los podemos
> vender o no. (Konetzke 1953–62, 1:3)

By 2 June 1495 the Crown had received the memorandum and apparently
had decided not to wait any longer for advice from their body of consultants.
Ignoring the second item in Columbus's memorandum to Torres, the Crown
agreed with the first:

> [Since the Indians had been sent not to be sold but] to be given to cer-
> tain people so that they might learn the language; and since these nine

heads are not for sale but for language training, we order that you give
them over so that we might proceed as the Admiral advised.

[Dado que los indios enviados por Colón no habían sido enviados para
vender sino] para que los diese á algunas personas para que apren-
diesen la lengua; y pues estas nueve cabezas no son para vender salvo
para aprender la lengua, vos mandamos que se las fagais entregar luego
para que faga dellos lo quel dicho Almirante escribió. (Konetzke 1953–
62, 1:5)

For now, the cannibal Indians were still a novelty, and the Crown remained
somewhat cautious in its pronouncements. But as other factors came into the
picture, the cannibal Indians gradually ceased being novelties and became a
problem requiring a drastic solution. That process may be followed in the
documents transmitted to Spain between 1494 and 1503 and in the reactions
of people in Spain to the stories coming out of the New World.

At first, reports of cannibals continued to be influenced largely by the hermeneutical tradition concerning monsters and other fabulous beings. Such
reports particularly affected, as will be seen, the history of New World cartography, even from the beginning. For instance, in Columbus's diary[12] the following islands are identified as belonging to cannibals: Española and Cuba[13]
(5 December 1492) and Carib and Matinino (15 January 1493). It was on Matinino, said Columbus, that cannibal women lived. They were supposedly
visited by their men only during certain times of the year, a story obviously
derived from the Amazon tradition. On today's maps, the island called Carib
and the Amazon island called Matinino have disappeared; not so on early
New World maps. In fact, on the first map we possess of the New World,
known as the Zorzi sketch map (dated 1500), which was drawn according to
Columbus's instructions, two of the islands are identified as belonging to cannibals (see fig. 2.2). One was located exactly where the Indians told him during his first voyage that it was: "the second one at the entrance to the Indies"
("la segunda a la entrada de Las Indias"; Varela 1982, 144). The other, closer
to the mainland, became known as being "of cannibals" during his later voyages. It is difficult to find the equivalent of either island on today's maps, and
yet, through the powerful credence given to cartography, Columbus's remarks began to acquire an almost ontological validity. Attributions became
facts; rumors became part of science.

Some of the early rumors of cannibal islands or cannibal lands were, in

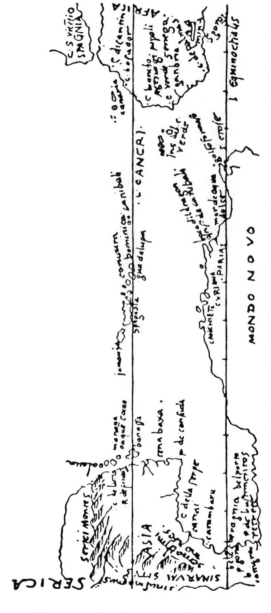

FIGURE 2.2. Alessandro Zorzi's sketch map of the New World, drawn according to instructions from Christopher Columbus, 1500. (Fite and Freeman 1926, 14; courtesy of the University of Illinois at Urbana-Champaign Library.)

fact, later substantiated. From 1494 on, beginning with Columbus's second voyage, reports concerning cannibals often described not imaginary beings but European contacts with real Indians. The first island on which the Spaniards landed on Columbus's second voyage, Guadalupe (now Guadeloupe), was characterized by Peter Martyr in his summary of that voyage as "the principal dwelling place of the Caribs" ("la principal morada de los caribes"; Martyr 1944, 16).

Europeans viewed the cannibals sent back by Columbus at the end of the second voyage with both horror and fascination. Martyr himself confessed that he traveled to Medina several times just to look at the cannibals, who were put on display like circus animals (Martyr 1944, 18). These trips occurred in October 1494. Later, on 5 December in a letter to Pomponio Leto, Martyr tried to make sense of what he had seen and learned:

> And do not doubt that there are [people like] Lestrygonians and Polyphemus [in the New World] who feed on human flesh. Listen and pay attention to what I have to say, even if your hair should stand on end. On leaving the Fortunate Isles—which some wish to identify as the Canaries—and proceeding in the direction of Hispaniola—that's the name of the island where [the Spanish] have settled—if one angles down a bit toward the equator, one comes upon a group of innumerable islands belonging to fierce men who are called cannibals or caribs and who—though naked—are noteworthy warriors. . . . They attack the villages of peaceful Indians, and the men that they capture they eat raw. They castrate the boys, just as we do chickens; and when they are grown and are fat they decapitate them and eat them. Proof of this was obtained by our men when, on nearing land with their ships, they so frightened the caribs, who had never seen ships of such size, that they abandoned their homes, fleeing to the mountains and the dense forests. Our men, on entering the houses of the cannibals (circular houses built from small logs), found men's legs hanging from stakes and salted in the same way we generally salt swine, and [they found] the head of a young man who had recently been killed, still flecked with blood, and [there were] pieces of the same young man in pots to be cooked together with ducks and parrots, and other [pieces of flesh] placed at the fire on spits.

> Y no dudes que hay Lestrigones o Polifemos [en el Nuevo Mundo] que se alimentan de carne humana. Escucha y ten cuidado no sea que

de horror se te pongan los pelos de punta. Cuando se sale de las Afor-
tunadas—que algunos quieren sean las Canarias—en dirección a la
Española—pues con este nombre llaman a la isla en que han fijado su
asiento—, si se enfila proa un poco hacia el Mediodía, se viene a dar
en un grupo incontable de islas de hombres feroces, llamados caníbales
o caribes, los cuales—aunque desnudos—son notables guerreros. . . .
Atacan [las] aldeas [de indios pacíficos] y a los hombres que cogen se
los comen crudos. Castran a los niños, como nosotros a los pollos; y
cuando han crecido y engordado, los degüellan y los comen. Prueba
de ello tuvieron los nuestros cuando, al arrimar las naves, aterrori-
zados los caribes a causa del tamaño nunca visto de los navíos, aban-
donaron sus casas y huyeron a las montañas y a los espesos bosques.
Entrados los nuestros en las casas de los caníbales—construídas con
maderos de pie, de forma esférica—encontraron colgadas de las esta-
cas piernas de hombres saladas en la misma forma que nosotros sole-
mos hacer con las de cerdo, y la cabeza de un joven recién matado,
salpicada aún de sangre, y pedazos del mismo joven en ollas para co-
cerlos junto con carne de patos y papagayos, y otros puestos al fuego
en asadores. (Martyr 1953, 269)

In order to communicate the substance of what he had learned, Martyr found
it useful to appeal to beings that Europeans recognized from Homer's *Odyssey*
(elsewhere he also appealed to the rhetorical tradition of teratology in general). In addition, Martyr described cannibalism as an occupation like raising
chickens or pigs for slaughter. In this way, perhaps, the incredible became
more credible, the incomprehensible more understandable, but by the same
token the gap between the practices of these Indians and those of civilized
Europeans was also emphasized. It is also equally clear that the people so
described are not characters in mythology, legend, or story, for Martyr had
spoken to eyewitnesses. It was his task as "historian of the Indies" to inter-
view the returning voyagers.

Already by Columbus's second voyage the presence of cannibals was being
used to justify European activities in the New World. For instance, at one
point during that voyage Columbus was asked by an old Indian chief why
Europeans had come to his part of the world. Here, in Martyr's words, was
Columbus's answer:

The king and queen of Spain had sent him there to pacify all those
regions of the world, unknown until now, for the following purpose:
to conquer the cannibals and all the other evil men of the country and

to sentence them to deserved punishments, but to defend the peaceable [Indians] and to honor them for their virtues.

El rey y la reina de las Españas le habían enviado para que apaciguase todas aquellas regiones del mundo desconocido hasta ahora, es a saber: para que debelara a los caníbales y demás hombres malos del país y les impusiera los merecidos castigos, pero a los inofensivos los defendiera, y honrara por sus virtudes. (Martyr 1944, 40)

All this has the air of a post hoc justification; in Martyr's re-creation it sounds like a kind of set piece trotted out for the occasion. Of course, there was no hint of such thinking in the documents preceding the first voyage—in, for instance, the capitulations between Columbus and the Crown in the spring of 1492.

In one way or another, cannibals or reputed cannibals played a part in many of the initial negative experiences of Europeans in the New World. For instance, in the first battle in the New World (which occurred on Hispaniola toward the end of the first voyage on 13 January 1493), the Spanish engaged Indians so belligerent that Columbus speculated that they were probably Caribs who ate human beings (Varela 1982, 116). In *Historia de las Indias*, Las Casas (1951, 1:305) comments that Columbus was wrong, that there never were any Caribs on that particular island. Even the first blameworthy actions by Europeans toward Indians were related to cannibals and cannibalism. For example, the first discussion about enslaving Indians was, as has been noted, ostensibly motivated by the wish to eradicate cannibalism. The first description of the rape of an Indian woman, which Michael de Cuneo boasts about in his letter to Annari of 28 October 1495, identified the victim as "a woman of the cannibals" ("una mujer de los caníbales"; Cuneo 1965, 42).[14] The first act of conquest—that is, the first deliberate and unprovoked use of arms against a people of the New World—was undertaken against Indians identified as Caribs. That happened in 1498 when Columbus decided to take the island of Dominica by force because, he wrote, it was controlled by Caribs and he needed to take on water (Las Casas 1951, 2:9). What emerges from these and other documents is that Europeans in the fifteenth and sixteenth centuries did not doubt that cannibals existed in the New World. The only doubt was whether a particular tribe or group of people engaged in cannibalism.

Between 1499 and 1503, Spaniards and Caribs often clashed. In 1499, for instance, Alonso de Ojeda, having received numerous complaints from certain "good" Indians that other Indians on a nearby island had been making war on them, capturing them, and eating them, decided to help them to exact vengeance. He joined forces with the good Indians and attacked the Caribs, defeating them and capturing fifteen while losing only one soldier (Herrera [1601; reprinted 1726–30] 1944, 1:127). In 1500 Pedro Alonso Niño and his men were attacked by cannibals. Fending them off, Niño managed to liberate some of the cannibals' prisoners. He also captured one of the cannibals and handed him over to the former prisoners, who took their revenge, beating him unmercifully "with sticks, fists, and kicks" ("a palos, puñetazos y pata-das"; Martyr 1944, 85). Europeans and the good Indians, or *guatiaos*, were con-sistently seen, then, as "allies, brothers in arms" (see Herrera [1601; reprinted 1726–30] 1944, 1:164).

Between 1499 and 1503, a number of islands were identified as inhabited by cannibals. Some of the islands were named—Dominica, Guadalupe, Los Jardines, Granada, and Trinidad, among others—but some were designated simply as "of cannibals." Encounters with cannibals were not confined to islands, however. Between 1499 and 1503 Europeans also came upon canni-bals in Brazil who gained notoriety from Vespucci. Also during those years, on what was then known as Tierra Firme or Terra Firma,[15] the northern part of Venezuela and Colombia, cannibals were said to have been encountered frequently.

One encounter is particularly noteworthy because Herrera directly linked it to the cannibal law of 1503. The background of the encounter, according to Herrera, was the Crown's explicit instruction to Nicolás de Ovando not to "scandalize" or "offend" the Indians of Hispaniola or of other islands and Terra Firma. Ovando was also forbidden to capture these Indians and to take them to Castile. Nevertheless, in the words of Herrera,

> since in previous years the [Indians] had been scandalized by Christo-val Guerra and by others, especially in Cartagena, where [Guerra] did them great harm, the [Indians] did not let them [the Spanish] land on their lands, and they defended themselves with their weapons, and they killed some Christians,[16] and great complaints were made about this to the Catholic Kings, who were told that these [Indians] were Cannibals, now called Caribs, that is, those who ate human flesh; and it was so, and since these Indians always fled from having anything to do with Christians, the Queen, abhorring this news about [Indians] eating human flesh, which for her was something very frightful, and

hearing about their barbarous and bestial practices, ordered a law to
be written.

> como en los años passados quedaron escandalizados de Christoval
> Guerra, y de otros, especialmente en Cartagena, adonde hizo violen-
> cias, y no los dexavan saltar en sus tierras, y con las armas se defen-
> dian, y mataron algunos Christianos, de que formaron grandes quexas
> a los Reyes Catolicos, y les informaron que eran Canibales, que aora
> dizen Caribes, a los que comen carne humana: y era assí, que estos
> tales siempre huyeron la conversación de los Christianos: por lo cual,
> aborreciendo la Reyna esta nueva de comer carne humana, que para
> ella fue muy espantosa, y la relacion de sus barbaras y bestiales cos-
> tumbres, mandó dar una patente. (Herrera [1601; reprinted 1726–30]
> 1944, 1:203–4)

What follows in Herrera's narrative is a long and accurate summary of the
cannibal law of 1503. Significantly, the Spaniards seem to have been the initial
aggressors here, but the impression given is that the queen was reacting to
cannibalism rather than to the Indians' resistance. As we have seen, and as
suggested by their contiguous placement in the above quotation, cannibalism
and armed resistance to the Spaniards were closely and perhaps inextricably
linked in the minds of Spaniards both in the New World and in Spain.

The more salient motives behind the cannibal law may now be summarized and briefly glossed. These motives were, of course, interrelated:

1. The peace and security motive: Enslaving cannibals (necessary because of
   their belligerence) would ensure peace in the region, both among groups
   of Indians and between Indians and Spaniards.
2. The religious motive: Enslaving cannibals (necessary because of their pagan
   beliefs and customs and their continuing refusal to hear the word of God)
   would lead them toward Catholicism and eventual salvation.
3. The civilizing motive: Enslaving cannibals (necessary because they were incapable of political autonomy and true self-government) would, by bringing them to live among Spaniards, teach them to live like civilized human
   beings.
4. The economic motive: Enslaving cannibals (advisable because of the costs
   of colonizing the New World) would mean greater revenues—legally—for
   the Crown and more wealth for the slave traders, an argument that the
   Crown had earlier rejected in its response to the Memorandum to Torres.

5. The judicial motive: Enslaving cannibals (necessary because of their unre-
pentant criminality) would punish them for their crimes against Spaniards
and against other Indians, crimes that included (but were not limited to)
eating other human beings.

Peace and security, salvation, the civilizing process, money, justice—powerful
motives all. Taken together, they overwhelmed most objections to establishing slavery in the New World and helped to pave the way—when labor shortages developed—for the importation of slaves from Africa.

The enslavement of Indians, which had been expressly forbidden from the
beginning of the European venture in the New World, was legally permissible
from 1503 onward, but only an Indian identified as a cannibal could be "mis-
treated," legally separated from his family, removed from his home, transported to other lands, and sold without penalty. From 1503 on, therefore, the
designation of *cannibal* became economically useful and justified certain activities in the New World. In effect, a law ostensibly designed to bring peace
to the New World actually converted it into a battlefield and a slave market.

The cloak of legality increasingly served to justify militant activities. In 1509,
for instance, Diego de Nicuesa attacked the Island of Santo Domingo, capturing "more than a hundred Indians, which he sold as slaves, stating that he had
done it with the permission of the King because they were Caribs" ("ciento y
tantos Indios, que vendio por esclavos diziendo que lo avia hecho con licencia del Rey por ser Caribes"; Herrera [1601; reprinted 1726–30] 1944, 1:242).
Some even declared the aggression against the Indians to be a "just war," in
accord with principles developed by St. Augustine and other theologians of
the Middle Ages, for whom a war against the "enemies of Christ" was fully
justified. In 1510, Alonso de Ojeda indicated that "according to the scholars,
theologians, and canon lawyers, it was legally permissible to make war on
[Carib] Indians who resisted Christianization and to capture them for slaves"
("de acuerdo de los Letrados, Teologos, y Canonistas, que haziendo resistencia estos Indios [Caribes], y no queriendo admitir la Fe, les hiziessen guerra,
y fuessen tomados por esclavos"; Herrera [1601; reprinted 1726–30] 1944,
1:250). In that same year, testifying under oath, Juan Ponce de León affirmed
that the death of Cristóbal de Sotomayor in Puerto Rico caused "the first declaration of war against the Caribs by King Ferdinand. It was toward September
of 1510 that the Indians killed Don Cristóbal" ("de la primera declaración de
guerra a los Caribes por don Fernando [Rey]. Mataron a don Cristóbal hacia
septiembre de 1510"; Murga Sanz 1956–61, 1:xxxiv). On 23 February 1512,

two months after he signed the second cannibal law (on 23 December 1511), the king confirmed in a royal decree that the "war on the Caribs from the island of Hispaniola" ("guerra a los Caribes desde la Isla Española") was lawful and in the best interests of the island's pacification. Such Caribs could therefore be enslaved without the Crown being paid its customary royal fifth (Konetzke 1953–62, 1:36–37). By 1515 a general and declared state of war existed with the Caribs. A few years later, in 1519, the lawyer Zuazo asked for permission "to bring Caribs from Terra Firma as slaves and to bring as servants Indians from the Lucayos and other useless islands" ("para traer por esclavos los caribes de Tierra Firme, é por naborias los de Lucayos é otras islas inútiles"; Pacheco et al. 1864–84, 1:362). Two months after that, Zuazo, writing now in an official report, again confirmed that the king intended to "destroy and to capture the said Caribs" ("la voluntad del Rey fue destruyr e cativar los dichos caribes"; Castañeda 1980, 82). These (and other) Spaniards, then, considered the Crown's policies toward the Caribs to be clear and unambiguous.

After 1503, more and more cannibals were suddenly "discovered" to inhabit more and more places: Santa Marta, Cartagena, the Island of Dominica, some islands near Cartagena that became known as "nests of ferocious cannibals" ("nidos de feroces caníbales"; Martyr 1944, 248), and other islands near Guadalupe and Jamaica, in and around the Gulf of Uraba. Island after island was designated as "of cannibals" or "of Caribs," even islands previously known to be inhabited by noncannibals.[17] The redefinition of the region was accomplished both legally and cartographically. Legally, it occurred on island after island by means of depositions to the effect that the people of that particular island were man-eaters. Such statements were officially witnessed by a Spanish bureaucrat and duly notarized. An example of the cartographical redefinition of the region may be noted in Martín Fernández de Enciso's *Suma de geographia*, published in 1519. After listing the islands of Trinidad, Paria, Mayo, Tabaco, Santa Lucia, Barvada, Matinino, La Dominica, Guadalupe, Monserrate, La Redonda, San Cristoval, Sant Bartolomé, Sant Martin, La Anegada, Las Virgenes, Santa Cruz, and Sant Juan, and indicating their locations, Fernández de Enciso says the following:

> From Trinidad to San Juan is a distance of 240 leagues. All the other islands I have named are between these two. And all of them belong to cannibals who eat human flesh. They take to the sea in canoes in order to make war on other [Indians] and on other [cannibals]. And those that they can they take to their own lands, and if they are men, they eat them, and if women, they use them for slaves. And if one of

the captured men is thin they fatten him up; and once he is fat, they eat him; and they say that the most delicious parts of men are the fingers and the lean portions of the flank. These [cannibals] use bows and arrows a great deal. If the cannibals are attacked and they realize that their attackers are stronger than they are, they leave that particular island and go to another one. And on all these islands it is said that there is gold.

Aly desde la trinidad, fasta a Sant Juan dozientas i quarenta leguas. estan todas las otras que he nombrado entre medias destas dos. i son todas de Canibales que comen carne umana. i vanse por la mar en canoas a hazer guerra a otras partes i unos a otros. i a todos quantos pueden los llevan a sus tierras i si son hombres comenselos i si mugeres sirvense dellas como de esclavas. i si algun hombre delos que llevan esta flaco ponenlo a engordar: i desque esta gordo comenselo: i dizen que lo mas sabroso es los dedos delas manos i lo delgado delas ijadas del hombre. Estos usan mucho los arcos i flechas. Si van a hazerles guerra i conoscen que los que van son mas poderosos que no ellos dexan la isla y vanse a otras. En todas estas islas dizen que ay oro. (Enciso 1519, fol. 68r and v; I have slightly modernized the Spanish orthography)

All of these islands belong to today's Lesser Antilles. That they were identified as "de caribes" or "de caníbales" on sixteenth-century maps may be seen, for example, in figure 2.3. Eventually, in the cartographical and cultural imagination of Europeans, cannibals came to inhabit an entire sea, the Caribbean, which etymologically means the "sea of cannibals."

In 1530 something unexpected happened. On 2 August, in Madrid, the king signed a royal provision completely prohibiting the capture and enslavement of all Indians, including those who formerly had been declared enemies of the Crown and of Christ and who had been captured in a just war. "We revoke and suspend," entoned the provision, "all the permissions and declarations made up to the present" ("Revocamos y suspendemos todas las dichas licencias y declaraciones hasta oy hechas"; Encinas 1596, 364–66). For many years the enslavement of cannibals had been the norm. The economy of the region depended on it; slavery had become part of the New World way of life. Thus the reaction in the colonies was predictable. The number of official reports, petitions, and complaints concerning cannibals, which had radically

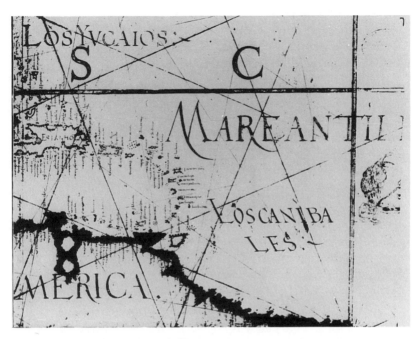

FIGURE 2.3. Detail from a Dutch (?) planisphere, attributed to Andreas Homem, 1559, identifying the Lesser Antilles as inhabited by "los caníbales." (From the Newberry Library collection of the Bibliothèque Nationale [Paris] map collection; courtesy the Newberry Library.)

diminished during the 1520s, increased again. For example, in 1532 the lawyer Espinosa wrote the Crown about the difficulty Spaniards were having in subduing the Indians on the Gulf of Uraba "because they act like Caribs who do not allow themselves to be subjugated" ("por ser como son caribes que no se dejan sojuzgar"; Friede 1955–60, 2:287). Near Cartagena, wrote Pedro de Heredia at about the same time, some Indians had to be punished (just how was not specified) "because we discovered a province where Indians habitually ate each other" ("porque hallamos una provincia [en] que se comían unos a otros"; Friede 1955–60, 3:25). It is unclear whether Heredia was basing his characterization of the Indians' cannibalism as "habitual" (which is the sense of the Spanish imperfect tense here) on any eyewitness accounts. On 23 February 1533, the town council of San Juan in Puerto Rico petitioned the Crown to be allowed—again—to enslave the Caribs "because they deserve to be enslaved more than any other Indians on account of their practices and infidel

beliefs" ("pues que sus obras e infidelidad los merecen más que otros ningunos"; Murga 1955–61, 1:18).

Besieged on all sides, the Crown yielded. Recalling yet again the great
danger that the Caribs posed to Europeans, citing their "continual resistance"
(*continua resistencia*) and their "abominable practice" (*práctica abominable*) of eating people, the king signed another cannibal law on 13 September 1533. This
new law permitted and, I would say, even encouraged the declaration of just
wars and the enslavement of Caribs "because the said Caribs eat human flesh
and commit other grave transgressions in great offense to God" ("porque los
dichos caribes comen carne humana y hacen otros excesos grandes en gran
ofensa de Dios"; Konetzke 1953–62, 1:145–46). Parts of this law were often
repeated, and its general message restated, in correspondence with individuals who petitioned the Crown after 1533. In 1534, for instance, the king gave
official permission to Pero Ortiz de Matienço to make war for three years on
"the Carib Indians [living near Cubagua], who were either enemies or declared as such by our law-officers and our royal chancery" ("a los indios caribes [cerca de Cubagua, la isla de las perlas] henemigos que están o fueren
declarados por la nuestra audiencia e chancillería real"; Otte 1961, 1:169).[18]
"Declared as such"—the phrase is revealing. Even the *requerimientos* of those
years, unlike the first *requerimiento*, directly referred to cannibalism.[19] Immediately upon landing on Terra Firma—so ordered the government of Santa
Marta—Spaniards were required to inform the Indians by means of interpreters of the European intention "to teach them good customs and to wean
them from vices and from eating human flesh, and to instruct them in our
Holy Faith" ("para les enseñar buenas costumbres y apartarlos de vicios y
comer carne humana, y a instruirlos en nuestra Santa Fe"; Friede 1955–60,
3:206). This statement repeats, verbatim, instructions given on 17 November
1526 (see *Recopilación* [1681] 1943, 1:1–2). If the Indians resisted, the Spaniards
again had the right to conquer them by force and to enslave them.

Such policies concerning the Indies were not arrived at without controversy. In truth, the sixteenth century was a chaotic battlefield on which polarized opinions clashed and debate flourished (Hanke [1949] 1965; Hanke 1974;
Monica 1952). Doubts about the Spanish role in the Indies arose long before
the famous debate at midcentury between Bartolomé de Las Casas and Ginés
de Sepúlveda. In 1511 the Dominican friar Antonio de Montesinos ascended
his pulpit in Santo Domingo and, in ringing tones, preached a sermon denouncing the Spaniards' treatment of the Indians. Montesinos's censorious
words caused an uproar, both in Santo Domingo and back in Spain. A com-

mission was established to investigate the entire matter. The result was the
Laws of Burgos (1512–13), dedicated principally to humanizing the institution
of the *encomienda*.[20] Given the Spanish obsession with cannibals, it may be
puzzling that Caribs are not mentioned in this set of laws.[21] They did not figure
in them, I believe, because—unlike the *guatiaos*, or "good" Indians—they
were not considered subjects of Spain. The Laws of Burgos were instruments
of governance, not of conquest.[22]

Montesinos was but the first of a long line of clerics and scholars—among
them Vitoria, Cayetano, Soto y Carranza, Cano, and Las Casas—who discussed
the Spanish presence in the Indies, thus casting the royal mind into what is
known as "the doubts about the Indies" (*la duda indiana*; see, e.g., Carro 1951).
Such doubts arose because of reports from the Caribbean, Central America,
and Peru. At one point in the 1530s the Crown seriously considered abandoning its project in the Indies. According to the documents of the time, it was
the moral and "political" condition (giving politics its Aristotelian sense here)
of the Indians that persuaded the Crown to continue colonizing the New
World.

For example, even Francisco de Vitoria, one of the most reasonable and
"liberal" of the scholars and theologians who wrote about the Indies, concluded in his *Relectio de Indis* (1539): "The Christian princes [can justifiably]
make war on the barbarians [the Aztecs in this instance] because they eat human flesh and because they sacrifice men" ("Principes christianorum possunt
inferre bellum barbaris quia vescuntur carnibus humanis et quia sacrificant
homines"; Vitoria [1539] 1967, 110). Such a war, undertaken in defense of the
cannibals' innocent victims, could legally be declared under the principle of
the "law" or "right of people" (*ius gentium*), or what today we would call human rights. Once the war against such man-eaters had ended, the Spaniards
were obliged to withdraw from the captured territories and give back the
cannibals' property (Vitoria [1539] 1967, 110–11).[23]

The debate culminated in Spain at midcentury with the so-called *controversia
de Indias* between Sepúlveda and Las Casas. Sepúlveda's arguments were based
on Aristotelian thought and on the intellectual tradition of the monster. In his
work on the subject, entitled *Democrates alter o secundus, sive de justis belli causis apud
Indus* (Democrates the Second; or, On the just causes of the war against the
Indians), Sepúlveda invoked the concept of a just war in order to justify—
logically and morally—both war against the Indians and their enslavement.
The Indians, he said, were sodomites, cowards, sacrificers of other human
beings, and cannibals. Therefore they were not like other men; he called

them *homunculi* (little men), a term indicative of the tenor and sophistry of the debate. As Paracelsus, for example, maintained in his *De homunculis et monstris*, the term *homunculus* identifies a kind of monster or deformed creature associated in medieval medicine with artificial insemination. Being monstrous, *homunculi* need not be treated like other men.

Sepúlveda, who never traveled to the New World, knew of Indians only through documents; Indians were textual abstractions to him. But Las Casas, who lived in the Indies for many years, wrote from the perspective of personal experience as well as from theological conviction and canon law. For Las Casas, all Indians, even the cannibals, were human and were always capable of living as "political" beings. For him, all Indians could learn the ways of Christ. The debate between Las Casas and Sepúlveda was won by Las Casas.[24] His victory, however, was not as decisive as we are taught in school, for even after midcentury, problems with cannibals persisted, and laws allowing or even mandating their enslavement were enacted.[25] Reports of cannibalism continued to be sent to Spain throughout the century, reports which, as Las Casas had noted earlier in that century, were less than pure in their motivation. Moreover, the intellectual tradition of the monstrous and savage Other, evident in the arguments of Sepúlveda, continued to have currency throughout the century. In some respects, tradition rewrote reality.

It is in the iconographic aspects of the history of cartography and cosmography that we find some of the more dramatic and conclusive evidence for the continuing influence of the rhetorical tradition of describing and locating monsters. Curiously, sixteenth-century Spain did not develop an iconographic tradition concerning cannibals in the New World. That seems to have been the specialty of nations less centrally involved in colonizing the New World in the sixteenth century, nations like England, Germany, and Italy. Why this should be so, no one can be certain, but a reason or two may be essayed. First, Spain's involvement was continuous, shaped by bureaucratic and legalistic thinking, and it covered a vast amount of territory and many different peoples. These included the Aztecs in the 1520s and the Incas in the 1530s, both of which had empires reminiscent of those in Europe. For Spain, cannibals eventually came to be regarded as simply one of a great number of "problems" to be solved; in brief, cannibals became commonplace and familiar. Second, such a familiarity with cannibals—or with alleged cannibals—did not happen in the case of England, Germany, and Italy. For those countries, cannibals remained exotic and perhaps were therefore easily de-

Die figur anzaigt vns das volck vnd insel die gefunden ist durch den cristenlichen künig zü Portgal oder von seinen vnderthonen. Die leüt sind also nackent hübsch. braun wolgestalt von leib. ir heübter halß.arm.scham.füß. frawen vnd mann ain wenig mit federen bedeckt. Auch haben die mann in iren angesichten vnd brust vil edel gestain. Es hat auch nyemantz nichts sunder sind alle ding gemain. Und die mann haben de weyber welche in gefallen. es sy mütter. schwester. oder freündt. darinn haben sy nit vnderschayd. Sy streyten auch mit ainander. Sy essen auch ainander selbs die erschlagen werden und henckens. Den das selbig flaisch in den rauch. Sy werden alt hundert vnd fünffzig iar. Vnd haben kain regiment.

FIGURE 2.4. The woodcut "Amerikaner" of 1505, the first "ethnographic" depiction of New World peoples. (Honour 1976; courtesy the Newberry Library.)

picted and graphically vivid as a cultural symbol. It was in Germany, for instance, that the very first "ethnographic" picture was created of New World peoples, a 1505 woodcut illustrating a German edition of a letter by Vespucci and labeled "Amerikaner." This woodcut, shown in figure 2.4, depicts several cannibal scenes (see Sturtevant 1976). The only apparent exception to this rule of the relationship between familiarity (or the lack of it) and iconographic representation seems to be the Portuguese cartographic school, and it is an exception which in its way proves the rule. Portuguese cartographers, having at their disposal the unexplored areas of Brazil's vast interior, filled them with cannibals and other Indians, as well as exotic animals (see Cortesão 1935, 1960).

Descriptions of terrae incognitae as being inhabited by monsters were based, as suggested earlier in this essay, on a long rhetorical and historiographical tradition. Sometimes descriptions were solely by means of labels added to a map, as was the case, for example, with the 1522 edition of Ptol-

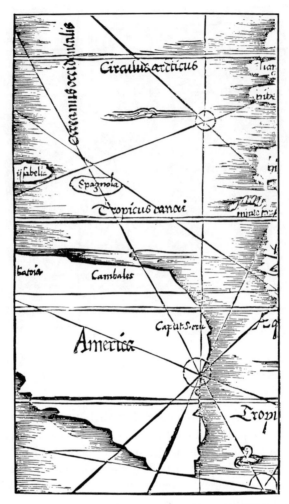

FIGURE 2.5. Ptolemy's *Geography* of 1552 employed simple labels to indicate
the presence of cannibals. (Winsor 1892; courtesy of the University of Illinois at
Urbana-Champaign Library.)

emy (fig. 2.5). Sometimes images carried the brunt of the message, as was the
case with Sebastian Münster's 1540 edition of Ptolemy. Münster also made
sure that no one mistook his meaning, for he identified the people in northeastern Brazil as "canibali" (fig. 2.6). Or cannibal activities could be but one of
several scenes on a map, as in Diogo Homem's 1558 map of South America
(fig. 2.7).[26]

FIGURE 2.6. Sebastian Münster, "The New World," from his edition of Ptolemy's *Geographia universalis, vetus et nova* (Basel 1540). (Sanz 1970, p. 121; courtesy of the University of Illinois at Urbana-Champaign Library.)

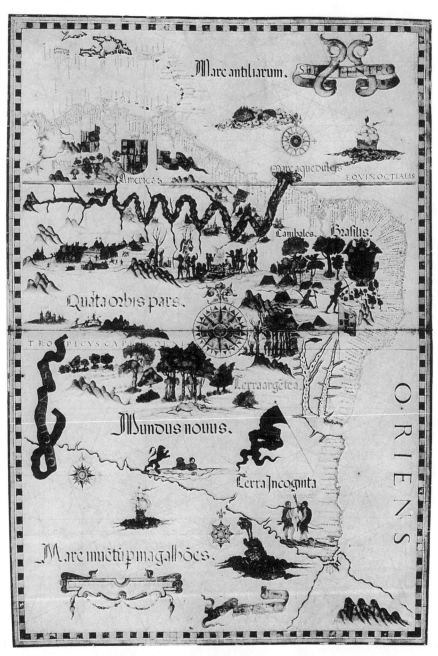

FIGURE 2.7. Diogo Homem's 1558 map of South America, which depicted a scene of cannibalism as one of its views of life in the New World. (Honour 1975a, pl. 21; source: British Library, Dept. of Manuscripts; courtesy the Newberry Library.)

In labeling South America the "fourth part of the world" (*quarta orbis pars*), Homem, a Portuguese cartographer, reflected the fact that the European discovery and exploration of the Americas changed the Western cosmographical conception of the world. Before 1492, or rather before the New World was considered to be truly new and not a part of Asia, Europeans had traditionally divided the world into three parts: Europe, Africa, and Asia. When iconographically summarized by a symbolic figure, each of these parts was represented by a person, usually a woman. In sixteenth-century cosmographical divisions, the New World was represented most often by a cannibal. Such a tactic complemented other symbolizing tendencies in other kinds of documents. Examples have been put forward here from cartography and early ethnography. Other examples include Vespucci's letters, Hans Staden's *True History*, Jean de Léry and André Thevet's contributions, Montaigne's famous defense of cultural relativism in his essay on cannibals, the illustrations in the many volumes on the New World published by the De Bry brothers in the late sixteenth and early seventeenth centuries, and Shakespeare's use of the word *canibal* (it was usually spelled with one n in sixteenth-century English) to form his anagram *Caliban* in *The Tempest*. All these examples, when added to those cited earlier, contributed to the ideological stereotyping of that fourth part of the world. Unfortunately, space limitations prevent any extended analysis of these documents here.

One cosmographical and cultural symbolic representation, however, is particularly relevant to this essay. In 1595 Paolo Farinati, working in Italy, created a work entitled *America* (fig. 2.8) which depicts, in a nutshell, the basic conflict concerning cannibalism and cultural or civilizational identity in the sixteenth century. America is here depicted as a male cannibal (that in itself is unusual, though it accords with the documents, most of which treat men rather than women). Seated in the middle of the picture and engaged in roasting a human shoulder and arm, the cannibal has turned his face to his right (not to his left, or sinister, side of the body) in order to contemplate the crucifix. The message is clear: by turning away from cannibalism and toward Christianity— and all that European Christendom implied in the sixteenth century—the savage is turning toward civilization. This turn symbolizes both socialization and salvation. Here, in iconographic terms, is depicted the dynamics of legal documents like the cannibal laws of 1503, 1511, 1533, and even 1569.

Who, then, was the New Man of the New World to sixteenth-century Spain and to Europe? He was a cannibal, a Carib. And what was the newly discovered fourth part of the world? It was a world of cannibals. There were, of course, other conceptions of the New World, some even Edenic, and there

FIGURE 2.8. Paolo Farinati's painting *America* (1595), which depicts the turning away of an Amerindian from cannibalism in favor of Christianity. (Honour 1975b, pl. 92; courtesy of the University of Illinois at Urbana-Champaign Library.)

were other conceptions of the New Man, some even Adamic. But the conception documented and discussed in this essay, so long ignored or minimized by many historians and yet so unavoidably important to an understanding of early New World history, leads one to think that the "true history" of the New World has yet to be written. This essay attempts to recapture a portion of that truth. Moreover, perhaps the negative image of Latin American culture and society as primitive, savage, and barbarous, an image that persists even today in Europe and the United States, may be due in part to the vestiges of a historical memory as powerful as it is repressed: the memory of cannibalism—real, rumored, and attributed—in the New World in the fifteenth and sixteenth centuries.

NOTES

1. The research leading to this and my other essays on this subject (all work toward a book) has been supported by grants from the National Endowment for the Humanities (Senior Fellowship, 1987–88), from International Programs and Studies (The William and Flora Hewlett Fund) and the Center for Latin American and Caribbean Studies at the University of Illinois, from the Newberry Library, and from the John Carter Brown Library. My thanks to all these institutions and foundations. A preliminary and much briefer version of this essay, written in Spanish and not accompanied by illustrations, appeared in Colombia in 1989: "La ley de los caníbales: Cartagena y el Mar Caribe en el siglo XVI," in De ficciones y realidades: Perspectivas sobre literatura e historia colombianas, ed. Alvaro Pineda Botero and Raymond Williams (Bogotá: Tercer Mundo Editores, 1989), 123–37.

2. In recent years the term discovery has become problematic and controversial. Many scholars are of the opinion that the term is too imperialistic and that a more neutral term should be used, such as encounter (other terms include finding, inventing, and imagining). After all, one version of the argument goes, the people in the New World were not a passive object in nature that needed to be identified by the scientific European mind in order to become useful to human consciousness or in order to exist. During the colonial period in the New World, two or more radically different societies were actually seeing each other for the first time, and each society interpreted the encounter according to its own hermeneutic norms. In the politically correct rush toward more value-free terms, however, it may be forgotten that what took

place was indeed a discovery—at least from the European perspective of the fifteenth and sixteenth centuries—and that discovery was followed by an appropriation of lands and peoples (in other words, by a conquest). The possible and unintended result of transforming a discovery into an encounter may be to mitigate the physical, moral, and intellectual violence of what happened. In the context of the present essay, the actions and thoughts of Europeans in and about the New World were those of discoverers and conquerors.

3. For instance, in John Alden's thematic index to his magnificent chronological guide to the New World, entitled *European Americana*, there are but ten entries on cannibalism, four of which refer to works by Ronsard and Montaigne. Five of the remaining six entries refer to a book on the Kingdom of the Congo by D. Lopes. Hans Staden, author of perhaps the most famous sixteenth-century work on cannibalism, is not mentioned in this entry, though he is given a heading of his own (without a cross-reference to cannibalism). By way of comparison, syphilis has more than 250 entries even though cannibalism was far more important than syphilis in determining Europe's conception of the New World.

4. To his credit, Peter Hulme in his 1986 book *Colonial Encounters* did not overlook the subject of cannibalism. His first chapter, based in part on an earlier article entitled "Columbus and the Cannibals" (1978), treats some of the same material I treat in this essay. His perspective and mine, however, are radically different. In this essay I am less theoretically oriented and more interested in bringing long-forgotten documents back into the historical record and into historiographical consciousness.

5. Arens is not the only anticannibalist, though he thinks he is. Apparently ignorant of either Spanish or Portuguese, he overlooks the work of Julio Salas (1920) and of J. Fernando Carneiro (1946). Arens is correct in calling attention to imperialist motives in descriptions of cannibalism, but he undermines his analysis by overstatement and by absolutist claims.

6. Unless otherwise noted, all translations in this essay are my own.

7. For the sake of readability, I have divided the law into paragraphs and have broken some extremely long series of clauses into sentences. In the original manuscript version, this law is all one flowing paragraph.

8. The *taínos* were the first Indians Columbus encountered. They were said to be a peace-loving people. The term was generalized to include all friendly Indians. The *guatiaos* are defined by Antonio de Herrera and others as allies.

9. See the entries for 4, 23, and 26 November 1492; for 11, 12, 17, and 26 December 1492; and for 2, 13, 14, 15, and 16 January 1493.

10. Samuel Eliot Morison (1963, 89) comments in his translation and edition of Columbus's diary that Bartolomé de Las Casas indignantly dissented from Columbus's remarks. Las Casas said that no such monsters could be found in those islands, though it was possible that the people being referred to were the inhabitants of the islands of the Caribs (see Las Casas 1951, 1:228).

11. The exception here is Sicily—probably due to the influence of Homer—on which, according to the Waldsperger Map, cyclopes were noted; see Harley and Woodward 1987, 331.

12. It is true that Columbus's diary was not published until the nineteenth century and that therefore it could not directly affect the ideology formation of Europeans in the fifteenth and sixteenth centuries. Nonetheless, Peter Martyr reported on its contents in the *Decadas de orbe novo*, published toward the end of the fifteenth century, and in succeeding editions until the complete version was published in 1530. Further, the letter to Santángel is a reasonable condensation of many of the diary's salient issues. Moreover, Hernando Colón's life of his father, entitled *Vida del Almirante Don Cristóbal*, contained a detailed account of the first voyage; it was first published in Italian in Venice in 1571 (Iglesia 1947, 17).

13. Las Casas comments in the margins of the diary that the Indians of Hispaniola were not man-eaters. That he remains silent about those in Cuba suggests that he considered that they were.

14. The veracity of Cuneo's letter has been questioned, but even if it is proved that Cuneo was making things up, it cannot be denied that the letter was composed in the fifteenth century and that it represents a point of view then current.

15. In the fifteenth and sixteenth centuries, the term *Terra Firma* did not mean the mainland in general but specifically the northern coast of South America.

16. In the sixteenth century the terms *Christiano* and *Cristiano* were generic terms for person or Spaniard. The connotation is that such a person is civilized.

17. Other parts of the New World were similarly redesignated. Las Casas, for instance, complained in his *Historia de las Indias* that the Indians of the Yucatán peninsula had been wrongly identified as man-eaters and that this was done solely to justify Spanish atrocities in the area and the taking of slaves (Las Casas 1951, 3:231)

18. Cubagua was the center of the pearl-gathering industry early in the sixteenth century. Apparently the Caribs were impeding—or rather, were declared to be impeding—the industry.

19. The *requerimiento* was a declaration required of the Spanish whenever they came into contact with a new group of Indians. In it they were supposed to inform the Indians of the Spanish government and Christian cosmology and to offer them the opportunity of allowing the Spanish peaceful entry into their territory in order to carry out the mission of civilizing and Christianizing them. Should they refuse, the Spanish had the legal right to use force. It is a rather odd requirement in many ways, not the least of which is that it was delivered in Spanish—in the early years without translators—to Indians who had no idea what was being said, if they were even within earshot. Its principal function was to ensure the "legality" of all that transpired. The Spanish conquest and colonization of the New World was a lawyer's paradise.

20. The *encomienda* was an institution in which Indians were "commended" to certain Spaniards for the care and salvation of their souls. It required collecting Indians in groups, housing them, teaching them Christianity and, in general, caring for them. In return, the Indians were supposed to give the Spanish a certain number of days of labor per year. Needless to say, abuses of the system were the norm.

21. There is a veiled reference to the Caribs or to cannibal Indians in Article 27, which deals with Indians who "are daily being brought from the neighboring islands." As we know from other documents, only Indians identified as cannibals and "enemies of Christianity" could be legally transported from one island to another. These Indians, says the article, are to be indoctrinated and "taught the things of the faith." If such Indians are "slaves," then they "may be treated by their owner as he pleases," but they were not to be treated with the same harshness with which other slaves were generally treated (Gibson 1968, 75).

22. Before 1518, according to Demetrio Ramos Pérez, the word *conquest*, and therefore the policy, did not appear in Spanish documents concerning the New World (Ramos 1985, 48). Ramos maintains that before 1518 Spanish policy advocated exploration, evangelization, and colonization, not conquest.

23. Obviously, Vitoria's argument (conclusion 5 on the "just war" question outlined earlier) was conceived and developed with little regard for the psychology of human behavior. Conquerors were unlikely to return con-

quered territories simply because a theologian in Spain said that it was the right thing to do.

24. In a sense, in the forum in which the debate took place (the School of Theology in Valladolid), the debate's outcome was almost predetermined. The beneficent view of the Indian had received intermittent but powerful support for the previous fifty years, particularly from the papacy. In 1537, for instance, Pope Paul III issued a bull (called *Sublimis Deus Sic Dilexit*) which proclaimed the essential humanity of all Indians. Being men, they had to be treated accordingly. See Gibson 1968, 104–5.

25. One such law, dated 25 January 1569, reads as follows: "The inhabitants of the Windward Islands are legally permitted to make war on the Carib Indians, who are harassing those islands with armed incursions and who eat human flesh, and [the inhabitants] can enslave those [Caribs] that they capture, as long as they are fourteen years or older, and they may not enslave women of any age. We order that this be done in this way, in keeping with the instructions that might be given by the Court of Santo Domingo in additional justification" ("Tienen licencia los vecinos de las Islas de Barlovento para hacer guerra á los Indios Caribes, que las van á infestar con mano armada, y comen carne humana, y pueden hacer sus esclavos á los que cautivaren, con que no sean menores de catorce años, ni mugeres de qualquiera edad; Mandamos que así se execute, guardando las instrucciones, que diere la Audiencia de Santo Domingo para mas justificación"; *Recopilación* [1681] 1943, 2:204–5).

26. This is but one of a series of maps by Diogo Homem portraying South America, most of which follow the same iconographic pattern (cannibals in Brazil, especially the Northeast, and giants in Patagonia) and carry the same legends: *Mundus novus, terra incognita, quarta orbis pars,* and *canibales.*

BIBLIOGRAPHY

Alden, John, ed. 1980. *European Americana: A Chronological Guide to Works Printed in Europe Relating to the Americas, 1493–1776.* 2 vols. New York: Readex Books.

———. 1953. *Epistolario.* Vol. 9 of *Documentos inéditos para la historia de España.* Madrid: Góngora, S. L.

Arens, W. 1979. *The Man-Eating Myth: Anthropology and Anthropophagy.* New York: Oxford University Press.

Carneiro, J. Fernando. 1946. *A Antropofagia entre os indígenas do Brasil.* Rio de Janeiro: Imprensa Nacional.

Carro, P. Venancio D. 1951. *La teología y los teólogos-juristas españoles ante la conquista de América.* Vol. 18. 2d ed. Salamanca: Biblioteca de Teólogos Españoles.

Castañeda Delgado, Paulino. 1980. La política española con los Caribes durante el siglo XVI. *Revista de Indias* (Madrid) 119–22:73–130.

Colón, Hernando. [1571] 1947. *Vida del Almirante Don Cristóbal Colón.* Mexico City: Fondo de Cultura Económica.

Cortés, Vicenta. 1956. Los indios caribes en el siglo XVI. *Proceedings of the Thirty-Second International Congress of Americanists,* 726–31. Copenhagen: Munksgard.

Cortesão, Armando. 1935. *Cartografia e cartógrafos portugueses dos séculos XV e XVI (Contribuição para um estudo completo).* 2 vols. Lisbon: Edição da Seara Nova.

Cortesão, Armando, and Avelino Teixera da Mota. 1960. *Portugaliae monumenta cartographica.* 6 vols. Lisbon: Comissão Executiva das Comemorações do V Centenario de Morte do Infante D. Henrique.

Cortesão, Jaime. 1965. *História do Brasil nos velhos mapas.* 2 vols. Rio de Janeiro: Instituto Rio Branco.

Cuneo, Michele de. 1965. Do novitatibus insularum occeani Hesperii repertarum a Don Christoforo Columbo Genuensi (Carta a Geronimo Annari). Trans. and ed. Marisa Vannini de Gerulewicz. *Revista de Historia* (Caracas) 24:33–64.

Encinas, Diego de, ed. 1596. *Provisiones, cédulas, capítulos de ordenanças: Instrucciones y cartas, libradas y despachadas en diferentes tiempos por sus Magestades . . . hasta agora.* Vol. 4. Madrid: La Imprenta Real.

Fernández de Enciso, Martín. 1519. *Suma de geographia.* Madrid.

Fite, Emerson, and Archibald Freeman, comps. 1926. *A Book of Old Maps Delineating American History Down to the Close of the Revolutionary War.* Cambridge, Mass.: Harvard University Press.

Forsyth, Donald W. 1983. The Beginnings of Brazilian Anthropology: Jesuits and Tupinamba Cannibalism. *Journal of Anthropological Research* 39:147–78.

Friede, Juan, ed. 1955–60. *Documentos inéditos para la historia de Colombia.* 10 vols. Bogotá: Academia Colombiana de Historia.

Friedman, John Block. 1981. *The Monstrous Races in Medieval Art and Thought.* Cambridge, Mass.: Harvard University Press.

Gibson, Charles, ed. 1968. *The Spanish Tradition in America.* Columbia: University of South Carolina Press.

Hanke, Lewis. [1949] 1965. *The Spanish Struggle for Justice in the Conquest of America.* Boston: Little, Brown.

————. 1974. *All Mankind Is One: A Study of the Disputation Between Bartolomé de Las Casas and Ginés de Sepúlveda in 1550 on the Intellectual and Religious Capacity of the American Indians.* De Kalb: Northern Illinois University Press.

Harley, J. B., and David Woodward, eds. 1987. *Cartography in Prehistoric, Ancient, and Medieval Europe and the Mediterranean.* Vol. 1 of *The History of Cartography.* Chicago: University of Chicago Press.

Herrera, Antonio de. [1601; reprinted 1726–30] 1944. *Historia general de los hechos de los castellanos, en las islas, y Tierra-Firme de el Mar Occeano.* 5 vols. Asunción, Paraguay: Guarania.

Honour, Hugh. 1975a. *The European Vision of America.* Cleveland: Cleveland Museum of Art.

————. 1975b. *The New Golden Land: European Images of America from the Discoveries to the Present Time.* New York: Pantheon Books.

————. 1976. *L'Amérique vue par l'Europe.* Paris: Editions des musées nationaux.

Hulme, Peter. 1978. Columbus and the Cannibals. In *Ibero-Amerikanisches Archiv,* 4:115–39.

————. 1986. *Colonial Encounters: Europe and the Native Caribbean, 1492–1797.* London: Methuen.

Iglesia, Ramón. 1947. Prologue to *Vida del Almirante Don Cristóbal Colón,* by Hernando Colón, 7–19. Mexico City: Fondo de Cultura Económica.

Konetzke, Richard, ed. 1953–62. *Colección de documentos para la historia de la formación social de Hispanoamérica, 1493–1810.* 3 vols. Madrid: Consejo Superior de Investigaciones Científicas.

Las Casas, Bartolomé de. 1951. *Historia de Las Indias.* 3 vols. Mexico City: Fondo de Cultural Económica.

Martyr, Peter, de Anglería. 1944. *Décadas del Nuevo Mundo, 1530.* Trans. Joaquín Torres Asensio. Buenos Aires: Bajel.

Monica, Sor M. 1952. *La gran controversia del siglo XVI acerca del dominio español en América.* Madrid: Ediciones Cultura Hispánica.

Morison, Samuel Eliot (trans. and ed.). 1963. *Journals and Other Documents on the Life and Voyages of Christopher Columbus.* New York: Heritage.

Murga Sanz, Vicente. 1956–61. *Historia documental de Puerto Rico.* 3 vols. Río Piedras, Puerto Rico: Plus Ultra.

Navarrete, Martín Fernández de, ed. 1945. *Colección de los viajes y descubrimientos que hicieron por mar los españoles desde fines del siglo XV.* Vol. 2. Buenos Aires: Guarania.

Otte, Enrique. 1961. *Cedulario de la monarquía española relativo a la Isla de Cubagua,* 1523–1550. 2 vols. Caracas: Fundación John Boulton and the Fundación Eugenio Mendoza.

Pacheco, Francisco, Francisco de Cárdenas, Luis Torres de Mendoza, et al., eds. 1864–84. *Colección de documentos inéditos, relativos al descubrimiento, conquista y colonización de las posesiones españolas en América y Oceanía.* 42 vols. Madrid: Archivo de Indias.

Palencia-Roth, Michael. 1985. Cannibalism and the New Man of Latin America in the Fifteenth- and Sixteenth-Century European Imagination. *Comparative Civilizations Review* 12:1–27.

———. 1989. La ley de los caníbales: Cartagena y el Mar Caribe en el siglo XVI. In *De Ficciones y realidades: Perspectivas sobre literatura e historia colombianas,* ed. Alvaro Pineda Botero and Raymond Williams, 123–37. Bogotá: Tercer Mundo Editores.

———. Forthcoming. Mapping the Caribbean. In *The History of Caribbean Literatures and Cultures,* ed. James Arnold. International Comparative Literature Asssociation. Amsterdam: John Benjamins.

Ramos Pérez, Demetrio. 1984. El hecho de la conquista de América: Estudio preliminar. In his *La ética en la conquista de América: Francisco de Vitoria y la escuela de Salamanca,* 17–63. Madrid: Consejo Superior de Investigaciones Científicas.

Recopilación de leyes de los reynos de Las Indias. [1681] 1943. 3 vols. Madrid: Consejo de La Hispanidad.

Rosien, Walter. 1951. *Die Ebstorfer Weltkarte.* Hannover: Niedersächsisches Amt für Landesplanung und Statistik.

Sahlins, Marshall. 1985. *Islands of History.* Chicago: University of Chicago Press.

Salas, Julio. 1920. *Los indios caribes: Estudio sobre el origen del mito de la antropofagia.* Madrid: Editorial América.

Sturtevant, William C. 1976. First Visual Images of Native America. In *First Images of America: The Impact of the New World on the Old,* ed. Fredi Chiappelli, 417–54. Berkeley: University of California Press.

Varela, Consuelo, ed. 1982. *Cristóbal Colón: Textos y documentos completos.* Madrid: Alianza.

Vitoria, Francisco de. [1539] 1967. *Relectio de Indis, o la libertad de los indios,* ed. L. Pereña and J. M. Pérez Prendes. Madrid: Consejo Superior de Investigaciones Científicas.

Winsor, Justin. 1892. *Christopher Columbus and How He Received and Imparted the Spirit of Discovery*. New York: Houghton Mifflin.

Wittkower, Rudolf. [1942] 1972. Marvels of the East: A Study in the History of Monsters. *Journal of the Warburg Institute* 5 (1942):159–97. Reprinted in Wittkower's *Allegory and the Migration of Symbols*, 46–74. London: Thames and Hudson.

3

Writing and Evangelization in Sixteenth-Century Mexico

José Rabasa

A few years ago in a squabble with the French ethnohistorian George Baudot, Edmundo O'Gorman (1978, 448) ridiculed French scholars for referring to the early missionaries' texts as *enquêtes ethnographiques*, as if one could speak of the activities of marital love as "gynecological investigations." Unfortunately, O'Gorman's implicit differentiation between the scientific objectives of ethnography and the evangelical ends of the missionaries ignores the pious "my people" syndrome, very common among cultural anthropologists. Moreover, Bernardino de Sahagún, at least in one instance, seems to combine "love" and "obstetrics" when he recommends in his prologue to the *Arte adivinatoria* (1570) that confessors know the proper and symbolic meanings of words "so that they can understand and pursue and extract them (as if with a hook [*garabato*] or *manu obstetricante*)" (García Icazbalceta 1982, 384). Medicine thus provides a visual metaphor for the conversion of Indians to Christianity and for the field of ethnographic inquiry. The difference between the Franciscan corpus and contemporary ethnographies, then, does not reside in an opposition between loving missionary work and objective research but instead, perhaps, in how anthropology defined itself as a modern science distinct from the texts produced by travelers, missionaries, and government officials.

The debate between O'Gorman and Baudot would actually be over different understandings of what it means to write ethnography in different epochs, and therefore it would not make sense any longer to speak of a history of ethnography but of a history of ethnographies, and likewise of a history of reli-

gions even when confining ourselves to Catholicism.[1] Neither religion nor
ethnography retains a uniform meaning in different moments in the history
of the West. Moreover, as we write today about the encounter of cultures in
sixteenth-century Mexico, we ought to be aware of how our own discourses
on religion and ethnography differ from those in the sixteenth century, as
well as from those in the nineteenth and early twentieth centuries, when
ethnography was institutionalized as a science.

By these last remarks I am not suggesting a notion of historical consciousness and a hermeneutic approach à la Hans-Georg Gadamer, in which a
reader would take full cognizance of his or her prejudices in the process of
interpretation (Gadamer 1979; cf. Keber 1988). Rather, I am suggesting that
the study of the past is fundamentally a debate over the present. This concern
with the present should not be confused with writing a history of ethnography from a contemporary understanding of the discipline but fully consistent
with the history of disciplines or forms of life in the plural, as well as with
current critiques of the scientific status and rhetorical devices of modern anthropology (see, e.g., Clifford 1988; Clifford and Marcus 1986; Fabian 1983;
Marcus and Fischer 1986). It is my belief that in the way we approach the
conquest and evangelization of Mexico we define perspectives on contemporary issues affecting Indian peoples in the Americas. Although this paper
focuses exclusively on early colonial historiography, a subtext suggests how
particular modes of writing ethnography, which first emerged in the sixteenth-century Spanish conquest of the New World, have affected the constitution and reconstitution of colonial subjects up to our time.

If the lack of precedent in Europe for understanding Amerindian cultures
is one way of defining the complexity of early Spanish-American chronicles,
this same unique situation prompted new functions of writing with political
and ideological ramifications without antecedents in the Middle Ages.[2] We
can, in fact, trace the transition from a medieval exemplary sense of history to
a modern transformative concept of history: Missionaries in the New World
were practicing the writing of history as an instrument of change long before Vico advanced the principle that man makes history. A study of missionaries spanning the first hundred years of the Spanish colonization of Mexico
will enable us to (1) assess the practice, nature, and efficacy of conversion;
(2) document different conceptualizations of indigenous religious beliefs; and
(3) trace patterns in the transformation of native cultures. I am establishing a
corpus of texts in which the earliest samples belong to the first evangelical
efforts by such Franciscans as Pedro de Gante and Toribio de Benavente,
better known as Motolinía, both of whom wrote in the first half of the six-

teenth century, while the later texts pertain to such secular priests as Hernando Ruiz de Alarcón and Jacinto de la Serna in the first half of the seventeenth century. What interests me is not so much to provide an accurate representation or true interpretation of such complex figures as Sahagún or the Dominican Diego Durán as to clarify, on the basis of sixteenth-century historiography, the following three questions on how writing culture shapes colonial situations:

1. How are ethnography, conversion, and resistance articulated in terms of syncretism and the formation of a colonial subject?
2. What rhetorical devices and strategies inform the writing of Nahua culture?
3. What epistemological transformations underlie the trajectory from early representations of a highly civilized Nahua to those of a later ignorant Indian?

Syncretism and the Colonial Subject

It is common knowledge that if ethnography constitutes an integral component in modern colonial enterprises, it is perhaps particular to the Spanish conquest of America that the knowledge of other cultures is intimately bound up with the justification of imperialist policies and the conversion of the colonized to Christianity. But in defining differences with other European enterprises in Africa and India, especially in the nineteenth century, scholars tend to exaggerate, for instance, the respect of the English for Indian customs and political structures. Without necessarily ignoring the specificity and relative autonomy of each colonial enterprise, one can derive new insights on colonial modes of domination from comparative studies. Although much research in the humanities and social sciences would gain by attending to the position of imperialism and colonialism in the production of the West, the history of imperialism is not necessarily the best version of history. As Gayatri Chakravorty Spivak has put it, the deconstruction of the colonial subtext "is rather, to offer an account of how an explanation and narrative of reality was established as the normative one" in both metropolitan and colonial contexts (1987, 281). Spivak's proposed narrative would account for the epistemic violence that constituted the colonial subject as an Other alongside the complete overhaul of the episteme in the redefinition of sanity that Foucault locates at the end of the European eighteenth century. Instead of assuming a dichotomy between colonial-colonized and colonial-colonizer subject positions, we are interested here in seeing how a colonial subject is constituted as a subjectivity at fault, obviously with racist overtones (cf. Adorno 1988; Bhabha 1986; JanMohamed 1986). Moreover, we should note that epistemic violence in the colonies often preceded, if it did not provide a laboratory for, forms of domination later implemented in the metropolis.

This is not the place to elaborate on differences and parallelisms between sixteenth- and nineteenth-century colonialisms, though some brief prefatory remarks will help us visualize how colonial discourses articulate different projects in history. But first let us assess how changes in the meaning of religion in the course of the sixteenth century themselves affected the criteria by which native behavior was defined as aberrant.

The Reformation and the Council of Trent (1543–65) were the two most important religious events in the sixteenth century. The Reformation affected the evangelization of Mexico by giving it an excessive concern for heretical interpretations by the Indians. The Reformation partially explains what George Foster has called the "stripping down process" of Catholicism to its basic dogmas. I say partially because European pagan residues were also carefully avoided by the missionaries. On the other hand, the Council of Trent institutionalized the uniformity, prohibition, and control of local practices, with a special emphasis on a visual register of unacceptable behavior, thus isolating a social body for the inscription of the law (see, e.g., Gruzinski 1982, 178; Certeau 1975, 135). During the early years of the conquest there was not, indeed, a clear consensus about the place of earlier customs within the new order.

The differences between the religious sixteenth century and the secular nineteenth century are self-evident. One does not find in India the destruction of temples or the burning of books. One certainly does find, however, the programmatic formation of an elite in India that in many ways paralleled the training of trilingual Nahuas at the Franciscan College of Tlatelolco as described by Sahagún in a prologue to the *Historia general de las cosas de la Nueva España*, also known as the *Florentine Codex* (ca. 1579):

> After we came to this land to implant the Faith, we assembled the boys in our houses as is said. And we began to teach them to read, write, and sing. . . . For this training [teaching grammar] a college was formed. . . . The Spaniards, and other religious who knew this laughed much and made fun. . . . But on our working with them for two or three years, they came to understand all the subjects of the grammar book and to speak Latin, and understand it, and to write Latin, and even to compose hexametric verses. (Sahagún 1950–82, 13:82)

Some students were trained as interpreters to aid the Franciscans in translations from Nahua to Spanish and Latin and vice versa, as preachers to teach the doctrine, and as young wardens to survey and inform on their elders. Even if the Franciscan pedagogical programs were commendable, one ought not to overlook the colonial logic in their institutionalization of European knowledge (Gómez Canedo 1982, 131–46; Kobayashi 1974; Mignolo 1989). The training of an elite does not exclude racist policies, and it certainly furthers hegemonic rule. For the record, let me quote Macaulay's "Minute on Indian Education" (1835):

> We must at present do our best to form a class who may be interpreters between us and the millions whom we govern; a class of persons, Indian in blood and colour, but English in taste, in opinions, in morals, and in intellect. To that class we may leave it to define the vernacular dialects of the country, to enrich those dialects with terms of science borrowed from the Western nomenclature, and to render them by degrees fit vehicles for conveying knowledge to the great mass of the population. (Quoted in Spivak 1987, 282)

The education of colonial subjects for proselytizing—in this case science, in the other Christianity, though as we will see religion always implies more than a set of beliefs or even an ethic—suggests a form of violence perhaps even more insidious than the destruction and persecution of the exterior manifestations of belief. It is an epistemic violence that seeks to implant an institution of knowledge and European subjectivity. Yet ethnography, the writing of an *ethnia*, in spite of its will to dominate the other culture by means of its objectification within a system, not only registers forms of resistance but also provides a space where "ethnicity" inscribes itself. By ethnicity I do not mean a pristine form of authenticity but instead a tension resulting from the institutional forms imposed by the dominant culture and the need to convey a sense of the self or a meaning of history that is alien to the colonial order.[3] The supposition that the subject is an empty and homogeneous substance that holds different beliefs, and consequently that conversion merely implies the acceptance of articles of faith, is a recurrent commonplace in both the Christian doctrines used by the missionaries and the definition of syncretism from the sixteenth century onward.

One of the earliest observations on the conversion of Mexico, in Cortés's *First Letter* (1519), actually written by the Cabildo of Veracruz before the march to Tenochtitlan, defines the process of conversion as one in which "Our Lord God would be very pleased if . . . the devotion, trust and hope in [their] idols were transferred to the divine power of God; for it is certain that if they were to worship the true God with such fervor, faith and diligence, they would perform many miracles" (1986, 36). Though this statement is carefully crafted in terms of the three theological virtues, the Indians would convert to Catholicism by a simple change of the object of faith, hope, and charity. This same proposition underlies Cortés's appropriation of the temples in the *Second Letter*: "The most important of these idols, and the ones in whom they have most faith, I had taken from their places and thrown down the steps . . . and I had images of Our Lady and of other saints put there, which caused Moctezuma and other natives some sorrow" (106). According to Cortés, Moctezuma's affliction was due to a concern that the people, seeing that their gods were being treated disrespectfully, would become angry and give them nothing, leaving them to die of hunger. Cortés then tells Charles V how he informed Moctezuma that there was only one God, and so on. In Cortés's words, Moctezuma replies that "I [Cortés] would know better the things they should believe, and should explain to them and make them understand, for they would do as I said was best" (107). Thus the image of an "ideal native" is construed as a docile subject receiving information and knowledge about what to believe.

Whether the Indians were forced or chose out of their free will to baptize and marry within the Church, the process of conversion presumes a homogeneous subject. The converts must first accept the articles of faith and then be taught to genuflect, make the sign of the cross, and murmur prayers by rote. The instruction and memorization of the letter of the doctrine remains a future task. Confession itself is designed to reinforce doctrinal teachings. As the confessor reviews the list of commandments and mortal sins, along with the basic articles of faith, he is regimenting memorization from two perspectives: (1) he polices, as it were, those who have been doing their homework; and (2) he implants an artificial memory designed to register as sinful behavior what otherwise would not be perceived as such. (This last form amounts to quite literally inscribing the body with a new law.)

As Alonso de Molina puts it, he designed his *Confesionario mayor* ([1569] 1984) as a memory aid, "So that you can see and read how you are to search and know the sins" (fol. 7r). Molina proceeds to list things that must be recalled in order to have a thorough examination of conscience and build the habit of bringing one's life to memory from childhood on. To those reared as Catholics, all this must seem like a common confessional format (cf. Tentler 1977, 28–53). But what sets this confessionary apart from European counterparts are its questions concerning specific Nahua beliefs and practices: "Did you ever ask a sorcerer to draw your fortune, or to draw a spell from your body and to apply suction? Did he cut your hair superstitiously? Did you call on one to discover something you had lost, or to divine something about you in water?" (Molina 1984, fol. 20v). All these customs are well codified in such histories as Sahagún's and Durán's.

In passing we may note that, as expected, Molina not only quotes the Psalms in support of the sacrament of penance and the examination of conscience but also alludes to Socrates' dictum "Know thyself" as the true wisdom of philosophy. But confession constitutes the subject to be examined as it is defined and mapped out by the loci of an artificial memory; it also makes the sinner the depository of a truth to be extracted and for which he or she must accept full responsibility.[4]

It is precisely in the call for thorough examinations of conscience that Sahagún, Durán, and other missionaries writing in the second half of the sixteenth century denounced the sham of the early conversions. Sahagún accused the Nahuas of lying; Durán diagnosed deep-seated habits that had distorted the teachings of the Church. In their condemnations, both Sahagún and Durán seem to reflect the strict and rigid guidelines first defined and reinforced by the Council of Trent, and such doctrinal changes become especially evident when we compare their positions with those of Fray Pedro de Gante and Motolinía.

For instance, Gante readily adopts dances and pagan songs to communicate the Christian doctrine: "Since I had seen this [pagan songs and dances] and that all their songs were dedicated to the gods I composed a very solemn song about the law of God and the faith. . . . I also gave them patterns to paint on their mantles so they could dance with them because this was the way the patterns had been used by the Indians. . . . In this way they first came to show obedience to the church and the patios were full of people" (quoted in Madsen 1961, 377). In a parallel passage, Motolinía corroborates the early Franciscan approval of native ways and creativity in the Indians' production of ornaments and practice of rituals: "Shortly afterwards they began in Huexotzingo to make very rich and beautiful veils for the crosses and platforms for the images of the Saints in Gold and feather work. Then they began to adorn their churches and make altarpieces and ornaments and have processions, and the children learned dances with which to enliven the latter" (Motolinía 1973a, 129). All this is very far from what today smacks of hysteria in Durán's assertion that "these people used superstitions, sorcery, and idolatry in everything" (Durán 1971, 397). Thus Durán saw haircuts, sowing and reaping, sweeping, and—practically speaking—the totality of everyday life as invested with superstition:

"Heathenism and idolatry are present everywhere: in sowing, in reaping, in storing grain, even in plowing the earth and in building houses" (55). Apparently, a viable Hispanization comforts Durán: "In some places, however, the natives are becoming more like us" (407). The post-Tridentine emphasis on the visual corroboration of behavior is manifest in this last statement. Sahagún also exposes heresy and errors in the new songs: "And if . . . they sing some songs they have composed, which deal with the things of God and His saints, they are surrounded by many errors and heresies" (Sahagún 1950–82, 13:81). Gante, Motolinía, and the first missionary efforts in general built on native culture as a vehicle for Christianity; moreover, it was expected that the old would mingle with the new. In the early evangelical efforts there was certainly no room for more than one god, and the missionaries were generally rigid about other articles of faith, but pagan ceremonies that did not overtly contradict Catholicism were accepted and encouraged. This tolerance for a coexistence of ceremonies and allowance for specific local practices was also common in Europe before the Tridentine Church.

Sahagún deplores the error the early missionaries committed when they allowed such mixtures. Dissimulation is one of his favorite topoi. Native leaders were questioned at the time of their conversion, and as Sahagún puts it in the prologue to the *Arte adivinatoria*, "when questioned if they believed in God the Father, the Son and the Holy Spirit, and the rest of the articles of the faith, they would say yes, *quemachca*, in conformity with their conspiracy and custom [of incorporating other gods into their pantheon]" (García Icazbalceta 1982, 382). Sahagún's denunciation of open heathen practices would suggest a change of criteria to measure thorough conversions rather than a change in the Indians' behavior. Conversion in this context would imply more than the "obedience" (read "submission") Gante and Motolinía considered a sufficient basis for granting baptism. For Sahagún the same techniques of the confession should be applied beforehand to guarantee a thorough and sincere acceptance of the faith.

Though it is Sahagún who gives us some of the earliest information on the cult of Guadalupe, in denouncing it he should perhaps be credited for inventing the phenomenon we have come to recognize as syncretism. Syncretism is intimately bound to questions of conversion and implies the notion of an autonomous, homogeneous subject. It is not therefore a cultural phenomenon that lends itself readily to observation but rather a diagnosis of sincerity or the capacity to embody the type of subjectivity requisite for a true conversion. Syncretism is generally defined according to two criteria that imply either an accepted conversion or the deceit Sahagún denounces. Deceit boils down to the idols-behind-the-altar syndrome. It is neither Guadalupe nor Saint Ann that the Indians pray to but Tonantzin and Toci, our mother and grandmother in the ancient pantheon (see Sahagún 1950–82, 13:90–91).[5] The Indians just said yes without meaning it when they were asked if they accepted the sole existence of one god. A concept of resistance could be formulated in these terms, but this yes/no type of understanding of conversion and resistance ignores native culture or, if you wish, an ethnic unconscious that cannot be emptied and at once refilled with another set of beliefs.[6] It is precisely this complication that has led modern anthropologists, perhaps already anticipated by Durán's insistence on deep-seated habits, to advance a model of syncretism based on the supposition that the Indians had converted and invented a new church. Since this process could be described as a phenomenon of cultural production, albeit under colonial rule, I do not see the need to classify it as syncretic, especially when the boundaries of the indigenous and the European are difficult if not dangerous to draw. William Madsen, in perhaps the authoritative text on the subject, has defined this second type not so much as a mosaic but as "a process of fusional syncretism that eventually almost eliminated all visible vestiges of paganism" (1961, 378). Syncretism, then, implies a combination of two or more cultural traditions, as does resistance when couched in culturalist terms. But cultural explanations of this sort tend to ignore the ideology that defines the position of the colonial subject as a neophyte at fault and furthermore to naturalize a teleology in which pagan components are condemned to disappear. Somehow we are led to believe that some invisible force is eliminating paganism and to ignore the fact that syncretism was first constituted as an error. Madsen's notion of an eventual elimination of paganism implies a progressive civilizing process and consequently an evolutionary model. Syncretism represents a phenomenon that cultural anthropologists celebrate, but its archaeology conveys discrimination and exclusion on the basis of an ethnic deficiency. We must now ask ourselves how the colonial subject is constituted as a problematic neophyte.

The Writing of Nahua Culture

Tzvetan Todorov (1984) has commended Sahagún for writing about Nahua culture without glossing the contents, as was commonly practiced by other missionaries; this absence of value judgments and the role given to informants in the production of Sahagún's *Historia general* appear exceptional even by today's scientific standards and experimental writings in ethnography (cf. Clifford 1988; Clifford and Marcus 1986). But the "uncontaminated" text is perhaps even more striking when we read the prefatory remarks that frame the *Historia general* as an arsenal to ward off the devil: "I know of a certainty that neither does the devil sleep nor is the reverence these natives render him forgotten; and that he is awaiting an opportunity, that he may return to the dominion he has held. . . . And for that time it is good that we have weapons on hand to meet him with" (Sahagún 1950–82, 13:59).

Needless to say, the intentions of Sahagún and those of contemporary ethnography differ as to the politics as well as the poetics of experimental writings. Politically they correspond to opposite points in the history of Western expansionism. Sahagún manifests the beginning of a European colonization of the planet in which indigenous cultures are recorded as inferior if not plainly evil. This asymmetry constitutes the position of the colonial subject and legitimizes his or her domination and reduction to the status of subaltern. Experimental ethnographies, in contrast, picture themselves as seeking to contribute to processes of decolonization. The success of these enterprises eludes their corresponding intentions to dominate and liberate. On the one hand, contemporary ethnographical experiments with dialogue tend to be more encroaching upon other cultures than their systematic critique of the power of objectifying devices in realist representation would lead us to believe (Rabasa 1987, 137–41; cf. Clifford 1988, 41–46; Fabian 1990; Marcus and Cushman 1982). On the other hand, Sahagún's will to knowledge leads him to provide a space in which native informants can inscribe their ethnicity. But we should note that such a critique occurs in spite of the intentions of both Sahagún and the informants and the collegians from Tlatelolco. We should not, then, categorize the poetics of Sahagún's *Historia general* on the basis of this clearing within the discourse of power, nor should we allot a privileged place to poetics in the avowed politics of Sahagún. To propose a hidden intention that would negate Sahagún's overt political statements on the grounds that the information contained in the *Historia general* exceeds its linguistic and anthropological needs for evangelization is to second-guess Sahagún without direct testimony to support a "scientific" hidden agenda (cf. Klor de Alva 1988a, 45–48). How much Sahagún believed it was necessary to know about the other culture in order to build an arsenal against the devil is a question we cannot answer. However, the collaboration of informants and collegians in the production of the texts certainly provides a space for the inscription of ethnicity regardless of censoring by Sahagún or even self-censoring on the part of the collegians and informants. These methodological observations obviously do not seek to exclude possible readings of Sahagún as an invaluable source of information on pre-Hispanic culture but rather to probe the ideology underlying his elaboration of a total reconstruction of Nahua culture.

Sahagún envisions the *Historia general* as a storehouse—indeed, as a linguistic thesaurus that could be readily consulted for interpreting songs, dances, dreams, confessions, and whatnot if they were suspected of being idolatrous: "This work is like a dragnet to bring to light all the words of this language with their exact and metaphorical meanings, and all their ways of speaking, and most of their ancient practices, the good and evil" (13:47). Sahagún, however, further specifies that he is not writing a dictionary but preparing a preliminary corpus of proper forms of Nahuatl speech: "Through my efforts twelve Books have been written in an idiom characteristic and typical of this Mexican language . . . as well verified and certain as that which Virgil, Cicero, and other authors wrote in the Latin language" (13:50).

The implication of this last statement is that Sahagún is indeed inventing a form of classical Nahuatl (Klor de Alva 1989). It is an invention not because the samples of an "idiom characteristic and typical" that he collects do not approximate the language of the elite in pre-Hispanic times but because the literary corpus he constructs precisely intends to illustrate how high-ranking Nahuas used to talk before the conquest and therefore to correct what the missionaries perceived as a deterioration of its proper use. Thus, besides being a linguistic register of voices and metaphorical meanings, the *Historia general* fulfills a normative function. It dictates a linguistic ideal and raises the image of a foregone orderly pre-Hispanic society. Classical Nahuatl enables missionaries and Christianized members of the native elite to assert a legitimate ascendancy as the new bearers of culture in their sermons, translations of religious literature, and everyday teachings of doctrine. The bulk of the elite (except for those trained) cannot claim any sort of authority besides the instrumental political position allotted to them by the colonial order.

The invention of classical Nahuatl complements the elaboration of a storehouse of symbols and metaphors for the interpretation of religious phenomena. Missionaries from Sahagún to Ruiz de Alarcón also complained of an opaque and difficult language, that is, "an esoteric language, *nahualahtolli*, that was ostensibly used to communicate with supernatural beings" (Klor de Alva 1989, 157). For Sahagún, sacred songs are an invention of the devil: "The songs which, in this land, he [the devil] contrived to be prepared and utilized in his service and for his divine worship, his songs of praise, in the temples as well as beyond them, are this forest or brambled thorny thicket. Said songs contain so much guile that they say anything and proclaim that which he commands. But only those he addresses understand them" (Sahagún 1950–82, 13:58). Likewise, half a century later Ruiz de Alarcón forewarned his readers about difficult metaphors and allegories in the conjurings and incantations he recorded in the *Treatise on the Heathen Superstitions* (1629): "And that which is found written about the subject among the likes of these is all in a difficult and almost unintelligible language, both because the Devil, its inventor, influences his veneration and esteem by means of the difficulty of the language found in all the conjurings, invocations, and spells, and because the more figures and tropes the language has, the more difficult it is to understand" (Ruiz de Alarcón 1984, 40). As a linguistic storehouse, Sahagún's *Historia general* would provide an indispensable instrument for deciphering the allegorical sacred speech reported by Ruiz de Alarcón, but as a literary corpus it also provides a model for writing sermons and translating from Latin and Spanish into Nahuatl (Dibble 1988, 108–10 and passim). The *nahualahtolli*, insofar as it is attributed to the devil, would be disqualified as legitimate speech, which amounts to a usurpation of language and authority from indigenous men and women of knowledge.

We cannot overestimate the role the collegians from Tlatelolco played in the production of classical Nahuatl. Not only Sahagún but many other Franciscans as well acknowledge their debt to the Nahua scholars they had trained in early days of the College of Tlatelolco. Thus Fray Juan Bautista, in the prologue to his *Sermonario* (1606), after giving credit to his native assistants and praising some of them for speaking Latin ex tempore, deplores the void their deaths left behind: "Today there remain so few Indians we can consult about their language, that they are few in numbers, and many of them use corrupt words, as they are used by the Spaniards" (García Icazbalceta 1982, 475). Juan Bautista exalts the older disciples of Tlatelolco for their translations of "anything in Latin and in Romance, attending more to sense than to the letter" (475). There is certainly a concern for the distortion of the doctrine, but it would be unfair to reduce their view of language to some sort of "pipeline" theory of communication. Indigenous scribes are praised for their translation of the sense, not just the letter, of a document. As for his own translations, "The Mexican language is in itself so elegant, copious, and elaborate, that one can barely translate a line from Castilian or Latin into it, that is not doubled" (478). This suggests that by *sense* (*sentido*) Juan Bautista did not mean merely a correct translation of the *tenor*, which a word-for-word translation would actually miss because of the different symbolism present in each language, but also an adoption of the Nahuatl vehicle and rules of composition. So his preoccupation with the corruption of the letter cannot be reduced to such errors as, "I have found Indians, very bilingual (ladino) and with a Bachelor degree, that talking to me have said: 'Dios itlaneltoquilitzin,' which means the faith with which God believes; when it should be: 'Dios ineltococatzin,' the faith by means of which he is believed in; and of this sort I could draw many examples" (475). This concern with proper terms is part of a larger strategy of translating and composing sermons in Nahuatl following the style of precontact oratory.

Although Juan Bautista's emulation of the "elegant, copious and elaborate" speech of old would entail a Nahuatlization of Christianity, the Catholic doctrine must remain intact in the process (cf. Dibble 1974). The system of interpretation and a privileged historical narrative must inform the production of Nahuatl texts. An asymmetry is thus preserved by severing language from culture. But in order to guarantee the prevalence of a European master code, Nahuatl culture must be reduced to Sahagún's type of encyclopedic text, and it is indeed the pre-Hispanic world that the *Historia general* reconstructs. Nahuatl culture is written in a quite literal sense of the term *writing*: it is inscribed—as well as given an order—on a blank piece of paper (cf. Certeau 1975). As a result of the destructuring of pre-Hispanic society, the friars faced a proliferation of cultural forms whose significance they had no way of recognizing. Having burned the books and destroyed the native religious institutions, they were forced as early as the 1530s to reconstruct the past in order to interpret the present. This project, however, had a double edge since Nahua culture is meaningful in its own right beyond the friars' interpretations. Thus the missionaries created the materials for an indigenous counter-memory insofar as their ethnographies potentially conveyed an alternative to the Christian worldview. It is perhaps this counter-memory that Sahagún was trying to correct, along with some "factual" errors, when he revised book 12 ("The Conquest of Mexico") in 1585 (Cline 1988). Missionary ethnographers from Sahagún to Ruiz de Alarcón were often accused of promoting the problem they were supposed to be solving. One cannot but agree with the critics.

Cultural asymmetry becomes evident in Sahagún's translation into Spanish of book 1 ("The Gods"). What in Nahuatl reads as: "Uitzilopochtl [Hummingbird from the Left] was only a common man, just a man, a sorcerer, an omen of evil; a madman, a deceiver, a creator of war, a war-lord, an instigator of war" (Sahagún 1950–82, 1:1) becomes, "The God Vitcilupuchtli was another Hercules, exceedingly robust, of great strength and very bellicose, a great destroyer of towns and killer of people" (Sahagún 1932, 25). Here we can trace a passage from a predominantly paratactical style in the Nahuatl text to a syntactical Spanish—a recasting in the vehicle of the dominant language. But there is also a semantic rewriting in the comparison with Hercules. The comparison with Greco-Roman myth privileges a historical narrative in which paganism, having been superseded by Christianity, may now nevertheless illuminate Nahua numina. The allusion to Hercules in the translation seemingly does not add any meaning to Huitzilopochtli other than the commonplace one of physical strength. It functions more as a metaphor than as a fragment of comparative ethnography or mythology. Nevertheless, in the process pre-Hispanic deities are accommodated within a system in which the Greco-Roman pantheon has been reduced to a repertoire of symbols. As Klor de Alva (1988a) has pointed out, the emphasis on the human origins of Huitzilopochtli might betray a Hispanized informant. The Nahuatl version, notwithstanding self-censoring, would fulfill its function as a thesaurus of terms and forms of speaking about the gods.

Sahagún's prologues to the *Historia general* betray a historical schema that leaves no room for a reciprocal rewriting of European history from a New World perspective. One thing is for certain in Sahagún's schema: Spaniards will always rule the country. The only salvation for the Indians is indeed Spanish rule: "If they were left alone, if the Spanish nation were not to intercede, . . . in less than fifty years there would be no trace of the preaching which has been done for them" (13:98). Sahagún briefly entertains the possibility that the Gospel was preached before the Spaniards arrived, but if that was the case, the Indians soon "reverted to their idolatries which they previously held. And I conjecture this from the great difficulty I have encountered in the implanting of the faith in this people" (13:97).

Sahagún did not share the millenarian aspirations of the first twelve Franciscans (see, e.g., Baudot 1977; Phelan 1970). On the contrary, all his statements on history seem to undermine, if not to mock, the early Franciscan dreams. This difference may be because he did not come to New Spain with the first twelve in 1524 but later in 1529, or perhaps because by the 1570s, when he wrote most of his prologues, there was no room for the early optimism. The Council of Trent had regimented mysticism as well as doctrinal flexibility toward local customs, and the arrival of the Jesuits in 1572 severely curtailed the power of the regulars, as the former allied themselves with the secular branch.

In this respect Durán's pessimism reflected a parallel predicament for the Dominicans. His is also a pessimistic history. Durán's long elaboration on Topiltzin as St. Thomas in the first chapter of the *Libro de los ritos y ceremonias en las fiestas de los dioses y celebración de ellas* (1581) arrives at a parallel conclusion to

Sahagún's: "We also know that this apostle was a preacher to the Indians but that, having become discouraged there, he asked Christ (when the Lord appeared to him at a fair) to send him wherever He wished except to the Indians" (Durán 1971, 59). It would seem that, for both missionaries, the Indians were thick and slow to understand Church doctrine.

From the Civilized Nahua to the Ignorant Indian

Let us take Motolinía's description of the hummingbird as a point of entry to the epistemic violence that reduced the Nahuas to the status of "ignorant" Indians:

> If God thus preserves some small birds and afterward resurrects them, and year by year one sees these marvels in this land, who would doubt of human bodies, which are buried corruptible, that God shall not resurrect them incorruptible by Jesus Christ, and that he will dress and adorn them with the four gifts, and sustain them with the tenderness of his divine fruition and vision, since he sustains these small birds with the dew and honey of flowers, and dresses them with such gracious feathers, that not even Solomon in his splendor was dressed as one of these. (Motolinía 1973b, 334)

The colorful feathers of hummingbirds and their sustenance by dew and the honey of flowers demonstrate the power of God to dress and sustain the resurrected body with his vision and fruition. But by implication the hummingbird is also a sign of the care God has taken in dressing the New World landscape with metaphors that prove an article of faith. Whereas the phoenix as myth symbolizes the resurrection, the hummingbird as nature reveals it through analogy.

Motolinía had no qualms about using the Huitzilin as a symbol of the resurrection even though the hummingbird would bring to mind the main Aztec deity, Huitzilopochtli (Hummingbird from the Left), if not the trials by Inquisition of Don Carlos Ometochtzin and Puxtecatl Tlayotla (known as Don Miguel after his baptism). Both were accused of apostasy, among other crimes. Don Carlos, who had been one of the first disciples at the College of Santa Cruz in Tlatelolco and whose sedition and dogmatizing consequently were an embarrassment to the college, was burned at the stake in 1539 after Bishop Zumárraga relaxed him to the secular arm (see Greenleaf 1965; Padden 1970, 240–70). The investigation of Don Carlos led to the discovery of a great stone image of Tlaloc and a cult center. Though Tlayotla was spared the stake, he was identified as leading a conspiracy to bring back the reign of Huitzilopochtli. According to rumor, the statue of this god was successfully concealed after the fall of Tenochtitlan. Meanwhile, in the midst of all these scandals, Motolinía, quite unshaken, praised the success of the early missionaries and seemingly mocked the Huitzilopochtli scandal. After all, in spite of subjecting Tlayotla to torture, the idol of Huitzilopochtli was never discovered. Tlayotla was incarcerated in the Franciscan convent of El Grande, where we lose track of him but where he most likely died.

Martin Ocelotl's case enables us to trace one more distinction between Motolinía and the more strict views of Sahagún and Durán, now with regard to the calendrical system of the Tonalpohualli (the count of the days; Klor de Alva 1981; *Proceso Inquisitorial* 1910, 34 and passim). Among the charges against Martin Ocelotl, that of diviner took precedence over being a *nahual*—literally, "an entity that can be interposed" i.e., "a mask, a disguise; a sorcerer" (Andrews and Hassig, 1984, 313n12)—or even talking to the devil. In the process Martin Ocelotl was asked if he knew that to divine the future was forbidden. He answered in the affirmative but denied practicing divination. Changing opinions on the Tonalpohualli in the course of the sixteenth century convey a transformation in the evaluation of pre-Hispanic culture.

Motolinía again conceived of the Tonalpohualli as culturally compatible with conversion to Christianity. First, he believed the Tonalpohualli was a calendar based on astronomical observations: "This table can be called a calendar of the Indians of New Spain, which they counted by a star that in the fall first appears in the afternoons in the west" (Motolinía 1973b, 54). As we will see, the astronomical basis of the Tonalpohualli was a highly debated topic in the sixteenth century. What interests me here about Motolinía's position is his praise of the astrological system and the Nahuas who invented it: "And it is to be known that this two hundred and sixty days are so measured by this number, because so many were the signs or fates, dispositions of the planets in which human bodies were born, according to the philosophers and astrologers of Anahuac" (Motolinía 1973b, 54). As this passage makes evident, Motolinía is praising the Nahuas not just for their observations of the planet Venus but precisely for the divinatory function of the calendar. For details on the Tonalpohualli, he refers the reader to the books of the Nahuas: "If you want to further inquire into this topic, see their books" (55). We would not be too far off track if we were to assume that Motolinía was referring, if not specifically to *Codex Borbonicus*, at least to a similar Tonalamatl (book

of days). At any rate, the opinion of the philosophers and astrologers of Anahuac, which according to Motolinía's etymology means "what is surrounded
by water," does not contradict the introduction of Christianity. Their astrological system is comparable with its European counterparts: "It is not a new
opinion of those from Anahuac, because we know that in our nations there
are philosophers or their writings that hold it" (Motolinía 1973b, 55).

In accommodating Christianization, or at least in finding the Tonalpohualli
compatible with it, Motolinía separated the validity of the Indian system and
its organization based on Venus from its cosmogonical underpinnings: "The
cause and reason for counting the days by this star, and that they revered and
sacrificed to it, was because these deceived natives thought and believed that
one of their main gods, named either Topiltzin or Quetzalcohuatl, became
that resplendent star when he died and parted from this world" (Motolinía
1973b, 56). In brief, the genesis of the myth can be separated from its divinatory system. Some corrections in the line of faith would make its organization
of daily life compatible with Christianity.

If we now turn to Durán's perspective on the calendar, we find a completely opposite position. I have already noted Durán's conception of everyday life as impregnated with idolatry and superstition. After complaining of
the burning of books in the 1530s—which, by the way, coincided with the
political climate under Archbishop Fray Juan de Zumárraga that led to the
imprisonment of Martin Ocelotl and Puxtecatl Tlayotla, and the burning of
Don Carlos Ometochtzin—Durán explains the content of some of the now
lost books: "These characters also taught the Indian nations the days on which
they were to sow, reap, till the land, cultivate corn, weed, harvest, store, shell
the ears of corn, sow beans and flaxweed" (Durán 1971, 396). Durán obviously was not concerned with how this lost knowledge could enlighten his
contemporaries about how to reverse the destruction of the Indian economy.
Instead, he sought to further its destruction by emphasizing superstition and
hence the irrationality of native knowledge. Like Motolinía, Durán compares
Nahua and European astrological calendars: "The reason for all this was that
some signs were held to be good, others evil, and others indifferent, just as
our almanacs record the signs of the zodiac, where we are told that some
influences are good, others bad, and others indifferent regarding the sowing
of crops and even the health of our bodies. Wise and experienced doctors
wait, consider, and know when bloodletting or a cathartic is beneficial or
harmful" (Durán 1971, 396). If the first sentence seems to convey an equivalence, the second statement on health previews a refutation of Indian knowl-

edge on empirical grounds. The phrase "wise and experienced doctors" obviously does not refer to Nahua healers. He immediately moves on to differentiate Indian beliefs from those of Spanish farmers: "Spanish farmers observe the rules of the almanac and are governed by them when they sow. They observe the date, and through experience they know whether there will be drought or barrenness. But this Indian nation observed different rules" (396).

The rules of the Spanish almanac entail observation and experience, just as the Spanish doctor waits for the proper signs. Furthermore, Spanish farmers trust God, and moreover, "each does his share and all the necessary work" (Durán 1971, 396). Durán contrasts this attitude of work and observation of nature with the Indians' uncritical adherence to the calendar and the sorcerers' instructions: "They could have gathered the crop earlier, at their leisure; but since the old sorcerer found in his books or almanac that the day had come, he proclaimed it to the people, and they went off in great speed" (397). Leisure is not what is at stake here but rather the difference between an arbitrary system and one that is informed by empirical observation. The arrogance of the friar as he suggests that Amerindians for millennia never bothered to understand and follow nature entails a disaccreditation of Nahua leaders. His final judgment sums up a reduction of native knowledge to superstition on the basis of a normative science: "And I believe that there was no science here; all was sorcery and superstition" (404). Durán similarly undermines medical knowledge with rhetorical questions that I believe need no commentary; for example: "Is there a man of average intelligence willing to believe that by sucking the hair of the head with the mouth a headache will disappear?" (60).

Durán attacks Indian knowledge on both the medical and agricultural fronts. So-called sorcerers mislead the people and consequently should be persecuted in the extirpation of all forms of heathen practice. All Durán's concerns with heathenism are ultimately connected with an economic program and a medical system. Before examining these topics in Durán, it is worthwhile noting that Jacinto de la Serna's *Manual de ministros de indios* (1656) gives the most explicit condemnation of Nahua medical knowledge when he explains epidemics as follows: "And all this is due to their lack of faith in our medicines, and not wanting to use them, preferring their mistaken and sacrilegious doctors that not only cannot cure their body, but indeed kill them, and their soul, which is the most important part, and that is why God our Lord punishes them" (Serna [1892] 1987, 287). After making this religious point about native doctors, de la Serna underscores the importance of the Indian nation and hence of caring for their bodies and souls, and for very economic reasons: "Nothing can be done without them, not the mines, the fields, the factories, the buildings, because they are the blood of the mystical body of the Monarchy" (287).

Likewise, Durán's concern with the calendar and its regulation of agriculture and health inevitably leads him to condemn the economy of feasts: "I heartily believe that all this merrymaking is not in honor of God or of the saint but in honor of the natives' sensuality, their bellies. Their aim is simply to eat, to drink, and to get drunk. This, in sum, was the ultimate aim of the ancient feasts" (Durán 1971, 407). Beyond a preoccupation with idols behind the altar, what we find here is the implementation of a work ethic. Durán's ultimate question seems to be, Why spend and waste so much? Economic reform is clearly on his agenda for Hispanization. Take, for instance, how the notion of *nepantla* ("in the middle") is expressed in economic terms:

> Once I questioned an Indian regarding certain things. In particular I asked him why he had gone about begging, spending bad nights and worse days, and why, after having gathered so much money with such trouble, he offered a fiesta, invited the entire town, and spent everything. Thus I reprehended him for the foolish thing he had done, and he answered, "Father, do not be astonished; we are still in Nepantla." . . . Or, better said, they believed in God and also followed their ancient heathen rites and customs. And this is what the Indian meant in his despicable excuse when he stated that the people still were "in the middle" and were "neither fish nor fowl." (Durán 1971, 410–11)

As this passage on nepantla makes evident, economic considerations set the two religious systems apart and were integral to conversion programs. Idleness, as Durán puts it, "comes to us from ancient times" (408). Several passages illustrate the Indians' resistance to an incipient capitalist economy and its work ethic, among them: "Instead of hiring themselves out to a Spaniard, earning three reales a week, they prefer to go from market to market, trading things which are hardly worth twenty cacao beans. They will offer the Spaniard four reales to be given their liberty in order to return to their little houses or huts" (53).

In reading this passage, one cannot but wonder why Durán did not question the denial of liberty by the Spaniards. He does describe how abuse led to a kind of mental state that Frantz Fanon (1968) categorized as an instance of the psychopathology of the colonized: "Their spirit has been so hurt, so damaged, that they live in fear" (Durán 1971, 53). In passing, it is worthwhile recalling a passage in which Sahagún, after praising the muchachos who in the early days terrorized their elders, complains that the friars have been "forbidden to imprison or punish anyone in their houses for any infraction" (Sahagún 1950–82, 13:81). Implicit in these distinct views on violence and terror are Durán's understanding of conversion in terms of transforming the cultural habitus and Sahagún's in terms of verifying the sincerity of the Indians' acceptance of the faith. Both coincide, however, in their condemnation and subjugation of native knowledge.

In an appendix to book 4, Sahagún quotes and refutes Motolinía's opinion on the lack of idolatries in the calendar, stating that "there is no reason to condemn it" (Sahagún 1950–82, 4:140). Especially noteworthy is Sahagún's refutation of Motolinía's assertion that "the Indians [who] devised this count showed themselves to be natural philosophers: this is most false. For they do not carry out this count according to any natural order; for it was the invention of the devil and an art of soothsayers" (4:141). In terms reminiscent of Durán, Sahagún here disqualifies native knowledge, first by placing the calendar outside a normative science, a natural order, and second by reducing the practitioners to soothsayers following the whims of the devil. Further on in this appendix, Sahagún again insists on the unscientific nature of the Tonalpohualli, and compares it to European astrology: "For the art of judiciary astrology, common among us, is founded upon natural astrology, which is the signs and planets of the heavens and in their course and aspect" (4:145). He also underscores the devilish origin of the Tonalpohualli: "It hath no foundation in any science nor in any natural order. . . . I say it was fraud and deceit in order to dazzle and derange people of low capacity and little understanding" (4:145). Not only does the Tonalpohualli lack any correspondence with a natural order, it is specifically designed "to dazzle and derange" people with inferior intellects.

Thus Sahagún's critique of Motolinía passes judgment not just on the populace but on the "ministers" of the devil themselves. Sahagún certainly praises the disciplinary regime and moral philosophy that in pre-Hispanic times "taught these natives through experience that, to live morally and virtuously, rigor, austerity, and continuous concern for things beneficial to the state was necessary" (Sahagún 1950–82, 13:75). What Sahagún chooses to ignore is the fact that the calendar had a vital social function since the tonalli (forces linking the individual with the cosmos) was determined on a given day that would be beneficial to the newborn and thus functioned as a modeling system and regulator of the social order (López Austin 1980, 1:223–33).

The prologues, appendixes, notes, exclamations, and other remarks in

Sahagún's *Historia general* do not mark a clear separation between an ethnographic text and metatextual commentaries. Sahagún's reconstruction of a total pre-Hispanic culture seeks to illuminate fragments, superstitions, and residues of idolatry, all of which was perceived as a conspiracy to return to Satan's ways; it presumes a destructuring of postconquest society in which the Indians are defined as perpetual minors. Thus we find two ethnographic texts: one reconstructs pre-Hispanic antiquity, the other reveals a fragmented condition. From Sahagún (as well as from the other texts we have examined) we learn how the missionaries themselves subjected the Indians to psychological and corporal punishment, not to mention the brutal abuse inflicted under the *encomienda* and *repartimiento*. Friars terrorized Indian leaders and promoted self-loathing and contempt for their culture. Missionaries not only subjugated native knowledge but also sought to implant a constant vigilance of thought through confession and a constant sermonizing on the inferiority of their culture. We are thus witnessing a systematic undermining and destruction of Indian subjectivity.[7]

By the time Ruiz de Alarcón wrote his treatises, the policing of native ways was building on concrete day-to-day case studies of superstitions and sorcerers' conjurings that no longer required a reconstruction of pre-Hispanic culture. In fact, Christian motifs often form an integral component of what he calls fictions and incantations. No more does Ruiz de Alarcón allude to the Mexican grandeur, as Durán referred to ancient Mexico in his narrative of the rise and fall of the Aztecs.[8] Instead he writes about "ignorant" Indians, about a subaltern class plagued by what he views as superstitious beliefs and opportunistic sorcerers. Between Cortés's dictum on Mexican civilization in the *Second Letter* (1520) ("considering that they are barbarous and so far from the knowledge of God and cut off from all civilized nations, it is truly remarkable what they have achieved in all things" [1986, 108]) and Ruiz de Alarcón's and de la Serna's recommendations on the *congregaciones*, the forced resettlement to enhance the effectiveness of the friars' vigilance ("only much later were the Indians grouped into congregations where their vices may be noticed more easily" [Ruiz de Alarcón 1984, 40]), we can trace the creation of a colonial subject. Cortés's reference to them as barbarians, although he recognized their achievements, already implied the subjugation of native knowledge through the imposition of a normative science. The medical and economic categories that we have traced in Durán's and Sahagún's reduction of the Tonalpohualli to superstition recur in Ruiz de Alarcón's and de la Serna's writings, but there is no longer any admiration to be found, nor do they find a need to reconstruct pre-Hispanic culture and history.

NOTES

1. For a critique of histories of anthropology that are written from a contemporary definition of the discipline, see Rabasa 1987, 131–59. On the history of religions, see Certeau 1975, 131–38 and passim; cf. Klor de Alva 1988a, 31–52. Unless indicated otherwise, all translations are mine.

2. For detailed discussions of writing in the Middle Ages and the Renaissance in the context of New World texts, see Rabasa 1989a and 1989b. Also consult Certeau 1975, 215–48.

3. Frank Salomon (1982) analyzes colonial Peruvian Indian historians in terms of a tension between a Spanish diachronic temporality and a narrative of events significant from a specifically Indian perspective. This inherent contradiction leads Salomon to define the texts he studies as "chronicles of the impossible," but it is precisely in this tension that ethnicity asserts itself. This notion of the "impossible" might provide an affirmative response to Spivak's otherwise negative answer to the question and title of her essay "Can the Subaltern Speak?" (1987).

4. Klor de Alva (1988b), in his study of the process of conversion and the function of the confession to develop a new self, draws from Michel Foucault's 1985 analysis of the transformation of the ethical substance in the transition from heathen Greek and Roman sexual mores to Christian sin. For an analysis of confessionaries following Foucault's distinction, in the *History of Sexuality* (1978), between grids pertaining to family alliances and to sexuality, see Gruzinski 1987. Gruzinski quite correctly reminds us that Foucault's chronology must be corrected by attending to how the colonial situation in sixteenth-century Mexico constituted a sort of testing ground for measures, strategies, and techniques that were later deployed in Europe during the seventeenth century. Both Gruzinski and Klor de Alva have documented how a sense of sin and penitence was implemented to forge a new ethical self. Here I am suggesting not so much how desire is transformed into discourse in the confession as how discourse transforms otherwise acceptable behavior into sinful desires and practices.

5. For a critique of versions of Guadalupe as a syncretic popular Indian cult in place since the sixteenth century, see Taylor 1989. Also consult O'Gorman 1986, 138–41 and passim.

6. For an analysis of the process of the Westernization of Mexico in terms of a colonization of the "imaginary," or ethnic unconscious, see Gruzinski 1988. Though Gruzinski's analyses raise questions and illuminate areas not

addressed before, his insistence on avoiding facile syncretic explanations of residual heathen practices leads him to overlook completely resistance or the production of new cultural forms that cannot simply be reduced to manifestations of a thorough Westernization. On the notion of an ethnic unconscious, see Fischer 1986, 231: "The recreation of ethnicity in each generation, accomplished through dream- and transference-like processes, as much as through cognitive language, leads to efforts to recover, fill in, act out, unravel, and reveal."

7. See Spivak 1987, 280–81: "The clearest available example of such epistemic violence is the remotely orchestrated, far-flung, and heterogeneous project to constitute the colonial subject as Other. This project is also the asymmetrical obliteration of the trace of that Other in its precarious Subject-ivity."

8. Durán's *Historia de los Indios* ([1579–81] 1967) has two main parts; while the part dedicated to the gods, rites, and calendar has extirpation as its dominant metaphor, the narrative of the rise and fall of the Aztecs has resurrection as its dominant motif. Resurrection indeed suggests the possibility of healing the psychopathological state I mentioned above. It is beyond the scope of this essay to explore how Durán might reconcile these two dominant metaphors, but for the record I will cite a couple of passages on the resurrection of Mexican grandeur: "My desire has been to give it life and resuscitate it from the death and oblivion in which it has rested for such a long time" (2:28), and "the Mexican historians and painters painted with vivid histories and tints, with the brush of their curiosity, with vivid colors, the lives and feats of these courageous knights and lords, so that their fame would fly, with the clarity of the sun, over all nations. Whose fame and memory I wanted to relate in this my history, so that conserved here, it lasts for the time it may last, so that the lovers of virtue take fancy to follow it" (2:99). Doris Heyden and Fernando Horcasitas did not include these passages in their translation of Durán's history of Mexico-Tenochtitlan (Durán 1964).

BIBLIOGRAPHY

Adorno, Rolena. 1988. El sujeto colonial y la construcción cultural de la alteridad. *Revista de Crítica Literaria Latinoamericana* 14 (28): 55–68.

Andrews, J. Richard, and Ross Hassig. 1984. Introduction, notes, and appendixes in *Treatise on the Heathen Superstitions That Today Live Among the Indians*

Native of this New Spain, by Hernando Ruiz de Alarcón. Norman: University of Oklahoma Press.

Baudot, George. 1977. *Utopie et histoire au Mexique: Les premiers chroniqueurs de la civilization mexicaine, 1520–60.* Toulouse: Privately printed.

Bhabha, Homi. 1986. The Other Question: Difference, Discrimination and the Discourse of Colonialism. In *Literature, Politics, and Theory*, ed. Francis Barker et al., 148–72. London: Methuen.

Certeau, Michel de. 1975. *L'écriture de l'histoire.* Paris: Gallimard.

Clifford, James. 1988. *The Predicament of Culture: Twentieth-Century Ethnography, Literature, and Art.* Cambridge, Mass.: Harvard University Press.

Clifford, James, and George E. Marcus, eds. 1986. *Writing Culture: The Poetics and Politics of Ethnography.* Berkeley: University of California Press.

Cline, S. L. 1988. Revisionist Conquest History: Sahagún's Revised Book XII. In *The Work of Bernardino de Sahagún: Pioneer Ethnographer of the Sixteenth Century*, ed. Jorge Klor de Alva, H. B. Nicholson, and Eloise Quiñones Keber, 93–106. Albany and Austin: Institute of Mesoamerican Studies and the University of Texas Press.

Cortés, Hernán. 1986. *Letters from Mexico.* Trans. Anthony Pagden. New Haven, Conn.: Yale University Press.

Dibble, Charles E. 1974. The Nahuatlization of Christianity. In *Sixteenth-Century Mexico: The Work of Sahagún*, ed. Munro S. Edmonson, 225–33. Albuquerque: School of American Research and the University of New Mexico Press.

———. 1988. Sahagún's Appendices: "There Is No Reason To Be Suspicious of the Ancient Practices." In *The Work of Bernardino de Sahagún: Pioneer Ethnographer of the Sixteenth Century*, ed. Jorge Klor de Alva, H. B. Nicholson, and Eloise Quiñones Keber, 107–18. Albany and Austin: Institute of Mesoamerican Studies and the University of Texas Press.

Durán, Diego. [1579] 1964. *The Aztecs: The History of the Indies of New Spain.* Trans. Doris Heyden and Fernando Horcasitas. New York: Orion Press.

———. [1579–81] 1967. *Historia de las Indias de Nueva España e islas de la Tierra Firme.* 2 vols. Ed. Angel María Garibay K. Mexico City: Porrúa.

———. [1581] 1971. *Book of the Gods and Rites and Ancient Calendar.* Trans. Doris Heyden and Fernando Horcasitas. Norman: University of Oklahoma Press.

Edmondson, Munro S., ed. 1974. *Sixteenth-Century Mexico: The Work of Sahagún.* Albuquerque: School of American Research and the University of New Mexico Press.

Fabian, Johannes. 1983. *Time and the Other: How Anthropology Makes Its Object*. New York: Columbia Univerity Press.

———. 1990. Presence and Representation: The Other and Anthropological Writing. *Critical Inquiry* 16:753–72.

Fanon, Frantz. 1968. *The Wretched of the Earth*. Trans. Constance Farrington. New York: Grove Press.

Foucault, Michel. 1978. *The History of Sexuality*. Vol. 1: *An Introduction*. Trans. Robert Hurley. New York: Vintage.

———. 1985. *The History of Sexuality*. Vol. 2: *The Uses of Pleasure*. Trans. Robert Hurley. New York: Pantheon Books.

Gadamer, Hans Georg. 1979. The Problem of Historical Consciousness. In *Intepretative Social Science: A Reader*, ed. Paul Rabinow and W. Sullivan, 103–60. Berkeley: University of California Press.

García Icazbalceta, Joaquín, ed. [1886] 1981. *Bibliografía mexicana del siglo XVI*. 2d ed. of Agustín Millares Carlo's edition of 1954. Mexico City: Fondo de Cultura Económica.

Gómez Canedo, Lino. 1982. *La educación de los marginados: Escuelas y colegios para indios y mestizos en la Nueva España*. Mexico City: Porrúa.

Greenleaf, Richard E. 1965. The Inquisition of the Indians of New Spain: A Study in Jurisdictional Confusion. *Americas* 22:138–66.

Gruzinski, Serge. 1982. La conquista de los cuerpos: Cristianismo, alianza y sexualidad en el altiplano mexicano; Siglo XVI. In *Familia y sexualidad*, 177–206. Mexico City: SEP/80.

———. 1987. Confesión, alianza y sexualidad entre los indios de Nueva España: Introducción al estudio de los confesionarios en lenguas indígenas. In *El placer de pecar y el afán de normar*, 171–215. Mexico City: Instituto Nacional de Antropología e Historia/Joaquín Mortiz.

———. 1988. *La colonisation de l'imaginaire: Sociétés indigènes et occidentalisation dans le Mexique espagnol, XVIe–XVIIIe siècle*. Paris: Gallimard.

JanMohamed, Abdul R. 1986. The Economy of Manichean Allegory: The Function of Racial Difference in Colonialist Literature. In *"Race," Writing, and Difference*, ed. Henry Louis Gates, Jr., 78–106. Chicago: University of Chicago Press.

Jara, René, and Nicholas Spadaccini, eds. 1989. *1492–1992: Re/Discovering Colonial Writing*. Hispanic Issues series, 4. Minneapolis: Prisma Institute.

Keber, John. 1988. Sahagún and Hermeneutics: A Christian Ethnographer's Understanding of Aztec Culture. In *The Work of Bernardino de Sahagún: Pioneer*

Ethnographer of the Sixteenth Century, ed. Jorge Klor de Alva, H. B. Nicholson, and Eloise Quiñones Keber, 53–63. Albany and Austin: Institute of Mesoamerican Studies and the University of Texas Press.

Klor de Alva, J. Jorge. 1988a. Sahagún and the Birth of Modern Ethnography: Representing, Confessing, and Inscribing the Native Other. In *The Work of Bernardino de Sahagún: Pioneer Ethnographer of Sixteenth Century Mexico*, ed. J. Jorge Klor de Alva, H. B. Nicholson, and Eloise Quiñones Keber, 31–52. Albany and Austin: Institute for Mesoamerican Studies and the University of Texas Press.

———. 1988b. Contar vidas: La autobiografía y la reconstrucción del ser nahua. *Arbor* 515–16:49–78.

———. 1989. Language, Politics, and Translation: Colonial Discourse and Classical Nahuatl in New Spain. In *The Art of Translation: Voices from the Field*, ed. Rosanna Warren, 143–62. Boston: Northeastern University Press.

Klor de Alva, J. Jorge, H. B. Nicholson, and Eloise Quiñones Keber, eds. 1988. *The Work of Bernardino de Sahagún: Pioneer Ethnographer of Sixteenth Century Mexico*. Albany and Austin: Institute for Mesoamerican Studies and the University of Texas Press.

Kobayashi, José María. 1974. *La educación como conquista (empresa franciscana en México)*. Mexico City: El Colegio de México.

López Austin, Alfredo. 1980. *Cuerpo e ideología: Las concepciones de los antiguos mexicanos*. 2 vols. Mexico City: Universidad Nacional Autónoma de México.

Madsen, William. 1961. Religious Syncretism. In *Handbook of Middle-American Indians*, vol. 6: *Social Anthropology*, ed. Manning Nash, 369–91. Austin: University of Texas Press.

Marcus, George E., and Michael M. J. Fischer. 1986. *Anthropology as Cultural Critique*. Chicago: University of Chicago Press.

Mignolo, Walter. 1989. Literacy and Colonization: The New World Experience. In *1492–1992: Re/Discovering Colonial Writing*, ed. René Jara and Nicholas Spadaccini, 51–96. Hispanic Issues series, 4. Minneapolis: Prisma Institute.

Molina, Alonso de. [1569] 1984. *Confesionario mayor en lengua mexicana y castellana*. Ed. Roberto Moreno. Mexico City: Universidad Nacional Autónoma de México.

Motolinía [Toribio de Benavente]. [1541] 1973a. *History of the Indians of New Spain*. Trans. Elizabeth Andros Foster. Westport, Conn.: Greenwood Press.

———. [1544] 1973b. *Memoriales; o, Libro de las cosas de la Nueva España*. Ed.

Edmundo O'Gorman. Mexico City: Universidad Nacional Autónoma de México.

O'Gorman, Edmundo. 1978. Al rescate de Motolinía: Primeros comentarios al libro de Baudot. *Historia Mexicana* 27:445–78.

————. 1986. *Destino de sombras: La luz en el origen de la imagen y culto de nuestra señora de Guadalupe del Tepeyac.* Mexico City: Universidad Nacional Autónoma de México.

Padden, R. C. 1970. *The Hummingbird and the Hawk: Conquest and Sovereignty in the Valley of Mexico, 1503–1541.* New York: Harper and Row.

Phelan, John Leddy. 1970. *The Millenial Kingdom of the Franciscans in the New World.* 2d ed. Berkeley: University of California Press.

Proceso Inquisitorial del Cacique de Texcoco. 1910. Publicaciones del Archivo General de la Nación, vol. 1. Mexico City.

Rabasa, José. 1987. Dialogue as Conquest: Mapping Spaces for Counter-Discourse. *Cultural Critique* 6:131–59.

————. 1989a. Utopian Ethnology in Las Casas's *Apologética.* In *1492–1992: Re/Discovering Colonial Writing,* ed. René Jara and Nicholas Spadaccini, 263–89. Hispanic Issues series, 4. Minneapolis: Prisma Institute.

————. 1989b. Columbus and the Scriptural Economy of the Renaissance. *Dispositio* 14 (36–38): 271–301.

Ruiz de Alarcón, Hernando. [1629] 1984. *Treatise on the Heathen Superstitions That Today Live Among the Indians Native of This New Spain.* Trans. J. Richard Andrews and Ross Hassig. Norman: University of Oklahoma Press.

Sahagún, Bernardino de. [ca. 1579] 1932. *A History of Ancient Mexico.* Trans. Fanny R. Bandelier. Nashville: Fisk University Press.

————. [ca. 1579] 1950–82. *Florentine Codex: General History of the Things of New Spain.* 13 vols. Trans. Arthur J. O. Anderson and Charles Dibble. Santa Fe and Salt Lake City: School of American Research and the University of Utah.

Salomon, Frank. 1982. Chronicles of the Impossible: Notes on Three Peruvian Indigenous Historians. In *From Oral Expression to Written Expression: Native Andean Chronicles of the Colonial Period,* ed. Rolena Adorno, 9–39. Syracuse, N.Y.: Maxwell School of Citizenship and Public Affairs, Syracuse University.

Serna, Jacinto de la. [1892] 1987. *Manual de ministros de indios para el conocimiento de su idolatrías, y extirpación de ellas.* In Pedro Ponce, Pedro Sánchez de Aguilar, et al., *El alma encantada,* facsimile edition of the Anales del Museo Nacional de México, 6:261–480. Mexico City: Fondo de Cultura Económica. Written in 1656.

Spivak, Gayatri Chakravorti. 1987. Can the Subaltern Speak? In *Marxism and the Interpretation of Culture*, ed. Cary Nelson and Lawrence Grossberg, 271–313. Urbana: University of Illinois Press.

Taylor, William. 1987. The Virgin of Guadalupe in New Spain: An Inquiry into the Social History of Marian Devotion. *American Ethnologist* 14:9–33.

Tentler, Thomas N. 1977. *Sin and Confession on the Eve of the Reformation.* Princeton, N.J.: Princeton University Press.

Todorov, Tzvetan. 1984. *The Conquest of America: The Question of the Other.* Trans. Richard Howard. New York: Harper and Row.

4

Early English Transfer and Invention of the Black in New Spain

Carolyn Prager

The sixteenth- and seventeenth-century English literature of conquest and discovery reconfigures the image of the African, amplifying older metaphoric valuations with newer economic and political ones. In the early quest for empire in the New World, the English literally transferred and verbally invented the African destined for the Americas within the seemingly incompatible constructs of ally and slave. In the course of a war of attrition designed to undermine Spanish control of and access to the Americas, British slavers and would-be slavers actively pursued collaboration with those fugitive black bondmen in New Spain known as the Cimaroons. For nearly a century, from the earliest accounts of Hawkins's slaving ventures to New Spain to Davenant's theatrical recollections of the Drake-Cimaroon Panamanian campaign, the English saw the African destined for the New World as both slave and free, enemy and friend, thing and person, savage and sage, the transferred and the invented.

When in *Considerations Touching a War with Spain*, Francis Bacon counseled James I in the 1620s about the inadvisability of military confrontation in the Americas, he did so in terms of the poverty of British intelligence about the fortifications along the American coast, the strength of Spanish overseas garrisons, and the condition of the natives. At one point he questioned specifically the currency of English knowledge about the state of the "Cymerownes or slaves, whether it be matter at this time of any consequence as formerly it hath been" (14:504). Derived from a Spanish word connoting "wild,"

"fierce," and "unbroken," the Spanish first applied the word *cimarrones* to do-
mestic cattle gone wild in Hispaniola, then to fugitive Indian slaves, and by
the 1530s principally to escaped Africans (Price 1973, 1–2). The word entered
the English lexicon in the Elizabethan period in connection with the black
legend of Spanish atrocities against subject peoples.[1]

In 1642, sixty-nine years after the event, Thomas Fuller recalled how "Negroes, called Symerons" helped Drake make off with an "infinite masse" of
Spanish gold in the memorable 1573 raid on Nombre de Dios ([1938] 1966,
135). Fuller's pointed reference to "Negroes, called Symerons," like Bacon's
to "Cymerownes or slaves," looks backward and forward to the only consistently positive categorical English image of the black in the sixteenth and seventeenth centuries. And the distinction implied between ordinary "Negroes"
and those called "Symerons" serves as a cultural marker of exceptionality, a
peculiarly restrictive differentiation between those New World Africans known
as Cimaroons and those known as blacks and slaves.

In the main, precolonial English writing describes the African in three
ways. The first is as a metaphoric agent—an exotic, alien, and slavish incarnation of the dark side of the soul. This image is found, for example, in the
characters Aaron and Zanche, the Moors in Shakespeare's *Titus Andronicus* and
John Webster's *White Devil*, respectively. The second way is as a commercial
object, a commodity to be bought and sold like a bolt of cloth or a cask of
wine. And the third is as an imperial ally, a nation of black fugitives escaped
to mountainous or other inhospitable areas of New Spain from where they
ready themselves to join with those who would help them take revenge on
their former masters. The Cimaroons add a political dimension to the essentially commercial English image and treatment of the black in Spanish
America. Because of actively sought alliances forged between these former
slaves and other European powers frustrated in their economic and colonial
aspirations in the Americas, the Cimaroons were regarded throughout the
sixteenth and seventeenth centuries as potential and willing associates in England's continuing contest with Spain.[2]

Few Londoners of the period had ever seen a "blackamoor." Those who
knew about them—or thought they did—had met them mainly as icons of
depravity or monstrosity, Shakespeare's Othello the most notable exception.
In English Renaissance creative works, the bondage of people of color helps
refurbish images of ancient provenance of men and women darkened and
enslaved by sin. As actual contact with Africa increased during the Renaissance, the figure of the black often served as a convenient representation for

conceptions of slavery defined centuries before in Hellenic, Judaic, and Christian tradition. This fusion of commonly held conceptions of slavery and the slave derived from the past and confirmed by the present receives its finest poetic exposition with Caliban in The Tempest, the first English play with a major black character to be set in the New World.[3]

Unlike contemporary poets, theologians, and dramatists, the corsairs, merchants, travelers, and preachers who provided the initial corpus of literature written by Englishmen about the New World seldom had need for or recourse to the iconic black who personified the servile appetites of his or her European captors and owners. Very infrequently the reader finds in the voyage and travel literature of English authors the association of race, color, and sin with a servile estate that resonates throughout the poetry, drama, and scriptural commentary of the period. Thomas Gage's firsthand description of dark-skinned prostitutes in seventeenth-century Mexico is, therefore, unusual, for it was written by an actual English visitor to the Spanish Main. In a particularly racy passage, the renegade Dominican preacher describes bare-breasted and bejeweled blacks in language more common to poetic, dramatic, and theological representations of the African found outside of the newly discovered continents. "Most of these," he says in The English-American, "are or have been slaves, though love have set them loose at liberty to enslave souls to sin and Satan" (1648, 87). By now a commonplace in more creative documents, Gage's literary employment of lustful black slaves who tempt those enslaved to lust owed more to the profession and education of the writer than to the genre in which he wrote.

As the unseen gave way to the seen, however, Britain's earliest encounter with Spanish America foretold the end of the symbolically crafted black. Othello might woo Desdemona with stories of monstrous creatures spawned in Africa and known from Pliny through Mandeville such as the "anthropophagi, and men whose heads / Do grow beneath their shoulders" (1.3:144–45). Yet eight years before Othello appeared on the stage, Sir Walter Raleigh discredits, if not actual belief in such fabulous creatures, at least the importance of that belief. In recounting his "discoverie" of Guiana in 1596, Raleigh found credible the vivid testimony of certain natives about a warlike race with eyes in their shoulders and mouths in their chest. He even regretted that he could not bring one of them to England "to put the matter out of doubt" (1596, 70). While acknowledging that the inquiry might be of interest to others, however, he questioned its actual worth: "whether it be true or no the matter is not great, neither can there be any profit in such imagination, for mine owne part

I saw them not, but I am resolved that so many people did not all combine, or forethinke to make the report" (70).

Raleigh's emphasis upon the tangible and profitable devalued a long-held belief in the existence of monstrous peoples in much the same way that the period set aside the figurative black in favor of the material slave in the Americas. Indeed, the earliest printed record of English contact with the African in the New World is of Africans forcibly transported there for profit by the English themselves. In 1562, John Hawkins carried the first English cargo of slaves to the New World, having been "amongst other particulars assured, that Negros were very good marchandise in Hispaniola, and that store of Negros might easily bee had upon the coast of Guianea" (Hakluyt 1903–5, 10:7). In violation of strong Spanish interdiction of foreign travel and trade in her overseas territories, Hawkins easily disposed of his living "wares" to a labor-starved America (65). "And the most principal thing of al is, to send more Negros," the governor of Havana pleaded in a letter to Philip of Spain intercepted by the English and printed in the *Voyages* along with Hawkins's accounts of his three slaving ventures to New Spain (Hakluyt 1903–5, 10:162).

The Hawkins material was the principal but not the only source of information available to sixteenth-century English people that equated the Africans in or intended for the Americas with slaves. The merchant William Fowler deposed that "the best trade in those places is of Negroes: the trade whereof he hath used, and hath sold Negroes at the said places; and seen other merchants likewise sell their Negroes there, divers times" (Arber [1903] 1964, 1:107).[4] Hakluyt's and Purchas's widely read collections of voyages announce that blacks are being carried across the ocean to labor in the mines, fields, and waters of the Spanish territories. Of the Margarita Islands "those which have people have some Negros, slaves unto the Spaniards, which occupie themselves in labour of the Land, or in fishing for Pearles" (Purchas 1906, 17:187). Of the Africans, those "which be caried continually to the West Indies" are "rich wares" (Hakluyt 1935, 7:98). Of the Congo, the Portuguese there "have divers rich Commodities . . . but the most important is every yeere about five thousand Slaves, which they transport from thence, and sell them at good round prices in . . . the West Indies" (Hakluyt 1935, 6:110). Of a captured Portuguese ship, it is "bound for Angola to load Negroes, to be carried and sold in the River of Plate: It is a trade of great profit, and much used. . . . It is a bad Negro, who is not worth there five or six hundreth peeces, . . . for there is no other Merchandize in those parts" (Purchas 1906, 17:99).

Hawkins's third slaving voyage ended with his capture and the loss of considerable property at San Juan de Ulúa. Depositions to the English Admiralty

Court after the disastrous voyage of 1567–68 shed light on the English under-standing of a profitable trade. Seemingly called as an independent witness to lend credibility to claims for damages against the Spanish Crown, Fowler, for example, testified that a fardel of English cloth sold ordinarily at Vera Cruz for between 226 and 250 pesos and a butt (130 gallons) of sherry for 100 pesos, but "a Negro of a good stature and young of years" sold for 400 to 600 pesos (Arber 1903, 1:106, 107). Hawkins claims to have lost the value of fifty-seven slaves, forty-five of whom were "Negroes, of goodly stature, shape, and per-sonage; and young of years, being the choice and principal of all the Negroes which were gotten and purchased in the last voyage at Guinea" (1:119).

By so documenting the loss of real property, the English apparently hoped to establish that theirs was a peaceful commercial venture. Spanish docu-ments confirm Hawkins's loss of the blacks. Their physical condition can only be conjectured, but it seems highly unlikely that they were in the prime con-dition upon which Hawkins insisted, considering that slave viability was no-toriously poor in the Middle Passage and that they were what remained from among those who had already been picked over and sold elsewhere on the coast. Only seven of the ten or twelve that were on the Minion when it fled back to England, for example, survived the trip homeward, according to other sworn testimony before the Admiralty Court.[5]

Concern for the plight of the slave rather than that of the slaver is a rela-tively recent phenomenon in the long history of slavery. Hawkins concludes his True Declaration of the Troublesome Voyage, published in the same year as the Admiralty Court hearings (1569), with a self-serving passage conveying the impression that the extremities experienced by the English almost defy ex-pression: "If all the miseries and troublesome affaires of this sorowfull voyage should be perfectly and thoroughly written, there should neede a painefull man with his pen, and as great a time as he had that wrote the lives and deathes of the Martyrs" (Hakluyt 1903–5, 10:74).

What Hawkins does describe in some detail is the physical and emotional toll of slave-catching on the slavers. They were shot at and wounded with poisoned arrows at Cape Verde, "where we landed 150 men, hoping to ob-taine some Negros, where we got but fewe, and those with great hurt and damage to our men" (Hakluyt 1903–5, 10:64). They were betrayed by an African king in Sierra Leone who enlisted their aid against a neighboring tribe in return for a share of the human booty, eliciting Hawkins's comment, "but the Negro (in which nation is seldome or never found truth) meant nothing lesse: for that night he remooved his campe and prisoners, so that we were faine to content us with those few we had gotten our selves" (65–66). On their return home, the English faced the prospect of disease, death, and "the greatest miserie of all," that of shipwreck (marginalia, p. 74). Of the anonymous slaves we learn little, not even their exact number, except for reference to some four or five hundred with whom Hawkins had left Africa.

To the extent that human exploitation has linguistic correlatives, the depersonalized and dehumanized image of the black slave in New Spain voiced in the writings of English voyagers to New Spain is also assimilated across the Atlantic into more creative and reflective literature. Reflecting the intercontinental merging of the literal with the literary, Valdes in Marlowe's play claims that Faustus's powers shall make the elements serve them "as Indian Moors obey their Spanish lords" (Marlowe 1963, 122). In Chapman's *Masque of the Middle Temple*, Moors are introduced attired "like Indian slaves." In Brewer's *The Love-Sick King*, the bailiff compares his coal miners to the pearl-diving African slaves of the Indies: "Seven hundred black *Indians*, or *Newcastle* Colliers, your Worship keeps daily to dive for Treasure five hundred fathom deep for you" (1907, lines 952–53). Browne uses the fact that the "swarms of Negroes serving under the Spaniards" were "all transported from Africa, since the discovery of Columbus" (1964, 464) as one of several proofs that complexion results from genetic makeup rather than climate, a minority view of the cause of pigmentation in his day. Burton compares the buying and selling of "African negroes" used as beasts of burden to that of horses and tells of a Spaniard in the Yucatán who sold a hundred "negro slaves" for a horse ([1932] 1961–64, 1:351) to illustrate the emotional and social depression of poverty in *The Anatomy of Melancholy*.

In *Slavery and Social Death* (1982), Orlando Patterson analyses the processes of dehumanization common to most societies condoning institutional servitude that ready both slave and master for the acceptance of bondage. Patterson tentatively defines slavery as the "permanent, violent domination of natally alienated and generally dishonored persons" (13). The contemporary citations in the paragraphs above reflect these servile dynamics. In the language of traders, voyagers, poets, and philosophers alike, Africans in New Spain are depersonalized by their anonymity or by generic naming. They are assigned animal rather than human characteristics, they are the hunted rather than the hunter, they are likened to swarms of insects, and they are used as beasts of burden. They are branded, in this case by the fact of pigmentation, a genetic sign reflected in the "black" or "negro" racial nomenclature. Above all, they are relegated to the category of things with only chattel value. Because the precolonial English text linguistically debases the forcibly displaced African in Spanish America to accommodate a servile status, the Cimaroon had to be textually elevated with properties befitting people sought as political and military confederates of the English nation. The Cimaroon is invested, therefore, with human attributes, some historical and some invented. The result is a figure that is only nominally black or bond, Bacon's "Cymerownes or slaves" and Fuller's "Negroes, called Symerons." In Nichols's *Sir Francis Drake Revived* ([1628] 1932), for example, which is the major contemporary account of the Panamanian campaign, some of Drake's black benefactors have Christian (but not family) names (e.g., Pedro, the "cheefe *Symeron*"; 297). Nichols records how in their mountain retreats the Cimaroons exhibit civilized standards of hygiene and dress that impress the English party. They "lived verie civilly and cleanely, for as soone as wee came thither, they washed themselves in the river, and changed their apparrel, which was verie fine and fitly made . . . (as also their women doe weare) somewhat after the Spanish fashion" (298).

In English accounts, however, their pursuit of freedom and revenge is chief among the historical elements humanizing the Cimaroons, and their invitation of British imperial governance is chief among the invented ones. In Patterson's sense, the Cimaroons are reclaimed from the social death of slavery through restoration of their honor. In contemporary literary accounts, this manifests itself primarily through frequent references to their love of freedom and pursuit of revenge against those who had subjugated them.

According to a passage in Hakluyt's *Voyages*, blacks in New Spain "doe daily lie in waite to practice their deliverance out of that thraldome and bondage, that the Spaniards do keepe them in" (9:430). Richard Hawkins describes the Cimaroons as they are most frequently understood for almost a century in connection with their assistance to the English in Panama in the 1570s: "These are fugitive Negroes, and for the bad intreatie which their Masters had given them, were then retired into the Mountaines, and lived upon the spoil of such Spaniards, as they could master, and could never bee brought into obedience, till by composition they had a place limited them for their freedome, where they should live quietly themselves" (Purchas 1906, 194). To Fulke Greville in his life of Sir Philip Sidney, the former slaves Drake hoped to recontact in 1585 were the "relics of those oppressed Cimaroons [who] would joyfully take arms with any foreigner to redeem their liberty and revenge their parents' blood" (1986, 65–66).[6]

Determined to demonstrate a large chink in Hispanic American armor to a cautious Queen in pre-Armada England, Hakluyt claims in the 1584 *Discourse of Western Planting*: "Those Contries wherof the Spaniarde is Lorde, are partly ruinated, dispeopled, and laid waste by their incredible and more than barbarous and savage endeles cruelties, and partly grevously infested by the Indians, Symerons, Moores, Chichimici revolted, and consequently he is easie to be driven thence" (1935, 2:263). Indeed, Hakluyt strove to make the "incouragemente of the Symerons" (249) a major instrument of public policy, offering up repeatedly the reassuring image of rebellious organized outlaw blacks friendly to the British as major proof of Philip II's colonial weakness, a public posture that would be echoed a generation later by Bacon to yet another regent. The discourse resonates with the exploits of ex-slaves who sap the strength of their former masters through their "frontier warres," who hold Sir Francis and other Englishmen in high regard, and who would join with anyone who was ready to provide them with arms and leadership against the Spanish foe (248).[7]

Drake's collaboration with the blacks of Panama is certainly the most famous of several made by English corsairs and the one most frequently recalled for nearly a century through every phase of Anglo-Spanish conflict by Anglican, Puritan, and Catholic alike. This strange alliance of convenience between slaver and ex-slave in the 1570s fortified British policy toward the Spanish in the New World for almost a century. Drake most certainly learned of the rebellious blacks firsthand during the five to six voyages he made to America before his first independent command in 1572–73. At least two of these involved trade in Africans. He was with Lovell in 1567 when the latter landed some ninety blacks in Río de la Hacha and with Hawkins on the third voyage which brought five or six hundred blacks to the Mexican coast and which ended so poorly for the English at San Juan de Ulúa in 1569.

Reviewed by Drake before his death, Nichols's *Sir Francis Drake Revived* (1628) is the major contemporary firsthand account of Drake's American campaigns of the 1570s. The subtitle of the text is informative: *Calling upon This Dull or Effeminate Age, to Follow His Noble Steps for Gold and Silver.* According to the document, the Cimaroons did everything for Drake during the Panamanian expedition, providing thirty of his forty-eight fighting men, feeding his party and him, guiding them, sheltering them, spying for them, and literally dying for them. With the help of his black benefactors and campaigners, Drake seized a mule train so rich in gold and silver that he had to leave the silver behind.

The British wanted only gold and glory; the Cimaroons, only revenge in exchange for their aid. When John Oxenham joined forces with the Cimaroons in 1575 and 1576, it was reportedly with the understanding that their part of the booty would be "onely the prisoners, to the end to execute their malice upon them, such was the rancour they had conceived against them, for that they had beene the Tyrants of their libertie" (Purchas 1906, 195). To feed their "insatiable revenges," Richard Hawkins states that the blacks would roast and eat the heart of any Spaniard upon whom they could lay their hands (195).

Interest in the Drake-Cimaroon material waxed and waned in the seventeenth century, varying with the status of England's relations with Spain. Nichols's *Sir Francis Drake Revived* was reprinted in 1653 and Gage's *The English-American* in 1655, the latter at Cromwell's order, to incite Hispanic sentiments appropriate to English military expeditions in the Spanish New World fostering the Western Design. Near the end of the Commonwealth period, William Davenant exploited commonly understood perceptions about the Spanish treatment of Indians and Africans in New Spain for two dramatic entertainments: *The Cruelty of the Spaniards in Peru* (1659) and *The History of Sir Francis Drake* (1658), both of which he used again in the Restoration dramatic miscellany *A Playhouse to Be Let* (1663).

Part opera, part drama, part masque, and part spectacle, *The History of Sir Francis Drake* consists of six entries, each preceded by musical accompaniment, three set in Peru and three in areas around Panama, episodically drawn primarily from the Nichols material. Davenant assumed a level of audience familiarity with the past and present context of the piece, belying its simple dismissal as mere entertainment. Stage directions are very specific. Those for scene two, for example, in which Drake solidifies an alliance with the Cimaroons, state that it is to be one "in which is discern'd a Rockie Country of the Symerons, who were a Moorish People, brought formerly to Peru by the Spaniards, as their Slaves, to dig in Mines; and having lately revolted from them, did live under the government of a King of their own Election" (353). Those for the fourth require a tree, from "the top of which Pedro (formerly a slave to the Spaniards . . .) had promis'd sir Francis Drake to shew him both the North and the South Atlantick Seas" (2:357).

Despite fidelity to his major source and the historical moment, however, Davenant has some difficulty in separating the figure of the honorable Cimaroon from that of the stereotypical lustful African. In entry five he intrudes a sexually and racially charged episode more consistent with received ideas about the savage and unrestrained black, the content of which is only suggested in Nichols. In the latter, Drake strives to keep the Cimaroons from taking their revenge on Spanish prisoners, especially women and unarmed men (see, e.g., 2:294, 308). In Davenant, the Cimaroons are represented as having captured a Spanish bride and bridegroom at their nuptial feast,

> To whom the Sym'rons now
> Much more than fury show;
> For they have all those cruelties exprest
> That Spanish pride could e're provoke from them
> Or Moorish Malice can revenge esteem. (2:98)

A graphically described painted backdrop depicts a "Beautiful Lady ty'd to a Tree, . . . with her hair deshevel'd and complaining, with her hands towards Heaven: About her are likewise discern'd the Symerons who took her prisoner" (98). Prepared to harm her in unstated but implied ways for revenge against those who "Have forc'd our Brides" (2:99), the "trusty" (2:93) and "brave" (2:103) Cimaroons of entries three and six now become the "cruel Symerons" (2:99) whom an outnumbered Drake would fight to preserve the national honor, an honor, he declares, that "must revengeful be / For this affront to Love and me" (2:99).

At one point in Davenant's Drake, the entire chorus sings

> All order with such clemency preserve,
> That such as to our pow'r submit,
> May take delight to cherish it,
> And seem as free as those whom they shall serve. (2:93)

The patriotic fiction that the English would be more benevolent rulers of the Indians and Africans than the Spanish was an early part of England's imperial vision. Raleigh's claim that Guiana was ripe for the plucking was based on its untapped wealth, its distance from Spanish strongholds, and the implicit allegiance to England he claimed for its inhabitants: "All the most of the kings of the borders are already become her Majesties vassals: & seeme to desire nothing more than her Majesties protection, and the returne of the English nation" (A4). In a celebratory poem prefaced to his account of Keymis's second voyage to Guiana written in 1596, Chapman builds from an image of a virgin land "whose rich feet are mines of golde" (line 18) making "every signe of all submission" (22) to the Queen, to the concluding one: "Where new Britania, humblie kneeles to heaven, / The world to her, and both at her blest feete, / In whom the Circles of all Empire meet" (182–84).

Similarly, in 1579–80, at the beginning of his career, Hakluyt proposed that the English take control of the Straits of Magellan by planting a colony of "Symerone," to be transported there by their friend Drake or others, "hundreds or thowsands, how many as we shal require," and governed by a "few good English captens" (1935, 1:142). Despite the freezing climate, the Cimaroon was ideally suited to the enterprise, Hakluyt maintained, because, al-though born in a hot climate, "yet by meane he has been bredde as a slave" (143). Well-fed, clothed, and lodged, he will "think himself a happy man" because he has been "by our nation made free from the tyrannous Spanyard, and quietly and courteously governed by our nation" (143).

The idea that England has American allies from among those subjugated by the Spanish pervades sixteenth- and seventeenth-century writing in sup-port of an aggressive military policy against Spain through erosion of her colo-nies, as well as the writing that urged English colonization of the New World. In the *Discourse of Western Planting* (1584), Hakluyt assures the Queen that "the Spaniardes have executed moste outragious and more than Turkishe cruelties in all the west Indies, whereby they are every where there, become moste odious unto them, whoe woulde joine wth us or any other moste willingly to shake of their moste intollerable yoke" (1935, 2:212). In 1648, the year of the first printing of *The English-American*, Gage claimed that the English would find support against the Spanish from the latter's "own slaves the blacka-moors who doubtless to be set at liberty would side against them in any such occasion" (1928, 230). Perpetuating the myth of invitation, he maintained that the main reason the Guatemalan Cimaroons had fled to the mountains was to prepare for joining forces with the English or Dutch, "for they know, from them they may enjoy that liberty which the Spaniards will never grant unto them" (209).

By 1648, however, the English had already established colonies in Barba-dos and elsewhere in the Lesser Antilles (as Gage himself noted in the pref-ace) and had begun the switch from cotton and tobacco to sugar, which led to the large-scale introduction of black slaves in the 1640s. A Barbadian planter in 1642 wrote, "Here are come lately about five hundred Negroes and more daily expected" (James Browne to James and Archibald Hay, cited in Puckrein 1984, 70). George Downing could report that Barbadian households in 1645 bought no fewer than "a thousand Negroes, and the more they buy the better able they are to buy" (43). Ligon's map of Barbados circa 1640 depicts a man on horseback in pursuit of two runaway blacks near a mountainous area.[8]

The idea of the English as liberators of the black slaves or ex-slaves of New Spain must be viewed within the limitations of a period that could condemn certain aspects of institutional slavery but not the institution itself. Las Casas, you will remember, argued the case against Spanish enslavement of the Indian on very narrow grounds and proposed as the economically expedient alter-native that African slaves be introduced to spare the suffering natives. The English promised liberation not from slavery but from "the moste intollerable yoke" of Spanish cruelty. Contemporary English writing does not deplore the enslavement of Africans in New Spain. Instead, it explores the opportunities that the circumstances of slavery presented to trade in slaves, to collaborate with them against a mutual enemy, and to promote an imperial vision of English benevolence toward subject races. It is a vision sadly at variance with history.

NOTES

1. According to Spedding, the text of Bacon's *Considerations Touching a War with Spain* printed in the *Works* represents an expansion of notes previously prepared for a speech that may have been presented before Parliament in 1623–24 during debates over the proposed Spanish marriage and restitution of the Palatinate. Bacon enlarged the notes into a fuller discussion of the question of Anglo-Spanish relationships for presentation to the prince. Although the first two divisions of the treatise were published in 1629, the third division, from which the citation is taken, was considered too politically sensitive for publication at the time (Bacon [1862–1901] 1901, 456, 469). The standard work on English literary anti-Hispanicism is still Maltby 1968. Citations are by page number, unless otherwise indicated. The modern equivalents for u, v, j, and i are used throughout, except for contemporary variations of *Cimaroon(s)*.

2. Jordan (1968, 3–124) provides the best introduction to the complex topic of perceptions of race and slavery in England before the African "became preeminently the slave" (43); Jones supplies a convenient summary of the period's conception of Africans; and Cawley summarizes contemporary references to the Cimaroons (391–94) in documentary and creative literature.

3. Hunter traces the iconographic tradition of the black man which Shakespeare reversed in depicting a noble Othello. The generally negative symbolic use of the African has been well documented and analyzed by Jones (1965) and by Tokson (1982). Davis 1966 is the major study of ancient legacies connecting "slavery to ideas of sin, subordination, and the divine order of the world" (91).

4. The Admiralty Court testimony has been preserved in State Papers, Dom. Eliz., July 1569, vol. 53, Public Records Office, London. That cited here is from the text in Arber [1903] 1964.

5. See, for example, the testimony of John Tommes in Arber [1903] 1964, 120.

6. Greville's *Dedication to Sir Philip Sidney*, commonly known as the *Life of Sir Philip Sidney*, was probably completed sometime after March 1610, possibly in 1615 or later, according to Gouws. The text of the Gouws edition is from the *editio princeps* of 1652. Greville, who considered Drake but a "mean-born subject to the crown of England" (1986, 64), gives Sidney undue credit for the conception of Drake's 1585 West Indian campaign, including the idea for renewing relationships with the Cimaroons.

7. Wright (1932) provides a good summary of English interaction with the Cimaroons and Spanish reaction during the 1570s in her introduction to vol. 2, especially xxxvi–lxiv. According to Mellafe, Drake's sacking of Nombre de Dios with the aid of the Cimaroons "confirmed Spanish fears of the political potential of such slaves" (105). Bowser (1974) threads references to the threat of English invasion and complicity throughout his detailed analysis of Spanish problems with the "control of the African" in chapters 7 and 8. Spanish depositions taken from those previously seized by Drake off the coast of South and Central America in 1579 suggest how intensely the Spanish feared the prospect of further collaboration between the English and the Cimaroons. See, for example, that of Nicholas Jorje, in which he was asked specifically if he had "heard the said Englishmen discuss anything concerning the Cimaroons of this kingdom and answered that he heard the said Captain Francis saying that he loved them, speaking well of them and enquiring every day whether they were now peaceful" (Nuttall 1914, 140).

8. Ligon's map is reproduced opposite the title page of Puckrein 1984.

BIBLIOGRAPHY

Arber, Edward. [1903] 1964. *An English Garner: Voyages and Travels Mainly During the Sixteenth and Seventeenth Centuries*. 2 vols. New York: Cooper Square Publishers.

Bacon, Francis. 1862–1901. *The Works of Francis Bacon*. Ed. James Spedding, Robert Leslie Ellis, and Douglas Denon Heath. 14 vols. London: Longmans.

Bowser, Frederick P. 1974. *The African Slave in Colonial Peru, 1524–1650*. Stanford, Calif.: Stanford University Press.

Brewer, Anthony. 1907. *The Love-Sick King*. In *Materialien zur Kunde des alteren Englishen Dramas*, ed. A.E.H. Swaen. Louvain: A. Uystpruyst.

Browne, Sir Thomas. 1964. *The Works of Sir Thomas Browne*. Ed. Geoffrey Keynes. 4 vols. Chicago: University of Chicago Press.

Burton, Robert. [1932] 1961–64. *The Anatomy of Melancholy*. 3 vols. London: Dent.

Cawley, Robert R. 1938. *The Voyagers and Elizabethan Drama*. Boston: D. C. Heath.

Chapman, George. [1913] 1961. *The Plays of George Chapman: The Comedies*. Ed. T. M. Parrott. 2 vols. New York: Russell and Russell.

———. 1941. *The Poems of George Chapman*. Ed. Phyllis Brooks Bartlett. New York: Russell and Russell.

Davenant, William. [1673] 1968. *The Works of Sir William Davenant*. 2 vols. New York: Benjamin Blom.

Davis, David Brion. 1966. *The Problem of Slavery in Western Culture*. Ithaca, N.Y.: Cornell University Press.

Downing, George. 1929–47. *Winthrop Papers*. 5 vols. Cambridge: Massachusetts Historical Society.

Fuller, Thomas. [1938] 1966. *Thomas Fuller's* The Holy State and the Profane State. Ed. Maximilian Graff Walten. 2 vols. New York: AMS Press.

Gage, Thomas. [1648] 1928. *The English-American: A New Survey of the West Indies, 1648*. Ed. A. P. Newton. London: Routledge and Son.

Greville, Fulke. 1986. *The Prose Works of Fulke Greville, Lord Brooke*. Ed. John Gouws. Oxford: Clarendon Press.

Hakluyt, Richard. 1903–5. *The Principal Navigations Voyages Traffiques and Discoveries of the English Nation*. 22 vols. Glasgow: James MacLehose.

———. 1935. *The Original Writings and Correspondence of the Two Richard Hakluyts*. Ed. E.G.R. Taylor. 2 vols. London: Hakluyt Society.

Hunter, G. K. 1967. *Othello and Colour Prejudice*. Proceedings of the British Academy. Reprinted in *Dramatic Identities and Cultural Tradition: Studies in Shakespeare and His Contemporaries*, 31–59. Liverpool: Liverpool University Press, 1978.

Jones, Eldred D. 1965. *Othello's Countrymen: The African in English Renaissance Drama*. London: Oxford University Press.

———. 1971. *The Elizabethan Image of Africa*. Folger Booklets on Tudor and Stuart Civilization. Charlottesville: University Press of Virginia.

Jordan, Winthrop D. 1968. *White Over Black: American Attitudes Toward the Negro, 1550–1812*. Chapel Hill: University of North Carolina Press.

Ligon, Richard. 1657. *A True and Exact History of the Island of Barbados*. London.

Maltby, William S. 1968. *The Black Legend in England: The Development of Anti-Spanish Sentiment, 1558–1600*. Durham, N.C.: Duke University Press.

Marlowe, Christopher. 1963. *The Complete Plays of Christopher Marlowe*. Ed. Irving Ribner. New York: Odyssey Press.

Mellafe, Rolando. 1975. *Negro Slavery in Latin America*. Berkeley: University of California Press.

Nichols, Philip. [1628] 1932. *Sir Francis Drake Revived:* . . . *Documents Concerning English Voyages to the Spanish Main, 1569–80*. Ed. Irene A. Wright. London: Hakluyt Society.

Nuttall, Zelia, ed. and trans. 1914. *New Light on Drake: A Collection of Documents Relating to His Voyage of Circumnavigation, 1577–80*. London: Hakluyt Society.

Patterson, Orlando. 1982. *Slavery and Social Death: A Comparative Study*. Cambridge, Mass.: Harvard University Press.

Price, Richard, ed. 1973. *Maroon Societies: Rebel Slave Communities in the Americas*. Garden City, N.Y.: Anchor.

Puckrein, Gary A. 1984. *Little England: Plantation Society and Anglo-Barbadian Politics, 1627–1700*. New York: New York University Press.

Purchas, Samuel. 1905–7. *Hakluytus Posthumas; or, Purchas His Pilgrimes*. . . . 20 vols. Glasgow: James MacLehose.

Raleigh, Sir Walter. 1596. *The Discoverie of the Large, Rich, and Bewtiful Empire of Guiana*. . . . London.

Shakespeare, William. [1948] 1968. *Shakespeare: The Complete Works*. Ed. G. B. Harrison. New York: Harcourt.

Tokson, Elliot H. 1982. *The Popular Image of the Black Man in English Drama, 1550–1688*. Boston: G. K. Hall.

Wright, Irene A., ed. 1928–32. *Documents Concerning English Voyages to the Spanish Main, 1569–80*. 2 vols. London: Hakluyt Society.

II   Mediating Political Discourse

5

Taking Possession and Reading Texts

Establishing the Authority of Overseas Empires

Patricia Seed

> The Admiral [Christopher Columbus] went ashore in the armed launch, and Martín Alonso Pinzón and his brother Vicente Yañes, who was captain of the Niña. The Admiral brought out the royal banner and the captains [brought] two flags of the green cross . . . with an F [Ferdinand] and a Y [Isabella], and over each letter a crown, one [letter] on one side of the [cross], and the other on the other [side]. . . . The Admiral called to the two captains and to the others who had jumped onto land, and to Rodrigo d'Escobedo, the notary and registrar of the whole fleet, and to Rodrigo Sánchez de Segovia; and he said that they should bear faith and witness [as to] how he, in the presence of all, was going to take, and in fact, did take possession of said island for the king and for the queen, his lords, making the solemn declarations required to preserve their rights, as is contained at greater length in the legal instruments of proof made there in writing.[1]

Columbus's son Ferdinand's version of the events of 12 October 1492 is that "The Admiral . . . took possession of it in the name of the Catholic Sovereigns *with appropriate ceremony and words*" (emphasis added; Columbus [1571] 1959, 59).

Even as the conquest of the New World was often accomplished by military means or by occupation, its authority—that is, the right to rule—was established by language and ceremony. For Columbus, it was the ritual landing of the royal banner and twin flags, together with the language of his well-witnessed solemn declarations, that established the right of the Crown of Castile to this territory, later known as the New World. Columbus's first step was to mark his presence on the land—the customary first element in the Roman tradition of taking possession. Like the Venetian John Cabot, who had planted a cross and two flags on the coast of Cape Breton only a few years later, Columbus borrowed the ceremonial elements marking his arrival in the New World from his Mediterranean seafaring predecessors.[2]

But ceremonies of arrival, marking physical presence on the land—no matter how compelling, frequently used, or well witnessed—were only the first step. The second part of the Roman-derived concept of possession was manifesting intent to remain, which Columbus did, in his son's report, by "appropriate ceremony and words." Columbus's solemn declaration and due recording of the intent to claim the land were far from improvised. By the terms of his agreement with Ferdinand and Isabella, Columbus was required to make a grave declaration of the intent to remain and to record those words for posterity by writing them down (Rumeu de Armas 1985, 239–41). The Spanish monarchs considered such statements critically important to establishing their possession and rightful power.[3] No specific device or words need be employed; what mattered was the solemnity of the utterance.

In the first English effort at New World settlement, at St. John's Harbor in 1583, Sir Humphrey Gilbert gathered together the Portuguese, French, and English merchants and shipmasters trading and fishing off the banks of Newfoundland and informed them of his written authorization to possess the territory for England. He then "had delivered unto him (after the custom of England) a rod [a small twig] and a turf of the same soil."[4] No banners were unfurled, no elaborate ceremonies were observed upon landing. Whereas Columbus declared the intent of the Spanish Crown to remain by a solemn speech duly recorded by notaries, Gilbert indicated his intent to settle by having a twig and a piece of earth brought to him.

Immediately after Columbus's return to Spain, the monarchs sought formal legal authorization for their title from the pope. For much of the sixteenth century, the Spanish Crown's right to rule the New World was embedded in the 1493 donation of Pope Alexander VI and constituted by reading a text containing an account of that donation, called the Requirement.

For English monarchs the language used to constitute their right was also embedded in a written text (a letter patent), but the right was executed in the act of settling on land in the New World. In June 1578, four years prior to the voyage to Newfoundland at which he received the "rod and turf," Sir Humphrey Gilbert received a royal patent authorizing him to "discover . . . such remote, barbarous, and heathen lands, countreis, and territories not pos-sessed by any Christian prince or people nor inhabited by Christian people and the same to have, holde, occupy and enjoy." This patent was subse-quently renewed on behalf of Gilbert's half brother, Sir Walter Ralegh, and used to found the first semipermanent English settlement in the New World, the colony at Roanoke in the territory later known as Virginia (Hakluyt [1598–1600] 1904, 8:17–23, 289–96). By contrasting the language of the offi-cial authorizations for empire—the English letter patent and the Spanish pa-pal bull—and their divergent forms of cultural expression—taking possession and reading texts—this essay contrasts English and Spanish practices in estab-lishing the authority of overseas empire.[5]

The word *patent* comes from the Latin *patente*, signifying "open." Letters patent are open letters, as distinguished from letters close, private letters closed up or sealed.[6] Letters patent came from a sovereign (or other person in authority) and were used to record an agreement, confer a right, title, or property, or authorize or command something to be done. Queen Elizabeth's letters patent to Gilbert and Ralegh authorized—that is, literally established—the authority for Englishmen to venture into the New World. From similar and sometimes identical patents in the next century came the authorizations for the settlement of Virginia, New England, Maryland, and the Carolinas. The patent makes explicit what the queen legitimated. Her twin authorizations, on the one hand, to "discover, find, search out, and view" and on the other, "to have, holde, occupy and enjoy" relate not to the peoples of the New World but to the lands, which are described as "remote, barbarous, and hea-then." There is a critical elision at the core of this definition because, while land can be remote, it cannot be barbarous or heathen; only people can have these qualities. If, as is sometimes alleged, attributing a characteristic of a people to a place is common in English, this simply tells us that the language itself allows for suppressing knowledge of the existence of peoples. But far from being an insignificant or merely rhetorical feature of the English lan-guage, this oxymoronic omission of persons plays a central role within a cru-cial political document, the first formal authorization that actually led to En-glish settlement in the New World and the model used for all subsequent English patents for occupying the New World.

Elizabeth's letter patent specifies what Gilbert was entitled to "have, hold, occupy and enjoy," namely, "all the *soyle* of all such lands, countreis, and territories . . . and of all Cities, Castles, Towns and Villages, and *places* in the same" (emphasis added).[7] The official authorization is limited to subduing space that is implicitly occupied but to whose inhabitants the patent does not refer. It is the "soyle," not the people (whose metonymic presence is noted only in passing), that Gilbert and Ralegh were granted rights to hold and enjoy. The very definition of what is to be possessed elides—that is to say, suppresses by omission—the question of inhabitants by focusing on the "soyle." And it is possession of the soil that Gilbert then ceremonially enacted on the banks of Newfoundland in 1583.

Furthermore, the Gilbert and Ralegh patents both state, these lands were granted "with full power to dispose thereof, and of every part in fee simple or otherwise, according to the order of the lawes of England."[8] In other words, the land of the New World is given to use and to distribute "according to . . . the lawes of England," as though full title were already established by virtue of the royal patent.

In English law of the time, only the monarch enjoyed full dominion over land, and hence the ultimate authorization for control over land—including the power to dispose of it—had to originate with the Crown (Aylmer 1980, 87–96). To justify the right to rule New World "soyle" in terms of England's legal code, official permission to distribute land had to be bestowed by the queen.

By what right did Elizabeth I authorize Gilbert and Ralegh to "have, hold, occupy and enjoy" with the additional "full power to dispose thereof . . . according to . . . the lawes of England" territories that she did not actually own? The patent lays out two rationalizations to justify English dominion over the New World: the authority of the Crown and the eminent domain of Christian princes.

The authority invoked by Elizabeth originated first, in the words of the patent, from her own "especial grace, certaine science, and mere motion." "Special grace" designated the source of royal authority in medieval English thinking—the idea that royal authority derives from God and comes to the Crown by grace. The queen's special grace is therefore a power that comes to her directly from God, a concept of kingship unique in western Europe in medieval and early modern times.[9] Grace also signified favor or benign regard on the part of a superior, as the ground of a concession (as opposed to a right or an obligation) or manifestation of favor. In the sixteenth century, *science* signified knowledge, but knowledge as a personal attribute. And "motion" was either moving, prompting, urging, instigating, or bidding—grounds or a cause for action. The adjectives that qualify the three bases of royal authority are *special* (favor), *certain* (knowledge), and *mere* (motion), all personal: they depend solely on the distinctive qualities of the queen. The queen's authority derives from her direct personal relationship with the ultimate source of power. Neither popes nor compacts with the people or commonwealth disturb the singular assertion of that authority in granting land.

The second source of the queen's authority is the absence of dominion over the lands by any other Christian ruler. Her grants are to those "lands, countreis, and territories not possessed by any Christian prince . . . nor inhabited by Christian people." Here, for the first and only time, the letters patent refer to human beings, but the word *people* only encompasses Christians: the presence of native peoples is still suppressed by omission. In making possession possible for Christian sovereigns, the letters patent tacitly acknowledge the legitimacy of dominion of other Christian (that is, European) rulers while passing over in silence the potential legitimacy of the New World's inhabitants. Although this right of other European rulers was not always respected in practice, it was at least enshrined in theory.[10]

The authorization to occupy lands not possessed by another Christian monarch suggests that Elizabeth's jurisdiction was also implicitly grounded in the right of eminent domain of Christian rulers. While Anglican preachers such as Richard Hakluyt and Samuel Purchas and many Puritans advanced conversion as one reason for conquest,[11] the letters patent fail to make English occupation of the land contingent upon proselytizing Indians.[12] Only twice in subsequent patents did the Crown make Christianization its goal. On both occasions its aim was to solidify rule over its own subjects, not to assert authority over the Indians.[13] However, all other sixteenth-century patents— French, Spanish, and Portuguese alike—insisted that legitimacy (the right to rule or even be present in the New World) was contingent on evangelizing the natives.[14] In papal bulls and letters dating from as early as the fifteenth century, this was the condition of the right to conquer infidel or pagan territory accorded the Crowns of Spain and Portugal.[15] For the English queen, rather than being an aim of conquest, religion legitimated the power of the state. It was the Christian (European) *prince* who had a right to the land. And the dominion of the Christian sovereign was justified simply by his or her possession of Christianity, not by the desire to spread it. In the constitution of English rule over the New World, religion functioned as a prop for the authority of the state but not as a means of controlling subjects.[16]

After obtaining the patent, the next step was for European adventurers to establish the authority articulated therein. Elizabeth's formula for instituting her authority was the phrase "to have, holde, occupy and enjoy," used synonymously with the phrase "to possess." The royal patent to Gilbert states that "Wee doe by these presents graunt, and declare, that all such countries so hereafter to be possessed and inhabited as afore sayd, from thesefoorth shall bee of the allegiance of us, our heires, and successours" (Hakluyt [1598–1600] 1904, 8:20). In other words, all that is necessary for the territories of the New World to belong to the queen, her heirs, and successors is that the authority of the letters patent be enacted by taking possession.

Possession in Roman law (from which English as well as Spanish law derives) signifies two things: physical presence and intention to hold the territory as one's own.[17] It is both an act and a mental process, an intention. Taking possession means establishing the intent to own and hence is incomplete or inchoate ownership. It is occupation on the way to ownership. Taking possession occurs at the moment when the authority created by the text of the letters patent is activated. The English style of taking possession was culturally distinctive. In the classic English legal treatise on possession, Frederick Pollock and Robert Samuel Wright declare that "in the eyes of [English] medieval lawyers, that possession largely usurped not only the substance but the name of property."[18] Not only was the authority in the New World over land, but to the English the concept of property (dominion over land) was synonymous with possession.

Another dimension of English thinking on possession is expressed most vividly in a popular version of the old legal proverb: "possession is nine points of the law"[19]—meaning that possession constitutes nearly all of the legal claim to ownership. Pollock and Wright establish this principle succinctly: "possession is the root of title," and the right to ownership (unaccompanied by actual possession) is merely a right to sue the possessor.[20] Whereas Roman law differentiated between possession and the right to possess, English law collapsed the two categories.[21] Thus in English law and, interestingly, in English law alone, the fact of possession creates a virtually unassailable right to own as well.

For the most part, the act of taking possession in the English colonies was neither ritualized nor ceremonialized. Ceremonies of arrival are absent from English accounts of voyages to the New World. Neither the New England narratives of William Bradford and John Winthrop, nor the Virginia tales of John Smith and William Strachey, nor the report of the initial voyage of Philip Amadas and Arthur Barlowe describe a ritual of arrival.[22] Nor do most of them note a ceremony marking the transition of the land into the possession of the monarch. "English practice required no particular symbolic action or form of words, provided the intention was clearly expressed . . . and followed by actual entry," writes Frederick Pollock, a prominent English authority on land laws.[23] Ceremonies were not necessary; the authority of England over the land was already created by the letters patent, and taking possession—the placing of the bodies of Englishmen on American soil with the intent to remain—was sufficient to activate that authority.

While Gilbert's reception of the twig and turf of ground was the ceremonial declaration of the intent to remain—the second critical element of possession—it was rarely observed subsequently.[24] In the medieval Anglo-Saxon tradition, the intent to remain was most commonly established through occupation—the building of fences or other boundary markers—and the construction of permanent edifices on the land (Lightwood 1894, 13). In the New World, building houses, forts, or other property (Winthrop 1825, 1:290; Purchas 1906, 18:315), which the letter patent describes as habitation, was sufficient to prove possession. Building permanent dwelling places or boundary markers manifested the intention to remain that was essential to taking possession.

The culturally distinctive characteristics of the English act of taking possession become apparent when contrasted with the practices of other European powers. Europeans in the New World, as well as in Asia and Africa, used a variety of symbolic acts to mark their presence or their contact with lands or peoples.[25]

Beginning in 1483, Portuguese explorers placed *padrões* (pillars of stone) bearing the royal arms along the coasts of Africa, India, and Brazil. The first Portuguese to sail to Brazil in 1500 erected a cross similarly emblazoned.[26] A Dutch expedition to the East Indies landed on the uninhabited island of Mauritius, where the vice admiral nailed a wooden board bearing the arms of Holland, Amsterdam, and Zeeland to a tree.[27] Jacques Cartier raised a cross with a shield bearing the fleur-de-lis and the slogan "Long live the King of France" at Gaspé harbor on the Saint Lawrence River in 1534. On the coast of Florida in 1562, Jean Ribault set up pillars with the arms of the king of France.[28] Vasco Núñez de Balboa built a pile of stones to note his sighting of the Pacific Ocean and carved the names of the kings of Castile on some tall trees.[29] Some of these devices were not related to formal acts of authority but were designed to ceremonialize the occasion. When the discoveries were unexpected, as was Balboa's, the signs of possession—the stones and graffiti—were hastily improvised on the spot. But other actions, such as the placing of the stone pillars by the Portuguese, crosses by the Spanish, and wooden boards by the Dutch, were regarded by their rulers as official acts indicating their dominion over the territory. The Portuguese saw the stone pillars as signaling their possession of territory following the Roman tradition of stone markers; the French and Spanish envisioned the cross as a sign of their having taken possession of the territory;[30] and the Dutch similarly regarded nailing the arms of the States General to a tree (Jameson 1909, 293–354).

Because their concept of dominion was bound up with residence on the land and with the nearly synonymous use of "possession" and "property," the English believed that symbolic manifestations such as crosses, shields, and stone pillars functioned merely as mnemonic devices or at best as navigational beacons.[31] This is how such markers were seen by many of the earliest English explorers. A member of a 1580 expedition searching for a northeast passage to the Far East described a cross he left for a fellow explorer: "Upon the said crosse Master Pet did grave his name with the date of our Lourde . . . to the end that if the William did chaunce to come thither, they [sic] might have knowledge that wee had beene there."[32] During the voyage resulting in the memorable wreck of the *Sea-Venture* in Bermuda, the fleet that reached Virginia left a cross at Cape Henry to signal that it had sailed that way.[33] On occasion, the English planted crosses with the name of the monarch to replace those of other powers, as a sign of supersession. When the English attacked a French settlement at Saint Sauveur on Mount Desert Island, they took down the cross that the French fathers had erected and placed their own, inscribed with the name of James I (Champlain [1632] 1922, 1 : 152).

Placing a cross, even if ceremonial rather than official, was a political act directed not at the natives but at other Europeans. "And this we diligently observed," wrote Captain George Waymouth, "that in no place . . . wee could discerne any token or signe that ever any Christian had beene before; which either by cutting wood, digging for water, or setting up Crosses (a thing never omitted by any Christian travailours) wee should have perceived some mention [written or spoken commemoration]."[34] The Dutch carved the name of their religion in *Spanish* on a board in Mauritius, clearly warning Spaniards to stay away; Queen Isabella in 1501 ordered one of her subjects to "place landmarks with the coat of arms of their Highnesses, or with other known signs . . . in order to obstruct the *English* from discovery" (Navarrete 1945–46, 3 : 100). These markers functioned in much the way that the placing of national flags on the North Pole, the South Pole, and the moon have functioned in the nineteenth and twentieth centuries.[35] The medium of the cross defined dominion over territory at a time when the dream of a universal Christian empire still prevailed; the additional decorations of the coats of arms of cities or kings symbolized the connection to secular power—the divisions within that dream.

Unlike other European powers, the English rejected the idea that signs—

markers, pillars, plaques, or piles of stone—could establish dominion over a territory or that anything other than "taking possession" (constructing permanent residences) constituted dominion. Whereas Portuguese sovereigns saw their stone pillars with crosses and royal arms "as a sign of how they saw said lands and islands . . . and acquired . . . dominion over them," the English refused to recognize anything other than occupation or settlement (Biker 1881, 1:55). Because the concepts of what constituted possession were mutually exclusive, and the respective imperial aims competitive, conflict over the meaning of sovereignty was inevitable.

In 1562 the Portuguese ambassador to Elizabeth's court lodged a formal protest against English trading in Guinea on the west coast of Africa, justifying an exclusive claim on the basis of Portugal's discovery, propagation of Christianity, and peaceful domination of the commerce of that territory for sixty years. He further complained that the English had placed an arbitrary interpretation on the concept of dominion and asked the queen to forbid her subjects to trade in Portuguese areas. "They [the English] decide that he [the Portuguese king] has no dominion but where he has forts and receives tribute . . . but as the words are doubtful, he desires her [Queen Elizabeth] . . . to change them into such others [words] as may comprehend all the land *discovered* by the Crown of Portugal" (emphasis added).[36] The queen replied that "her meaning . . . is . . . to restrain her subjects from haunting [frequenting] . . . land . . . wherein the King of Portugal had obedience, dominion, and tribute, and *not* [to prevent their trading] from all places *discovered* whereof he had no superiority at all" (emphasis added).[37] An annoyed ambassador responded that "his master *has* absolute dominion . . . over those lands already discovered" (emphasis added).[38]

At the core of this exchange were two fundamental cultural and linguistic differences between the Portuguese and the English. First, to the Portuguese ambassador the word *discovery* signified the establishment of legitimate dominion. For the Portuguese, the concept of discovery was linked to the technology and knowledge that they had pioneered. They had invented the navigational skills, found the most efficient sailing routes to West Africa, and located the African groups willing to supply the goods most desired by the European market. Expressed in more modern terms, discovery was the insistence that the Portuguese held a patent on the technology—maps, sailing devices, and a knowledge of trading seaports, latitudes, and sea lanes that they had invented.[39] The English Crown refused to consider discovery, so understood, as a legitimate source of the right to rule.[40]

A second and greater difference concerned the understanding of the word *possession.* The phrase closest to the English "taking possession" that appears in Portuguese charters of exploration and discovery is *tomar posse* (to hold something with the objective of taking some economic advantage from it), a form of economic *jouissance.* Dom João III's 1530 instructions to Lopalverez, for example, ordered him to *tomar posse*—that is, "to hold with the intention of taking economic advantage, whatever land, places and islands which said captains . . . discover or see, to hold and thus in my name acquire dominion over said places, lands, and islands." After ordering his captains to *tomar posse* the lands that had been "discovered"—the territories to which the Portuguese had located the sea-lanes—João went on to specify how Portuguese dominion was to be exercised, the precise object of Portuguese "taking possession." João's captains were to "take with the intention of obtaining economic benefit the navigation, trade, and commerce of said lands, places and islands"—in other words, anything that could be reduced to money.[41] The principal object was not land, as for the English, but trade and commerce.

In the Portuguese conception of dominion, imperial authority over the "important transactions, commerce and trade" was usually asserted either by a formal agreement, such as a treaty with the native inhabitants,[42] or by informal agreements that the Portuguese termed "introducing and maintaining the rules of prudence" (what we now call the market). Portuguese authorities claimed to be bringing prudence and market discipline to communities they described as previously operating solely on individual greed.[43] No permanent physical presence or fixed dwellings were necessary for the Portuguese to assert dominion, only a set of contractual agreements or customary practices relating to trade. Portuguese dominion was that of a market economy.

The Portuguese ambassador further argued, as evidence of his king's dominion over the commerce of the Guinea region, the king's longtime peaceful possession of the title "Lord of Guinea, of the Conquest, Navigation and Commerce of Ethiopia, Arabia, Persia, and India." The title, which dated from news of Vasco da Gama's return in 1499, described the geographic reach of Portuguese vessels in the spice trade's sea-lanes and ports where vessels of other nations customarily sought Portuguese safe-conduct passes in order to navigate.[44] The failure of other powers to contest the monarch's use of that title constituted acceptance of his right to dominate the economic markets of the region.

The English responded by denying Portuguese dominion. Their arguments derived from differing cultural and linguistic conceptions of discovery and taking possession.[45] The role of translation in fixing the meanings was critical, for in this dispute Robert Cecil read the ambassador's *tomar posse* as taking possession, thereby imposing the English concept of possession as property (land) on the Portuguese conception of economic arrangements as the core of dominion.[46] Cecil's translation guaranteed that each side could remain convinced that the other was engaged in an outrageous violation of obvious principles. The act of translation was thus involved in shaping the political misconceptions of the two sides in this cross-cultural dispute.

Nearly two decades later, a similar dispute erupted between England and Spain, turning on mutually exclusive concepts of the legitimate means of establishing political empire. In 1580 the Spanish ambassador protested Francis Drake's intrusions into territory claimed by Spain during his voyage around the world (1577–80). The official chronicler of the reign of Queen Elizabeth, William Camden, reported that the queen responded by denying Spanish dominion over the territory in the following words: "[Spaniards] had touched here and there upon the Coasts, built Cottages, and given Names to a River or Cape which does not entitle them to ownership. . . . Prescription without possession is worth little."[47] Elizabeth was quoting to the Spaniards a commonplace of medieval English law: "A man cannot by prescription [that is, by declaration or decree] make title to land,"[48] an understanding, as already noted, not shared by Spaniards or, indeed, by any other European power of the time. Her observations on the lack of relationship between naming and the establishment of sovereignty denied legitimacy to Spanish cultural and linguistic conceptions of taking possession. These conceptions can be seen as early as the actions of Columbus during his first journey to the New World.

The account of Columbus's son Ferdinand of the events of 12 October 1492 begins with his father's going ashore, bearing banners with a cross and the symbols of the Crowns of Castile and Aragon. Before the solemn declarations that Ferdinand and Isabella had required of him in order to assure Spanish dominion, and "after all had rendered thanks to Our Lord, kneeling on the ground and kissing it with tears of joy, . . . the Admiral arose and gave the island the name San Salvador." Beginning with this small strip of land, on his first voyage Columbus claimed to have named 600 islands, leaving 3,000 islands unnamed and thus unpossessed, only "scattered on the waves."[49] On some days he plunged into what one commentator calls "a veritable naming frenzy" (Todorov 1984, 27). At midnight on 11 January 1493

> He left the Rio de Gracia . . . sailing east four leagues as far as a cape that he called Bel Prado; and from there to the southwest is the mountain to which he gave [the name] Monte de Plata. . . . From there . . . [to] the cape he called Del Angel is 18 leagues. . . . From [cape] Del

Angel east by south there are four leagues to a point that he gave [the name] [Punta] Del Hierro and in the same direction four leagues further is a point that he called Punta Seca. And from there on the same course at six leagues is the cape that he said was Redondo, from there to the east is the cape Del Francés. . . . One league from there is the Cape of Buen Tiempo; from this [cape] south by southeast there is a cape he called Tajado.[50]

Columbus's practice of naming—or more accurately, renaming—rivers, capes, and islands as part of the ceremony of taking possession was repeated throughout the conquest of the New World and constituted one of the culturally specific acts of Spanish imperial authority.[51] The practice represents a form of ritual speech that undertakes a remaking of the land. Naming geographical features in effect converts them from their former status to a new European one: the external body of the land remains the same, but its essence is redefined by a new name. The use of ritual speech to name territory is analogous to the process of baptism practiced upon the peoples of the New World. These two key elements—the renaming of places and the ceremonial declarations—instituted Spanish colonial authority through an act of speaking, a dramatic enactment of belief in the power of words.

For the English, naming was merely symbolic, in the same category as planting crosses. George Percy, who visited the shores of the Virginia territory in 1606, described the conjunction between naming and placing a cross: "The ninth and twentieth day we set up a Crosse at Chesupioc Bay, and named that place Cape Henry" (Purchas, 1906, 18:409). Naming for the English had no connection with the establishment of the authority of empire. For the Spanish, it was critical.

Elizabeth dismissed other components of Spanish possession in this dispute as merely touching "here and there upon the Coasts," building "cottages" as a substitute for setting up residence. Both rejections relate to the way in which Spaniards established a relation to land. In place of settling on the land, they merely glanced off its fringes, "touched . . . upon the Coasts"; rather than erecting substantial buildings, they constructed a few cottages.[52] Thus one part of Elizabeth's response stemmed from her objections to the Spanish understanding of taking possession as an essentially symbolic act, the other from the allegedly impermanent character of Spanish relationships to the land.

Finally, a linguistic difference lay at the core of the misunderstandings between Spaniards and English in this dispute. By taking possession, the English meant residing or inhabiting. When Spanish officials referred to settlement, they used the verb "to people" (*poblar*). But even this word bore connotations and significance that diverged sharply from the English word *habitation*. *Poblar* defines the arrival of people, rather than the construction of buildings or dwellings, as the critical step in occupying a region. Furthermore, to the Spanish Crown, peopling (*poblando*) did not establish the right to rule but was an activity sometimes taken after imperial authority had been established by naming and solemn declarations.[53] From the Spanish perspective (one shared by other European powers), the English had no respect for international conventions or rights but simply marched into a territory, settled, and declared it theirs.[54]

While described legally in the same Roman-inspired terms as the Spanish—placing a body over the land with the intention of remaining—the English customarily manifested *both* by erecting permanent dwelling places or homes. But even though sixteenth-century Englishmen denounced other nations for invoking mere "signs" or symbols to hold overseas territory, these same English failed to realize that their own belief in taking possession or the creation of rights to suzerainty through the construction of permanent buildings was itself a symbolic act, as culturally distinctive as that of any other European power of the time. The only difference was that the primary symbolism of the English conception of sovereignty was architectural.

At the core of the differences were incompatible cultural and linguistic concepts of what constituted the right to rule colonial territory: possession, appropriate ceremony and words, or *tomar posse*. Allied to these linguistically irreconcilable ideas about the basic nature of entitlement to overseas rule were incompatible cultural images of how such rights were ceremonially enacted over territory.

Like the English, the Spanish in the New World used a written document to ensure the legitimacy of imperial authority. For the English, authority was established by letters patent; for the Spaniards it was created by a papal bull. In 1493 the bull *Inter caetera* of Pope Alexander VI gave Spain the exclusive right to present the Gospel to the natives of the New World and guaranteed Spain's right to rule the land in order to secure the right to preach.[55] Alexander VI granted the New World on these terms: of his "own motion, mere liberality, certain science, and apostolic authority" ("motu proprio, mera liberalitate, et ex certa scientia, ad de Apostolicae potestatis"; *Bullarium* 1858)—language near that used by Queen Elizabeth—"special grace, certain science, mere motion." The parallels are even greater than this. Not only the language but also the parchment form, scribal style, and great seals of Elizabethan patents are identical to those of medieval papal bulls. Finally, "letter patent" was the most common sixteenth-century English translation of the Latin *bula*. At the time, the word *bull* more often referred to the lead seal than to the document itself.[56]

Although Elizabeth's language in the royal patent differs only slightly from that of the papal bull, the differences are instructive as to the origins of both sources of authority. The word *grace* in Elizabeth's terms meant both a special authority from God and the queen's own freely bestowed favor—the latter being the exact sense of the papal "liberality." As for the "apostolic authority," by the mid fifteenth century Edward IV was using the phrase "of our special grace, ful power, and authority royall" on royal charters, substituting "authority royall" for the papal "authority apostolic."[57] In using the formula of the Roman pontiff to establish authority over the New World, the queen implicitly asserted her authority as equal to his.

As with the English letters patent, the papal bull granted Spaniards territory "not possessed by any Christian prince." (In many Spanish translations this is rendered as "the right which any Christian prince has gained" and the word *possession* is not used.) Just as the letters patent conceded the authority to dispose of the New World, so too did the bull give the New World to Spain "with free and absolute power, authority, and jurisdiction." But the English patent altered the papal formula to characterize the grant of absolute authority over the New World as decidedly English—"according to the lawes of England."

The most profound changes made by the English in the papal formula restricted the category of dominion to the "soyle" and added the phrase "remote, barbarous, and heathen lands" to characterize the object of English empire. These alterations to the papal format reveal English cultural biases regarding the target of imperial authority.

For the twenty years following Columbus's arrival in the New World, Spaniards employed the methods described above. Upon landing at or entering into a new territory (an enterprise they termed "discovery" or "entry"),[58] Spaniards ritually invoked the Crown of Castile and the pope in a solemn fashion, often renaming the land as well.[59] Spanish officials did not require any specific language in the ceremonies that inaugurated their rule.[60] But while the practice of activating Spanish authority through ceremony and ritual speech continued to be practiced throughout the colonial period, the speech itself was altered in the third decade of Spanish settlement in the New World.

Because the pope's grant was contingent upon converting the natives, a challenge was not long in coming. It came from Dominicans newly arrived on the island of Hispaniola. In a December 1511 sermon, Father Antonio de

Montesinos attacked Spanish officials on the island (including one of Columbus's sons) in a scathing critique that focused on their failure to convert the
natives (Las Casas 1986, 2:440–42). The criticism found its mark, for the following year King Ferdinand ordered a reconsideration of the matter of Spanish title to the New World. He convened a commission to draw up new laws
governing the treatment and conversion of Indians (the Laws of Burgos) and
asked a canonist and a jurist to consider how the authority of the Spanish
empire might be better legitimated. The canonist was the Dominican Fray
Matías de Paz of the University of Salamanca; the jurist, Juan López de Palacios
Rubios.[61] Their respective treatises expanded and elaborated the reasons for
the conquest. From Palacios Rubios's essay government officials extracted a
portion that could be used to justify Spain's future conquests of New World
peoples. This text became known as the *Requerimiento* (Requirement), which
required the natives to submit to the authority of the Spanish Crown. Used in
explorations of the Caribbean after 1512, it would be employed whenever
Spaniards encountered people in the New World. It was invoked in the conquests of Mexico and Peru, as well as in hundreds of other encounters with
hunter-gatherers and small agricultural and fishing communities.[62] The Requirement served to legitimate Spanish authority over the New World until it
was replaced in 1573 by a revised, less demanding version, the Instrument of
Obedience and Vassalage.[63]

In the instructions issued by the Crown for discoveries and conquests after
1512, the Requirement was ordered to be read to the New World natives. In
other words, from then on, the Crown specified a ritual speech to be used in
enacting the authority of its empire over a people. No longer would any "appropriate ceremony and words," as employed by Columbus, be sufficient; the
words had to be those of the Requirement.

Just as the English did, the Spanish claimed a right to rule based on their
possession of Christianity, a (self-proclaimed) superior religion. But the relationship between religion and the power of the Christian state was delineated
differently in the Requirement than in the English letters patent. The opening
phrases announce the status of the person reading as a messenger and servant
of the king of Castile, whose sources of authority are provided by tracing a
genealogy of power beginning with God and extending in an unbroken line
to St. Peter, the pope, and finally to the papal donation made to Ferdinand
and Isabella by virtue of which "Their Highnesses are kings and lords of these
islands and the mainland" (Sanz 1916, 1:293).

The Requirement concludes by demanding two things: that the Indians
recognize the genealogy of power and that they allow Christian priests to

preach the faith. "Therefore, as best I can, I beg and *require* you to understand well what I have said . . . that it is just and that you recognize the Church as lady and superior of the universal world, and the Pontiff . . . in her name, and the King and the Queen our lords in his place as superiors and lords and monarchs of these islands and mainland . . . and that you consent . . . to having the religious fathers declare and preach to you on this subject" (Sanz 1916, 294). If natives refused to acknowledge the papal donation and to admit preachers, the Spaniards considered themselves justified in commencing hostilities. In practice, the document, according to Lewis Hanke, "was read to trees and empty huts. . . . Captains muttered its theological phrases into their beards on the edge of sleeping Indian settlements, or even a league away before starting the formal attack. . . . Ship captains would sometimes have the document read from the deck as they approached an island, and at night would send out enslaving expeditions, whose leaders would shout the traditional Castilian war cry 'Santiago!' rather than read the Requirement before they attacked" (Hanke 1949, 33–34).

Gonzalo Fernández de Oviedo, an early sixteenth-century conquistador and chronicler of the conquest, wrote, "I would have preferred to make sure that they [the Indians] understood what was being said; but for one reason or another, that was impossible. . . . I afterwards asked Doctor Palacios Rubios, the author of the Requirement, whether the reading sufficed to clear the consciences of the Spaniards; he replied that it did."[64] No demonstration of understanding was required: rather, the issue of reception was studiously ignored. It was the *act of reading the text* that constituted the authority. The only other action needed to legitimate Spanish rule was to record that the act of reading had taken place. Just as Columbus had been required to register his solemn declarations in written legal instruments, the final step in implementing the requirement and establishing its legality was the order that a notary preserve a record of this reading with "a signed testimony."

During the sixteenth-century debates over the Requirement, occasional consideration was given to the issue of translation (Oviedo 1944, bk. 29, chap. 8) but none to the strangeness of the act of reading to people who had not only never read but had never seen the act of reading. We who have grown up with reading can only imagine the questions. Why is someone holding up an object (a written document) in front of himself and looking at it while he speaks? Is it an avoidance taboo? Is he afraid? ashamed? Why is the speaker's glance or gaze not directed at the listener but at the object he is holding? To New World societies with different body language and conventions for speech, European reading (and even speaking) practices must have appeared strange.[65]

While most of the commentators upon the Requirement, from Walter Ralegh and Bartolomé de Las Casas to modern historians, have interpreted it in a derisive or ironical way, there is more to it than simple absurdity (Hanke 1938, 25–34; Verlinden 1970, 41–42). First, it expressed a traditional European form of establishing authority (the letters patent or papal bull) derived from the practices of the papal chancery. Second, if the idea that the act of reading to an uncomprehending audience seems a bizarre or unusual way of legitimizing power, it should be remembered that there are dozens of similar examples in contemporary American criminal and civil law. The most obvious instance is the United States Supreme Court's *Miranda* decision, which legitimates the authority of the American government over an often uncomprehending suspect when he is *read his rights*. The dominion of the American criminal justice system is also established by reading. What the act of reading accomplishes, in contradistinction to English architectural symbolism or Portuguese erecting of stone posts and flag-planting, is the establishment of authority over *people*. The central, most important act legitimating Spanish rights over the New World articulated authority over persons rather than over land or commerce.

For the Spaniards, the principal target of imperial authority was people, and all the major institutions of the first century of Spanish colonial rule established public and private authority over people. In addition to slavery, the Spaniards brought with them two other institutions that exerted authority over persons. The *encomienda*, the principal reward sought by Spanish settlers in the New World, was a grant of Indian labor to private citizens; the *repartimiento* was a bureaucratic process for organizing rotating weekly pools of Indian workers. The major institutions of the first century of Spanish rule thus exerted authority over people. Grants of land (*mercedes de tierra*) came relatively late in the conquest and were subsidiary to grants of labor.[66]

It might be argued that the Spaniards came to rule over people, and the English over land, due to ecological exigencies rather than cultural predispositions: the English in North America encountered a lightly inhabited terrain, while the Spaniards encountered the most densely populated regions of the Americas. Three facts refute this thesis.

First is the historical timing of the development of the Requirement and the institutions of Spanish rule over people. Indian slaving began with Columbus, and the New World *encomienda* or practice of granting settlers rights to

Indian labor originated in 1503.[67] The doctrine of the Requirement asserting imperial authority over people was created in 1512. Even by this late date, Spanish settlement was restricted to a few Caribbean islands whose population densities were closer to those of North America than they were to the heavily settled regions of Peru and Mexico.[68] In other words, the institutions of rule over people were established long before the discovery of Central and South America, with their sizable native populations.

Second is the timing of the English focus on land as their primary object. English concern with authority over land was apparent as early as the letter patent of 1578, *before* any expedition to settle the New World was launched, and it remained a constant feature of official authorizations thereafter. Furthermore, the English patents were issued after news of the Inca, Maya, and Nahua empires had spread throughout Europe, and there was the distinct (but unrealized) possibility that a similar empire would be found on the North American continent.

Finally, to answer the question of what the English might have done had they encountered such an empire, one can look to the eighteenth century, when they began to rule a continent more densely populated than central Mexico or highland Peru. In India the first act of English officials was to *survey native land laws* and to try to organize a system of taxation based on land ownership (Guha 1981). They subsequently invented the modern techniques of land survey in order to rule the Indian subcontinent.[69] Spanish officials in highland Peru and Mexico counted people; the English in India surveyed the land.[70] Spanish colonialism taxed natives by a census; British colonialism, by a map. It was not the ecology of the peoples encountered but cultural conceptions that defined the central objects of European authority.

The Requirement officially ceased to be the means of enacting the authority of the Spanish empire overseas in 1573, when it was replaced by a new set of instructions, called the Instrument of Obedience and Vassalage. Eliminating reference to the papal bull, it described the king as "the only and singular defender of the Church." The Indians were invited to obey him so that in exchange for protection from their enemies they might become beneficiaries of Spanish political and economic power. But although the source of authority was redefined, the method of enacting it was not. The Instrument of Obedience and Vassalage was still to be read to the natives, with the added provision that efforts be made to secure translators. In its new form, the instrument was read not only in the New World but also in the Philippines to legitimize Spanish conquest (Hanke 1938, 16:88–142). While the obvious implausibility of asserting a papal donation was eliminated in an era that had witnessed the end of papal universality, the method of implementation (reading) continued.

Each of these separate targets of imperial authority—land for the English, labor for the Spaniards—was also the principal focus of internal struggle and contention over the legitimacy of imperial rule. English and Anglo-American critics of English imperial policy such as Roger Williams attacked the means by which the English acquired land. Their Spanish counterparts—Las Casas and Juan Zumárraga—criticized the means by which Spaniards acquired the right to Indian labor. Neither developed substantial critical assessments of the other empire's principal object. The enslavement of Indians never came in for the scathing critiques in England or Anglo-America that it received in the Spanish empire, nor did the gradual dispossession of native peoples from their lands receive the same attacks in Spain that it did in the English empire. Discourses critical of imperial authority centered on the aspects each culture defined as crucial. In English culture, what mattered was the title to land; in Spanish culture, the right to use labor. The difference centered on the priorities of the two societies: the conquest of land and the conquest of peoples.

The differing constructions of the authority of empire additionally illuminate the very different responses to the problem of native depopulation. For the Crown of Spain, widespread deaths of natives from disease and other causes were evidence of God's disfavor. Charles V in 1523 ordered Hernán Cortés to take into consideration "the monumental harm and losses received by the said Indians through their deaths and dwindling numbers and the great disservice that Our Lord has received because of it."[71] In a similar royal order to Ponce de León two years later, Charles added: "not only has our duty to God Our Lord not been performed because such a multitude of souls have perished . . . but we ourselves [the Crown] have been ill-served by it as well."[72] James I of England, on the other hand, in his 1620 letter patent for the Plymouth Colony wrote: "Within this late yeares there hath by God's Visitation raigned a Wonderfull Plague . . . to the utter Destruction, Devastacion and Depopulation of the whole Territorye, so that there is not left for many Leagues together in a Manner any [person] that doe claim or challenge . . . Where by We in our Judgment are persuaded and satisfied that the appointed Time is come in which the Almighty God in his great Goodness and Bountie towards Us and our People hath thought fitt and determined that those large and goodly Territoryes, deserted as it were by their naturall inhabitants should be possesed and enjoyed" (Hazard 1792, 1:105). Not only are the massive numbers of native deaths not to be either mourned or taken as evidence of unjust and tyrannical conduct, they are proof positive of divine intervention on behalf of the English, "a Wonderfull Plague" demonstrating God's "great Goodness and Bountie towards Us and our People."

This sentiment was echoed by Puritan settlers as well as Catholic monarchs. John Winthrop, for example, suggested that the plague that hit the natives just before the Puritans arrived was evidence of God's hand in creating a vacant land: "God hath consumed the Natives with a great plague in those parts soe as there be few inhabitants left."[73] The Spanish critique of empire found its fulcrum in the devastating losses of people, losses that threatened the basis of the empire's wealth in human beings. For the English, native deaths were more than unproblematic; they were declared to be signs of divine favor.

The English and Spanish empires in the New World were Christian imperialisms, founded at the core on a belief in the right of the religion of the West to rule the other religions of the world. For the English, religion functioned as a prop for the authority of the state; for the Spaniards it was a means of coercing Indians into European ways of thinking. In their invocation of Christian imperialism as the authority for expansion over the rest of the world, both the English and the Spanish empires addressed medieval tradition. The Spanish king appealed to the authority of the papacy, and Elizabeth I similarly drew upon the same sources as the medieval Roman pontiffs in her letters patent. The assertions of the English and Spanish monarchs were thus the effort to assert a traditional medieval authority at the very start of the age of European expansion.

It is ironic that, by using letters patent, English rulers continued to invoke both the form and the substance of the medieval papal bull to legitimize rule over the New World through the middle of the seventeenth century. The English made little effort to alter their adaptation of the authority of the pontiff even after Spain ceased to regard the bull as a legitimate source of authority.[74] While this can be seen partly as the result of the position of the English monarch as head of the church, its formulas were invoked unself-consciously by Oliver Cromwell—no friend of the Church of England—to justify the settlement of Nova Scotia (Hazard 1792, 616–17). Although the Spanish are most often considered the most medieval of European powers, it was the English—whose formula for establishing empire became fixed in the late sixteenth century—who continued for the longest period to assert medieval concepts of sovereignty overseas. The language of Gilbert's 1578 patent was used for the last time in letters patent issued for Australia at the end of the eighteenth century. Spanish imperial authority relied centrally upon articulating a relationship between Europeans and a living, breathing Other rather than simply demarcating space. It had to constitute its authority primarily through possession not of territory but of bodies and minds, by authority over persons rather than places. If in the medieval English world, possession was synonymous with property, in the Spanish world it signified dominion over people. When the English conquered, they aimed to conquer territory, and when they took over an area, they sought to possess the land, not the people. Spanish authority was textual imperialism par excellence: the reading of a Western text to uncomprehending natives. Whereas the ultimate authority of each empire was founded on written language, that of the English empire in the New World was established by habitation, "taking possession," while that of the Spanish empire was enacted by reading.

Historical memories of the origins of these two empires have been built around the central aims of each. We commemorate the origins of English settlement in the New World by place: Plymouth Rock, Jamestown, even Roanoke. But we do not remember the start of the Spanish empire by a location. Exactly where Columbus landed is uncertain in our memories as well as our scholarship. We do remember the date on which he made his solemn declarations, ceremony, and words. We mark the conquest of land by the place where it began; we remember the ceremonies that initiated the conquest of people by commemorating a time: a date, 12 October, and a year, 1492.

ACKNOWLEDGMENTS

My colleague Ira Gruber provided invaluable advice on colonial Anglo-America, as did (in different areas) Ranjit Guha, George Stocking, George E. Marcus, John E. Wills, Jr., Peter Hulme, Susan Deeds, and Tamsyn Donaldson. The Institute for Aboriginal Studies at Australian National University, Canberra, the History Department of Northern Arizona University, and the Getty Center for the History of Art and the Humanities have heard this presented as a ceremonial speech. This essay is from a forthcoming comparative history of the politics and ceremony of European expansion in the New World.

NOTES

1. Dunn and Kelley 1989, 62, 64. I have used Dunn and Kelley's transcription of the Las Casas text rather than the translation. A *protestación*, for example,

in Spanish law is and was "a solemn declaration for the purpose of preserving one's right"; *testimonio* is both "proof by witness" and "an instrument legalized by a notary."

2. Lorenzo Pasquligo to his brother, 23 August 1497, in Harrisse [1882] 1968, 322; also Williamson 1962, 208. According to Harrisse, Cabot was Genoese by birth, like Columbus, but Venetian by adoption (1–41). The use of banners and insignia was also recommended in Henry VII's letters patent; Hakluyt [1582] 1850, 21.

3. "Seyendo por vos descubiertas e ganadas las dichas islas . . . e fecho por vos . . . el juramento e solemnidad que en tal caso se require" "Carta de merced . . . a Cristóval Colón" (Rumeu de Armas 1985, 239–41). See also Fernández 1987.

4. Hakluyt [1598–1600] 1904, 8:53–54; "Vortigerne þe king Bi•tæhte heom al þis lond [and] ne bilæfde him an heonde a turf of londe," *Laȝamon's Brut or Chronicle of Britain* [ca. 1205], cited in the *Oxford English Dictionary* in entry for turf.

5. In medieval times, the term *imperium* (empire) was synonymous with the Holy Roman Empire, but in the fourteenth century it began to acquire in popular works the more general meaning of a great realm, a usage current in the period of European expansion (Koebner 1961, 46–47; Folz [1953] 1969).

6. Scargill-Bird 1896, 34–35. Letters patent were first used in 1201. The forms became fixed early in the thirteenth century, though minor modifications occurred between 1460 and 1482. By the early sixteenth century, they had replaced earlier forms of both the writ and the royal charter. Hall 1908–9, 1:24–25, 53–54.

7. Hakluyt [1598–1600] 1904, 8:18. Subsequent patents only expand the basic idea of space—"lands, woods, soil, grounds, havens, ports, rivers, mines, minerals, marshes, waters, fishings, commodities, and hereditaments" (Virginia, 10 April 1606; Brown [1890] 1964, 540), "land, soyles, grounds, havens, ports, rivers, waters, fishing, mines and minerals" (Massachusetts, 4 March 1628); "soil, lands, fields, woods, mountains, fens, lakes, rivers, bays and inlets" (Lord Baltimore, 28 June 1632); "lands, tenements, or hereditaments" (Connecticut, 23 April 1662); "tract or part of land" (William Penn, 28 February 1681). The last four statements are quoted in Lucas 1850, 32, 89, 48, 106.

8. Maryland's charter (1632) reads "in fee simple or in fee tail or otherwise"; Connecticut's (1662) more fulsomely grants the right to "Lese [sic], grant, demise, alien bargain, sell, dispose of, as our other liege people of this our realm of England"; Lucas 1850, 89, 48.

9. Kantorowicz 1957, 48. "Special grace" was first used in letters patent in the first quarter of the fourteenth century during the reign of Edward II; Hall 1908–9, 25.

10. James I of England granted to the Virginia Company five-sixths of the territory between 40° and 46° N, which Henry IV of France had already granted to the Sieur de Monts. James I's grant (10–20 April 1606) came just three years after the Sieur de Monts's (8 November 1603). De Monts's first charter is in Lescarbot [1611] 1866, 2:408–14.

11. Hakluyt [1582] 1850, 8–18. For other Anglicans, including the bishop of London, see Wright [1943] 1965, 12, 53, 93, 124, 138–39. John Winthrop expressed this as "the propagation of the gospell to the Indians . . . tendinge to the inlargment of the Kingdome of Jesus Christ"; Winthrop n.d., 1. See also R. C. [Robert Cushman], "Reasons and Considerations Touching the Lawfulness of Removing out of England and into the Parts of America" (1621) in Young 1844, 239–49.

12. Some American historians have erroneously claimed that the letters patent express a desire to spread Christianity as an official goal of colonization; see, e.g., Beer 1959, 29; Miller 1956, 101. The actual wording of the letters patent on which Miller based his assertion is simply that the Crown is "greatly commending, and graciously accepting of, their [the colonists'] desires . . . in propagating of Christian religion to such people" (emphasis added; Brown [1890] 1964, 53–54). The charters to Cecil Calvert (28 June 1632) and William Penn (28 February 1681) similarly acknowledge the grantee's desire to convert the Indians, but religious dominion is not the Crown's concern (Lucas 1850, 100).

13. The Massachusetts Colony Charter (4 March 1628) states: "Our said people in inhabiting there may be so religiously, peaceably, and civilly governed, as theire goode life and orderly conversation may winne and invite the natives of that countrey to the knowledge and obedience of the onlly God and Savior of mankind and the Christian faith, which in our royal intention and the adventurers' free profession is the principal end of this plantation" (Lucas 1850, 43). In the second Virginia Charter (23 May 1609, sec. 29), the reason given is to exclude Spaniards from Virginia (Brown [1890] 1964, 236; Lucas 1850, 18). Mention of Christianization was dropped from subsequent patents for these areas.

14. François I's 1540 commissions to Jacques Cartier and the Seigneur de Roberval introduce the aim of French conquest: "to more easily bring the other peoples of these countries to believe in our Holy Faith." The authoriza-

tion for Spain's declaration of war is the refusal of the natives to listen to the preaching of the priests. Roberval's commission is in *Collection de manuscrits contenant lettres, mémoires, et autres documents historiques relatifs à la Nouvelle France* (1883), 1:19, 30–36.

15. *Romanus pontifex*, 15 September 1436, and *Dudum cum ad nos*, 6 November 1436, in *Monumenta Henricina* 1962, 5:281–82, 347–49.

16. Neither the English nor the Dutch refer to Christianizing the natives as an authorization for their discovery or presence in the New World; see Keller 1938, 134–35; Trelease 1962, 137–46.

17. Lightwood 1894, 9; *Digest of Justinian* 1985, sec. 41.2.3.

18. Pollock and Wright 1888, 5. For examples of the importance of possession in sixteenth- and seventeenth-century English law, see the legal handbook *The Compleat Clerk* . . . (London, 1677), 98–104, 157–58, 316–18, 320–21, 742–44, 780–81, 867. Many of the formulas date from the reign of Elizabeth I.

19. According to the *Oxford English Dictionary*, the seventeenth-century legal expression of possession may be eleven points of the law (out of a total of twelve points), that is, a majority of the points of the law. For its subsequent legal use, see James William Norton-Kyshe, *The Dictionary of Legal Quotations* (London: Sweet and Maxwell, 1904).

20. Pollock and Wright 1888, 22. "It is one of the most general and long-settled rules of law that a person who is in apparent possession has all the rights, remedies and immunities of a possessor. . . . He cannot be disturbed except by another person who is able to show a present right to the possession" (Pollock and Wright 1888, 147). Furthermore, the "right to possession . . . is merely a right in one person to sue" (145). For an example of the operation of this principle in colonial America, see *Colonial Laws of Massachusetts* 1890, 123–24.

21. In Roman law the distinctions are called *possidere* (a right) and *in possessium esse* (physical possession); Pollock and Wright 1888, 47.

22. One of the few examples of an arrival ritual is described in Harris 1928, 77.

23. Pollock 1896, 75. Charters emerged later for the purpose of maintaining a record. In English law, recording was not an important part of either the ceremony of possession or the proof of ownership, although it was in the Spanish world.

24. Bradford 1968; Winthrop 1825, 1:290; Purchas 1906, 18:459–540; Smith [1580–1631] 1986; Strachey 1849; Purchas 1906, 18:459–540. Amadas

and Barlow are the first to state they took possession of Virginia for the Queen; see "First Virginia Voyage, 1584," in Hakluyt 1986, 65–76.

25. A study that fails to make the distinction between official and unofficial acts and that often makes errors of fact but that is nonetheless interesting is Keller 1938. Wagner (1938) provides some critical commentary on Keller but no notes. Morales Padrón 1955 contains several interesting descriptions of ceremonies but ignores the extensive sixteenth-century Spanish legal literature on "discovery" and "possession" (see note 60 below). Juricek 1976 unfortunately relies heavily on Morales Padrón.

26. The first stone pillar was placed probably around May 1483, at the mouth of the Congo River; Baião et al. 1937–40, 1:366. See also the notice of the subsequent placement of pillars by Dias and Almeida in Malheiro Dias 1924–26, 1:380, 2:104, 3:xxxi; Lopes de Castanheda [1551] 1924–33, 1:6; Alguns documentos 1892, 108–21, esp. 119.

27. *The Journall or Dayly Register Containing a True Manifestation, and Historicall Declaration of the Voyage, Accomplished by Eight Shippes of Amsterdam, under the Conduct of Jacob Corneliszen Neck Admirall, Wybrandt van Warwick, Vice Admirall, which Sayled from Amsterdam the First Day of March, 1598* . . . ([1601] 1974, 7): "In this Island, our Vice Admirall caused a shield of wood to be made and fastened to a tree, to the end that if any ships arrived at that place they might perceive that Christians had been there; and thereupon was carved these words 'Christians Reformados,' reformed Christians, with the armes of Holland, Zealand, and Amsterdam." The Dutch version is in Commelin 1646, vol. 1, voyage no. 3, fol. 4. The previous Dutch voyage (under Cornelius Houtman) had followed well-known routes and had landed only in places well populated with other Europeans.

28. Cartier [1580] 1975, 21 (a similar action of cross planting on Cartier's second voyage is noted in Marion 1923, 5); Hakluyt [1598–1600] 1904, 7:457, 462. In 1613 Samuel de Champlain also placed crosses with the arms of France; see Champlain [1632] 1922, 2:15, 34–35. Seventeenth-century French missionaries on the Mississippi appear not to have attached regal emblems to the crosses; Shea 1903, 16.

29. Las Casas 1986, 2:595. In the absence of trees, Francisco Cano in 1568 carved crosses into nopal cactuses; Morales Padrón 1955, 362.

30. For the French, see note 28 above. On Roman stone markers in the Iberian peninsula, see Scott 1910, 348. Fernández Navarrete [1825–37] 1945–46, 3:149–50; "Instrucción de Don Antonio de Mendoza," in *Colección de Documentos Inéditos Relativos al Descubrimiento . . . en América y Oceanía* [hereafter

CDI], 3:325–28; "Ordenanzas sobre descubrimiento nuevo y población" of Phillip II (13 July 1563), CDI, 3:484–538, esp. 490. For examples of actions, see CDI, 2:549–56, 3:337, 4:470, 5:286ff, esp. 370–71, 14:134–35; Hakluyt [1598–1600] 1904, 10:434–38. Ironically, when it came to the dispute between the Portuguese and the Spanish in the Moluccas, the Spanish argued a position closer to the English; Charles V to D. João III, 18 December 1523, in Fernández Navarrete [1825–37] 1945–46, 4:283–90.

31. This is also the argument that Cartier used in addressing the native leaders at Gaspé harbor; see Ramusio [1556, repr. Venice, 1606] 1967, fol. 375: "And then we showed them by sign, that the said cross had been planted as a marker (and signal) for entering the harbor" (Dipoi su mostrato con segni, che detta croce era stat piantata per sar dar segno, & cognoscenza come s'hauesse da entrar in detto porto). The French original was discovered in 1867 and is reproduced in Biggar 1924, 66: "Et puis leurs monstrames par signe, que ladite croix avoit eté plantée pour faire merche et ballise, pour entrer dedans le hable."

32. "The discoverie made by M. Arthur Pet and M. Charles Jackman of the Northeast parts" (1580) in Hakluyt [1598–1600] 1904, 3:288.

33. "To sett up a cross upon the pointe . . . to signify our coming in [the harbor]"; Governor and Council of Virginia to the Virginia Company of London, 7 July 1610, in Brown [1890] 1964, 403.

34. Waymouth reported: "Wee carried with us a Crosse to erect at that point" (Purchas 1906, 18:353). They are called "testimonies of Christians" in *A True and Sincere Declaration of the purpose and ends of the Plantation begun in Virginia set forth by the authority of the Governors and Councellors established for that Plantation* (1609) in Brown [1890] 1964, 338–353, esp. 348–49.

35. "Before we went from thence, our generall cause to be set up, a monument of our being there; as also of her majesties, and successors, right and title to that kingdome, namely, a plate of brasse, fast nailed to a great and firme post; whereon is engraven her graces name, and the day and yeare of our arrivall there, and of the free giving up, of the province and kingdome, both by the king and people, into her majesties hands"; Drake 1652, 80.

36. Replication of the Portuguese ambassador, 7 June 1562, in Stevenson 1867, 77.

37. Answer to the Portuguese ambassador, 15 June 1562, in Stevenson 1867, 95.

38. Second replication of the Portuguese ambassador, 19 June 1562, in Stevenson 1867, 106.

39. The idea of "invention" continues to play a more important role in the meaning of discovery in Portuguese than in English. Contrast the *Oxford English Dictionary*'s definition of discovery with that in Pereira Victoria 1970. The argument for invention or innovation did apply to the Portuguese South Atlantic voyages but was considerably more difficult to make for navigation in the Indian Ocean, which had been sailed for millennia; see Thomaz 1985, 526.

40. From 1940 to the early 1960s, the debate about discovery seems to have focused primarily on the intention of the individual *actor* rather than on imperial intention; see Bataillon and O'Gorman 1955; Morison 1940, 5–10; O'Gorman 1961; Washburn 1962.

41. "Tratado de paz entre El Rey D. João II e os habitantes da ilha de Sunda, e auto de posse que se tomou en nome do dito Rey, da mesma ilha," in Biker 1881, 55–57. In contemporary Brazilian law, the object of *posse* is still "anything that can be reduced to money"; Nascimento 1986, 130–31.

42. For examples of the conditions of trade established in the treaties with India, see Biker 1881.

43. "[São] gentes sem ley nem regras de prudencia, sômente se governava & regia pelo impeto da cobiça que cada huũ tinha; nos o reduzinos & possemos em arte [do commerço] com regras universaes & particulares como tem todas las sciençias"; Barros [1534] 1932, 10.

44. Baião et al. 1937–40, 2:359. In an earlier diplomatic incident, the Portuguese envoy to Bengala in 1522 had defended the title on the grounds that "The King, our lord, is called by his titles. . . . [F]or this reason, where his ships sail, no others may sail without his permission [*seguros*]." Barros elaborates the reasons for the title "Senhor da conquista, navegação, e comercio da Etiopia, Arabia, Persia e India"; see Barros [1534] 1932, dec. 1, bk. 6, chap. 1. For a modern critical history of safe-conduct passes, see Thomaz 1985, 522, 525.

45. The only semiofficial enunciation of the Portuguese position in terms of international law is Freitas 1625, a response to the publication of Grotius 1608.

46. Contrast the original version of the Portuguese ambassador's remarks in Santarem 1854, 15:128–34, 136–45, with William Cecil's translation in Stevenson 1867, 41–42, 54–55, 75–79, 106–7.

47. "Nec alio quopiam jure quam quod Hispani hinc illinc appul erint, casulas posuerint, sslumen [*sic*] aut Promontorium denominaverint quae proprietatem acquirere non possunt . . . cum praescriptio sine possessione haud valeat" (Camden 1625, 328). The widely cited twentieth-century translation of this passage by Edward Cheyney (1905, 660) differs significantly from the 1635

English translation by R. N. Gent on several points. Most important for the discussion here, Cheyney renders the final phrase categorically as "prescription without possession is not valid." The seventeenth-century English translation, historically closer to the Latin original, is more equivocal. The 1635 translation, "prescription without Possession is little worth," accepts symbolic acts as valid but demeans their importance.

48. Herber 1891, 2. Similar sentiments are expressed in *Nova Britannia: Offring Most Excellent Fruites by Planting in Virginia* (1609), excerpted in Brown 1964, 262.

49. Columbus [1571] 1959, 59; Anghiera 1907, 45. Martyr interviewed members of Columbus's expedition, including Columbus himself.

50. Columbus 1989, 322–25. I have worked from the Dunn and Kelley transcription.

51. "Llegados alla con la buenaventura, lo primero que se ha de fazer es pone nombre general a toda la tierra general, a las ciudades e villa e logares," Ynstrucción para el Gobernador de Tierra Firme (Pedrarias Dávila), 4 August 1513, in Serrano y Sanz 1916, 1:279–84, esp. 280. Bernal Díaz del Castillo ([1633] 1960) cites literally hundreds of instances of renaming, a point that Ranajit Guha noted while reading Díaz for *An Indian Historiography of India* (Calcutta: K. P. Bagchit and Co., 1988); personal communication.

52. Spanish authorities would sometimes order the erection of a symbolic house and gallows on a hill visible from the ocean in order to discourage other Europeans from entering the territory; see the instructions for Juan de Solís for Golden Castile and lands south (1514) in Fernández Navarrete [1825–37] 1945–46, 3:149–50.

53. On the subsidiary role of instructions to *poblar* even in early agreements, see Fernández 1987; for a later example from 15 May 1522, see Cortés 1970, 165.

54. "Instrucción que dió el Rey a Juan Díaz de Solís," 24 November 1514, in Fernández Navarrete [1825–37] 1945–46, 3:149–50. For French comments on English practices, see Marion 1923, 38–39. Dutch observations are in de Vries 1911, 233, and Van der Donck et al., *Vertoogh van Nieuw Nederland* (1650), translated in Jameson 1909, 309.

55. *Bullarium* 1858, 5:361ff. Portugal received the same rights for Africa and Asia, as well as, it later turned out, a tiny portion of South America that was expanded into the territory now known as Brazil. For the negotiations and intrigue surrounding the acquisition of these bulls, see Giménez Fernández 1944, 171–430, and the critique by Alfonso García Gallo (1958).

56. *Dictionnaire de théologie catholique* (1910), 2:1255–64; A. Amanieu, ed., *Dictionnaire de Droit Canonique* ... (1925), 2:1126–32; *A Treatyse of the Donation Gyven unto Sylvester Pope of Rome by Constantyne* ([1534] 1979). On the clerical origins of English charters generally, see Hall [1908] 1969, 167–77.

57. Charter of Edward IV, 16 April 1462, in Hakluyt [1598–1600] 1904, 2:147–58. Cabot's patents use "grace especial" (3 February 1498) and "special goodness" and "own motion" (19 March 1501); Williamson 1962, 226, 243. The substitution of royal for apostolic authority was common practice in other European courts. The Portuguese kings, when making land grants, used the phrase "de nosso moto proprio, çierta çiencia, livre vomtade, poder reall e aussoluto." Note, however, the omission of "special grace." "Carta de donação de El Rei D. Manuel a Miguel Corte Real," 15 January 1502, in *Alguns Documentos* (1892), 131–32.

58. Real provisión, 10 April 1495, Fernández Navarrete [1825–37] 1945–46, 2:196–99; 8 June 1501, to Alonso de Hojeda (3:99–102); 12 June 1523 to Lúcas Vásquez de Ayllón (3:166–73); Queen to Juan de Agramonte, October 1511 (3:137–40); Instrucción to Ferdinand Magellan, 8 May 1519 (4:123); Cortés 1970, 163. Pedrarias used a white banner; CDI, 2:549–56.

59. See note 51, also CDI, 2:558–67; 3:337; 4:467–70; 5:211–15, 221–29, 370; 10:12–18; 14:128–35; 15:306–7, 320–23; 16:165–373.

60. For some examples of the variety of language used, see Morales Padrón: "Descubrimiento y toma de posesión" (347–48). This often fascinating collection of ceremonies is marred by a misunderstanding of "possession" in sixteenth-century Spanish legal theory. An excellent English-language introduction to the subject is Scott 1934, esp. 116–36.

61. Altamira 1938, 4:5–79; Rubios 1954; Paz 1954; Bullón y Fernández 1933, 4:104–5.

62. Original rationales are in Rubios 1954, 36–37, and Paz 1954, 250–52. For dozens of examples of its use in small communities prior to the discovery of Mexico and Peru, see CDI, 20:14–119. Examples of the text of the Requirement as issued for Peru are in Encinas [1596] 1945, 4:226–27; for Panama, see Serrano y Sanz 1916, 1:292–94, and Fernández de Oviedo 1944, vol. 7, bk. 29, chap. 7; for Chile, see Toribio Medina 1920, 2:287–89; see also Hanke 1938a, 231–48. When no people were encountered, no specific speech was required in possession ceremonies.

63. See the text of an Instrument of Obedience and Vassalage in CDI, 16:142–87. For examples of use, see CDI, 9:30–45 and 16:88ff., esp. 188–207. One interpretation of the reasons for the shift is Hanke 1959, 86–88.

64. Fernández de Oviedo 1944, 131–32; the manner in which the Requirement was read appears at the start of chap. 7.

65. On the strangeness to North American Indians of one form of European speech behavior (preaching), see Johannes Megapolensis's 1644 essay in Jameson 1909, 177–78. On the reaction of the Peruvian Indians to writing, see Seed 1990. Mexican pictographs appear to have been used as mnemonic devices rather than being "read" in the Western style; see Gibson 1975 and Glass 1975.

66. Simpson 1929; Zavala 1973; Sherman 1979; Chamberlain 1970; Colección de Documentos Inéditos . . . de Ultramar, 1 : 105–6.

67. The encomienda received its first legal recognition in the instructions sent to Nicolás de Ovando, governor of Hispaniola, in 1503; CDI, 31 : 209–12.

68. When the Requirement was promulgated, only three Caribbean islands had Spanish settlements: Jamaica, Hispaniola, and Puerto Rico (Las Casas 1986, 2:456).

69. The modern land survey's colonial origin in British India was acknowledged at length in the 1911 Encyclopaedia Britannica but had disappeared by mid-twentieth-century editions. In later editions, the actual historical colonial origins are concealed by apparently neutral descriptive language, e.g., "the land survey is."

70. The remarkable Suma de visitas, the partial summaries in Juan López de Velasco's Geografía y descripción universal de las Indias, and other counts of people are described in Gerhard 1972, 28–33. Similar reports exist from the reign in Peru of Viceroy Francisco de Toledo; see Cook 1981, 7. Their experience in North America did not place the English in contact with sufficient numbers of people, so techniques of surveying remained relatively primitive; see Marshall and Peckham 1976 and Harley et al. 1978.

71. Real cédula a Hernán Cortés, 20 June 1523, in Encinas [1596] 1945, 2:185.

72. Encinas [1596] 1945, 2:186.

73. Winthrop n.d., 7. Similar sentiments were expressed by Edward Johnson: "The Indians . . . began to quarrell with them [the English] about their bounds of Land . . . but the Lord put an end to this quarrell also, by smiting the Indians with a sore Disease. . . . Thus did the Lord allay their spirits, and made roome for the following part of his Army" (Johnson [1654] 1937, 79–80).

74. For its use by Oliver Cromwell, see letters patent for Arcadia and Nova Scotia, 6 August 1656, in Hazard 1792, 616–17.

BIBLIOGRAPHY

Albuquerque, Luis de, and Inácio Guerreiro, eds. 1985. *Actas do II Seminario internacional de história Indo-Portuguesa.* Lisbon: Instituto de Investigação Científica Tropical.

Alguns documentos do archivo nacional da torre do Tombo acerca das navegacões e conquistas portugezas. 1892. Lisbon.

Altamira, Rafael. 1938. El texto de las leyes de Burgos de 1512. *Revista de historia de América* 4:5–79.

Amanieu, A., ed. 1925. *Dictionnaire de Droit Canonique . . .* Paris: Letouzey et Ané.

Anghiera, Pietro Martiro d'. 1907. *De orbe novo de Pierre Martyr Anghiera.* Trans. Paul Gaffarel. Paris: E. Leroux.

Aylmer, G. E. 1980. The Meaning and Definition of "Property" in Seventeenth-Century England. *Past and Present* 86:87–96.

Baião, António, Hernani Cidade, and Manuel Múrias. 1937–40. *História da expansão portuguesa no mundo.* 3 vols. Lisbon: Editorial Atica.

Barbour, Philip L., ed. 1986. *The Complete Works of Captain John Smith (1580–1631).* Chapel Hill: University of North Carolina Press.

Barros, João de. [1534] 1932. *Asia: Primeira decada.* 4th ed., rev. Ed. António Baião. Coimbra, Portugal: Imprenta da Universidade.

Bataillon, Marcel, and Edmundo O'Gorman. 1955. *Dos concepciones de la tarea histórica, con motivo de la idea del descubrimiento de América.* Mexico City: Imprenta Universitaria.

Beer, George Louis. 1959. *The Origins of the British Colonial System, 1578–1660.* Gloucester, Mass.: P. Smith.

Biggar, Henry Percival. 1924. *The Voyages of Jacques Cartier.* Ottawa: F. A. Acland.

Biker, Julio Firmino Judice. 1881. *Colecão de tratados e concertos des pazes que o estado da India portugesa fez com os reis e senhores . . . da Asia e Africa oriental . . .* Lisbon.

Bradford, William. 1968. *History of the Plymouth Plantation, 1620–1647.* 2 vols. New York: Russell and Russell.

Brown, Alexander. [1890] 1964. *The Genesis of the United States.* New York: Russell and Russell.

Bullarium diplomatum et privilegiorum sanctorum romanorum pontificum. 1858. Rome.

Bullón y Fernández, Eloy. 1933. "El problema jurídico de la dominación española en América antes de las Relecciónes de Francisco Vitoria," *Anuario* 4:99–128.

Camden, William. 1625. *Rerum Anglicarvm et hibericarvm Annales regnante Elizibetha.* London. Translated into English in R. N. Gent, *Annals; or, A History of the Most Renowned and Victorious Princess Elizabeth, Late Queene of England.* 3d ed. London, 1635.

Cartier, Jacques. [1580] 1975. *A Shorte and Briefe Narration of the Two Navigations and Discoveries to the Northwest Partes called Newe France.* Trans. John Florio. Amsterdam: Theatrum Orbis Terrarum.

Chamberlain, Robert S. 1970. The Roots of Lordship: The Encomienda in Medieval Castile. In *From Reconquest to Empire: The Iberian Background to Latin American History.* Ed. H. B. Johnson, Jr., 124–47. New York: Knopf.

Champlain, Samuel de. [1632] 1922. *The Voyages and Explorations of Samuel de Champlain.* Trans. Annie Nettleton Bourne. New York: AMS Press.

Cheyney, Edward. 1905. "International Law Under Queen Elizabeth." *English Historical Review,* 20:659–72.

Colección de Documentos Inéditos . . . de Ultramar. 25 vols. 1885–1932. Madrid.

Colección de Documentos Inéditos Relativos al Descubrimento . . . en América y Oceanía (CDI). 1864–84. 43 vols. Madrid.

The Colonial Laws of Massachusetts, Reprinted from the Edition of 1672. 1890. Boston.

Columbus, Christopher. 1989. *The Diario of Christopher Columbus' First Voyage to America, 1492–1493: Abstracted by Fray Bartolomé de Las Casas.* Transcribed and translated by Oliver Dunn and James Kelley, Jr. Norman: University of Oklahoma Press.

Columbus, Ferdinand. [1571] 1959. *The Life of Admiral Columbus by his Son Ferdinand.* Trans. Benjamin Keene. New Brunswick, N.J.: Rutgers University Press.

Commelin, Isaäk. 1646. *Begin ende Voortang van de Vereenighde Nederlandtsche geoctroyeerde Oost-indische Compagnie.* Vol. 1. Amsterdam.

Cook, Noble David. 1981. *Demographic Collapse in Indian Peru, 1520–1620.* Cambridge: Cambridge University Press.

Cortés, Hernán. 1970. *Cartas de relación.* Mexico City: Porrúa.

Díaz del Castillo, Bernal. [1633] 1960. *Historia verdadera de la conquista de la Nueva España.* Mexico City: Porrúa.

Dictionnaire de théologie catholique. 1910. Paris: Letouzey et Ané.

Digest of Justinian. 1985. 4 vols. Latin text edited by Theodor Mommsen. Translated by Alan Watson. Philadelphia: University of Pennsylvania Press.

Drake, Sir Francis. 1652. *The World Encompassed.* London.

Encinas, Diego de. [1596] 1945. *Cedulario indiano.* Vols. 2 and 4. Madrid: Ediciones Cultura Hispánica.

Fernández, Rafael Diego. 1987. *Capitulaciones colombianas (1492–1506).* Zamora, Michoacán, and Mexico City: Colegio de Michoacán.

Fernández de Oviedo, Gonzalo. 1944. *Historia general y natural de las Indias.* 14 vols. Asunción, Paraguay: Editorial Guaranía.

Fernández Navarrete, Martín. [1825–37] 1945–46. *Colección de los viajes y descubrimientos que hicieron por mar los españoles . . . 5* vols. Buenos Aires: Editorial Guaranía.

Folz, Robert. [1953] 1969. *The Concept of Empire in Western Europe from the Fifth to the Fourteenth Century.* Trans. Sheila Ann Ogilvie. New York and London: Edward Arnold.

Freitas, Justo Seraphim de. 1625. *De iusto imperio lusitanorvm asiatico.* Valladolid, Spain.

García Gallo, Alfonso. 1958. Las bulas de Alejandro VI y el ordenamiento de la expansión portuguesa y castellana en Africa e Indias. *Anuario de história del derecho español,* 461–829.

Gerhard, Peter. 1972. *A Guide to the Historical Geography of New Spain.* Cambridge: Cambridge University Press.

Gibson, Charles. 1975. Prose Sources in the Native Historical Tradition. In *Handbook of Middle American Indians,* vol. 15, pt. 4, ed. Howard F. Cline, 313–15. Austin: University of Texas Press.

Giménez Fernández, Manuel. 1944. Las bulas alejandrinas de 1493 referentes a las Indias. *Anuario de estudios americanos* 1 : 171–430.

Glass, John B. 1975. A Survey of Native Middle American Pictorial Manuscripts. In *Handbook of Middle American Indians,* vol. 14, ed. Howard F. Cline, 7–11. Austin: University of Texas Press.

Grotius, Hugo. 1608. *De mare liberum.* Valladolid.

Hakluyt, Richard. [1582] 1850. *Divers Voyages Relating to the Discoverie of America, and the Islands Adjacent . . .* London.

———. [1582] 1986. *Voyages to the Virginia Colonies.* London: Century Press.

———. [1598–1600] 1904. *Principal Navigations, Voyages, Traffiques, and Discoveries of the English Nation.* 12 vols. Hakluyt Society Publications, Extra Series. Glasgow: MacLehose.

Hall, Hubert. [1908] 1969. *Studies in English Official Historical Documents.* New York: B. Franklin.

————. 1908–9. *A Formula Book of English Official Historical Documents.* 2 vols. Cambridge: Cambridge University Press.

Hanke, Lewis. 1938a. A aplicaçã do requerimento na America Hespanhola, 1526–1600. *Revista do Brasil* 3:231–48.

————. 1938b. The "Requirimiento" and Its Interpreters. *Revista de Historia de América* 1:25–34.

————. 1949. *The Spanish Struggle for Justice in the Conquest of America.* Philadelphia: University of Pennsylvania Press.

————. 1959. *Aristotle and the American Indians: A Study in Race Prejudice in the Modern World.* London: Hollis and Carter.

Harley, J. B., Barbara B. Petchenik, and Lawrence W. Towner. 1978. *Mapping the American Revolution.* Chicago: University of Chicago Press.

Harris, Alexander, ed. 1928. *A Relation of a Voyage to Guiana by Richard Harcourt, 1613.* London: Hakluyt Society.

Harrisse, Henry. [1882] 1968. *Jean et Sébastian Cabot: Leur origine et leurs voyages.* Amsterdam: R. B. Grüner.

Hazard, Ebenezer. 1792. *Historical Collections: Consisting of State Papers and Other Authentic Documents.* Philadelphia: T. Dobson.

Herber, Thomas Arnold. 1891. *The History of the Law of Prescription in England.* London.

Jameson, J. Franklin, ed. 1909. *Narratives of New Netherland, 1609–64.* New York: Charles Scribner's Sons.

Johnson, Edward. [1654] 1937. *Wonder-Working Providence, 1629–51.* Ed. J. Franklin Jameson. New York: Barnes and Noble.

The Journall or Dayly Register Containing a True Manifestation, and Historicall Declaration of the Voyage, Accomplished by Eight Shippes of Amsterdam, Under the Conduct of Jacob Corneliszen Neck Admirall, Wybrandt van Warwick, Vice Admirall, which Sayled from Amsterdam the First Day of March, 1598. [1601] 1974. New Haven, Conn.: Research Publications.

Juricek, John T. 1976. English Territorial Claims in North America Under Elizabeth and the Early Stuarts. *Terrae Incognitae* 7:7–22.

Kantorowicz, Ernst H. 1957. *The King's Two Bodies: A Study in Mediaeval Political Theology.* Princeton, N.J.: Princeton University Press.

Keller, Arthur S. 1938. *The Creation of Rights of Sovereignty Through Symbolic Acts, 1400–1800.* New York: Columbia University Press.

Koebner, Richard. 1961. *Empire.* Cambridge: Cambridge University Press.

Las Casas, Bartolomé de. 1986. *Historia de las Indias.* 3 vols. 2d ed. Ed. Agustín Millares Carlo. Mexico City: Fondo de Cultura Económica.

Lescarbot, Marc. [1611] 1866. *Histoire de la Nouvelle-France.* 3 vols. Paris: Librarie Tross.

Lightwood, John M. 1894. *A Treatise on Possession of Land.* London.

Lopes de Castanheda, Fernão. [1551] 1924–33. *Historia do descobrimento e conquista da India pelos portugueses.* 9 vols. 3d ed. Coimbra, Portugal: Imprenta da Universidade.

Lucas, Samuel. 1850. *Charters of the Old English Colonies in America.* London.

Malheiro Dias, Carlos, ed. 1924–26. *História da colonização portuguesa no Brasil.* 3 vols. Oporto, Brazil: Litografia Nacional.

Marion, Séraphin. 1923. *Relations des voyageurs français en Nouvelle France au XVIIe siècle.* Paris: Les Presses Universitaires de France.

Marshall, Douglas W., and Howard H. Peckham. 1976. *Campaigns of the American Revolution: An Atlas of Manuscript Maps.* Ann Arbor: University of Michigan Press.

Miller, Perry. 1956. *Errand into the Wilderness.* Cambridge, Mass.: Belknap Press/ Harvard University Press.

Monumenta Henricina. 1962. 5 vols. Coimbra, Portugal: Comissão Executiva das Comemorações do V Centenario da Morte do Infante D. Henrique.

Morales Padrón, Francisco. 1955. Descubrimiento y toma de posesión. *Anuario de Estudios Americanos* 12:321–80.

Morison, Samuel Eliot. 1940. *Portuguese Voyages to America in the Fifteenth Century.* Cambridge, Mass.: Harvard University Press.

Nascimento, Tupinambá Miguel Castro do. 1986. *Posse e propriedade.* Rio de Janeiro: Aide Editora.

O'Gorman, Edmundo. 1961. *The Invention of America: An Inquiry into the Historical Nature of the New World and the Meaning of Its History.* Bloomington: Indiana University Press.

Paz, Matías de. 1954. *Del dominio de los reyes de España sobre los indios.* Trans. Agustín Millares Carlo. Mexico City: Fondo de Cultura Económica.

Pereira Victoria, Luiz Augusto. 1970. *Pequeño dicionário de sinónimos.* Rio de Janeiro: Editorial de Ouro.

Pollock, Frederick. 1896. *The Land Laws.* London.

Pollock, Frederick, and Robert Samuel Wright. 1888. *An Essay on Possession in the Common Law.* Oxford.

Purchas, Samuel. 1906. *Hakluytus Posthumus; or, Purchas His Pilgrimes*, . . . Glasgow and New York: MacLehose.

Ramusio, Gian Battista. [1556; repr. Venice, 1606] 1967. *Navigationi et Viaggi*. 3 vols. Amsterdam: Theatrum Orbis Terrarum.

Rubios, Palacios. 1954. *De las islas del mar Océano*. Trans. Augustín Millares Carlo. Mexico City: Fondo de Cultura Económica.

Rumeu de Armas, Antonio. 1985. *Nueva luz sobre las capitulaciones de Santa Fe de 1492 concertadas entre Los Reyes Católicos y Cristóbal Colón*. Madrid: Consejo Superior de Investigaciones Superiores.

Santarem, Visconde de. 1854. *Quadro elementar das relacões politicas e diplomaticas de Portugal*. Vol. 15. Paris.

Scargill-Bird, S. R. 1896. *A Guide to the Principal Classes of Documents Preserved in the Public Record Office*. 2d ed. London.

Scott, James Brown. 1934. *The Spanish Origin of International Law: Francisco Vitoria and His Law of Nations*. Oxford: Clarendon Press.

Scott, S. P., trans. 1910. *The Visigothic Code*. Boston: Boston Book Company.

Seed, Patricia. 1990. "'Failing to Marvel': Atahualpa's Encounter with the Word." *Latin American Research Review* 26:7–32.

Serrano y Sanz, Manuel. 1916. *Orígenes de la dominación española en América*. Vol. 1. Madrid: Bailly-Baillière.

Shea, John Gilmary. 1903. *Discovery and Exploration of the Mississippi Valley*. 2d ed. Albany, N.Y.: J. McDonough.

Sherman, William L. 1979. *Forced Native Labor in Sixteenth-Century Central America*. Lincoln: University of Nebraska Press.

Simpson, Lesley Byrd. 1929. *The Encomienda in New Spain: Forced Native Labor in the Spanish Colonies, 1492–1550*. Berkeley: University of California Press.

Smith, John. [1580–1631] 1986. *A True relation of . . . Virginia: The Complete Works of Captain John Smith (1580–1631)*. Vol. 1. Ed. Philip L. Barbour. Chapel Hill: University of North Carolina Press.

Stevenson, Joseph, ed. 1867. *Calendar of State Papers, Foreign Series, of the Reign of Elizabeth, 1562* . . . London.

Strachey, William. 1849. *Historie of Travaile into Virginia Britannia* . . . London.

Thomaz, Luis Filipe Ferreira. 1985. *Estructura politica e administrativa do Estado da India no século XVI*. In *Actas do II Seminario internacional de história Indo-Portuguesa*, ed. Luis de Albuquerque and Inácio Guerreiro. Lisbon: Instituto de Investigação Científica Tropical.

Todorov, Tzvetan. 1984. *The Conquest of America: The Question of the Other*. Trans. Richard Howard. New York: Harper and Row.

Toribio Medina, José. 1920. *El descubrimiento del Océano Pacífico*. 2 vols. Santiago de Chile: Imprenta Universitaria.

A Treatyse of the Donation Gyven unto Sylvester Pope of Rome by Constantyne. [1534] 1979. Amsterdam: Theatrum Orbis Terrarum.

Trelease, Allen W. 1962. Indian-White Contacts in Eastern North America: The Dutch in New Netherland. *Ethnohistory* 9:137–46.

Verlinden, Charles. 1970. *The Beginnings of Modern Colonization*. Ithaca, N.Y.: Cornell University Press.

Vries, David Pietersz de. 1911. *Korte historiael*. S'Gravenhage, Netherlands.

Wagner, Henry R. 1938. The Creation of Rights of Sovereignty Through Symbolic Acts. *Pacific Historical Review* 4:297–326.

Washburn, Wilcomb E. 1962. The Meaning of "Discovery." *American Historical Review* 68:1–21.

Williamson, James A. 1962. *The Cabot Voyages and Bristol Discovery Under Henry VII*. Cambridge: Hakluyt Society.

Winthrop, John. 1825. *The History of New England from 1630 to 1645*. Boston.

———. n.d. *Winthrop's Conclusions for the Plantations in New England*. Reprinted in Old South Leaflets, No. 50. Boston.

Wright, Louis B. [1943] 1965. *Religion and Empire: The Alliance Between Piety and Commerce in English Expansion, 1558–1625*. New York: Octagon Books.

Young, Andrew. 1844. *Chronicles of the Pilgrim Fathers of the Colony of Plymouth from 1602 to 1625*. Boston.

Zavala, Silvio A. 1973. *La encomienda indiana*. 2d ed. Mexico City: Porrúa.

———. 1988. *Las instituciones jurídicas en la conquista de América*. 3d ed. Mexico City: Porrúa.

6

The Counter-Discourse of
Bartolomé de Las Casas

Stephanie Merrim

During its first fifty years the Hispanic presence in the New World produced a diverse and unwieldy corpus of writings. These writings encompass a trajectory that proceeds from the Creation, with Columbus's claims, beginning in his *Diario de a bordo* (Diary of navigation), that the New World was an earthly paradise, to the destruction and Fall, with Bartolomé de Las Casas's denunciations in the *Brevísima relación de la destrucción de las Indias* (Most brief relation of the destruction of the Indies) in 1542: "[I], friar Bartolomé de Las Casas, . . . go about this court in Spain trying to expel the inferno from the Indies" ("[Yo], fray Bartolomé de Las Casas, . . . ando en esta corte de España procurando echar del infierno de las Indias"; 1987, 174). They take us from the pastoral "barbarism" of Columbus's West Indies to the refined civilization of the Aztecs. Attitudes toward the Amerindians undergo several convolutions. Fray Ramón Pané's *Relación acerca de las antigüedades de los indios* (Relation of the ancient ways of the Indians), of 1498, outlines a policy advocating the forced conversion of the natives of the Antilles; Alvar Núñez Cabeza de Vaca, having shared the Amerindians' lives during his eight years of wandering across the North American Southwest and Mexico, assimilates the ways of indigenous peoples and argues for their humane treatment and peaceful conversion in his *Naufragios* (Shipwrecks) of 1542; the "Protector of the Indians," Bartolomé de Las Casas, laments the destruction of the Indies and their inhabitants in the *Brevísima*. Pané affords his contemporaries and us the first ethnography from the New World, and Gonzalo Fernández de Oviedo compiles the first natural history of the New World in his 1526 *Sumario de la natural historia*

de las Indias (Summary of the natural history of the Indies) as well the first
"encyclopedia," the massive Historia general y natural de las Indias (General and
natural history of the Indies), of 1535, which traces the history, ethnography,
flora, and fauna of all of the New World known to that date. So ambitious in
its intentions, the final version of Oviedo's Historia contains over 2,000 pages;
Columbus and Cortés each spent well over 400 (modern printed) pages in
the effort to keep the officials of Spain informed of their achievements.

This vast polymorphous body of writings nevertheless houses certain very
pronounced constants, both ideological and textual.[1] Europeans all, the writers share a larger cultural heritage—medieval in its religious fervor, Renaissance in its spirit of commercial and scientific initiative, Spanish in its sense of
honor. Each writer, to a greater or lesser degree, has been party to the conquest, and each subscribes in his own way to the goal of the religious conversion of native peoples. Every one of these works thus tells a tale of gold and
souls and provides its own portrait of the Amerindians. Consequently, the
same motifs—for example, of the Indians as tractable children, the New
World as a utopia, contrasts between civilization and barbarism—would float
from text to text, changing meaning according to the context and founding
an image of America for years to come. As they "invented America," to use
Edmundo O'Gorman's famous phrase, these men of arms turned men of letters also showcased their own roles in the events they were recounting. Autobiography thus invades history, and with it self-interest as the historians
wrote relaciones that petitioned for reward and recognition.[2] These "baggy
monsters," the first and hybrid writings from the New World, accommodated
not only history and autobiography but also many nascent fields of knowledge that would later become disciplines in their own right—geography, ethnography, natural history, myth, and so on.

All of these common traits allow us, at least for the purpose of analysis, to
view the historiographical writings of the first fifty years as something of a
textual family whose members at once share certain defining traits and retain
their own individuality.[3] To consolidate and make concrete the workings of
the proposed textual family, this essay focuses on its two outer poles, Las
Casas's Brevísima and Columbus's Diario de a bordo–works seemingly inimical
but curiously united by the contrary and polemical hand of Bartolomé de Las
Casas. Individually and together the two works allow us to form an idea, first,
of the evolution of the writings over the life of the textual family, and second,
of the relationship between its separate members. That is, as Michel Foucault
puts it, to see how they "derive from one another, regulate one another, and
are involved with one another" (1972, 69).

Las Casas's global and synoptic treatise, the *Brevísima relación de la destrucción de las Indias* was written in 1542 to right past wrongs and to promote the New Laws, which had just been promulgated to protect the Indians' rights. To these ends, the *Brevísima* reviews and demythifies not only the historical events that transpired throughout the known New World but also the tenets of the writings (notably of Columbus, Cortés, and Oviedo) that had legitimated them. As the author states, he takes issue with those who "think and say and *write* that the victories they have achieved by ravaging the Indians have all been God-given because their iniquitous wars are just" ("piensan y dicen y escriben que las victorias que han de los inocentes indios asolándolos, todas se las da Dios, porque sus guerras inicuas tienen justicia"; Las Casas 1987, 125; my emphasis). Las Casas's counter-argument in the *Brevísima* derives its vitriolic force by totally and overtly subverting the premises of the putative evangelical conquest. According to Las Casas, the Spanish conquerors, supposed bearers of the Word, have turned the paradisiacal Indies into an Inferno; the Spaniards haven't performed a single redeeming act, nor the Indians a single offense; if there is a just war, it is of the inherently saintly Indians against the "civilized" Spaniards, whose actions reveal them to be totally devoid of reason; service to the Crown under these circumstances constitutes disservice to God; and so on. Moreover, having read Columbus's early writings (see the *Brevísima*, p. 85), Las Casas ironically completes certain of their key assertions, showing how over time they have been taken to their logical—or absurd—consequences. The Indians of the *Diario* "gave of what they had like brutes" ("daban de lo que tenían como bestias"; Columbus 1985, 224); those of the *Brevísima*, in a realized metaphor, are *treated* as if they were beasts. The Indians keep on "giving of all they have," as in the *Diario*, but it is no longer sufficient for the Spaniards, whom the disillusioned natives now clearly understand as not "descended from heaven"—unless it is gold that sits on the heavenly throne. Whereas Columbus insists on his inability to put the new reality into words, reiterating that "this must be seen to be believed" ("no habría creencia sin vista"; Columbus 1985, 223), Las Casas can only repeat that to see is to disbelieve the atrocities that have been committed: "no human tongue nor news nor effort could suffice to recount these shocking actions" ("no podrá bastar lengua ni noticia e industria humana a referir los hechos espantables"; 1987, 105). Las Casas, we see, uses the language of the discovery to express the destruction.

Of equal import is Las Casas's revision of the discursive practices of the historiography of the Indies, a measure of the evolution in the ways of writing history over this period. Distancing himself from the particularized tangles of a history of the New World written from within, such as Oviedo's, Las Casas composes a "most brief summary of a very diffuse history" ("sumario brevísimo, de muy difusa historia"; 1987, 73) from a retrospective point of view. This transition from "diffuse" to "most brief" entails wide-ranging changes in the formal aspects of writing history. Columbus and Cortés, for the sake of expedience, resort to formulaic expressions, using the same descriptive epithets time and again. Las Casas's Brevísima, on the other hand, is entirely metaphorical (that is, repetitive), in its organization, description, and exposition. Flatly, tendentiously, and rather simplistically, Las Casas reduces all spaces and events to a single paradigm of Indian innocence and generosity abused by Spanish brutality and greed. Each section devoted to each territory displays an identical overall pattern: the land is a paradisiacal locus amoenus teeming with people; the Spanish arrive and are received generously by the Indians; they proceed to betray that generosity by brutalizing the natives and sacking their lands. Time, too, signifies not change but augmented repetition, the self-stated "rule" both of the events and of Las Casas's discourse: "And they [the cruelties] are so great, that they confirm the rule that we stated at the outset: that the more they proceeded to discover, and destroy, and lose people and lands, the more remarkable were the cruelties and iniquities against God and his children that they perpetrated" ("Y son tantas, que afirmaron la regla que arriba al principio pusimos, que cuanto más procedían en descubrir, y destrozar, y perder gentes y tierras, tanto más señaladas crueldades e iniquidades contra Dios y sus prójimos perpetraban"; p. 78). Particularity cedes to similarity on the stylistic plane as well in that Las Casas reduces all tyrants to a single model, suppressing the names of the individuals whom he accuses. Further, Las Casas frequently collapses many examples into a few, using a form of litotes, a rhetorical device of understatement—as when he writes: "To these two types of infernal tyranny can be reduced and summed up or subordinated . . . all of the other diverse and varied ways of ravaging these peoples, which are infinite" ("A estas dos maneras de tiranía infernal se reducen y se resuelven o subalternan . . . como á géneros todas las otras diversas y varias de asolar aquellas gentes, que son infinitas"; p. 78).

Most early writings from the New World accord with Aristotle's definition of history,[4] being particularized, asystematic, tales of singular events viewed from within. In Las Casas's effacing of the particular in order to bring to light the general principles of history, we encounter a vision approaching what Aristotle termed poetics. And this fact takes us to the larger, and much-debated, question of the "historicity" or truth value of the Brevísima. For it is well known that as it erases the particular the *Brevísima* also takes egregious liberties with facts and statistics, inflating them and disregarding those not considered pertinent to his argument. In the *Brevísima*, facts become mere stylistic devices, weapons in service of its monolithic vision of the history of the Indies.

Much as these transgressions may appear to discount the *Brevísima* as a history in modern terms, they are in fact the logical outcome of its place in a progression of writings that, with the passage of time, had perforce begun to accommodate new polemics and lines of thought. By 1535 the principal texts that would be used as empirical evidence on the debate on the Indies (e.g., Columbus, Pané, Martyr, Cortés, Jerez, and Oviedo) were in the public domain. With the advent of Spain's theological and juridical renaissance through the efforts of the so-called School of Salamanca, the question of the Indies, and the Indians, moved onto the more theological and philosophical plane that motivates and permeates the *Brevísima*. Las Casas's own thinking on the Indians, it has been established, is largely unoriginal, owing much to the *Relectio de Indis* of Salamanca's leading thinker, Francisco de Vitoria.[5] In his famous lectures at the University of Salamanca from 1529 to 1546, Vitoria disputed the title to the New World granted to Spain for the purpose of religious conversion by the papal bull of 1493 and argued that the Indians should be considered rational beings with the right of dominion over their own lands (see Pagden 1982, chap. 4). Juan Bautista Avalle-Arce's excellent analysis of the license the *Brevísima* takes with history ("Las hipérboles del Padre Las Casas"; [1960]) takes on even greater meaning when linked to this newly critical theological climate. Avalle-Arce argues that in the *Brevísima* Las Casas speaks more as an outraged moralist than as an historian. A moralist such as Las Casas, Avalle-Arce contends, moves within the realm of absolutes. He serves a higher truth—the Truth—and such a truth holds no truck with relativism or nuance. Hence, perhaps, the flagrant liberties Las Casas takes with facts and his disregard of mitigating historical data.

Rather than deny the *Brevísima* any historical value (it is, after all, a *relación*, or report), we might state the following. Monolithic as its argumentation appears, the *Brevísima* is in fact a multidimensional and transitional text, written at a point in which retrospective historical, as well as new moral, practical, and philosophical concerns were coming to the fore and demanding expression. These penetrate historical discourse, open it to new ideas, and render it many-tongued or, to use Bakhtin's term, dialogical (Bakhtin 1981). In combination with Las Casas's demythifying project, and with his telescoping of the "diffuse history" into a "most brief relation," such dialogism may well have resulted in a schematic history that appears to be monolithic but that in fact is clearly, and in determining ways, far from single-voiced or monological.

An inaugural work, the Brevísima opens new paths as wittingly or not it lays the groundwork for the ultimate counter-discourse, the 'black legend' of the Spanish conquest. A retrospective work, the Brevísima closes a cycle of stories that, as mentioned earlier, range from the discovery to the destruction of the Indies, from the Creation to the Fall. In this connection, we should not leave Las Casas's text without registering one obvious fact: Much as the Brevísima demythifies the Spaniards, in equal measure and to the same polemical ends does it mythify or idealize both the Indies and the Indians, representing both in utopian terms, as had, for different purposes but in notably similar terms and language, Columbus in his Diario. At times, in both the Brevísima and the lengthy Historia de las Indias, Las Casas speaks with a voice virtually indistinguishable from Columbus's, in effect turning the language of the oppressor to the benefit of the oppressed. As one of many examples, we take this passage from the Brevísima, with the idealized characterization of the Indians as well as the hyperbole and superlatives so typical of both authors: "All of these universal and infinite peoples a toto genero were created by God to be the simplest of beings, with no evil or duplicity, the most obedient and faithful . . . the most humble, most patient, most peaceful and tranquil, not rancorous, not quarrelsome, without grudges, without hatred, with no desire for revenge, of any in the world" ("Todas estas universas e infinitas gentes, a todo género crió Dios los más simples, sin maldades ni dobleces, obedientísimas, fidelísimas . . . más humildes, más pacientes, más pacíficas y quietas, sin rencillas ni bullicios, no rijosos, no querulosos, sin rencores, sin odios, sin desear venganzas que hay en el mundo"; Las Casas 1987, 75–76).

On a practical level, the confluence of Las Casas's and Columbus's voices is not all that remarkable, given Las Casas's involvement with Columbus's writings as well as his fascination with the discoverer himself: Las Casas not only composed an abstract of Columbus's Diario (the only copy of the text that we now possess) but also wrote extensively of the Admiral in his Historia de las Indias. In theoretical and textual terms, however, the implications of the overlapping voices are extensive, for they suggest that our cycle should be viewed as a circle, whose seeming beginning in the Diario contains its end. Let us now explore this circular route, with its reevaluation of the "origins" of the writings of Latin America, and examine the imprint of Las Casas's hand on Columbus's Diario. Here we will be arguing that, to understand fully the representation of the New World in the Diario, we must reach a fuller understanding of it as a function of Las Casas's counter-discourse, that is, at least in part, as Las Casas's text.

Our latter assertion is both somewhat unusual and, *latu sensu*, far from original. On the one hand, essential as Las Casas's role in shaping the *Diario* would appear to be, relatively few scholars have concerned themselves with ascertaining the year in which Las Casas transcribed the *Diario*. For those who have, the results have been inconclusive. Since we know that Las Casas spent time at the Columbian library in Seville in 1552, several scholars support that date.[6] Consuelo Varela, on the other hand, places the transcription during Las Casas's years in Santo Domingo, from 1522 to 1536—the same period in which he began to write the *Historia* and compiled material for what would eventually become the *Brevísima*—a theory with which we tend to concur.[7] On the other hand, much attention has been paid to another aspect of Las Casas's transcription of the *Diario*: his honesty. Henry Vignaud and Rómulo Carbia, among others, have accused Las Casas of fraudulently transcribing the *Diario* to suppress any hint that Columbus might have known that he was not sailing to the Indies.[8] We have no desire to take a stand on this important, if endless, polemic. We would, however, like to adduce some basic textual proof in support of Samuel Eliot Morison's conclusion that "the Las Casas Abstract [of the *Diario*] was well and honestly made" (239). First, when one juxtaposes the *Diario* as transcribed by Las Casas with Columbus's own 1492 Letter to Santángel, known as "Columbus's Letter Announcing the Discovery of the New World," which is something of a synopsis of the *Diario* itself, the two texts prove completely consonant in voice and ideas. Even more telling, those passages quoted directly from the *Diario* both by Las Casas, in his abstract and in the *Historia*, and by Columbus's son Hernando Colón, in his *Vida del Almirante* (Life of the Admiral), correspond practically verbatim, with discrepancies conceivably attributable to the copyists. Excerpts from the *Diario* quoted directly by Hernando Colón and paraphrased by Las Casas correspond faithfully in spirit and meaning if not in language. Finally, as an indication of his respect for the original texts, one should note the scrupulousness with which Las Casas demarcates his own interventions both in the *Diario* and in the *Historia*. Las Casas's abstract of the *Diario*, which alternates direct first-person quotations from Columbus's text with third-person summaries of the work's content, consistently and explicitly indicates when the narrative shifts to Columbus's "formal words."

Granting, then, Las Casas a good measure of integrity, we suggest that his imprint on the *Diario* is to be found in other dimensions, in a less duplicitous strategy. Rather than primarily editing the *Diario* with fraudulent intentions, we maintain that Las Casas transcribed it practically and strategically, as most clearly manifested in his use of direct quotations from Columbus's text—quotations that comprise a blueprint of Las Casas's own concerns. Reading the *Diario* in conjunction with the *Brevísima* and the *Historia*, it has appeared to us and to others that Las Casas abstracted Columbus's text in much the same fashion as we take notes on scholarly works for personal use, that is, with a clear eye to our own arguments.[9] The particular phrases, sentences, paragraphs, or entire entries that Las Casas quotes directly from the *Diario* (bolstered and reinforced, we note, by the third-person narration) are those which most transparently bespeak the Lascasian image of the Indies that emerges from the *Brevísima* and other of Las Casas's works. They insistently repeat a select cluster of issues: the Indies as a *locus amoenus*; the natural generosity, meekness, goodness, and physical perfection of the Indians; the ease with which they will become Christians; the greed of the Spaniards in their search for gold; the God-willed providentialism of the Discovery;[10] and Columbus's cognizance of his debt both to God and to his sovereigns. In these topoi of the discovery, we easily recognize the seeds of the argumentation against the destruction. The direct quotations—with their apologies for Columbus, their criticisms of his men, their emphasis on the commercial possibilities of the Indies as a corroboration of Columbus's belief that he had indeed found the Spice Islands, and so on—as well as Las Casas's suggestive comments in the margins, also lay the groundwork for certain pointed polemics of Las Casas's *Historia de las Indias*.[11] This topic merits a study unto itself.

Our brief discussion of the subject should, nonetheless, allow a fuller understanding of the two voices, and from there the two systems, at work in the *Diario*. Through his policy of direct quotation, Las Casas shapes Columbus's voice, and consequently that of the origins. The resulting voice, we have seen, at once responds significantly to Las Casas's personal preoccupations and serves as a model for his own voice in subsequent works. Much, then, as the two voices of Las Casas and Columbus may in effect converge, "Columbus's" voice in the *Diario* is in essence double-edged. By the same token, the *Diario* is what we could call double-directed because it operates simultaneously within the two distinct series of Columbus's writings and Las Casas's. The *Diario*, when viewed within the series of Columbus's works, is, of course, a very different text from the *Diario* when viewed within the series of Las Casas's works, because the meaning or inflection of particular statements changes according to the system within which we, as readers, insert them. Simply put, the same topics serve different purposes for Columbus and for Las Casas.

Though it would be interesting indeed to analyze all the passages directly quoted in the *Diario* and chart their function for each author, here we will limit ourselves to a few pointed examples. First, examples of the change of *meaning* according to the authorial context. In the directly quoted entry of 16 December, Columbus says of the Amerindians, "They have no arms, and they are all naked and with no skill in arms and very cowardly, for three could defeat a thousand of them, and thus they can easily be ruled and set to working and farming, or anything else that might be necessary" ("Ellos no tienen armas, y son todos desnudos de ningún ingenio en las armas y muy cobardes, que mil no aguardarán tres, y así son buenos para les mandar y les hacer trabajar y sembrar, y hacer todo lo otro que fuese menester"; Columbus 1985, 153). Columbus offers this statement, among other reasons, in proof of the easy exploitability of the native peoples as laborers or slaves. Las Casas conceivably quotes it to demonstrate their natural innocence and malleability. Or again, Columbus's observations to the Catholic kings on the ceremonial pomp encountered among the Indians of Hispaniola (18 December): "Your Majesties would undoubtedly be impressed with the status and reverence that all accord him [the "King," or chieftain], since they are all naked" ("Sin duda pareciera bien a Vuestras Altezas su estado y acatamiento que todos le tienen, puesto que todos andan desnudos"; Columbus 1985, 155). Columbus uses this remark to bolster his assertion that the highly civilized Hispaniola is actually Cipango/Japan. Las Casas conceivably quotes it to support his Aristotelian argument that the Indians are rational beings by virtue of their proven ability to form a polity. With regard to the change of *inflection*—that is, the way in which the emphasis or inflection falls on different parts of a statement according to the authorial context—we quote from the entry of 3 December: "They are peoples like the others that I have found and with the same beliefs, and they believed that we came from Heaven, and they give of what they have for whatever is given them . . . and I believe that they would do the same with spices and gold if they had them" ("Ellos son gente como los otros que he hallado, y de la misma creencia, y creían que veníamos del Cielo, y de lo que tienen luego lo dan por cualquier cosa que les den . . . y creo que así lo harían de especería y de oro si lo tuviesen"; Columbus 1985, 138). In Las Casas, the accent might fall on the Indians' intrinsic generosity and naive adulation of the treacherous Spaniards; in Columbus, the word *gold* leaps from the page. Needless to say, each of these statements hooks up with several other codes in each text and could thus be imputed various other motives and meanings on the part of each author.

The above examples give food for thought and, finally, for the conclusions of this essay. Particularly for those of us conditioned by ironic readings of the

Diario, such as Alejo Carpentier's in *El arpa y la sombra* (The harp and the shadow), it is truly intriguing to see a very different text—Las Casas's—emerge from Columbus's "formal words." According to Carpentier and others (see, e.g., Pastor 1983, chap. 1), that which in Columbus's *Diario* may be calculated distortion, self-serving strategy, and bad faith loses much of its duplicitous edge to become in Las Casas's version of the *Diario* a more direct, even noble, expression of philosophy and ideology. Cynical self-interest in Columbus cedes to larger interests in Las Casas. Consequently, what Beatriz Pastor has identified in Columbus's text as the origins of the discourse of colonialism[12] shares the same space as the seminal elements of Las Casas's discourse of anticolonialism. All of this places a final twist on what we might call the "limited economy" of our textual family. As suggested at the outset, it is customary in the early historiography of the New World for topics, motifs, and formulas to pass from text to text, often invisibly changing meaning according to the context. Considering, as we have, the *Diario* as a function of Las Casas's counter-discourse, it has become clear that within this single text the same statements speak with two contrasting tongues. Such a final twist inverts not only the direction of the textual family—its origins are now seen as contrived in full view of the fall—but also an adage that in both its forms describes the production of meaning in the textual family: The more things change, the more they remain the same; and here, The more things remain the same, the more they change.

NOTES

1. I refer the reader to my forthcoming essay "The First Fifty Years of Hispanic New World Historiography: The Caribbean, Mexico and Central America," in the *Cambridge History of Latin American Literature*, volume 1, for further elaboration of these general premises. The present essay had its inception in a paper I wrote for the Forty-first Kentucky Foreign Language Conference at the University of Kentucky at Lexington in April 1988. There I first elaborated the lines of the argument I would follow in the monographic essay for the Cambridge volume regarding the interconnections between Las Casas and Columbus. In the Cambridge essay the reader will find a more detailed and complete rendering of the issues addressed in the present study. I cite from the Arranz edition of Columbus's *Diario de a bordo*. All translations from the Spanish are mine.

2. *Relación* is a generic term for "report." I refer here more specifically to the *relación de hechos* ("relation of acts," also known as the "proof of merits and services"). This humble legal genre rooted in feudalism, the genre of which ordinary people would avail themselves to present their own life stories and legal cases in petitioning for reward for services rendered, held particular currency in early New World historiography. For discussions of the *relación* and its role in New World historical writings see Roberto González-Echevarría's essays "Humanismo, retórica y las crónicas de la conquista" (1983) and "The Law of the Letter: Garcilaso's *Commentaries* and the Origins of the Latin American Narrative" (1987).

3. Walter Mignolo, in his essay "Cartas, crónicas y relaciones del descubrimiento y la conquista" (1982), also views colonial historiography as a "textual family." For his definition, see page 58.

4. In his *Poetics* Aristotle wrote, for example: "Hence also poetry is a more philosophical and serious business than history; for poetry speaks more of universals, history of particulars" (1967, 51). For a discussion of Aristotle's notions of history versus poetics, see Gossman 1978, esp. 8–10.

5. See Carro 1971, which offers a precise correlation between key points of Las Casas's and Vitoria's thinking.

6. The reader will find a summary of this argument in Zamora 1989, 27. The final version of the present essay was completed before the publication of David Henige's *In Search of Columbus: The Sources for the First Voyage* (Tucson: University of Arizona Press, 1991), which also addresses the issues under consideration.

7. Varela (in Columbus 1984, 30) annotates the following statement of the diary entry for 11 October 1492: "What follows are the formal words of the Admiral in his book about the first navigation and discovery of *these Indies*" ("Esto que se sigue son palabras formales del Almirante en su libro de su primera navegación y descubrimiento d'estas Indias"; my emphasis), saying in note 31: "It seems to indicate that Las Casas made the copy of this *Diary* when he was in Santo Domingo" ("Parece indicar que Las Casas hizo el traslado de este *Diario* cuando se encontraba en Santo Domingo"). Admittedly, this is slim evidence, yet I would support Varela's assertion, given that (1) Las Casas began writing the *Historia general* in Santo Domingo in 1527 (as per his statement in the prologue to the *Historia apologética*); (2) he had access to Columbus's writings after he met Diego Colón in Madrid in 1516; (3) there is strong evidence that he transcribed the *Diario* in preparation for writing the

Historia de las Indias (see note 9 below); (4) Las Casas probably had already framed the chapters on Columbus for the *Historia* —for which the *Diario* was essential—before leaving Santo Domingo (see Hanke 1951, xxxv–xxxvi, n. 19); and (5) there is a striking similarity in style and thinking between Las Casas and Columbus in the *Brevísima*.

8. Columbus's lack of prior knowledge of the existence of new lands would, of course, enhance both the magnitude of his discovery as such and its God-willed providentialism. Vignaud's argument can be found in the second volume of his *Histoire critique de la grande entreprise de Christophe Columb* (1911). For works by Rómulo Carbia see, for example, his *La nueva historia del descubrimiento de América* (1936). For a summary of this whole debate, as well as further bibliography, consult Martínez 1955. For further bibliography on the argument against Carbia et al., see Hanke 1951, xlv–xlvi.

9. In this connection Hanke writes, "The world today knows the greatest document of a private nature about the discovery of America, the diary written by Columbus during his first voyage, because Las Casas transcribed it in order to utilize it in composing his *History of the Indies*" ("El mundo conoce hoy el más grande documento de carácter privado sobre el descubrimiento de América, el diario escrito por Colón durante su primer viaje, porque Las Casas lo transcribió para utilizarlo al componer su *Historia de las Indias*"; 1951, lxiv, n. 7). Zamora states that Las Casas "would have made the summary not for publication, which would have been absurd when there still existed a complete copy of the original, but rather to make use of it in the writing of his histories and treatises. . . . The important thing would be to transcribe precisely the passages that would be useful to Las Casas's future writing of his text" ("Habría hecho el sumario no para publicación, lo cual hubiera sido absurdo cuando todavía existe copia íntegra del texto original, sino para servirse de él en la redacción de sus historias y tratados. . . . Lo importante sería transcribir precisamente los pasajes que podrían ser útiles en la futura redacción de las obras lascasianas"; 1989, 27).

10. I believe that it would behoove those who argue for the marked messianic streak in Columbus's early writings to take into account the double voice of the *Diario*.

11. Las Casas's marginalia are particularly telling in this regard, for they signal arguments that would be made repeatedly in the *Historia* and the *Brevísima*. Both a facsimile and a transcription of Las Casas's marginal comments can be found in Carlos Sanz's edition of the *Diario de Colón* (Columbus 1962).

12. For example, Pastor suggests that the *Diario* initiated the Eurocentric historiography of the New World: "It initiates a long historiographical, philosophical, and literary tradition of representation and analysis of the American reality that would be characterized by an exclusively European historical-cultural perspective and by the systematic elimination of the indigenous perception of that reality" ("Inicia una larga tradición historiográfica, filosófica y literaria de representación y análisis de la realidad americana que se caracterizara por una perspectiva histórico-cultural exclusivamente europea y por la eliminación sistemática de la percepción indígena de esa realidad"; 1983, 81). And on page 83: "In the implicit selection of elements that constitute the imaginary Columbian model one finds expressed in a veiled way, and for the first time, the ideological structures that are part of the whole discovery of America and that would give shape to its later development" ("En la selección implícita de los elementos que constituyen el modelo imaginario colombino se expresan veladamente y por primera vez las estructuras ideológicas que están en el origen de la empresa del descubrimiento de América y que van a dar forma a su desarrollo posterior").

BIBLIOGRAPHY

Aristotle. *Poetics*. 1967. Trans. Gerald F. Else. Ann Arbor: University of Michigan Press.

Avalle-Arce, Juan Bautista. 1960. Las hipérboles del Padre Las Casas. *Revista de la Facultad de Humanidades* (Universidad Autónoma de San Luis Potosí) 11 (1): 33–55.

Bakhtin, Mikhail M. 1981. *The Dialogical Imagination*. Ed. Michael Holquist. Trans. Carol Emerson and Michael Holquist. Austin: University of Texas Press.

Carbia, Rómulo. 1936. *La nueva historia del descubrimiento de América*. Buenos Aires: Coni.

Carpentier, Alejo. 1979. *El arpa y la sombra*. Mexico City: Siglo XXI.

Carro, Venancio D. 1971. The Spanish Theological-Juridical Renaissance and the Ideology of Bartolomé de Las Casas. In *Bartolomé de Las Casas in History*, ed. Juan Friede and Benjamin Keen, 237–57. De Kalb: Northern Illinois University Press.

Columbus, Christopher. 1962. *Diario de Colón*. Ed. Carlos Sanz. Madrid: Biblioteca Americana Vetustissima.

———. 1984. *Textos y documentos completos*. Ed. Consuelo Varela. Madrid: Alianza Editorial.

————. 1985. *Diario de a bordo*. Ed. Luis Arranz. Madrid: Historia 16.

Foucault, Michel. 1972. *The Archeology of Knowledge*. Trans. A. M. Sheridan Smith. New York: Pantheon Books.

González-Echevarría, Roberto. 1983. Humanismo, retórica y las crónicas de la conquista. In his *Isla a su vuelo fugitiva*, 9–25. Madrid: José Porrúa Turanzas.

————. 1987. The Law of the Letter: Garcilaso's *Commentaries* and the Origins of the Latin American Narrative. *Yale Journal of Criticism* 1 : 107–32.

Gossman, Lionel. 1978. History and Literature: Reproduction or Signification. In *The Writing of History*, ed. Robert H. Canary and Henry Kozicki, 3–39. Madison: University of Wisconsin Press.

Hanke, Lewis, ed. 1951. *Historia de las Indias*. Mexico City: Fondo de Cultura Económica.

Las Casas, Bartolomé de. 1987. *Brevísima relación de la destrucción de las Indias*. Ed. André Saint-Lu. Madrid: Cátedra.

Martínez, Fr. Manuel María. 1955. *Fray Bartolomé de Las Casas: "El gran calumniado."* Madrid: Imprenta La Rafa.

Merrim, Stephanie. Forthcoming. The First Fifty Years of Hispanic New World Historiography: The Caribbean, Mexico and Central America. In *The Cambridge History of Latin American Literature*, vol. 1. Cambridge: Cambridge University Press.

Mignolo, Walter. 1982. Cartas, crónicas y relaciones del descubrimiento y la conquista. In *Historia de la literatura hispanoamericana*, ed. Luis Iñigo Madrigal, 1 : 57–116. Madrid: Cátedra.

Morison, Samuel Eliot. 1939. Texts and Translations of the Journal of Columbus's First Voyage. *Hispanic American Historical Review* 19 : 235–61.

O'Gorman, Edmundo. 1961. *The Invention of America*. Bloomington: Indiana University Press.

Pagden, Anthony R. 1982. *The Fall of Natural Man: The American Indian and the Origins of Comparative Ethnology*. Cambridge: Cambridge University Press.

Pastor, Beatriz. 1983. *Discurso narrativo de la conquista de América*. Havana: Casa de las Américas.

Vignaud, Henry. 1911. *Histoire critique de la grande entreprise de Christophe Columb*. Paris: H. Welter.

Zamora, Margarita. 1989. "Todas son palabras formales del Almirante": Las Casas y el diario de Colón. *Hispanic Review* 57 : 25–41.

7

Empowerment Through the Writing of History

Bartolomé de Las Casas's
Representation of the Other(s)

Santa Arias

In the sixteenth century, historiography functioned as an ideological apparatus that either legitimated and perpetuated the politics of the state or served as an instrument of political intervention and reform.[1] In Renaissance Spain, the eloquent official historians followed the humanist insight of Florentine historians and politicians such as Bruni, Bracciolini, Salulati, and Machiavelli, who understood the political power of historiography.[2] As Felix Gilbert has pointed out in referring to these Florentines, their "histories serve to strengthen loyalty to a ruler or a ruling family or to stimulate feelings of public spirit and civil pride" (Gilbert 1965, 219). Spanish official historians such as Gonzalo Fernández de Oviedo and Francisco López de Gómara, who dealt with the discovery and colonization of the new lands, wrote colonialist histories that infuriated the intellectuals and clergy who proposed a reformed political outlook toward the Indians.[3]

The Dominican friar Bartolomé de Las Casas became one of the most influential and polemical intellectuals of the sixteenth century through his writing and active political life, both of which challenged the imperialist ideological ground held by the state. His strategy of contention involved not only direct personal intervention in the debates concerning the rational capacity of the Indian but also the writing of theological and juridical treatises, as well as historical works in response to the official hegemonic histories of his political adversaries.

The *Historia de las Indias*, which occupied Las Casas for more than thirty years, sprang from these polemics and was his answer to the moral, juridical, and theological debates provoked by the conquest. Because of its combative yet rectifying character, the *Historia* is a complex work that is not a mere chronicle of discovery, conquest, and colonization. Las Casas took on the role of historian because it legitimated his position as a spokesman for a repressed community and served as a political instrument to denounce state policy and advise the Crown. In doing so, he placed himself and his work in the medieval literary tradition *de regimine principum*, which was perpetuated by the European Renaissance counselors and historians.

Las Casas stresses in his work that he is writing for the well-being of his country. He leaves aside superfluous praise of the Crown, however, a practice he criticizes in the prologue of the *Historia*. But in order both to legitimate his writings and to familiarize the intellectual elite with his version of history, he appeals to existing Christian values and uses rhetorical strategies known to Renaissance literary culture as well as the hegemonic language that he criticizes. His use and subversion, through writing, of the ideology of hegemonic culture is the base sustaining the radical critique that Las Casas presents through his writings. The present essay explores this central problem, taking as its main point of discussion the choices Las Casas made in the representation of otherness and their ideological consequences for his writing.

The description and representation of the discovered lands and cultures and the impact of the encounter with the conquistadors are central issues of the *Historia de las Indias*. Las Casas wants to persuade his designated reader by teaching about mistakes in history, following the Ciceronian idea of history as *magistra vitae*. The writing of history in the Renaissance was a hybrid activity that traversed genres and disciplines. In the *Historia*, the use of discourses such as biography, autobiography, jurisprudence, ethnology, and the sermon are central to Las Casas's reinterpretation of the historical details surrounding the discovery and conquest.

Bartolomé de Las Casas was faced with the question of the Other because of the point of view taken by the previous, colonialist histories. To rectify the historical record, he radically reinterpreted the indigenous culture and rewrote the history of the conquest. Through his writing and personal intervention in defense of the Indians, he contributed to the process of assimilation and acceptance of the Other that was a consequence of the ideological struggle with the exponents of the Spanish colonialist discourse.

Many recent studies have stated that the explorers' first oral and written descriptions reiterated the old themes and general attitudes of the popular culture of the High Middle Ages and of the Renaissance. The sixteenth-century writers' use of conceptual strategies of representation taken from prior literature has served to confirm that the discovery and exploration of the unknown lands did not have a great impact on the intellectual culture of the sixteenth and seventeenth centuries (Elliott 1976, 13; Febvre 1982, 416–17; Ryan 1981, 520–21). This "blunt impact," as Elliott has called it, may be explained by the ideological advantages that inhere in the failure or refusal to comprehend an unknown culture. Simply dismissing an unknown culture as barbaric made the work of the historians easier and assisted the state in legitimating conquest rather than peaceful coexistence. The historians simply assimilated their experiences to the fantastic and marvelous descriptions of the prior antiprimitivist texts.[4] This disavowal of difference flowed directly from the textual descriptions of classical and medieval encyclopedists, which had not accurately reflected actual cultural practices. Historians such as Pliny, Mela, Solinus, Saint Isidore, and Eneas Silvio served as models—both for content and form—for the explorers and missionaries of the High Middle Ages and the Renaissance (Hodgen 1964, 49–74). Oviedo, for instance, whose negative portrayal of the Indians moved Las Casas to write his own history, states at the beginning of his *Historia de las Indias* that Pliny was the model he intended to follow.

Colonialist representations such as those of Vespucci, Gómara, and Oviedo perpetuated the myth of the existence of the "wild man," "savage," or "barbarian" (Bernheir 1952; Hodgen 1964; Robe 1972). This category was used to portray pagans or peoples with whom Europeans had not had prior experience. The existence of the "wild man" was explained by citing knowledge assimilated from classical texts and art.[5] The Christian tradition explained such a condition of man as a direct result of sin (Ryan 1981, 520; White 1978, 151).[6] The wild man lived without civility, laws, or religion. He was the antithesis of civility and sanity, half animal, sinful, heretical, and insane (Hodgen 1964, 17–44; White 1978, 51).

As Hodgen and Rowe have shown, simple curiosity and the reading of classical historians led Renaissance missionaries and explorers to imitate the methodology of those historians in observing and recording unfamiliar cultural practices. Herodotus in particular had written extensively about the customs, linguistic differences, and religious practices he encountered during his travels. He investigated hearsay reports, interviewed eyewitnesses, and always explicitly or implicitly compared the unknown with the known (Hodgen 1964, 21–22; Rowe 1964, 4–5).

The ethnographic dimension of Las Casas's writings arises out of the necessity of demonstrating the rational capacity of the Indian in order to refute Oviedo's and Sepúlveda's propositions that the Indians deserved slavery because they had an inferior culture and committed unnatural crimes (Hanke 1985; Pagden 1982). To do so, Las Casas relied on the description of, and comparison between, Amerindian culture and the Western tradition. The ethnographical aspect of the *Historia*, including the description of the American biosphere, plays so central a part in the *Historia* that, as is well known, Las Casas decided to start another text dedicated exclusively to the study and interpretation of American Indian ethnology, the *Apologética historia sumaria*.[7] Nevertheless, the *Historia de las Indias*, because of its polemical nature and rhetorical strategies, contains much ethnography whose value to the text, and so to his political agenda, is undeniable.

In order to present a plausible reinterpretation of New World history, in which the cultural representation of the Other plays a large part, Las Casas had to justify his undertaking. To do so, in the prologue of the *Historia* he first states his ideas about history, critically assessing the practice of this discipline since antiquity. He then explains what moved him to write, namely, a need to disavow the previous histories and to rectify the historical record:

> With truth alone moving me to write this book, it remains for me to assert that for many years the greatest and ultimate need for all of Spain has been the light of truth and true information about all of the states of this east Indian sphere, the lack of which I have seen. . . .

> Resta, pues afirmar, con verdad solamente moverme a dictar este libro la grandísima y última necesidad que por muchos años a toda España, de verdadera noticia y de lumbre de verdad en todos los estados della cerca deste Indiano Orbe, padecer he visto. . . . (Las Casas 1986, 1 : 12)

Through the entire text, the lack of authority of other historians is called into question, and Las Casas demonstrates throughout the narration his superiority over the others. He stresses his age, his long experience in the New World, and his position as a Christian and a Church intellectual. This influences the point of view he adopts to persuade the reader that his version of history is correct. To establish his authority to write about the culture of the Other, he has to describe his own experiential relation to the Indians. He must show that he has established himself *within* the other culture. Referring to himself in the third person he states:

> and because the Indians saw what the padre was doing for them, defending them, praising them, and also baptizing the children, in all of which it seemed to them that he had more sway and authority than

the others, he received much respect and credit from the Indians throughout the island, and they also revered him just as they did their priests, sorcerers, prophets, or doctors.

> y porque vían los indios que el padre hacía por ellos, defendiéndolos y halagándolos y también baptizando los niños, en lo cual les parecía que tenía más imperio y auctoridad que los demás, cobró mucha estima y crédito en toda la isla para con los indios, allende que como a sus sacerdotes o hechiceros o profetas o médicos, que todo era uno, lo reverenciaban. (2:535)

Las Casas showed that he could write about the Indians with authority derived from the experience of having participated in and identified himself with their reality and, above all, from his acceptance by them. This deployment of personal narrative, a conventional component of ethnographies, serves to legitimate his version of the Other.[8]

Las Casas's historiographic practice consciously manipulates language and narrative structure in order to offer the reader descriptions that range from pleasant, bucolic descriptions of the landscape to chaotic, graphic, dramatic scenes of military conquest. The main characteristics of the ethnographic dimension of the text are the use of descriptive discourse treating indigenous culture and the narration of personal or historical episodes that serve to demonstrate the nature and attitudes of the Other. The narration of these carefully chosen episodes serves to convey a positive image of the Indian and to portray the conflictive nature of the encounter realistically.

The dual influence of classical and Christian myths and the great conflicts and changes that took place during the Renaissance influenced the development of the Christian utopian tradition in Renaissance texts, including histories of the conquest (Bataillon 1982; Cró 1983; Maravall 1974; Zavala 1947). The utopian dimension in Las Casas's representation of the Indian is obvious in his use of the Renaissance literary commonplaces of the noble savage and the Golden Age—previously used by Columbus and Peter Martyr to describe the discovered peoples. This utopian dimension, which has been noted by Antonio Maravall, José Luis Abellán, and Stelio Cró, describes the American countryside as a *locus amoenus* where abundance, peace, and harmony reign. Las Casas evokes Adam by describing the Indian as in a state of original purity:

> ... they went about as naked as their mothers gave birth to them, so carefree and simple, with such nonchalance and simplicity, with their private parts exposed, that it seemed they had not lost or had recov-

ered the state of innocence that our father Adam enjoyed, it is said, for
no more than six hours.

> . . . andaban todos desnudos, como sus madres los habían parido, con
> tanto descuido y simplicidad, todas sus cosas vergonzosas de fuera,
> que parecía no haberse perdido o haberse restituído el estado de ino-
> cencia, en que un poquito de tiempo, que se dice no haber pasado de
> seis horas, vivió nuestro padre Adán. (Las Casas 1986, 1:202)

The commonplace of the landscape as a garden, the belief in a state of original purity and perfection, and the notation of the communal character of
property are the most significant aspects that Las Casas sought to highlight.
Las Casas's description of the New World as an arcadia is found for the first
time in the *Historia de las Indias* when he relates the experience of Columbus
upon encountering land. That description is mediated by Las Casas's own
experiences in the New World, which dominate, clarify, and expand upon
what Columbus encountered.

> The long-awaited day came, the three ships arrived at the shore, the
> anchors were lowered, and they saw the entire beach full of naked
> people, who covered all the sand and earth. This land was and is an
> island fifteen leagues long, more or less, totally flat, with no moun-
> tains, a garden of green trees, very cool, as are all the islands of the
> Lucayos in that area. . . .

> Venido el día, que no poco deseado fué de todos, lléganse los tres na-
> víos a la tierra, y surgen sus anclas, y ven la playa toda llena de gente
> desnuda, que toda el arena y tierra cubrían. Esta tierra era y es una isla
> de 15 leguas de luengo, poco más o menos, toda baja, sin montaña
> alguna, como una huerta llena de arboleda verde y fresquísima, como
> son todas las de los lucayos que hay por allí. . . . (1:200)

The literary images of the classical *locus amoenus*, the Elysian Fields of antiquity, and the Garden of Eden all serve the description of an idyllic countryside. Renaissance Christian authors, including Las Casas, often confounded
pagan and religious literary commonplaces repeated from the Bible, Homer,
Virgil, Ovid, and medieval glosses on the biblical story of Adam in the Garden
of Eden (Giamatti 1966; Levin 1970; Tayler 1964). For Las Casas, the discovered islands have all the attributes of the blessed arcadia. They are "the
happiest and largest, most delightful, rich, abundant, and pleasant of the

world" ("las más felices y grandes, graciosas, ricas, abundantes, deleitables del mundo"; Las Casas 1986, 1:216).

Las Casas describes the social, religious, and political practices of the Indians with the goal of providing an interpretation completely different from that of the colonialist historians. The most notable strategy he uses to describe the cultural practices of the American Indians is to compare these discovered peoples with the heathen cultures described in the classics known to the Renaissance. In order to demystify the colonial stereotype of the Indian as a savage and a barbarian, Las Casas uses the same Eurocentric mode of representation, in which the unknown is compared to the known. He finds similarities between the Indians and the Germans described by Julius Caesar and Tacitus, as well as the African Seres tribe described in the histories of Pliny, Strabo, Solinus, Virgil, Boethius, Pompey, and Saint Isidore:

> Truly, to provide information in a few words about the good customs and the quality of these Lucayos, as we call the people of the small islands, and of the people of the island of Cuba as well, though I still say that the Lucayos were superior to all, I do not find any people or nation to whom I can compare them better than the ancients known as the Seres, oriental peoples of India, whom the ancient authors say are extremely calm and gentle and shun conversation with restless peoples, and who out of fear want no interaction with others. . . . Among them there are no adulterous women nor thieves taken to trial, nor is there ever anyone who kills another; they live in purity, they do not suffer bad times or pestilence; men never touch pregnant women nor those menstruating; they do not eat unclean meat, they never have sacrifices; in accordance with the laws of justice, each one is his own judge, living a long time and going through this life without illness, and because of this the historians describe them as very saintly and very happy.

> Y, verdaderamente, para en breves palabras dar noticia de las buenas costumbres y cualidad que estos lucayos y gente destas islas pequeñas, que así nombramos, tenían, y lo mismo la gente de la isla de Cuba, aunque todavía digo que a todas hacía ventaja esta de los lucayos, no hallo gentes ni nación a quien mejor la pueda comparar, que a la que los antiguos y hoy llaman y llamamos los Seres, pueblos orientales de la India, de quien por los autores antiguos se dice ser entre sí quietísimos y mansísimos; huyen de la conversación de otras gentes inquietas,

y por este miedo no quieren los comercios de otros. . . . Entre ellos
no hay mujer adúltera, ni ladrón se lleva a juicio, ni jamás se halló uno
que matase a otro; viven castísimamente, no padecen malos tiempos,
no pestilencia; a la mujer preñada nunca hombre la toca ni cuando
está en el tiempo de su purgación; no comen carnes inmundas, sacrificios ningunos tienen; según las reglas de la justicia, cada uno es juez de
sí mismo, viven mucho y sin enfermedad pasan desta vida, y por esto
los historiadores los llaman sanctísimos y felicísimos. (1:202–3)

The fragment that Las Casas quotes from Tacitus's *Germania* is important
not only because it confirms his argument in favor of the Indian but also
because it indicates that Tacitus provided a descriptive model for him. Tacitus
contrasted the virtues of the Germans with the vices and corruption of the
civilized Romans, using the literary motifs of the Golden Age and the noble
savage, and indicated the superiority of the "barbaric" culture. In the same
manner, Las Casas opposed the Indians to the Spaniards. The didactic aspect
of Las Casas's work and its critique of moral values made it a model for later
historians such as Campanella, Montaigne, and Lafitau, who also compared
civilization to the natural state of man.

Interestingly, the cultural traits Oviedo uses to demonstrate the Indian's
barbarism and wildness are the same ones Las Casas uses to demonstrate their
rational capacity and superiority to other peoples. The Indians' nudity, religious rites, and lack of private property are reinterpreted to emphasize their
disdain for luxury and power and thus to emphasize their natural inclination
toward Christian values. As in the texts of Renaissance reformers such as
More, Erasmus, and Vives, Las Casas describes the people as preferring peace,
love, and a tranquil life. With the aid of authorities such as Aristotle, Plato,
Albertus Magnus, and Saint Augustine, he shows the superior character of the
Indians' laws and methods of maintaining order.

Las Casas's role as catechist authorizes him to describe and interpret the
religious beliefs and practices of the Indians. It is precisely this aspect of the
ethnographic description that demonstrates the unjustness of Spanish military
aggression and the imperialist justifications that had been presented thereto-
fore. Las Casas stresses aspects that portray the Indian as an easy convert to
the Christian faith and refutes the belief that the Indians are pagans who practice satanic rites. He apologizes for the mistakes of the Indians because for
him they are like children who need to be taught. On the one hand, he rejects
the image as barbarians when he compares their religious practices to those
of the ancients and the earlier Iberians. On the other hand, he notes the simi-

larities between the religious practices of the European Christians and of the Indians. This sort of religious syncretism manifests itself in the reinterpretation of the rites, beliefs, and attitudes that the Indian held toward Christian symbols. Las Casas evokes the conception of the noble savage who, through a natural process, learns the truths of the faith. For example, he states that the Indians knew the place where souls go after death, that they knew about hell and paradise, that they knew of the Trinity and the Deluge. One of the best examples is the episode in which Las Casas describes the Indians of the Cuban village of Cueyba as Christian devotees by narrating how they voluntarily adored the statue of the Virgin left by Alonso de Ojeda. Las Casas commented:

> It was marvelous what devotion they all showed, the chief and his subjects, toward Saint Mary and her image. They had composed songs and motets and other things in praise of Our Lady, which they sang sweetly in their dances, called *areytos*, very melodious to the ear. . . .

> Era maravilla la devoción que todos tenían, el señor y subditos, con Sancta María y su imagen. Tenían compuestas como coplas sus motetes y cosas en loor de Nuestra Señora, que en sus bailes y danzas, que llamaban areytos, cantaban, dulces, a los oídos bien sonantes. . . . (2:534)

We see in Las Casas's description of the contact between the Spaniards and the Indians a dichotomy based on the Augustinian oppositional rhetoric that contrasts good and evil, which was also used by Erasmus and Thomas More. Las Casas accuses the Europeans of abandoning the Christian faith by acting in a way that appears completely satanical. This subversion of the representation—the European as the Other—is a fundamental ideologeme in the criticism of the conquest implicit in Las Casas's writings on the life of the Indian.[9] He criticizes the hypocrisy of the European Christians, just as had Erasmus in the *Enquiridion*, by inverting the religious preconceptions of the European—while the Indians adore the Virgin, the Europeans act like pagans:

> . . . the Spaniards adored two idols in these lands, one greater and one lesser: the greater was the person who distributed the Indians, for whom, so that he would give them Indians and not take them away, the Spaniards made a thousand types of ceremonies, praises, lies and honors, rather than sacrifices; the lesser idol was the unfortunate Indians, whom the Spaniards did not love and adore as people but rather as use, work, and sweat, as one does with wheat, bread, or wine.

... los españoles adoraban dos ídolos en estas tierras, uno mayor y
otro menor: el mayor era el que repartía los indios, al cual, por con-
tentarlo, por que diese a no quitase los indios, hacían mil maneras de
cerimonias, lisonjas y mentiras y honores, en lugar de sacrificios; el
ídolo menor eran los desventurados indios, a los cuales no estimaban
ni amaban y adoraban las personas, sino el uso, trabajos y sudores,
como se usa del trigo, del pan o del vino. (Las Casas 1986, 2:557–58)

The representation of the life and customs of the Indian requires an accompanying representation of the conquistador. Several chapters of the *Historia de las Indias* are dedicated to narrating the voyages and actions of various
conquistadors and important colonizers. Conquistadors and Spanish officials
such as Nicolás de Ovando, Alonso de Ojeda, Martín Fernández de Enciso,
Hernán Cortés, Francisco Pizarro, Vasco Núñez de Balboa, and Pánfilo Narváez are objects of criticism. Las Casas's narration of their lives contradicts the
heroic characters they assume in the official histories.

The use of historical episodes is morally strategic in Las Casas's denunciation of the anti-Christian actions of the Spaniards in the islands. In the second
and third books of the *Historia*, Vasco Núñez de Balboa and his men become
objects of the narration. The description of the Indians they find on the way,
a central aspect of travel journals, is converted into a secondary aspect. The
Spaniards' devastation, deceit, and exploitation is the main object of description. Las Casas turns to the rhetorical method of enumerative pictorial description to represent the evils of war.

The inclusion of the voyages of exploration of Núñez de Balboa serves the
strategic purpose of describing the shock of the encounter between two cultures, particularly for the Indian who has never seen a European. Las Casas
uses the travel motif because it offers him the opportunity to represent, from
a different point of view, the interaction between the cultures through the
narration of the daily actions of the Spanish toward the Indians they encounter at every step. The descriptions include encounters both violent and peaceful, dialogues between the Spaniards and the Indians, and the reaction of each
group to the other. The travel descriptions also serve to treat the lives and
customs of the natives so as to form a basis of comparison and invert the
description made by Fernández de Oviedo and Juan Ginés de Sepúlveda. The
latter, in the *Democrates secundus*, contrasts the Indians with the Spaniards in
order to justify the war on the Indians, "who, in prudence, wisdom, every
virtue, and humanity are as inferior to the Spaniards as children are to adults,
women are to men, the savage and ferocious to the gentle, the grossly intem-

perate to the continent and temperate" ("qui prudentia, ingenio, virtute omni, ac humanitate tam longe superantur ab Hispanis, quam pueri a perfecta aetate, mulieres a uiris saeui, et immanes a mitissimis, prodigiose intemperantes a continentibus, et temperatis"; Sepúlveda [1892] 1984, 33).

Las Casas, in describing the Indians, emphasizes their human qualities in their interactions with the Spanish. Violent encounters figure importantly because they contrast the gentleness, humility, and peacefulness of the Indian with the ferocity of the Spanish soldier. In the narration and description of the encounter between the two, Las Casas ideologically exploits the motif of *homo homini lupus*, that man against man is a beast. In treating the bellicose encounters between the Indian and the Spaniard, Las Casas persistently describes the Spanish soldier as a man-beast at war by using nouns such as tigers, lions, birds of prey, wolves, and serpents and adjectives such as hungry, ferocious, and destructive to describe him. The Indian, on the other hand, is described in biblical terms such as sheep or lamb.[10] This oppositional rhetoric served as a model for indigenous chroniclers in their criticism of the Spanish conquest.[11]

The grotesque but realistic description of the encounter functions as a catharsis for the reader when it demonstrates the total destruction, both natural and human, of Indian utopian society. While Oviedo and Sepúlveda diminish the figure of the Indian in history, Las Casas describes the encounter as the displacement of the morally superior Indian culture by the morally inferior culture of the conquistador.

Las Casas as a historian describes, interprets, and plays with the encounter between the Spaniard expanding his frontiers and the Indian being displaced. The *Historia*, as an amplification of the well-known *Relación de la destrucción de las Indias*, represents the conquistador as a murderer and an exploiter of Indians. The text also stresses the inter-Spanish disputes generated by the struggles for gold and power. Las Casas alludes to political actions and decisions as examples of immorality and a lack of respect for the Crown.

Las Casas's use of dialogue and monologue on the part of the protagonists in his history is among the most effective strategies he employs. Through this strategy he distances the narrator and lets the Spaniards speak and express their prejudice toward the Indians. On the other hand, the Indians' own dialogue or monologue dramatizes their reaction to the Other. Las Casas places the Indian in a position of equality and credibility by allowing him to speak and express his own perspective. This modification of the travel motif allows Las Casas to give the Other his own voice, silenced heretofore. In order to demonstrate the undeserved misfortune of the indigenous peoples, Las Casas, in a chapter entitled "Of the Cruelties of the Spaniards in Dabayba," quotes the *cacique* Abrayba as he speaks to his people:

> What misfortune is this, brothers, that has come over us and our homes? What have we done to this people who call themselves Christians, we unfortunate ones, living in our peace and tranquility and without offending them or any other person, that they have afflicted us and all our way of life and have destroyed and ruined us? How long must we suffer their cruelty, who treat and persecute us so perniciously?

> ¿Qué desventura es ésta, hermanos, que ha venido sobre nosotros y nuestras casas? ¿Qué habemos hecho a esta gente que se llaman cristianos, desdichados de nosotros, que viviendo en nuestra paz y tranquilidad y sin ofender a ellos ni a otra persona alguna, así nos han tornado afligido, y, de toda nuestra orden de vivir hecho ajenos y desvaratados? ¿Hasta cuándo habemos de sufrir la crueldad déstos, que tan perniciosamente nos tratan y persiguen? (Las Casas 1986, 2:581)

As we see, the authority of the text resides not only in the role of the narrator as participant-observer, as it does in all ethnography, but also in the authority of the voice of the Other. Las Casas gives free rein to the latter voice in order to strengthen his political and cultural critique. To dramatize the anguish that only the Indian can describe, the text is converted into a testimonial instrument of the Indian, converting the subjectivity of the voice of the Other into a form of authority that gives more force and power to the *Historia*. James Clifford, in his studies of ethnographic discourse, suggests that this dialogic aspect assures the authority of an ethnographic narrative, discrediting the traditional monologue of control. He states that the ethnographer alternates strategies of authority to convince (and thus is not merely a translator who describes the culture of the Other) and acts as a medium who records his own experience, other texts, and the historical context. According to Clifford: "It becomes necessary to conceive ethnography, not as the experience and interpretation of a circumscribed 'other' reality, but rather as a constructive negotiation involving at least two, and usually more, conscious, politically significant subjects" (1983, 133).

As we have seen, Las Casas emphasizes the abundance, order, and peacefulness of pre-Hispanic life and contrasts these qualities with the disorder caused by the Spanish on their arrival in the New World. The Renaissance literary commonplaces of the noble savage and the Golden Age function as nostalgic images of a destroyed paradise that contrasts with the corrupt world of the European. By including ethnographic details in his history, Las Casas demarginalizes the figure of the Indian and delegitimates the official stereotype based on a negative and deformed portrayal of the Other. The most revealing aspect is how the representation of the Other is expanded to include the description and evaluation of the life of the conquistador. With this Las Casas subverts the colonialist representation of the official historical discourse and represents the Spaniard as the only "wild man" lacking religion and law in the new lands. As Rolena Adorno (1988, 64–66) demonstrates in her discussion of the indigenous chronicles, the ideological function of such a subversion is the integration of the colonial subject into history and the deauthorization of colonial power that official versions of history seek to legitimate.

According to Homi Bhabha (1986, 171), the state justifies its colonial domination through official knowledge that allegedly gives it unique access to the Other. He also stresses that colonial discourse negates the capacity for self-government, independence, and civilization and gives unique authority to the official version of history and the mission of colonial power. When Las Casas re-presents the Indian, he calls into question the satanic and chaotic description of the official version and subverts it by describing the superior moral position of the Indian. As we have seen, he rejects the differences in customs, cultural values, religious practices, modes of production, and even race. With the positive representation of the Indian, he identifies the Other as those Europeans who fail to aspire to an ideal Christian status and denies and demystifies the extraneous and unknown otherness that had been attributed to the Indian. When Las Casas eliminated that otherness by acknowledging the "savage" peoples already known to the European, he replaced it with the representation of the colonizer. The Spaniard, in the *Historia*, is converted by means of his anti-Christian practices in the New World into that savage and barbaric Other that the Renaissance reader could recognize.

NOTES

1. My conception of ideological apparatus derives from Althusser 1971. Althusser points out that "the reproduction of labour power requires not only a reproduction of its skills, but also, at the same time, a reproduction of its submission to its rules of the established order, i.e., a reproduction of submission to the ruling ideology for the workers." Ideological state apparatuses

include institutions such as the Church, the army, the judicial system, and the universities that perpetuate the ideology of the state.

2. Ottavio di Camilo (1976), taking into consideration the manuscripts, books, and translations found in the inventories of Spanish libraries, has suggested that fifteenth-century Spain was influenced greatly by the humanist movement of the Italian Renaissance.

3. Homi Bhabha (1986, 171) defines the concept of colonial discourse as "racist stereotypical discourse [which] inscribes a form of governmentality that is informed by a productive splitting in its constitution of knowledge and exercise of power. Some of its practices recognize the differences of race, culture, history as elaborated by stereotypical knowledge, racial theories, and administrative colonial experience, and on that basis institutionalize a range of political and cultural ideologies that are prejudicial, discriminatory, vestigial, archaic, 'mythical' and, crucially, are recognized as being so."

4. The studies of Arthur Lovejoy (1935) and George Boas differentiate between primitivist, or antisavage, thought and antiprimitivist thought—a distinction used in contemporary studies of Renaissance texts. Their classification has been used particularly in the analysis of the first textual and artistic descriptions of the New World and of the more conflictive historical texts such as those of Oviedo, Gómara, Sepúlveda, Las Casas, Acosta, and Sahagún.

5. On the representation of Indians in art, see Hugh Honour 1975, 53–83.

6. Las Casas believed in the existence of the "wild man," following Saint Augustine. His apparent goal was to make those around him understand that the Amerindian did not fit within the category.

7. The possible influence of Sepúlveda's writing and of the debate in Valladolid in 1550 on the *Apologética historia sumaria* has been the subject of a lengthy disagreement. See the prologue in O'Gorman 1967 for a summary of the debate on the origins of the text. See also Pagden 1982, 119–45.

8. See Pratt 1986, 27–50, for a discussion of the function of personal narrative in ethnographies and travel journals.

9. In the second semantic horizon, the object of study is the ideologeme or the ideological motif, defined as the "smallest intelligible unit of the essentially antagonistic collective discourses of social classes." According to Jameson (1981, 87), its essential structural characteristic may be described as its capacity to manifest itself both as a pseudo-idea—a system of beliefs or a conceptual system, an abstract value, an opinion, or a prejudice—and as a proto-narrative, a type of class fantasy about the collective character of the

oppositional classes. The ideologeme is the basic material used to construct the cultural text.

10. This oppositional rhetoric, which we find throughout Las Casas's work, has been analyzed by Avalle-Arce (1960, 33–55) with respect to the *Relación de la destrucción de las Indias*. His article is one of the few studies that analyzes this aspect of Las Casas's language.

11. See the analysis by Adorno (1986, 126) of the use of such oppositional rhetoric by Guaman Poma de Ayala in the *Primer nueva crónica y buen gobierno*.

BIBLIOGRAPHY

Adorno, Rolena. 1986. *Guaman Poma: Writing and Resistance in Colonial Peru*. Austin: University of Texas Press.

———. 1988. El sujeto colonial y la construcción cultural de la alteridad. *Revista de crítica literaria hispanoamericana* 28:55–68.

Althusser, Louis. 1971. Ideology and Ideological State Apparatuses. In *Lenin and Philosophy and Other Essays*, 127–86. New York: Monthly Review Press.

Antelo, Antonio. 1975. El mito de la edad de oro en las letras hispanoamericanas del siglo XVI. *Thesaurus* 30:81–112.

Avalle-Arce, Juan. 1960. Las hipérboles del Padre las Casas. *Revista de la Facultad de Humanidades de Universidad Autónoma de San Luis de Potosí* 1:33–55.

Bataillon, Marcel. 1982. *Erasmo y España*. 2d ed. Mexico City: Fondo de Cultura Económica.

Bernheir, Richard. 1952. *The Wild Men of the Middle Ages: A Study in Art, Sentiment and Demonology*. Cambridge, Mass.: Harvard University Press.

Bhabha, Homi K. 1986. The Other Question: Difference, Discrimination and the Discourse of Colonialism. In *Literature, Politics and Theory*, ed. Francis Baker et al., 148–72. London: Methuen.

Camilo, Ottavio di. 1976. *El humanismo castellano del siglo XV*. Madrid: Fernando Torres.

Clifford, James. 1983. On Ethnographic Authority. *Representations* 1:118–42.

———. 1986. On Ethnographic Allegory. In *Writing Culture: The Poetics and Politics of Ethnography*, ed. James Clifford and George E. Marcus, 98–121. Berkeley: University of California Press.

Cró, Stelio. 1983. *Realidad y utopía en el descubrimiento y conquista de la América Hispana*. Troy, Mich.: International Book Publishers.

Elliott, John H. 1970. The Problem of Assimilation. In his *The Old World and the New*, 1492–1650, 28–53. Cambridge: Cambridge University Press.

———. 1976. Renaissance Europe and America: A Blunted Impact? In *First Images of America*, ed. Fredi Chiappelli, 1:11–23. Berkeley: University of California Press.

Febvre, Lucien. 1982. *The Problem of Unbelief in the Sixteenth Century*. Cambridge, Mass.: Harvard University Press.

Giamatti, Bartlett. 1966. *The Earthly Paradise and the Renaissance Epic*. Princeton, N.J.: Princeton University Press.

Gilbert, Felix. 1965. *Machiavelli and Guicciardini: Politics and History in Sixteenth Century Florence*. Princeton, N.J.: Princeton University Press.

Hanke, Lewis. 1959. *Aristotle and the American Indians*. Bloomington: Indiana University Press.

———. 1968. Bartolomé de las Casas: El antropólogo. In *Estudios sobre Bartolomé de las Casas*, ed. Lewis Hanke, 207–30. Caracas: Universidad Central de Venezuela.

———. 1985. *La humanidad es una*. 2d ed. Mexico City: Fondo de Cultura Económica.

Hodgen, Margaret. 1964. *Early Anthropology in the Sixteenth and Seventeenth Centuries*. Philadelphia: University of Pennsylvania Press.

Honour, Hugh. 1975. *The New Golden Land: European Images of America from the Discoveries to the Present Time*. New York: Pantheon Books.

Hulme, Peter. 1986. *Colonial Encounters: Europe and the Native Caribbean*. London: Methuen.

Jameson, Fredric. 1981. *The Political Unconscious: Narrative as a Socially Symbolic Act*. Ithaca, N.Y.: Cornell University Press.

Las Casas, Bartolomé de. 1967. *Apologética historia sumaria*, ed. Edmundo O'Gorman. 2 vols. 3d ed. Mexico City: Instituto de Investigaciones Históricas de la Universidad Nacional Autónoma.

———. 1986. *Historia de las Indias*, ed. Agustín Millares Carlo. 3 vols. 2d ed. Mexico City: Fondo de Cultura Económica.

Levin, Harry. 1970. *The Myth of the Golden Age in the Renaissance*. London: Faber and Faber.

Lovejoy, Arthur O., et al., eds. 1935. *The Documentary History of Primitivism and Related Ideas*. Baltimore: Johns Hopkins University Press.

Maravall, José Antonio. 1974. Utopía y primitivismo en el pensamiento de Las Casas. *Revista de Occidente* 141:311–84.

Momigliano, Arnaldo. 1977. *Essays in Ancient and Modern Historiography.* Middletown, Conn.: Wesleyan University Press.

Pagden, Anthony. 1982. *The Fall of the Natural Man: The American Indian and the Origins of Comparative Ethnology.* Cambridge: Cambridge University Press.

Pratt, Mary Louise. 1986. Fieldwork of Commonplaces. In *Writing Culture: The Poetics and Politics of Ethnography,* ed. James Clifford and George E. Marcus, 27–50. Berkeley: University of California Press.

Robe, Stanley L. 1972. Wild Men and Spain's Brave New World. In *The Wild Man Within,* ed. Edward Dudley and Maximilian E. Novak, 39–56. Pittsburgh: University of Pittsburgh Press.

Rowe, John H. 1964. Ethnography and Ethnology in the Sixteenth Century. *Kroeber Anthropological Society Papers* 30:1–19.

Ryan, Michael T. 1981. Assimilating New Worlds. *Comparative Studies in Society and History* 23:519–38.

Sepúlveda, Juan Ginés de. [1892] 1984. *Democrates secundus.* Madrid: Instituto Francisco de Vitoria.

Tayler, Edward William. 1964. *Nature and Art in Renaissance Literature.* New York: Columbia University Press.

Weckmann, Louis. 1967. The Middle Ages in the Conquest of America. In *History of Latin American Civilization,* ed. Lewis Hanke, 10–22. Boston: Little, Brown and Company.

White, Hayden. 1978. The Forms of Wildness: Archaelogy of an Idea. In his *Tropics of Discourse,* 150–82. Baltimore: Johns Hopkins University Press.

Zavala, Silvio. 1947. The American Utopia of the Sixteenth Century. *Huntington Library Quarterly* 4:537–47.

———. 1965. *La utopía de Tomás Moro en la Nueva España.* Mexico City: Editorial Porrúa.

III Decoding the New World

8

The Representation of New World Phenomena

Visual Epistemology and Gonzalo Fernández de Oviedo's Illustrations

Kathleen A. Myers

The early chroniclers of America share a common dilemma in writing about the New World: How does one convey the experience and novelty of America to the Old World? Edmundo O'Gorman has suggested that chroniclers and cosmographers "invented" America by constructing an image of it based on a variety of Old World sources and their own observations. This image reflected, among other things, the strategies for describing the New World and how these were linked to the political purposes of the account. Columbus, in his *Diario de a bordo* (1493) and *Relación del tercer viaje* (1498), used hyperbole to describe America as a haven for the Spanish empire's mercantile and religious interests, and invented an earthly paradise with his words.[1] At the same time, however, he encountered difficulty in pinpointing the exact nature of many of the things he saw: "there are a thousand kinds of trees and all bear fruit in their fashion, and they all have a most marvelous scent, so that I am the saddest man in the world not to know them, for I am sure each is a thing of great worth" ("ha árboles de mil maneras y todos de su manera fruto, y todos huelen que es maravilla, que yo estoy el más penado del mundo de no los cognoscer, porque soy bien cierto que todos son cosa de valía"; Columbus 1985, entry for 21 October 1492). Also employing the form of the *relación*, which bases itself on an autobiographical "I" (*yo*) who addresses a superior, Hernán Cortés talks of the indescribable marvels of New World civilizations but subordinates this to his own political purpose: to present himself as a heroic figure, loyal to the Crown, in order to mask his real status as a renegade whose insubordination to Diego Velázquez could be condemned by his addressee, the king. The first official chronicler for Charles V in the Indies, Gonzalo Fernández de Oviedo (1478–1557), who held this position from 1532 to 1556, continues this dual tendency of his predecessors. First, he inscribes an autobiographical *yo* into his history in order to persuade his reader of the credibility of his own words, and second, he comments on the difficulty of presenting his experience of America to the European reader.[2]

Oviedo shared with contemporary writers of America the autobiographical aspect of writing and the dilemma of depicting the New World, but he also significantly altered the relation between these two characteristics. The description of America is subordinate to personal political ends in both Columbus and Cortés, but Oviedo joins the two purposes and focuses equally on them. He persuades the reader that his *Historia general y natural de las Indias* (1535) is the very first comprehensive eyewitness account of the general and natural history of the Caribbean, Mexico, and Central and South America. He argues that his is the authoritative book on America's wonders: "this new and truthful history . . . [of] these wonders" ("esta verdadera y nueva historia . . . [de] estas maravillas"; Fernández de Oviedo [1535] 1944, 1:29),[3] and he viewed himself as a sort of Herodotus of the New World, writing about history, geography, and ethnography.[4] Unlike his Greek predecessor, however, Oviedo was not merely a systematic compiler, commentator, and judge of the truthfulness of previous texts; rather, his own presence and experience are the key to his argument with regard to his claim of credibility (authority) for his account as a truthful representation of the New World. Indeed, compared to other early chroniclers, Oviedo was more keenly self-conscious as an author addressing the difficulty of portraying America, and because of this, his more than 2,000-page account is permeated with passages concerning the predicament of early writers and his own working theories about the representation of America. That the early sixteenth century is characterized as a period of flux in the history of science, art, and representation further underscores the dilemma Oviedo encountered and attempted to resolve in the course of his *Historia*.

Like Columbus and Cortés, who established their own roles in the discovery and conquest as essential to their petitions to the Crown (Columbus as surveyor of riches and potential subjects for the Catholic kings; Cortés as loyal vassal conquering Mexico for Charles V), Oviedo made his role as a witness and writer an integral part of a complex argument in which he proposed that through the record of his own experience he would enable the king to know the Spanish empire, in particular the Indies. As the official chronicler, he constructed an equation in which seeing and experiencing the New World was equal to understanding its marvels and novelties (1:31). His experience as an eyewitness in turn granted him access to the truth and endowed his writing with the necessary authority to produce the official chronicle of America, which would enable his reader, the king, to formulate just laws based on truthful knowledge of the Indies and, upon beholding the secrets of New World phenomena, to praise God. The official chronicler thus places himself as the essential link between America and the king, and by extension God. His words become a powerful tool for imperial politics and the messianic vision:

> It is enough that I, as a man, as I have said, have seen these things for years, shall spend what life remains to me in leaving for posterity this sweet and pleasing *General and natural history of the Indies*, [with] all that I have seen. . . . Your Imperial Majesty . . . has been pleased to order me to write [these things] . . . so that they might thus be included in your glorious *Chronicles of Spain*: by which Your Majesty, besides serving God Our Lord, might publish and make known to the rest of the world all that beneath your royal Castilian scepter.

> Baste que, como hombre que ha los años que he dicho que miro estas cosas, ocuparé lo que me queda de vivir en dexar por memoria esta dulce agradable, *General é natural historia de Indias*, en todo aquello que he visto. . . . Vuestra Cesárea Magestad . . . ha seydo servido mandarme que las escriba . . . assi se vayan poniendo en su gloria *Chrónica de España*, en lo qual Vuestra Magestad, demas de servir a Dios, nuestro señor, en que se publique é sepa por el restante del mundo lo que está debaxo de vuestro real ceptro castellano. (1:28–29)

Yet, just as the laws of the empire were being formulated for the New World in the course of the first fifty years after Spain's contact with America—laws that reflect, at times, the emergence of a broadened worldview (the nature of man and the role of natural phenomena in understanding God's universe, for example)—Oviedo was formulating his own theories and practices for representing the New World and this new worldview.

Although Oviedo's history is a conglomeration of material that reflects both medieval and Renaissance influences and genres, for the purposes of this study I will focus on the manifestation of the equivalence between seeing and understanding and its relation to ideas on visual epistemology during the period. Elsewhere I have discussed Oviedo's use of the dialogue form to present his reliance on eyewitness testimony for his representation of historical events and to explicate his own historical methods.[5] The present study deals with another form employed in the *Historia* and its function: Oviedo's visual depiction of America's flora, fauna, and ethnographic items with his own field sketches and his theorizing on the role of sight, knowledge, representation, and authority.[6] To begin, I examine briefly how editions of Oviedo's history do not accurately reflect the complete drawings and how the sketches have traditionally been viewed by scholars. To understand better the significance of these illustrations, I recall the concept of visual epistemology during the Renaissance and how it affected ideas of history and representation. Lastly, I discuss the epistemological problem that the New World presented to the Old World and how Oviedo responded to this dilemma by supplying drawings, as epitomized by his chapter on the pineapple.

The full impact of Oviedo's drawings has never been completely felt because many of the illustrations have never been published in their original form and because they have been examined primarily for their documentary or artistic value, ignoring their role in the history as a whole. The thirty-two woodcuts in the sixteenth-century editions of the Historia were faithful to Oviedo's manuscript sketches. Most of the illustrations are embedded in the narrative itself and the style is not altered.[7] The majority of the drawings are in the first part of the history, which is more clearly devoted to depicting the natural wonders of America (later parts increasingly focus on historical events), and generally illustrate a single item in a non-narrative context.[8] However, only a quarter to a third of the text and drawings was published in the sixteenth century. Amador de los Ríos's nineteenth-century edition (1851–55) is the first complete edition of the history. He incorporated into this edition Oviedo's extensive manuscript revisions and additions, which included a number of previously unpublished drawings, but he drastically altered the original sketches. Making engravings based on the original sketches, de los Ríos rendered them according to nineteenth-century romantic conventions. In addition, he removed the illustrations from the narrative and placed them in an appendix. Unfortunately, subsequent editions have also followed this practice. Thus, many of Oviedo's more than eighty sketches have never been published in their original form and either have been lost or exist only in manuscript form.[9]

Given that Oviedo's sketches of American phenomena are among the earliest and that more than half of them are not accessible to most readers, it is not surprising that they have repeatedly caught the attention of scholars, though only for brief commentary.[10] In general, his illustrations have either been condemned for a "lack of artistic talent" or praised as among the first to depict "accurately" aspects of American flora, fauna, and ethnography.[11]

William Sturtevant's survey of ethnographic drawings of the New World, for example, lists only six works or artists published before Oviedo's work appeared on the scene. They range from items etched into early maps to a book for Maximilian I with 137 woodcuts of ethnographic items by Hans Burgkmair. By the second half of the sixteenth century there were other illustrators, such as the doctor Francisco Hernández (1570s), who was sent to the Indies by Philip II to report, collect, and draw plants with medicinal value, and in North America, Jacques Le Moyne (1580s) and John White (1580s), who portrayed American subjects with relative loyalty to what they actually witnessed. But Oviedo's work is one of the few early series of on-the-scene drawings of the New World's natural and man-made wonders in the early sixteenth century. Most sixteenth- and seventeenth-century artists' illustrations of America, argues Mercedes López Baralt, reflect the European ethnocentric mentality and serve the political ends of the text. The popular engravings of the New World by Theodore de Bry and family (1590–1634), for example, depict mythologized figures and create narrative scenes that promote the black legend, that is, the portrayal of the Spanish as cruel and inhuman conquerors of the Native Americans. Bernadette Bucher's insightful critical study of de Bry's work (Bucher 1981) analyzes his illustrations as an ethnographic record not of America but of Europe's integration of knowledge about the New World and of the Old World's inability to overcome its ethnocentrism. In doing so, she examines de Bry's illustrations for their symbolic value.

Taking a similar point of departure, I suggest that we leave aside questions concerning the documentary value of Oviedo's ethnographic and botanical illustrations and examine them for what Erwin Panofsky terms the "intrinsic" value of art. In other words, we should move beyond the identification of subjects—and the question of whether an image reflects the actual appearance of the object—in order to examine the basic underlying principles that informed the composition of the drawings, to focus on the ideas of representation.[12] By looking beyond the mimetic value of the drawings and examining them as a system that displays values as facts,[13] we can achieve a clearer understanding of why Oviedo wove illustrations into the fabric of his narrative history and what effect this visual, nonverbal form has on the history as a whole. Oviedo's own musings in his prologues and narrative about his role as official chronicler and the nature of history itself support this "reading" of his illustrations for their intrinsic value.

Throughout the *Historia* Oviedo asserts that his work follows the criterion of truth, that is, truth as linked with the sense of sight and therefore defined primarily as documentable fact rather than truth as solely moral or artistic truth. He maintains that if one has witnessed an event or experienced the nature of the New World firsthand, one may write about it with authority. In the general prologue to the *Historia*, Oviedo affirms: "the blind man cannot distinguish colors, nor can one who is absent bear witness to these matters like one who sees them" ("ni el ciego sabe determinar colores, ni el ausente assi testificar estas materias, como quien las mira"; 1:29). Oviedo perceived his role as author to be one in which he transcribed eyewitness experiences in order to give an accurate and authoritative image of Europe's encounter with America. To accomplish his purpose, he employed various modes of representation in his history, such as letters, dialogues, and drawings. He struggled to make his words and drawings the signs of things themselves; he strove to select a suitable mode of representation and an appropriate order for his material in order to reflect reality in his history, to serve as a mirror of the Indies that would inform the king and further the messianic mission of Spain's imperial destiny. Oviedo asserts that his experience and his words are to serve as the eyes for his most direct reader, the king, and by extension, his European readers: "I collected all that I write here in the course of two million trials and privations and dangers through twenty-two years and more that I have seen and experienced these things firsthand while serving my God and king in these lands of the Indies" ("yo acumulé todo lo que aqui escribo de dos millones de trabajos y nescessidades é peligros en veynte é dos años é mas que ha que veo y experimento por mi persona estas cosas, sirviendo a Dios é á mi rey en estas Indias"; 1:32–33).

When Oviedo set out to order and to record the nature and events of America, however, he encountered a difficult question, one that writers before him had also confronted: How can a European traveler write about a world in which European words and analogues are inadequate to convey its essence? Oviedo set forth this problem when he wrote:

> What mortal wit might comprehend such a diversity of languages, of costumes, and of customs among these men of the Indies? Such a variety of animals, both domestic and wild? Such an untilled wilderness of trees, abundant in their many kinds and fruits, and still others that are barren, and those too that are cultivated by the Indians, along with those that Nature itself produces with no help from human hands?

> ¿Quál ingenio mortal sabrá comprehender tanta diversidad de lenguas, de hábitos, de costumbres en los hombres destas Indias? Tanta varie-

dad de animales, assi domésticos como salvajes y fieros? Tanta multi-
tud innarrable de árboles, copiosos de diversos géneros de fructas, y
otros estériles, assi de aquellos que los indios cultivan, como delos
que la natura de su propio oficio produce, sin ayuda de manos mor-
tales? (1:27)

Such a proliferation of unfamiliar natural objects, languages, and customs
made the chronicler's task a difficult one. Furthermore, how does the historian who asserts that "without doubt the eyes are a great part of our intelligence of these things" ("sin dubda los ojos son mucha parte de la informa-
çion destas cosas"; 2:246) endow his text with the necessary authority for his
reader to participate in the sight and experience, and therefore the knowledge, of the New World? Reflecting on this problem, Oviedo echoes Pliny the
Elder, his most direct model for the external organization of his history (he
borrowed Pliny's title, geographical organization, and scientific taxonomy):
"It is difficult to make old things new, and to give authority to new ones" ("Es
cosa dificil hacer las cosas viejas nuevas, é á las nuevas dar auctoridad"), but
he then asserts, "Let the reader be satisfied that what I have seen and experienced at great risk, he enjoys and comes to know with none at all" ("Con-
téntese el lector con que lo que yo he visto y experimentado con muchos
peligros; lo goza él y sabe sin ninguno"; 1:32).[14]
    At the heart of this dynamic lies the epistemological and linguistic prob-
lems the New World presented to the Old. How does one know the New
World, and how does one portray it? Oviedo's task thus becomes one in
which American phenomena are simultaneously placed within the European
conventions for the representation of known objects and practices and also
described as something completely new. The sheer number of terms he borrowed from Amerindian languages rather than creating a semantic shift (a
word based on a European word) demonstrates Oviedo's response to no-
menclatorial pressure, "an immediate cognitive pressure" (Tuttle 1976, 603).
Oviedo's explanation for his practice once again is found in the opening prologue, and we see his dilemma about how to establish the authority of his
account:

If some strange and barbarous words be found here, the cause is the
novelty which they describe; and let no one question my good, plain
language, for I was born in Madrid and raised in the royal house and
have spoken with noble folk, and have read somewhat. Thus let it
not be suspected that I have mistaken the foreign words for my own
Castilian tongue, which is held to be best of all the vulgar languages.

Whatever terms in this volume do not accord with Castilian are names
or words put there to indicate those things that the Indians refer to by
those names.

Si algunos vocablos extraños é bárbaros aqui se halláren, la causa es la
novedad, de que se tracta; y no se pongan a la cuenta de mi romance,
que en Madrid nascí y en la casa real me crié y con gente noble he
conversado, é algo leydo, para que se sospeche que avré entendido mi
lengua castellano, la qual de las vulgares, se tiene por la mejor de todas; y lo que oviere en este volúmen que con ella no consuene, serán
nombres ó palabras puestas, para dar a entender las cosas que por ellas
quieren los indios significar. (1:31–32)

Oviedo strove to formulate new methods and forms to present his material. Many scholars argue that, to Oviedo, content was more important than
form (see Gerbi 1985 and Salas 1959), but I believe that, like many of his
Renaissance contemporaries, he was acutely aware of the interrelatedness of
form and content. Indeed, Oviedo's encounter with America forced him to
probe the limits of previous practices of representation, which were based on
the authority of written material, and to devise alternate strategies that would
include his own experience. Therefore, according to Oviedo, a new approach
to the concept of knowledge and its written expression had to be devised.
This search for a new method of recording history resulted in a renewed
interest by many in the Greek sense of the historian as "an individual who
sees and who recounts from the starting point of his own experience and
sight" (Franklin 1979, 130). While the role of sight in the apprehension of
knowledge was a common medieval topos, passages of Oviedo's history
show signs of moving away from medieval theories of visual epistemology
and practices of representation, and toward a new form of expression inspired by the works of classical antiquity and the emerging emphasis on empiricism and natural observation.

Oviedo lived in a time of change, change from a medieval view of the world
and its limits to a worldview increasingly based on experience and natural
observation, which was encouraged by the new, seemingly limitless, wonders
of the discovery of "one half" (una mitad) of the world, of which the authorities of classical antiquity "were ignorant, and which we see" ("ignoraron ellos
é vemos nosotros"; 2:198). In explaining the enormous task of writing about
this New World, Oviedo says: "I find myself almost standing on the threshold

of the innermost essence of the great and numberless secrets that are yet to be known in this second hemisphere" ("véome quassi al principio de la medula de los grandes é innumerables secretos que están por saberse del segundo hemispherio"; 11:5). The *Historia* manifests tendencies of both these worlds—the old and the new, the Middle Ages and the Renaissance—but the passages dedicated to reproducing visual images in the form of drawings and the verbal explanations of the items more clearly illuminate the Renaissance tendencies of the history as an empirical study than the medieval character of the history as a composite of previously written texts and information.

As Forrest Robinson notes in his study *The Shape of Things Known*, medieval scholars saw the universe as "reducible to a series of spatial relationships that may be reproduced in abstract pictures" (1972, 29). In this view, all material things, including art, thus hold a symbolic value. Accordingly, they attributed to the sense of sight a symbolic rather than an empirical value in apprehending knowledge and truth. For example, the revelation of truth—in particular, truth as God—was often described as coming in the form of light or a vision (Robinson 1972, 58). Likewise, medieval histories used historical events to illustrate God's judgment of people; history was considered a symbolic record of this judgment.

With the reinterpretation of the works of classical antiquity and the new focus on erudition and empiricism in the Renaissance, traditional theories about the relationship between the sense of sight and knowledge, and therefore the role of sight in art and history, shifted in emphasis. The focus "turned away from the divine itself and toward the divine found in nature," which encouraged a view of truth as quantifiable and based on the observation of nature (Robinson 1972, 59). The association of knowledge with the sense of sight had originated in Plato's theory of knowledge, and it was elaborated by Aristotle and Cicero (the latter being one of Oviedo's models). Both Plato and Aristotle, in their attempts to bridge the gap between the human mind and the external world, resorted to explaining the phenomenon of knowing as integral to sight but sight as linked to the intellect. Pliny summed up the classical view of visual epistemology: "The mind is the real instrument of sight and observation, the eyes act as a sort of vessel receiving and transmitting the visible portion of the consciousness" (quoted in Robinson 1972, 18). According to classical authors, then, the equation of seeing and knowing was largely figurative. Renaissance scholars, in reading and reevaluating the works of these authors, both revitalized and changed this formula.

The tradition of visual epistemology came to be taken more literally in the Renaissance. With the new emphasis on empiricism, a new relationship emerged between vision and the apprehension of knowledge. Renaissance artists and scientists sought truth in the observation of nature and experimented with mathematical relationships that placed objects in spatial relationships that attempted to reflect how things are perceived by the eye but that were also linked to the intellect, or the mind's eye. Using geometry, emblems, and images, they asserted that a direct relationship existed between a pictorial image and a higher reality—whether it was the Aristotelian concept that artists give expression to forms of nature or the Neoplatonic belief in the ideal, of Ideas within the mind. In turn, the belief that truth and knowledge are apprehended primarily through the sensation of sight influenced theories of perspective and representation. For example, Leon Alberti developed three-point perspective to create the illusion of three-dimensions and developed practices in which ideological points could be made with perspective.[15]

A parallel tendency emerged in Renaissance historical writing, in which a new emphasis on the role of perspective in examining the past resulted in a distancing from the events that permitted sixteenth-century interpreters of classical antiquity to allow for the particular—in other words, to see history not as a record of judgment but as a window onto a unique society at a specific time. Such a view contributed particularity and relativism to histories of the period, yet it did not deny a Christian framework or worldview. Along with the lively debates about the essence of truth, fiction, and history at the turn of the sixteenth century, the emerging concepts of perspective and relativity gave new importance to the role of sight and individual experience—for the author/artist as well as the reader/beholder—in the apprehension of truth and allowed for a new role for the particular in the scheme of God's world. Through his own examination and configuration of experience and experiment, the author/artist played a more important role than his medieval or classical counterpart in establishing truth, which in turn explains the increase in autobiographical tendencies among works of the period. To state it another way, the reliance during the Renaissance on the sense of sight led increasingly to the need for scientists, historians, and artists to experience through observation their subject of inquiry in order to establish their own authority to represent the subject.

The Renaissance impulse to quantify and visualize knowledge encouraged Oviedo to convey through pictorial images—both verbal and visual—what was accessible to him through his sense of sight. Through his drawings and words he attempted to make America comprehensible to the reader, that is, to place it in the mind's eye of his reader. Exposed to the ideas of the Renaissance during his years in Don Juan's court in Italy,[16] Oviedo often employed the strategy of comparing the exotic natural world, people, and artifacts of the New World with paintings and other visual arts of the period. To name a few, he evoked portraits of Suluman Ottoman, king of the Turks, and his head-piece to describe the marvelous feathers of an American bird (bk. 6, chap. 15); the manner in which Spanish painters rendered arabesques and florets to help the reader imagine some Amerindian clothing (bk. 24, chap. 11); and the gilding of a Castilian altarpiece to depict the color of a Yucatán mask (bk. 17, chap. 13).

When both the descriptive powers of words and the evocation of existing visual images fail to present an accurate picture, however, Oviedo resorted to his own graphic rendition of the object with a pen-and-ink illustration integrated into the narrative. Confronted with the inadequacy of language to set forth what he had witnessed, Oviedo employed drawings as a means of rendering the essence of an object for the reader, saying that "without a doubt the eyes play a great part in the information of these things, and given that they themselves cannot be seen or touched, the image of them is a great help to the pen" (quoted in Gerbi 1985, 390). He maintained that if direct observation was the most important element in the apprehension of a new subject, then a simple and relatively unembellished drawing was second best, the reader being, as it were, only once removed from actually observing the thing itself.

Focusing on Oviedo's drawings that depict indigenous objects and American flora, we see that he usually introduces the drawings into the narrative with a rather formulaic phrase or includes a more elaborate rationale for the drawing. The first category typically includes ethnographic objects straight-forwardly and analytically presented. In general, Oviedo employs a composite representation consisting of a discussion of the construction and utility of an item; a comparison with a European analogue; the introduction of the Native American name for the item and a drawing of it (as we will see in the case of the *caney*, hammock, and fire drill below). Oviedo's encounter with America's flora and its representation caused more difficulties because there were fewer analogues and more varieties, and often samples could not be sent to Europe. Thus his composite representation often includes a statement of the inadequacy of his drawings to represent the reality he sees.

After a long, detailed description (one that borrows no less than seven indigenous words) of the appearance, use, and utility—even for Christians—of the hammock, the author briefly introduces a drawing of it (see fig. 8.1): "and if I have been able to make it understood, this bed is of the kind that is

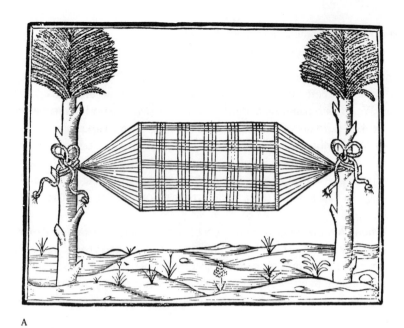

A

B

FIGURE 8.1. An Indian hammock from (a) the 1547 Salamanca edition of Oviedo's *Historia general de las Indias* (courtesy of The Lilly Library, Indiana University, Bloomington, Indiana); and (b) the "Monserrat Manuscript" of the *Historia general* (ca. 1547; courtesy the Real Academia de la Historia in Madrid).

depicted here" ("é si la he sabido dar á entender, esta cama es desta manera que aqui está pintada"; 1:241). Likewise, two pen-and-ink depictions of the native house, or *caney* (see fig. 8.2), follow a long passage that explains, using many Amerindian words, the construction and utility of the houses (bk. 6, chap. 1). They are then compared with the "field tents" (*tiendas de campo*) that Spanish armies carried. Finally, one drawing is presented with a short statement on the purpose it serves: "and that this may be better understood, I give here the manner or figure of this caney, so that it may be sufficiently well understood" ("y porque mejor se entienda esto, pongo aqui la manera ó figura del caney, como baste á ser entendido"; 1:294–95). Typical of Oviedo's method of presenting indigenous objects, he moves from a description of the utility of the caney to a comparison with the European analogue and finally to a relatively unembellished drawing of it. Furthermore, he attempts to make known the variety of caney found in America. Rather than reducing it to a single form, he emphasizes the particular; he not only distinguishes its likeness to and difference from Spanish objects but he also details the many varieties of caney, explaining,

> Because in certain provinces there they have a different shape, and some of these indeed are neither heard of nor seen save in that very land. But just as the shape of the caney, or round house, was depicted, I would like to include the second kind of house that I have mentioned, which is like this shown here, so that the reader may better understand what I have meant by the former and the latter.

> Porque allá en algunas provincias son de otra forma, y aun algunas dellas nunca oydas ni vistas, sino en aquella tierra. Pero pues se debuxó la forma del caney ó casa redonda, quiero assi mismo poner aqui la segunda manera de casas que he dicho, la qual es, como aquesta que está aqui patente, para que mejor se entienda lo que en la una y en la otra tengo dicho. (1:296)

Although these short introductions to drawings appear to be formulaic, a closer look at this device reveals Oviedo's belief in the power of linking a visual depiction with the new name for an object. The equation of seeing with understanding makes a "painted bed" (*cama pintada*) become a "hammock" (*hamaca*) and a "round house" (*casa redonda*) a caney for the European reader/viewer; he links the act of beholding a drawing with understanding its nature "so that it may be sufficiently well understood" ("baste á ser entendido").

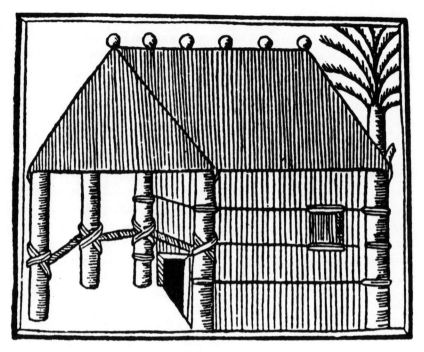

A

FIGURE 8.2. Two of Oviedo's depictions of an Indian hut, or *caney*: (a) from the 1535 Seville edition of his *Historia general de las Indias* (courtesy of The Lilly Library, Indiana University, Bloomington, Indiana); and (b) from the "Monserrat Manuscript" of his *Historia general* (courtesy the Huntington Library).

The representation of Native American objects in drawings aids the viewer in understanding the nature of these novelties.

Whereas Oviedo attempted to delineate the particular qualities of the caney through a composite of various methods of representing it, he inscribed his chapter on the canoe into the works of classical antiquity (bk. 6, chap. 4). The chapter opens with a reference to Pliny's *Natural History* and the "little boats of a single log" (*navecillas de un leño*) that Pliny describes. Oviedo deduces that these must be the same as those he sees on Hispaniola. As with previous descriptions, he borrows Native American words to name the object, "boat" (*canoa*) or "ship" (*piragua*); he explains in detail its construction, measurement, and utility; he employs European analogues, weighing the value of the American object against its European counterpart (*barca, navio*); and he incorporates

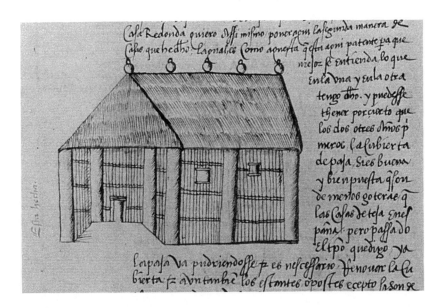

B

FIGURE 8.2. (*continued*)

two illustrations into the chapter "like the figure of it seen here" ("como aquí se ve la figura della"; 1:305); "just as the *nahe*, or rowboat, and the *canoa* are depicted here" ("segund aquí está pintado el nahe ó remo y canoa"; 1:306). The distinction of this passage lies in Oviedo's intent to discuss the texts of antiquity (he mentions Ovid and Virgil, too) and to elevate his own standing and history by comparing his experience to that recorded in written authorities. He asserts that his history is at least as authoritative as those of antiquity, since he can corroborate what they say, and is perhaps more authoritative because his history includes a new discovery for Europeans.

Indeed, the next chapter (bk. 6, chap. 5) questions the need to rely on the authorities of classical antiquity. After Oviedo's typical analytical description of a new item—in this case, the fire drill used in Hispaniola—he introduces a drawing of it and invokes Pliny again. This time, however, the official chronicler questions the conventional method of referring to traditional authorities and instead suggests that the reader play an active role in apprehending the idea of the fire drill:

This [object], at least, to draw fire from sticks, is included by Pliny in his *Natural History* . . . so that what Pliny relates and these Indians do (in

this case) are one and the same thing. . . . But why should I wish to call
on classical authorities regarding things that I myself have seen, much
less for those nature shows to all and are seen every day?

Esto á lo menos del sacar fuego de los palos pónelo Plinio en su *Natural Historia* . . . de manera que lo que Plinio dice y aquestos indios hacen (en este caso), todo es una mesma cosa. . . . ¿Mas para qué quiero
yo traer auctoridades de los antiguos en las cosas que yo he visto, ni
en las que natura enseña á todos y se ven cada día? (1:310–11)

He appeals to the reader's own observation of the sparks that fly from carriage
wheels in motion in order to secure in his reader's mind a better understanding of the nature of the fire drill: "thus, this is a thing commonly seen and
found in nature" ("assi que, esto es cosa que se vé é es natural"; 311). Although Oviedo encourages the reader to apprehend this device in the mind's
eye, based on the reader's own experience, he also acknowledges the role of
the corporeal eye in the cognition of the essence of the object: "Its form is
just as I show in the drawing since, even without the picture, what I have said
is sufficient to understand it. But it is still good to make as much use as possible of the picture so that the eyes may have direct intelligence of it and these
things may be better understood" ("La figura de lo qual es de la manera que
lo enseño debuxado, puesto que sin tal pintura basta lo que está dicho, para
lo entender. Pero todavía es bien en lo que fuere possible usar de la pintura,
para que se informen della los ojos é mejor se comprendan estas cosas";
1:310).

Oviedo apparently encountered few problems in the opening chapters of
his history when describing and depicting Native American ethnographic
items. Verbal descriptions are extensive there, and pictorial images are con-
cisely introduced, with only an occasional brief expression of doubt about
the effectiveness of the drawing. Such is not the case with the representation
of indigenous flora. In a chapter devoted to a meticulous description of the
planting of yuccas, the use of the fruit, and the varieties that exist, Oviedo
mentions in passing that he has resorted to depicting particular aspects of two
varieties of yucca leaves but that even this attempt is but a partial reflection of
the varieties: "I have drawn here the shape of both the one and the other,
notwithstanding the fact that even in the same types of leaves there are particular features and distinct sorts or varieties of yucca" ("puse la forma de la
una é de la otra aqui debuxadas, non obstante que en las mismas maneras de
hojas hay particularidades y diferenciadas suertes ó generaciones de yuca";

2:167). He points to the multiplicity of types of yucca plants and the problem of representing them.

The predicament recurs in other chapters, such as the famous one devoted to the wonders of the pineapple (bk. 7, chap. 14), which is one of the clearest illustrations of the author's dilemma in talking about unnamed, unordered American reality to the European reader and the effort required to move away from the reliance on naming alone to render the essence of an object or custom. In near rapture, Oviedo presents a dizzying proliferation of words, which begins with the problem of naming the fruit and continues with his struggle to classify and to describe accurately the marvels of the pineapple. First, the act of naming the fruit causes a variety of difficulties. Oviedo explains that because the fruit from the *cardo* looked like pinecones, the first Christians in the New World named it "pinecone" (*piña*). He asserts, however, that *piña* could be construed as a misnomer:

> A person might say, because it is a thistle, why do they not call this fruit an artichoke? I repeat that it was in the hands of the first Christians who saw them here to give them one name or another; and truly in my opinion a more fitting name would be to call it an artichoke, with regard to the thistle and thorns that grow on it, although it looks more like a pinecone than an artichoke. The truth is that it does not stray *totaliter* [Latin, "completely"] from being an artichoke.

> Podrá decir alguno que, pues es cardo, porque no llaman alcarchopha esta fructa: digo que en mano fué de los primeros chripstianos que acá la vieron darles un nombre ó el otro, y aun de mi parescer mas propio nombre seria decirla alcarchopha, aviendo respecto al cardo é espinos en que nasce, aunque paresce mas piña que alcarchopha. Verdad es que no se parte *totaliter* de ser alcarchopha. (2:190)

Oviedo points, perhaps unwittingly, to the apparently arbitrary nature of naming things. Why should the pineapple be named according to its resemblance to something else rather than according to its natural classification? Oviedo thus refers primarily to the fruit as "pinecone" (*piña*), but on occasion (at least three times in this passage alone), he resorts to a sort of double name, "pinecone or artichoke" (*piña o alcarchopha*). This relationship between a thing and its name in the New World is further complicated, as with the yucca, by the presence of many varieties of pineapples, which carry different indigenous names to identify them: "Some they call *yayama*; others have the name *boniama*; and others *yayagua*" ("A unas llaman yayama; a otras dicen boniama; é á otras yayagua"; 2:191).

Reducing the fruit that Oviedo believes is unequaled in the world to a single word proved problematic for the author. He therefore resorted to a detailed delineation of its qualities according to the four applicable senses that could experience the fruit. Here too, however, Oviedo finds words alone inadequate: they accumulate in a circular pattern in which the sensuous qualities of the pineapple are repeated several times—interspersed with information about its cultivation and medicinal uses—as though by pure repetition he could clarify for his reader the nature of this fruit. Moreover, using the dual strategy mentioned earlier, the author employs an analogue, saying that the fruit tastes like a mixture of peach and other fruits known in Europe, yet at the same time he asserts that the pineapple cannot be compared with any fruit he has known: "no other gives such contentment" ("ninguna otra da tal contentamiento"; 2:187); "it is beyond comparison with any other fruit I have seen" ("no tiene comparacion con ella otra fructa en las que yo he visto"; 2:189).

Halfway through this whirlwind of words, Oviedo acknowledges the obstacles involved in accurately portraying the fruit with words alone. Reflecting an uneasiness about things unseen that was characteristic of his times, Oviedo believed that all things could be represented to the sense of vision in some form,[17] so he introduces a drawing of it (fig. 8.3):

> The picture drawn by my pen and words cannot give such particular information nor so properly praise this fruit as to fulfill totally and sufficiently the particulars of the case without the brush, or, that is, the drawing; and even with the latter it would be necessary to include colors so that still more fittingly (*though only in part*) it might be better understood that I render it and say it, that in some way *the sight of the reader might better partake of this truth.* Nevertheless, I shall include it as best I can, as poorly drawn as spoken; but for those who have seen the fruit, this will suffice, and they will tell the rest. And for those who have never seen it save here . . . I hereby attest that if one day they see it, they will excuse me for not having known how nor been able to praise this fruit justly. (my emphasis)

> No pueden la pintura de mi pluma y palabras dar tan particular razon ni tan al proprio el blason desta fructa, que satisffagan tan total y bas-

FIGURE 8.3. Oviedo's drawing of a pineapple (piña) from the "Monserrat Manuscript" of his *Historia general* (courtesy the Huntington Library).

tantemente que se pueda particularizar el caso, sin el pincel, ó debuxo, y aun con esto serian menester las colores para que mas conforme (sino todo en parte) se diesse mejor á entender que yo lo hago y digo, porque en alguna manera la vista del lector pudiesse mas participar desta verdad: non obstante lo qual, pornéla, como supiere hacerlo, tan mal debuxada como platicada; pero para los que esta fructa ovieren visto bastará aquesto, y ellos dirán lo demás. Y para los que nunca la vieron sino aqui . . . les certifico que si en algun tiempo la vieren, me avrán por desculpado, si no supe, ni pude justamente loar esta fructa. (2:187–88)

Here we clearly witness, however, the limits of a literal interpretation of Ovie-do's idea that seeing equals understanding when it is applied to his drawings. He tells his readers that the drawings will help enable them to understand the wonders of the pineapple better but that their apprehension of it will be only partial. Achieving a visual epistemology through drawings, no matter how unembellished and faithful to nature they may be, is not equal to actually seeing the object firsthand. He expands on this view, saying, "And if, for lack of colors and of the drawing, I do not sufficiently *make known what I wished to be able to say*, blame my judgment, according to which in my eyes this is the most beautiful fruit of any I have seen, and the one with the best scent and flavor" (my emphasis) ("Y si, por falta de colores y del debuxo, yo no bastáre á dar á entender lo que querria saber decir, dése la culpa á mi juicio, en el qual á mis ojos es la mas hermosa fructa de todas que he visto y la que mejor huele y mejor sabor tiene"; 2:188).[18]

Besides the inability of a drawing to replicate nature exactly, Oviedo rec-ognizes another problem: his drawing attempts to depict a particular type of pineapple and in doing so leaves out the other varieties: "that which they call *yayama* is rather long in proportion and of the size I have depicted here, and the other two kinds or types of which I have spoken are more round" ("la que llaman yayama es algo en su proporcion prolongada é del talle de la que aqui he pintado, é las otras dos maneras ó géneros, de quien he hablado, son mas redondas"; 1:191). Although he sets out to depict the particular, Oviedo also wishes to represent all pineapples, and thus a tension emerges. He draws one type of pineapple, which becomes a schema for all pineapples, and with some misgiving he compensates with his words for depicting only a single variety.

Unlike da Vinci's sketches of plants and the herbals that began to circulate in the mid sixteenth century, Oviedo's work strives to portray the particular reality of America.[19] Unlike the woodcuts employed in herbals, which depict generic forms, in which the details of the particular types and the resulting multiplicity are replaced with a schema, Oviedo set out to portray the particular in his drawings. He encountered difficulties, however, that were similar to the problems he encountered in trying to make words represent America's novelties precisely. E. H. Gombrich, in writing about the use of the schema in art, explains the dilemma: "This tendency of our minds to classify and register our experience in terms of the known must present a real problem to the artist in his encounter with the particular" (1960, 168). He goes on to explain that seeing and knowing become seeing and noticing (172), where reality cannot be grasped by the intellect without some standard of comparison or interpretation (178). The tension between using analogies and schemas and attempting to fix an accurate verbal or visual image of the particular characteristics of American subjects is clear in Oviedo's text.

Oviedo did not reduce America to European formulas. He avoided the reductive tendency of other writers and attempted to reproduce the vast complexity of the New World with both words and drawings. Although Oviedo also included statements on the cultivation and utility of the pineapple, as well as different people's opinions about it, his primary impulse in this passage seems to be an attempt to understand for himself the process of representing this new wonder, to break the spiral of confusion caused by trying to settle on a single word that reflects the essence of the pineapple and to work out a standard for representing this novelty. He delineates the qualities of the object by using analogues, describing the empirical aspects of the fruit, and rendering a visual image of it. The fact that Oviedo underscores his partial representation of the pineapple emphasizes the "near-miss" quality of his and other chroniclers' endeavors and the importance of his own presence in America in order to approximate a truthful representation of the New World for the reader.

Time and again in subsequent introductions to his drawings, aspects of this near-miss quality emerge. Oviedo continues to draw new objects and periodically insists that the drawing aids the verbal description but does not replace the actual witnessing of the object for apprehending its essence. By asserting the superiority of a firsthand experience of America, Oviedo secured a place for his own authority about the New World as a chronicler who devoted forty-three years to living in and writing about America. His words and drawings, he maintains, are based on his own experience, but they cannot supplant the experience itself.

Typical of Oviedo, however, his insistence on this stance leads to an ironic situation with regard to later parts of the history. After part 1 of the Historia the number of drawings diminishes, and several of the later drawings are based on secondhand accounts. He illustrates, for example, a lookout tower that he has never seen, basing his drawing on a captain's verbal description of it: "and as they are a new shape of building, I have drawn here one of the same shape that this captain explained to me" ("y por ser nueva forma de edificios pinté aqui una de la misma forma queste capitan me la dió á entender"; 4:261). The new form of the tower justifies the inclusion of the drawing, but in the process Oviedo acknowledges both his own inability to experience everything for himself and his indebtedness to other individuals' firsthand accounts in order to complete his history.

On several other occasions, the official chronicler illustrates items from secondhand accounts and goes one step further, inviting others, including the reader, to participate and to judge the representation. He includes a map made by Diego de Almargo, verifying that it came from a reliable witness and therefore the chronicler considers it as good as his own firsthand evidence. On another occasion, the author invites the reader to judge the account and drawing of a volcano in Nicaragua for himself: "the reader may judge how it seems to him by comparing it to the things mentioned above, or to others; it has the following shape, and thus I have drawn or presented the shape of this Mount Massaya" ("el letor juzgue lo que le paresciere del que lo haya cotejado con las cosas sussodichas, ó con otras; é su figura es aquesta, y pues he pintado ó puesto la figura de aqueste monte de Massaya"; 11:128).

By examining Oviedo's drawings for their intrinsic value, we can see how he linked seeing with understanding, but we must also note the author's recognition that this formula is limited in two ways. First, the abundance of American marvels prohibits him from witnessing everything firsthand, so he must rely on accounts by others who were eyewitnesses. Second, the European reader can rely on the sense of sight to apprehend a picture of an American subject yet cannot witness the thing itself. In this case, the reader must rely on Oviedo's sense of sight and trust his methods of representing what he witnesses.

The 1535 general prologue to the Historia sets forth the manner in which the author was seeking to gain credibility and therefore the trust of his reader, and it also explains the explicit purpose of his work. By examining the repetition of certain words and their synonyms, as well as the manner in which they are linked together, we can see that Oviedo linked his travels in the New World with trials (*trabajos*) and dangers (*peligros*) that he underwent in order to witness (*ver*) and thus to understand (*entender*) the marvels of American phenomena. Furthermore, Oviedo asserts that being an eyewitness (*un testigo*) enabled him to name or represent (*nombrar*) American reality truthfully. This "truthful and new account" (*verdadera y nueva historia*), Oviedo maintains, gives him authority (*auctoridad*) as the official chronicler and enables the reader to praise (*loar*) God's creation and Spain's imperial destiny. According to Oviedo, the authority of his history depends on a chain of actions in which sight and experience are the crucial links; to travel (*viajar*), suffer (*padecer*), see (*ver*), experience (*experimentar*), understand (*entender*), write the truth (*escribir verdad*), and praise (*loar*) are all interconnected. In the instances in which he encounters the most difficulty in portraying American phenomena (as we see in his chapter on the pineapple), his words circle around the central issue of his *Historia*, pointing to his history as an authoritative medium through which the reader can praise the wonders of God's creation.

The multiplicity of forms that Oviedo employs to represent America are integral to the content of the history. We have seen that the illustrations are integral to the descriptions of the natural history of America as well as to the underlying principle of the history, whereby Oviedo attempts to follow the theory that everything is capable of visual representation. Images are not simply an important co-text to the *Historia*; image and text function as one.[20]

Basing his inclusion of drawings on theories of visual epistemology, Oviedo asserts the importance of the sense of sight in apprehending the essence of the New World. Yet the reader is unable in most cases to experience America firsthand. Thus, according to his theory, Oviedo's outer or corporeal eye must serve as a link to the reader's own corporeal eyes—vis-à-vis the drawings—and to the reader's inner eye, or mind's eye, in order to apprehend, if only in part, the wonders of America. By positioning himself and his text as the essential link between America and his reader, Oviedo proclaims the "official" nature of his history; that is, not only is he the first official chronicler of the New World, but his methods of historical representation also establish his text as the first official book on America. Edmundo O'Gorman asserts that Oviedo was one of the first to see new meaning in America ([1958] 1984, xv), and Antonello Gerbi observes that Oviedo brought a whole new reality to the writing of history (1985, 241).[21] Accepting his *Historia* as the first representation of America depends on accepting the empirical *yo* he

weaves into the text. Through his experience of New World natural phenomena and his methodology for representing them, he sought to bring the
original experience closer to his reader.[22] Responding to the Renaissance concern with the nature of truth and its relationship to history, as well as concern
with how best to apprehend a new reality, Oviedo resorted to creating visual
images of America and in the process constructed a theory of authority and
representation. He placed more importance on the image of America than on
words about it: "because it is a thing better seen in drawings . . . for it cannot
be understood with words" ("porque es mas para verle pintado . . . que no
para entender con palabras"; 6:117).[23]

If, as Helen Nader (1979, 14) suggests, Renaissance historical writing provides a record of the rhetorical achievements of the period, Oviedo's illustrations and musings about his drawings serve as a record of the first official
chronicler of America's theory and practice of representation, as well as of
European writers' predicaments and narrative strategies in general when writing about the New World. The *Historia* reveals much about the dilemma posed
by America—both in finding an adequate means for Europeans to convey its
essence and to establish a claim to credibility in writing about it. Since traditional European authorities did not apply to America, *authority* increasingly
became a relative term based on individual experience. Each chronicler therefore invented his own "true" picture of America according to his own particular point of view and purpose. What was begun by Columbus, Cortés, and
Oviedo continued through to chroniclers born in America. The Inca Garcilaso
de la Vega and Guaman Poma de Ayala, for example, employed deliberate
rhetorical structures and, in the latter case, illustrations to support the claim
of credibility.[24]

Indeed, sixteenth- and seventeenth-century visual representations of the
New World reflect a nonverbal method of discovering the meaning of
America. Through illustrations, authors and editors conveyed their view of
the New World, or at least one that they wished the European reader to believe. Through the use of drawings in his history, Oviedo reasserted the basis
for his criterion for the representation of history, both human and natural, as
sight and experience. In the process, he worked through various methods of
representation, both verbal and visual, to make known particular American
phenomena. As Oviedo journeyed through the New World and wrote about
it, he attempted to bridge the gap between the old authorities and formulas
and the reality of what he saw.[25] In grappling with this, he sought to become
both the author and the authority on America.

NOTES

All translations of Oviedo from the Spanish are by Amanda W. Powell.

1. See Beatriz Pastor's chapter on Columbus in her *Discurso narrativo* (1983).

2. Oviedo was not named official chronicler until 1532, but he began taking notes on the New World soon after his appointment as *veedor de oro* (overseer of Spain's gold foundries in America) in 1514.

3. All citations of Oviedo's work are from the 1944 edition by Editorial Guaranía. I cite the volume and page numbers.

4. For the composition and organization of Oviedo's history, see Stephanie Merrim's excellent article, "'Un *mare magno* e oculto': Anatomy of Fernández de Oviedo's *Historia*" (1984).

5. See my article "History, Truth and Dialogue" (1990).

6. I am indebted to Joseph Ewan, Amy Meyers, and Jane Munro, who assisted me in examining a portion of Oviedo's autograph manuscript, and to Rolena Adorno and Enrique Pupo-Walker, who made valuable suggestions on an earlier draft of this paper.

7. The impulse to record physical reality in the form of drawings is already apparent in Oviedo's first work about the New World, the *Sumario* (1526), which includes four woodcuts based on his own sketches. The first edition of the *Historia* (1535) includes three of these woodcuts and adds twenty-nine more, which were modified and republished in the 1547 edition. The 1557 publication of book 20 of the *Historia* includes a new woodcut of a Patagonian camp. See Turner 1985 for valuable information on manuscript drawings.

8. Parts 2 and 3 (the final thirty-one books of the *Historia*) have less than one-third of the illustrations found in part 1 (the first nineteen books).

9. I am indebted to the Huntington Library in San Marino, California, for granting me a fellowship to examine its portion of Oviedo's autograph manuscript of the *Historia general*. By far the majority of surviving illustrations are at the Huntington. There are twenty-four pen-and-ink drawings. The Real Academia de Historia in Madrid owns the only other known section of the autograph manuscript that contains original drawings. Although book 12 of part 1, which contains illustrations of New World fauna, was lost sometime after Turner's "Forgotten Treasures from the Indies" (1985) reproduced some

of the drawings, some photographic negatives of these and other lost Oviedo illustrations were at the Peabody Museum at Harvard University. The Peabody told me these negatives were loaned out and not returned. Other manuscript copies from the seventeenth and eighteenth centuries apparently faithfully transcribe Oviedo's illustrations, sometimes coloring them in. These partial copies, at the Biblioteca de Palacio in Madrid and the Biblioteca Colombina in Seville, provide us with an idea of the extent of Oviedo's drawings. My thanks go to Indiana University for a grant to study the extant manuscripts and copies. See also William C. Sturtevant's "First Visual Images of Native America" (1976), which mentions the whereabouts of Oviedo's drawing (447n23) and Daymond Turner's "Forgotten Treasures from the Indies" (1985), which provides a thorough study of the various manuscripts and copies. Turner makes only one significant error: the drawing that he considers Oviedo's "masterpiece," on the method used for ferrying horses, was not done by Oviedo. The artist of this piece used more elaborate contraposture and shading and more decidedly mannerist conventions than those seen in any of Oviedo's work. In addition, unlike Oviedo's other drawings, the illustration covers the whole folio and has been executed on different paper and inserted between the pages of Oviedo's manuscript.

10. Turner 1985 is an exception to the generally brief comments on Oviedo's drawings. Antonello Gerbi's extensive section on Oviedo in *Nature in the New World* (1985), for example, mentions only in passing the importance of the sense of sight and the role of art and illustrations in the *Historia* (181–85; 226–31; 390).

11. Paul Hulton and David Quinn are among the few researchers who have noted the novelty of Oviedo's approach. In *The Drawings of John White* (1964, 1:32), they note the liveliness of Oviedo's drawings and cite them as a "revolutionary achievement" not soon to be paralleled.

12. See Panofsky 1957. After the current essay was written it was brought to my attention that Rolena Adorno uses Panofsky's argument to illustrate the significance of Guaman Poma's drawings; see Adorno 1981, 54, 61.

13. Roland Barthes (1972, 123–31) is discussed in Adorno 1986a, 83. Adorno's book is an excellent example of a study that uses this approach. In chapter 4 she analyzes Guaman Poma's illustrations for their symbolic value.

14. Although sight and experience are not quite of the same order, sight being a part of experience, Oviedo equates the two in his prologue.

15. Many Italian Renaissance painters wrote treatises that discuss this re-

lationship, for example, Leon Battista Alberti's *Della Pintura* and Leonardo da Vinci's *Treatise on Painting*.

16. For a general discussion of this, see Amador de los Ríos's introductory study in his nineteenth-century edition of the *Historia* (Oviedo 1851–55). On Oviedo's knowledge of Italian Renaissance art, see García Sáiz 1982.

17. Robinson explains this phenomenon: "In a sense the Renaissance artist and scientist gave a local habitation to the airy nothingness of a predominately verbal philosophical tradition. They incorporated forms into their pictures, made concepts into visible objects, and thought of Ideas as things easily converted to images and emblems. The characteristic dissatisfaction with things unseen resulted in the belief that everything, including the activity of the mind, could be represented to the sense of vision" (1972, 94).

18. The actual drawing of the pineapple reveals, to a degree, Oviedo's confusion about how to represent it. He renders an image that is partially inspired by the pinecone.

19. The naming of American flora coincided with new efforts to delineate natural classifications. By the mid eighteenth century this activity had its effect in the abundant production of herbals. See J. Ewan 1976 and J. Sauer 1976.

20. Indeed, in the chapters that he revised or added to the history after its first printing, Oviedo took ever greater care to render the text and image as one. Sections of the manuscript copy at the Huntington Library show that the later illustrations were more often drawn first and the text fitted in around the image (see fig. 8.3, for example). Earlier illustrations are usually embedded in the narrative, but the words of the text are not as carefully interlocked with the image. The revised manuscript also documents Oviedo's keen interest in revising his earlier drawings to produce a more accurate depiction of American phenomena: he added a pair of hands to the drawing of the fire drill to show more clearly how it was used; the illustration of the canoe is done with more contraposture to demonstrate the motion necessary to move it; and he noted next to many of the illustrations whether they are to be printed as is or replaced with a new drawing. Figure 8.1b is a revised drawing in which Oviedo attempted to depict the hammock more accurately. He inserted a human figure to give the illusion of three dimensions. The 1535 and 1547 woodcuts (see fig. 8.1a) are based on Oviedo's original illustration of the hammock.

21. Enrique Pupo-Walker adds to this discussion of Oviedo's writing.

Oviedo occupies a unique position in historical discourse; his writings "were disquietudes favoured at the same time by the intellectual currents of the period and by the exigencies that planted a new historical reality without precedent" ("eran inquietudes favorecidas a un mismo tiempo por las corrientes intelectuales de la época y por las exigencias que planteaban una realidad histórica sin precedentes"; 1983, 88).

22. Stephanie Merrim argues that Oviedo's empirical *yo* is a subtext of the history, serving to assert his authority, which is achieved by establishing two "rhythms": the chronological passing of time and the revelation of life's mysteries (1984, 111–12). Furthermore, she suggests that Oviedo's natural history can be viewed as a teratology: "A teratology, or study in marvels (and monstrosities), the natural history submits the mysteries of its subjects to the reader's eyes as *herygma*, an ongoing parade of revelations, with the intent that reading about these mysteries should produce the same awe and reverence as the original reading of these miracles" (106).

23. The seventeenth-century Andean chronicler Guaman Poma de Ayala arrived at a similar, albeit more covert, theory of the relationship between words and images. Rolena Adorno (1986a) argues that Guaman Poma uses visual images to mediate between (Andean) oral and (European) written tradition and in doing so asserts that the message in his drawings is more powerful than that in the written chronicle.

24. See Zamora 1988 and Adorno 1986a, esp. chap. 4.

25. See Wayne Franklin's discussion of North American discoverers, who followed this same process (1979, esp. chaps. 1 and 2).

BIBLIOGRAPHY

Adorno, Rolena. 1981. On Pictorial Language and the Typology of Culture in a New World Chronicle. *Semiotica* 36:51–106.
————.1986a. *Guaman Poma: Writing and Resistance in Colonial Peru*. Austin: University of Texas Press.
————. 1986b. Visual Mediation in the Transition from Oral to Written Expression. *New Scholar* 10:181–95.
Alvárez López, Enrique. 1957. La historia natural en Oviedo. *Revista de Indias* 17:541–601.
Bakhtin, Mikhail. 1984. *Rabelais and His World*. Trans. H. Iswolsky. Bloomington: Indiana University Press.

Barthes, Roland. 1972. *Mythologies.* Trans. Annette Lavers. New York: Hill and Wang.

Bucher, Bernadette. 1981. *Icon and Conquest: A Structural Analysis of the Illustrations of deBry's Great Voyages.* Trans. Basia Miller Gulati. Chicago: University of Chicago Press.

Collins, J. L. 1951. Antiquity of the Pineapple in America. *Southwestern Journal of Anthropology* 7:145–55.

Columbus, Christopher. 1985. *Diario de a bordo.* Ed. Luis Arranz. Madrid: Historia 16.

Elliott, John H. 1970. *The Old World and the New, 1492–1650.* London: Cambridge University Press.

Ewan, Joseph. 1976. The Columbian Discoveries and the Growth of Botanical Ideas, with Special Reference to the Sixteenth Century. In *First Images of the New World,* ed. F. Chiappelli, 2:807–12. Berkeley: University of California Press.

Fernández de Oviedo, Gonzalo. 1851–55. *Historia general y natural de las Indias.* Ed. José Amador de los Ríos. Vols. 1–4. Madrid: Real Academia.

——. 1945. *Historia general y natural de las Indias.* Ed. J. Natálico González and José Amador de los Ríos. Vols. 1–14. Asunción, Paraguay: Editorial Guaranía.

Franklin, Wayne. 1979. *Discoverers, Explorers, Settlers: The Diligent Writers of Early America.* Chicago: University of Chicago Press.

García Sáiz, María Concepción. 1982. Acerca de los conocimientos pictóricos de Gonzalo Fernández de Oviedo. In *América y la España del siglo XVI: Homenaje a Gonzalo Fernández de Oviedo,* ed. Francisco de Solano and Fermín del Pino, 1:65–71. Madrid: CSIC, Instituto Gonzalo Fernández de Oviedo.

Gerbi, Antonello. 1985. *Nature in the New World: From Christopher Columbus to Gonzalo Fernández de Oviedo.* Trans. Jeremy Moyle. Pittsburgh: University of Pittsburgh Press.

Gombrich, E. H. 1960. *Art and Illusion.* New York: Pantheon.

Hernández, Francisco. 1615. *Quatro libros de la naturaleza y virtudes de las plantas y animales que estan recividos en el uso de medicina en la Nueva España.* Mexico City: Diego López Dávalos.

Hulton, Paul, and David Quinn. 1964. *The Drawings of John White.* 2 vols. Chapel Hill: University of North Carolina Press.

López Baralt, Mercedes. 1983. La iconografía política de América: El mito fundacional en las imágenes católica, protestante y nativa. *Nueva Revista de Estudios Hispánicos* 31:448–61.

Merrim, Stephanie. 1984. "Un *mare magno e oculto*": Anatomy of Fernández de Oviedo's *Historia general y natural de las indias*. *Revista de estudios hispánicos* 95:101–19.

———. Forthcoming. The First Fifty Years of Hispanic New World Historiography: The Caribbean, Mexico, and Central America. In *The Cambridge History of Latin American Literature*, vol. 1. Cambridge: Cambridge University Press.

Myers, Kathleen A. 1990. History, Truth, and Dialogue: Fernández de Oviedo's *Historia general y natural de las Indias* (Book XXXIII, Ch. XLVI). *Hispania* 73:616–25.

———. 1991. Imitation, Authority, and Revision in Fernández de Oviedo's *Historia general y natural de las Indias*. *Romance Language Annual* 3:523–30.

Nader, Helen. 1979. *The Mendoza Family in the Spanish Renaissance*. New Brunswick, N.J.: Rutgers University Press.

O'Gorman, Edmundo. [1526] 1950. *Summario de la natural historia de las Indias*. Ed. José Miranda. Mexico City: Fondo de Cultura Económica.

———. [1958] 1984. *La invención de América*. Mexico City: Fondo de Cultura Económica.

———. 1983. *Batallas y Quinquagenas*. Ed. Juan Pérez de Tudela. Madrid: Real Academia de la Historia.

Panofsky, Erwin. 1957. Iconography and Iconology: An Introduction to the Study of Renaissance Art. In his *Meaning in the Visual Arts*, 26–54. Garden City, N.Y.: Doubleday.

Pastor, Beatriz. 1983. *Discurso narrativo de la conquista de América*. Havana: Ediciones Casa de las Américas.

Pupo-Walker, Enrique. 1983. *La vocación literaria en el pensamiento histórico en América*. Madrid: Gredos.

Robinson, Forrest. 1972. *The Shape of Things Known*. Cambridge, Mass.: Harvard University Press.

Salas, Alberto M. 1959. *Tres cronistas de Indias*. Mexico City: Fondo de Cultura Económica.

Sauer, Carl O. 1966. *The Early Spanish Main*. Berkeley: University of California Press.

Sauer, Jonathan D. 1976. Changing Perception and Exploitation of New World

Plants in Europe, 1492–1800. In *First Images of America*, ed. Fredi Chiappelli, 2:813–25. Berkeley: University of California Press.

Sturtevant, William C. 1976. First Visual Images of Native America. In *First Images of America*, ed. Fredi Chiappelli, 1:417–54. Berkeley: University of California Press.

Turner, Daymond. 1985. Forgotten Treasure from the Indies: The Illustrations and Drawings of Fernández de Oviedo. *Huntington Library Quarterly* 48: 1–46.

Tuttle, Edward F. 1976. Borrowing versus Semantic Shift: New World Nomenclature in European Languages. In *First Images of America*, ed. Fredi Chiappelli, 2:595–605. Berkeley: University of California Press.

Vásquez, Josefina Zoraida. 1957. El Indio americano y su circunstancia en la obra de Oviedo. *Revista de Indias* 17:483–519.

Vives, Juan Luis. 1948. De ratione dicendi. In *Obras completas*, trans. L. Riber, vol. 2. Madrid: Ediciones Aguilar.

Zamora, Margarita. 1988. *Language, Authority and Indigenous History in the "Comentarios Reales de los Incas."* Cambridge Iberian and Latin American Studies. Cambridge: Cambridge University Press.

9

The Cross and the Gourd

The Appropriation of Ritual Signs in the *Relaciones* of Alvar Núñez Cabeza de Vaca and Fray Marcos de Niza

Maureen Ahern

> Two of their medicine-men gave us two gourds. Thence on-
> ward we carried gourds, which added greatly to our authority,
> since they hold these ceremonial objects very high.
> —*Alvar Núñez Cabeza de Vaca*

> Obligation is expressed in myth and imagery, symbolically
> and collectively; it takes the form of interest in the objects
> exchanged; the objects are never completely separated from
> the men who exchange them; the communion and alliance
> they establish are well-nigh indissoluble.
> —*Marcel Mauss*

In the two earliest reports of contacts between Europeans and Amerindians beyond the northernmost frontiers of New Spain, cultural interactions were carried out through the appropriation of ritual signs. The climax of Alvar Núñez Cabeza de Vaca's *La Relación* . . . ([1542] 1555)[1] turns on
the signifying power of the *calabaza*, or ritual gourd, and its use by Cabeza de
Vaca and his companions as a symbol of healing prowess and knowledge to
effect their safe passage from tribe to tribe through the Greater Sonoran Desert. In the report rendered to Viceroy Antonio Mendoza in 1539, Fray Marcos de Niza and Esteban de Dorantes used the Christian cross and the Indian
feathered gourd rattle as communication codes. A discursive reading of the
production and reception of these signs in the two reports demonstrates how
crucial a role the semiosis of cross-cultural communication played in deter-

mining the paradigms of cultural contact in this region. In the case of Cabeza de Vaca, the appropriation of signs became a bridge for cultural mediation. In the case of Fray Marcos and Estebanico, it produced cultural collision. An examination of how these earliest encounter texts articulate the complex processes of conflicting belief systems—of how "old" forms take on "new" meanings—offers another dimension to their significance in the formation of colonial discourse.

Alvar Núñez Cabeza de Vaca: The Calabaza as Cultural Mediator

The survivors of the Narváez expedition learned indigenous curing procedures at the Isle of Malhado off the Texas coast:

> On the island I have spoken of they wanted to make medicine men [shamans] of us without any examination or asking for our diplomas, because they cure diseases by breathing on the sick, and with that breath and their hands they drive the ailment away. So they summoned us to do the same in order to be at least of some use. We laughed, taking it for a jest, and said that we did not understand how to cure. Thereupon they withheld our food to compel us to do what they wanted. Seeing our obstinacy, an Indian told me that I did not know what I said by claiming that what he knew was useless, because stones and things growing out in the field have their virtues, and he, with a heated stone, placing it on the stomach, could cure and take away pain, so that we, who were wiser men, surely had greater power and virtue. At last we found ourselves in such stress as to have to do it, without risking any punishment [without any shame]. (chap. 15, p. 57 [fol. 21r and v])[2]

In this passage we note that the skeptical reactions of the Spaniards are set off by the phatic markers of indirect discourse: "We laughed [at them], taking it for a jest, and said that we did not understand how to cure" ("Nosotros nos reyamos dellos diziendo que era burla y que no sabiamos curar"; [fol. 21r] my emphasis). Here, then, where European logic met indigenous spirituality— which the skeptical narrator and his companions scoff at and dismiss as a joke—it is the Indian counter-arguments in the form of indirect discourse that convince them. Who "sees" here is not exclusively the authorial perspective that speaks but rather includes the perspective of the Indian informant. In the same paragraph we also note how elements of the reported speech of the author have intruded into the speech of the Indian informant as he repeats the narrator's words: "that I did not know what I said by claiming that what he knew was useless" (que yo no sabia lo que hazia en decir [fol. 21r]). Cabeza de Vaca seemed to feel it necessary to emphasize twice that he did not know how to cure, each time in a way that showed that these words belonged to another speaker, that they are "borrowed" from the other's speech. In this first presentation of healing, then, the perspectives of the author apprentice and that of his Indian master are merged in the same sentence in the text. As a result, while we perceive the feelings of the Indian participant from his own point of view, we are constantly listening to what Uspensky calls "the intonation of the narrator" (1973, 47).

This sequence is immediately followed by a detailed description of the curing procedures, which is rendered with interjections of the narrator's testimony to validate his curing: "They cauterize with fire, thinking it very effective, and [I have experienced it, and it worked well for me]" (1972, 57). Then he continues: "The way we treated the sick was to make over them the sign of the cross while breathing on them, recite a Pater Noster and Ave Maria, and pray to God, Our Lord, as best we could to give them good health and inspire them to do us some favors" (chap. 15, pp. 57–58 [fol. 21v]). In this initial representation of healing,[3] Cabeza de Vaca's discursive strategies first emphasize indigenous authority by supplying explicit descriptions of the native procedures, then he adds the accompanying prayers and evocation of the Christian Our Father and Hail Mary. Thus the curing episodes begin with a double inscription from Indian and Christian ritual.

Sometime later in 1533, Cabeza de Vaca and the three other survivors made their way farther down the Texas coast, where they were held captive by the Mariames and Yguazes, who journeyed each year to a vast prickly-pear harvesting area northwest of the lower Guadalupe River along the lower Nueces River (Campbell and Campbell 1981, 5–7). There the four survivors lived among the Mariames for at least eighteen months during 1533–34 and learned to speak their language. The acts of service rendered by the curing introduced the Spaniards to the ritual gift exchange, whose network of obligation and repayment motivated the neighboring Avavares to rescue them from starvation and danger and assign them lodging in the house of two shamans:[4]

> We told them in the language of the Mareames that we had come to see them. They appeared to be pleased with our company and took us to their homes. They lodged Dorantes and the Negro at the house of a medicine man [shaman], and me and Castillo at that of another. These Indians speak another language and are called Avavares. They were

those who used to fetch bows to ours [our friends] and barter with
them. . . . Forthwith they offered us many *tunas* [prickly pears], because
they had heard of us and of how we cured and of the miracles Our
Lord worked through us. (chap. 20, pp. 82–83 [fol. 29r and v])

Cabeza de Vaca relates how the Spaniards continued to cure the sick while
among the Avavares and reports the acts of healing performed by Castillo as
a contrast to his own superior prowess. Advancing from one prickly-pear
grove to another with the Avavares, with whom they remained for a period
of eight months during the years 1534 and 1535, they met tribes of many
different languages—Maliacones, Coayos, Susolas, Atayos, and Cutalchuches.[5]
The narrator describes the cures that Castillo, Dorantes, and Estebanico performed, as well as the extraordinary cure that Cabeza de Vaca worked on "an
Indian with eyes upturned, without pulse and with all the marks of lifeless-
ness. At least it seemed to me, and Dorantes said the same" (chap. 22, p. 88
[fol. 31r]. After Cabeza de Vaca makes the details of the procedure explicit, he
represents the results of the curing session through the accounts of indigenous witnesses:

> Our Indians to whom I had given the *tunas* remained there, and at
> night [they] returned telling that the dead man whom I attended to in
> their presence had resuscitated, rising from his bed, and walked about,
> eaten and talked to them, and that all those treated by me were well
> and in very good spirits. This caused great surprise and awe, and all
> over the land nothing else was spoken of. All who heard it came to
> us that we might cure them and bless their children . . . (chap. 22,
> pp. 88–89 [fol. 31v])

A pattern thus emerges for the discourse segments that narrate the curing.
First the *events* are introduced by reported speech, followed by explicit authorial descriptions of the details of the sessions. Then the *results* of each incident are added, nearly always represented in the text by the reported
speech of the Indians or one of the Spanish comrades. Usually these are followed by Cabeza de Vaca's stock comment giving us a sense of the scene and
context of the act: "This caused great surprise and awe, and all over the land
nothing else was spoken of" (chap. 22, p. 89). While it is Cabeza de Vaca as
witness and protagonist who simultaneously acts out and interprets the cures,
Cabeza de Vaca the narrator makes the Indians, through indirect discourse,
the authority for the events described in the report. This subtle interplay between the two modes of discourse constructs a representation of the Span-

iards that is enlarged by the power of indigenous ritual. It is also reported speech that effects the textual transformation of the four survivors into indigenous deities through the oral acclaim of the Avavares themselves. "During that time they came for us from many places and *said that verily we were children of the Sun*. Until then Dorantes and the Negro had not made any cures, but we found ourselves so pressed by the Indians coming from all sides, that we all became medicine-men [shamans]" (chap. 22, p. 89 [fol. 31v]; my emphasis).

Textual evidence points to the fact that two referential systems are operating simultaneously in the text. One is that of the shamans, who "were probably universal in this area" of southern Texas (Campbell and Campbell 1981, 36), as evidenced by the descriptions of ritual and ceremonial activity that involved dancing and feasting and gift payment or exchange that accompanied various healing episodes. The second is an analogous sign system of known value in the Christian register, that of miraculous signs. After Cabeza de Vaca's escape from the Mariames, miraculous signs delivered him to the friendly Avavares: the burning branch saved him from freezing to death in the desert, the dead returned to life, and throngs acclaimed Cabeza de Vaca and his comrades as they traveled from place to place. These referents evoke the semiosis of the Gospels of Mark and John and their system of meaning, which lies just below the textual surface throughout the biblical culture common to most Western readers of the time.[6] Now this connotative register can serve as a gloss or trope that points to an analogy between the curing that Cabeza de Vaca and his companions wrought among the Indian groups in the Greater Sonoran Desert and the miracles of Christ and the apostles as told in the Gospels. The signs manifested by the subtext offer a discursive solution to counter any criticism that the shamanistic curing of gentiles by Spanish soldiers and the self-attribution of near miracles might (and indeed did) generate among Spanish readers of the *relación*[7] as it simultaneously triggered associations of healing in the most authoritative tradition of miracles performed by Christ.

Into this narrative segment about the miraculous healing among the Avavares, without any punctuation or paragraph markers, Cabeza de Vaca inserted the Indian story of La Mala Cosa (the bad thing), a terrifying being who performed surgical operations, first cutting open his victims and then sealing their wounds back together. After the story of Mala Cosa's destructive feats are told by Indian friends, the skeptical reactions of their Spanish listeners follow: "We laughed very much at those stories, making fun of them, and then, seeing our incredulity they brought to us many of those whom, they said, he had taken, and we saw the scars of his slashes in the places and as they told" (chap. 22, p. 91 [fol. 32r]). The witnesses who experienced the event tell about it and then demonstrate its existence with concrete evidence—in this case, the scars left by the knife wounds—that attests to the authenticity of the experience. Nichols has identified the same strategy in the telling of miracles in medieval chronicles: "It is the representation of the event in *verbal accounts* that anchors and mediates all of the other elements. Without these accounts, there would be nothing else. The articulation of the event in narrative makes it available to the culture at large by transforming it into *mythos*, socially acceptable historical 'fact'" (1983, 78). Inserting the story of the Mala Cosa into the text at this point solves a critical narrative problem. The indigenous narrative itself is the element that verifies the Indians' truthfulness and provides credibility for incredible events. Inserted stories of this type demonstrate "the circular principal of mutual definition—a kind of narrative semiotic chain—whereby one text provided authority for a second text based upon a subsequent event" (Nichols 1983, 28). By building in an internal disclaimer ("We laughed very much at those stories"), the narrator sets up the chance to counter it by adding living proof that refutes all doubts ("and we saw the scars of his slashes in the places and as they told").

After the Spaniards departed from the friendly Avavares, they probably struck southwestward, where they met the Arbadaos and the Cuchendados at a location the Campbells place at "approximately 25 miles north of the river that is identifiable as the Rio Grande" (1981, 39).[8] There the travelers were asked to cure the sick and to place their hands on children. Cabeza de Vaca noted that these Indians regarded the Spaniards with such awe that food was given to them even when it meant that the Indians themselves had nothing to eat (chap. 29 [fol. 41r]). When the four survivors decided to travel northwestward,[9] they again struck the Río Grande, this time near its confluence with the Río Concho in eastern Chihuahua, where they made contact with Indians who lived in fixed houses at a point on or near "La Junta de los Ríos" in western Texas near Presidio. At this juncture, nomadic Athapascan-speaking peoples interacted with sedentary Puebloan peoples related to those along the northern Río Grande (Riley 1987, 290–94).[10] It was presumably here that the Spaniards reached a large town of more than a hundred houses, where they were received by a shouting crowd: "They carried perforated gourds filled with pebbles, which are ceremonial objects of great importance. They only use them at dances, or as medicine, to cure, and nobody dares touch them but themselves. *They claim that those gourds have healing virtues,* and that they come from Heaven" (chap. 27, p. 107 [fol. 37v]; my emphasis). It is among these same peoples that Cabeza de Vaca and his companions begin to use these insignia of the Indian shaman: "As we neared the houses all the people came out to receive us, with much rejoicing and display, and among other things, two of their medicine-men gave us two gourds. Thence onward we carried gourds, which added to our authority, since they hold these ceremonial objects very high" (chap. 29, p. 113 [fol. 40r]; my emphasis).

As Cabeza de Vaca and his companions traveled westward toward the Sonora Valley through the territories occupied by Upper Piman groups and Opatas, they were revered by growing throngs of admirers.[11] As they pass from tribe to tribe as shamans, the Spaniards translate their actions by means of the socioreligious codes of native authority. The discourse of the *Relación* now highlights that other authority in its remaining segments.

> They always accompanied us until we were again in the care of others, and all those people believed that we came from Heaven. What they do not understand or is new to them they are wont to say it comes from above. . . . We exercised great authority over them, and carried ourselves with much gravity, and in order to maintain it, spoke very little to them. It was the Negro who talked to them all the time; he inquired about the road we should follow, the villages—in short, about everything we wished to know. . . . In that part of the country those who were at war would at once make peace and become friendly to each other, in order to meet us and bring us all they possessed; and thus we left the whole country at peace. (chap. 31, pp. 129–30 [fol. 45r and v])

Johnson's study of the earliest sources on the Opatan tribes notes that they used gourd rattles (1971, 181) and that "Shamans were present in each community, and were respected and feared" (188). Another aspect of their social organization that may have favored the safe-conduct of the Cabeza de Vaca party was the importance that Opatan social organization placed on a formalized relationship with a male friend, or *noragua*. "The sources state that there was nothing that a man would not do for his *noragua*; he had to grant his every request. Should the *noragua* be about to start a dangerous trip, his friend would leave his own affairs and family to be with him and aid him in every way he could" (188).

The expanded segments that narrate the curing episodes in chapters 22 through 26 are followed by another enlarged segment consisting of chapters 27 through 31, in which Cabeza de Vaca incorporates the Spanish survivors into the ritual gift economy of giving, receiving, and repaying (Mauss 1967, 37–41), and its variant, ritual looting.[12] At a town the Spanish named Corazones, probably one of the sixteenth-century Sonoran statelets near present-

day Ures (Riley 1987), the travelers received gifts of cotton blankets, beads
and coral, fine turquoises, six emerald arrowheads of the type used in cere-
monials and six hundred dried deer hearts. When the party turned south
through Lower Piman country on the middle Yaqui River toward the Petateán
or Sinaloa River, accompanied by six hundred Indian friends, the first traces
of Christians in these lands proved alarming. The native population of Lower
Pimas (Upper and Lower Nebomes) and Cáhitan groups (Nures, Mayos, and
Yaquis; *Historia general de Sonora* 1985, 1:267) had fled into the mountains to
escape enslavement by Spanish raiding parties commanded by Captain Diego
de Alcaraz. Members of Nuño de Guzmán's expeditions in 1530 had pressed
northward up the west coast of México, and in 1533 his kinsman Diego de
Guzmán had penetrated as far as the Yaqui River. "Slaving groups, operating
from the Culiacán area, continued their activities for some years, and, in the
period between 1533 and 1536, there was a considerable depopulation of the
northern Tahue and Cáhitan areas because of slave raids" (Riley 1987, 78).
From 1530 on, wherever these Spanish troops ranged, the native inhabitants
preferred suicide to the cruelty and butchery they inflicted.[13]

> And they told us how the Christians had penetrated into the country
> before, and had destroyed and burnt the villages, taking with them half
> of the men and all the women and children, and how those who could
> escaped by flight. Seeing them in this plight, afraid to stay anywhere,
> and that they neither would nor could cultivate the soil, preferring to
> die rather than suffer such cruelties, while they showed the greatest
> pleasure at being with us, we began to apprehend that the Indians
> who were in arms against the Christians might ill-treat us in retaliation
> for what the Christians did to them. (chap. 32, pp. 133–34 [fol. 46v])

In this same segment Cabeza de Vaca explicitly anticipates the conflicts that
he and his Native American companions would face when they finally encountered a Spanish slave-raiding party. "Thereupon we had many and bitter
quarrels with the Christians, for they wanted to make slaves of our Indians,
and we grew so angry at it" (chap. 34, p. 139 [fol. 48v]).

At the climactic scene in chapter 34, when Cabeza de Vaca, Dorantes, Castillo, and Esteban, accompanied by six hundred Indian friends, meet the
Spanish raiding party, their cultural identity becomes the focus of conflict.
The discursive antitheses that represent this traumatic moment are set up by
the oppositions generated by the subject pronouns *nosotros* (we), used to refer
to Cabeza de Vaca, and *ellos* (they), employed to designate the Spanish.[14] In
this polarized discourse, the references to the Spanish are couched in terms

of separate and "other" beings with whom the narrating perspective does not identify. The embedded speeches of the Indians and their interpreters point out the fallacy of Spanish logic, as they contrast the categories of values that become their powerful arguments for the identification of Cabeza de Vaca and his party as indigenous, not Spanish: east/west, cure/kill, naked/clothed, without weapons/armed and mounted, give/withhold or rob. It is significant that the Cabeza de Vaca party initiates their meeting with the main body of Spanish troops with the cultural code of ritual giving by which they had survived, cured, and traveled ever since they left the Gulf Coast. The representation of this extraordinary encounter is well worth considering in its entirety:

> We gave the Christians a great many cowskin [buffalo] robes and other objects, and had much trouble in persuading the Indians to return home and plant their crops in peace. They insisted upon accompanying us until, according to their custom, we should be in the custody of other Indians, because otherwise they were afraid [they would die]; besides, as long as we were with them, they had no fear of the Christians and of their lances. At all this the Christians were greatly vexed, and told their own interpreter to say to the Indians how we were of their own race, but had gone astray for a long while, and were people of no luck and little heart, where as they were the lords of the land, whom they should obey and serve. The Indians gave all that talk of theirs little attention. They parleyed among themselves, saying that the Christians lied, for we had come from where the sun rose, while the others came from where the sun sets; that we cured the sick, while the others killed those who were healthy; that we went naked and shoeless, whereas the others wore clothes and went on horseback and with lances. Also, that we asked for nothing, but gave away all we were presented with, meanwhile the others seemed to have no other aim than to steal what they could and never gave anything to anybody. In short, they recalled all our deeds, and praised them highly, contrasting them with the conduct of the others. . . . Finally, we never could convince the Indians that we belonged to the other Christians, and only with much trouble and insistency could we prevail upon them to go home. (chap. 34, pp. 140–41 [fol. 48v and 49r])

The mediation of peace through the ritual signs of the *calabaza* and the *cruz* resolves a regional conflict in the final two chapters, when the mayor of Culiacán begs Cabeza de Vaca to persuade the Indians who had accompanied his party to return from the sierra. This transfer of power to the travelers is achieved through the powerful sign of the calabaza, or feathered gourd rattle. It is Cabeza de Vaca's use of the natives' sign of their own spirituality that compels the Indians to send their leaders to listen to his transmission of the mayor's request that they return to their lands and accept Christianity, a task that Cabeza de Vaca characterizes as dificultoso. He achieves it, however, by sending on ahead of him one of the ritual gourds that he had been given months before as a sign of healing prowess—gourds whose great power he had witnessed in the hands of many shamans during the past three years. Now it would serve as his sign of identification to his Indian friends:

> In order to insure their coming, we gave the messengers one of the
> large gourds we had carried in our hands—which were our chief insig-
> nia and tokens of great power. Thus provided and instructed, they left
> and were absent seven days. Then they came back, and with them
> three chiefs of those who had been in the mountains, and with these
> were fifteen men. (chap. 35, pp. 144–45 [fol. 50r])

In the ensuing discourse with these Indian ambassadors, Cabeza de Vaca skillfully uses dialogue to probe for the concept and name of their supreme deity, Aguar, whom he immediately equates with the Spanish Díos, making his own discourse witness to the production of syncretic signs in the application of the Spanish verbal sign to the indigenous concept of Aguar.

> Upon being asked whom they worshipped and to whom they offered
> sacrifices, to whom they prayed for health and water for the fields,
> they said, to a man in Heaven. We asked what was his name, and they
> said Aguar, and that they believed he had created the world and every-
> thing in it. We again asked how they came to know this, and they said
> that their fathers and grandfathers had told them, and they had known
> it for a very long time; that water and all good things came from him.
> We explained that this being of whom they spoke was the same one
> we called God, and that thereafter they should give Him that name
> and worship and serve Him as we commanded, then they would fare
> very well. They replied that they understood us thoroughly and would
> do as we had told. (chap. 35, p. 146 [fol. 50v])

When conversion of the Indians was sealed by this syncretism, they were entreated to mark their villages with the Christian emblem and to meet the Spanish with crosses, not bows. Later, when Cabeza de Vaca and his party reached San Miguel, Indian reported speech informed him how well these same allies were following his instructions and how extensive the exchange of their weapons for the cross had become: "Indians came and told us how many people were coming down from the mountains, settling on the plain, building churches and erecting crosses; in short, complying with what we had sent them word to do. Day after day we were getting news of how all was being done and completed" (chap. 36, p. 148 [fol. 51r]).

Thus, in Cabeza de Vaca's report of these first contacts the structures of the native healing networks have become reciprocal exchanges in which his success as a healer and the power it signified enabled him to act as a cultural mediator.[15] This he accomplished by the *inversion* of sacred signs. A form or signifier of Indian religion is appropriated and transmitted back to its original bearers in order to convey a Spanish message or signifier, which pacifies them and converts them to Christianity. Cabeza de Vaca's inversion of the function of the ceremonial rattle must be one of the very earliest documented examples of what Cummins has observed in Incan iconology: "that from the very first, part of Spanish strategy was to turn native expression back on itself so that Indians appeared to themselves as active participants in their own victimization" (1988, 284). As it articulates two different cosmologies, Cabeza de Vaca's *Relación* stands as testimony to his skill as a cultural negotiator. The healing rituals that he had learned among the tribes along the Texas coastal plain and throughout northern New Spain became not only the agent of his own survival but also the means of effecting a social healing in the region. The familiar sign of shamanic power overcame the perceived danger represented by the Spanish raiders, neutralizing their military power within the traditional space of indigenous fields and dwellings. But returning by the sign of the gourd, Cabeza de Vaca's allies are met by the sign of the cross, which converts that space of peace into one of acculturation and accommodation. His knowledge of two separate and apparently contradictory sign systems gave Cabeza de Vaca power over both, resulting in social control of a geographical space that still lay beyond the military control of New Spain.

Moreover, the representation of this particular contact episode—brought into the foreground of the narrative by its detailed telling and specific recall—can be likened to a palimpsest, where the original coded space, in which power and communication were inscribed onto it by the sign of the gourd, is partially effaced to make room for the inscription of power in a second code, which is the cross.[16] In the territory pacified by the gourd, it is the cross that imposes social and economic control. Together they form a new bicultural code that negotiates a peace, which facilitates political control. Thus emerges a sociopolitical discourse whose sense at the resolution of the encounter, while eminently bicultural, ultimately serves the Spanish colonial enterprise.

Cabeza de Vaca's unusual understanding and command of the older indigenous systems of power and knowledge resulted in the creation of new modes of cultural interaction in the Greater Sonoran Desert. In this sense, the calabaza as a sign of cultural negotiation lies at the heart of this frontier encounter. It is the author's skillful narration of those momentous events that make his *Relación* such a powerful text, whose reading, albeit through the filter of Spanish ideology, offers us a perspective on that Other with whom he so explicitly identified. His spectacular success with both orders established a new pattern of communication codes for initial encounters with many native peoples on the northern frontier. Little wonder that Estebanico would attempt to replicate such successful acts in his first contacts with Cíbola.

Estebanico at Zuni: Sign as Transgression

The powerful calabazas generate the climax in another myth-making text that is the sequel to Cabeza de Vaca's *Relación* in real historical time just as it is in narrative time: the *Descubrimiento de las siete ciudades*, the report that Fray Marcos de Niza wrote to the Viceroy Mendoza in 1539.[17]

When Fray Marcos left Culiacán in March of that year to scout the lands to the north, where the Cabeza de Vaca party had been told there were large, rich settlements, he took with him as guide Estebanico, who had already learned the curing rituals among the northern tribes three years earlier, and a large contingent of Indians. They were presumably a collection of Pima-speaking groups who had come south with the Cabeza de Vaca party three years before[18] and others, probably Cáhitan speakers from villages on the Sinaloa River. Cabeza de Vaca had reported, "It was the negro who talked with them all the time; he inquired about the road we should follow, the villages—in short, about everything we wanted to know" (chap. 31, p. 129 [fol. 45r]). With his experience as advance scout and interpreter for the Cabeza de Vaca party and the company of his old friends to serve as guides, it is not surprising that he pushed northward far ahead of the friar.

Fray Marcos and Esteban agreed upon a code of crosses that would transmit geographical information about the territory. The black scout would use them as he proceeded along "the way north, fifty or sixty leagues" up one of the major trade routes from central Mexico to the north, which since pre-Columbian times had been a corridor for the movement of both ceremonialism and trade contacts as far as the Hohokam, Mogollon, and Anasazi regions.[19] In the sixteenth century, Riley observed, "the entire Greater Southwest operated as an interacting entity with not only trade relationships but also ties of a sociopolitical and religious nature" (Riley 1987, 7). Fray Marcos described his system of signals as follows:

> And I agreed with him that if he received any information of a rich,
> peopled land, that was something great, he should not go farther, but
> that he return in person or send me Indians with this signal, which we
> arranged: that if the thing was of moderate importance, he send me
> a white cross the size of a hand; if it was something great he send me
> one of two hands; and if it was something bigger and better than New
> Spain, he send me a large cross. (Hallenbeck 18, [CDI 3:333])

Almost immediately Esteban sent back messages to Fray Marcos by his Indian interpreters, who brought larger and larger crosses. From this point on, their communication appropriated the sign system of Christian symbology to transmit information that was political as well as geographical, for the erection of a cross was part of the formal act of taking possession of new territories. Thus, in this first reconnaissance of the northern borderlands, the cross became a metasign that merged geopolitical space and spiritual space in Fray Marcos's report, as it also had in those of the medieval pilgrims.[20]

In May, now at Vacapá but still many days' journey from Cíbola,[21] Fray Marcos received the first news of Esteban's arrival at the famed city. A young Indian had managed to escape, bringing a report of ominous events: Esteban had sent his gourd rattles adorned with bells and "two feathers, one white and the other red" (29) to the lord of Cíbola, who threw them to the ground and sent the messengers back to tell Esteban that they would all be killed if they attempted to enter the city.[22] Disregarding the alarm that this news caused among his own guides, Fray Marcos pushed on ahead until he met two bloody and wounded Indians who had been with Estebanico at Cíbola and had witnessed the massacre they now related. At this textual juncture, the climax of the narrative is again articulated in terms of the sign of the calabazas adorned with red and white feathers and bells. Like Cabeza de Vaca's in Sinaloa, Esteban's faith in their power was so strong that he sent them on ahead to the lord of Cíbola as his own sign. The violent rejection they provoked in that leader, and Esteban's arrogant answer to it, are represented in the text by yet a second detailed telling of the same events, but on this occasion the narrator interjects the mode of direct discourse.

Finally, they told me that when Estévan arrived at one *jornada* from the city of Cíbola, he sent his messengers with his calabash to Cíbola, to the lord, to make it known to them that he was going to make peace and to cure them. When they gave him the calabash and he saw the cascabels, he angrily threw the calabash to the ground and said: "I know these people, for these bells are not of the fashion of ours; tell them to turn back at once; if not, no man of them will remain alive," and thus he remained much enraged. And the messengers returned, but feared to tell Estévan of what had happened; however, they finally told him, and he told them that they should have no fear; that he wished to go there, because although they had answered him badly, they would receive him well. So he went on and arrived at the city of Cíbola just before the setting of the sun, with all the people who went with him, which would be more than three hundred men, not counting the many women; and they [the Cíbolans] would not consent for him to enter the city, but [put them] into a large house with good apartments that was outside the city, and presently they took from Estévan all that he carried, telling him that the lord so ordered. . . . The next day, when the sun was a lancelength high, Estévan went from the house and some of the chiefs with him, and at once there came many people from the city and, when he saw them, he began to flee and we with him. We heard loud voices in the city, and on the terraces we saw many men and women watching. We saw no more of Estévan, but we believe that they shot him with arrows as they did the rest who were with him, of whom there escaped none but us. (Hallenbeck 31–32, [CDI, 3:345–46])

The shift from an indirect to a direct representation of Indian speech acts in this key episode highlights the fatal encounter, intensifying the suspense and sinister image created by the first sighting of the fabled Cíbola. It also creates a dramatic vignette of its lord reacting angrily to the gourds and arrogant message sent by Esteban. Thus at Cíbola there was no exchange or acceptance of the ceremonial objects but rather an explicit rejection that is twice told. The transmission of messages did not take place effectively. Freed from their "old context" among the Opatas and Pimas, the feathered rattles provoked rage and death when they were encoded into the new Zuni context. But the transmission of meaning was skewed when the positive cultural sign that had been appropriated from one context became a negative one when transmitted into a new one whose receptor encoded other values, producing a radical inversion of sign values from positive to negative.

Riley has established that, at the time of first Spanish contact, Cíbola-Zuni was the western terminus of the complex of trade routes running east, south and northwest, part of a larger network of the Greater Southwest where exchange of trade, information and ceremonial stretched from central Mexico, north to beyond Pecos (1987, 190–98).[23] Since the late fifteenth century the Zunis, like other Puebloan peoples, had been subject to increased pressure and aggression by nomadic Athapascan groups of Apaches or Jumanos who had moved into the area (Forbes 1960, Riley 1987). The lord of Cíbola could well have identified the gourds as those of one of these hostile groups. Or was the calabaza identified as an object that had demonic values, holding potential for what Bahr has translated as "the staying sickness," which in the Piman tradition is caused "by the strength of dangerous objects" (Bahr et al., 1974)? Was his feathered gourd a dangerous object that also involved transgression in the Zuni code? Bahr's study of shamanism and healing rituals among the Piman cultures points out that the shaman is the guardian not only of the tribal health but also of the Piman sense of cultural identity. "Rattles," he explains, "are part of the means by which the shaman gains access to spirits. This is the sound produced by his voice and his rattle" (1974, 206). Gourds function as aural enhancers because they extend the range of human presence beyond the range of the human voice.[24] We can only speculate about the extent to which Esteban had learned similar concepts, but—given the considerable evidence of the success of his previous curing experiences among Opatan and Upper and Lower Piman tribes with Cabeza de Vaca—he apparently understood that very well, sending them ahead of him as a way of projecting his power as a shaman. Still other factors that could have contributed to the hostile Zuni reaction were pointed out by Petersen (1985), who noted that there were Aztec artisans in Mexico who produced cascabeles of copper, gold, and silver. Did the Cíbolans "misread" Esteban's rattles with their attached bells as Aztec artifacts from Mexico because he was accompanied by more than three hundred "Mexican" Indians? Did they look upon Esteban as a scout for an army that would later come against them as well, which of course he was (Petersen 1985, 30)? It is not improbable that the gourd with its red feathers—in Zuni semantics, red signified the south (Tedlock 1979, 499) or violence (Cushing 1979, 175)—was read as a southern Athapascan or an Opatan or Piman sign. Twenty years after the fall of Tenochtitlan, the news of the defeat of the Mexicas by white strangers must have reached the Zuni through their extensive trade networks. The independent Zuni, on the defense against their Puebloan and Athapascan neighbors to the north, south, and east and the Hopis on the west, may easily have overreacted. Or this large group of strangers who demanded entry into their city may have arrived at the time of a secret society festival, whose ritual that entrance would have violated (Crampton 1977, 16).

The Spanish interpretations of the events at Cíbola recorded by Esteban's contemporaries point to the black man's violation of social codes, arrogance, and lack of credibility. The first is the account that Fernando de Alarcón picked up along the Colorado River west of Cíbola little more than a year later, which he reported to the viceroy from the Gulf of California in November 1540. When he inquired about the presence of other Spaniards at "Cevola" from an Indian informant who had been there, he wrote (as Hakluyt translated his report),

> He answered me no, saving one Negro which ware about his legs & armes certain things which did ring. Your lordship is to call to mind how this Negro which went with frier Marcos was wont to weare bels, & feathers on his armes & legs, & that he caried plates of divers colours, and that it was not much above a yeere agoe since he came into those parts. I demanded upon what occasion he was killed; and he answered me, That the lord of Cevola inquired of him whether he had other brethren: he answered that he had an infinite number, and that they had great store of weapons with them, and that they were not very farre from thence. Which when he had heard, many of the chiefe men consulted together, and resolved to kill him, that he might not give newes unto these his brethren, where they dwelt, & that for this cause they slew him, and cut him into many pieces, which were divided among all those chiefe lords, that they might know assuredly that he was dead; and also that he had a dogge like mine, which he likewise killed a great while after. (Alarcón [1540; 1598–1600] 1903–5, 304–5)

Pedro de Castañeda y Náçera, who reached Zuni in 1540 with Coronado's army, offered more explicit details, which he recorded in his *Relación de la jornada de Cíbola* twenty years later. In chapter 3, "How they killed the negro Esteban at Cíbola, and how Fray Marcos returned in flight," he notes Esteban's command of regional languages but also attributes his downfall to pride, arrogance, and transgression:

When Esteban got away from the said friars, he craved to gain honor and fame in everything and to be credited with the boldness and daring of discovering, all by himself, those terraced pueblos, so famed throughout the land. . . . As the negro had told them that farther back two white men, sent by a great lord, were coming, that they were learned in the things of heaven, and that they were coming to instruct them in divine matters, the Indians thought he must have been a spy or guide of some nations that wanted to come and conquer them. They thought it was nonsense for him to say that the people in the land whence he came were white, when he was black, and that he had been sent by them. So they went to him, and because, after some talk, he asked them for turquoises and women, they considered this an affront and determined to kill him. (Castañeda [ca. 1563; 1596] 1896, 112–13)

More significant evidence of transgression comes from Elsie Clews Parsons ([1939] 1974), who has studied the comparative values of the earlier cosmologies of the various Puebloan peoples in her monumental *Pueblo Indian Religion*. The Zuni, Parsons informs us, think by analogy, taking resemblance as an explanation of relationship. This use of resemblance "is controlling and fundamental in their ceremonial life. In such ideology . . . like causes or produces like, or like follows like; like may also preclude or cure like" (I:1:188). She notes that Cushing had remarked that to the Zuni the whole world is related on a basis of resemblance, a habit of mind that leads to reversing cause and effect, e.g., summer birds are supposed to bring summer instead of summer bringing summer birds (I:1:188). Therefore, the rattles of the black man who had come from the south could bring more of all that they symbolized. The line of sacred cornmeal "closes" a space against intrusion. Thus, Esteban would have been killed at Hawikuh by Horn Society guards if he crossed a line drawn on the trail against him by the Zuni warriors (I:2:363). Parsons states that Esteban was killed, "undoubtedly as a witch. He may have asked for turquoise and women, according to one report, but I surmise that the rattle was at the bottom of it. (Perhaps Esteban, *el negro*, was Chakwena Woman, the black-faced warrior whose heart was in her rattle!)" (I:2:385). Parsons points out that "Current Pueblo believe that anyone [who] may be a witch looks Spanish (or southern Athapascan)" (II:1:1067).

Another association of Esteban with danger from warring Athapascans is found in the ethnographic testimony of a Zuni tale from an oral tradition that dates back to the time of the first Spanish contact. It was collected by Frank Hamilton Cushing, who lived among the Zuni during the late nineteenth century, and it told of a time "when our ancients killed the Black Mexican at Kia-ki-me":

> But with these Black Mexicans came many Indians of Sóno-li, as they call it now, who carried feathers and long bows and cane arrows like the Apaches, who were enemies of our ancients; therefore these our ancients, being always bad tempered and quick to anger, made fools of themselves after their fashion, rushed into their town and out of their town, shouting, skipping and shooting with sling-stones and arrows and war clubs. Then the Indians of Sóno-li set up a great howl, and then they and our ancients did much ill to one another. Then and thus, was killed by our ancients, right where the stone stands down by the arroyo of Kia-ki-me, one of the Black Mexicans. . . . Then the rest ran away, chased by our grandfathers, and went back toward their country in the Land of Everlasting Summer. (Cushing 1979, 174–75)

Why Esteban, with multilingual interpreters and more experience in meeting new indigenous groups than any Spaniard of his time, ignored the warning from the Cíbolan war chief will never be known. But what our modern readings of this testimony from contemporary reports and oral tradition can detect is how the appropriation of older signs formed new codes to translate and transmit new situations of exploration, contact, and collision between cultural groups. Spanish survivors assume indigenous identity and learn to use the power of ritual healing and gift exchange to effect peace in the region. Indian signs relay Spanish conversion messages. A Catholic Spanish sign maps the first geography of Pimería Alta. At Cíbola positive values become negative. What was once power becomes transgression. Rejection triggers resistance and violence.

Certain ritual practices employed the same symbolic grammar, but the valence of the individual items changed as the codes and contexts changed. Used among many Southwest cultures, the ritual gourd as a semantically significant object could be read in different ways at different times and places. The Hispanized Esteban did not make the necessary distinctions among the tribes and their different values and rituals. In his hands the gourd lost its specificity, becoming a general cultural sign, yet the lord of Cíbola decoded it as a specific one. Although accompanied by indigenous guides whose worldview encompassed trade with and knowledge of the Zuni (Riley 1987), Esteban presumed that the power of his calabazas would prevail against Cíbola as they had among the Texan and Sonoran groups. And like the rattle, an aurality enhancer, the gourds became a geopolitical enhancer—the extension of the domination of the cross beyond the territories under the military control of New Spain. In these two earliest texts, the feathered gourd rattles are informed symbolically by the ancient Indian traditions of shamanism and its ritual healing. As such, their appropriation elicits a double response. In the contacts reported by the Cabeza de Vaca party, they voice an aesthetic of power and mediation. In Fray Marcos's and Estebanico's contacts, they represent an iconography of extension of the Spanish cross.[25]

In both narratives, the cross and the gourd mark the very first attempts of the Spanish to incorporate the northern borderlands—which had stood outside Aztec as well as Spanish imperial control—into the coded space of Spanish conquest and colonization. Closer to the political metropolis of the viceroyalty, the Indian groups who accepted the cross would soon acculturate (Johnson 1971; Spicer 1962; Riley 1976a), while beyond the edge of the world known to Spain, the fiercely independent Zuni would maintain their religious and political autonomy against many waves of imperial invaders (Simmons 1979). The telling of both sets of events epitomizes the contrasting nature of initial cultural contact in the Greater Sonoran Desert: mediation and conversion among the Opatas and the Lower Pimas in north central Mexico; rejection and resistance among the Zunis at Cíbola and beyond.

In this sense, these two *relaciones* stand as paradigms for the cultural interaction that would follow in this region during the next two centuries. An examination of sign function in Cabeza de Vaca's and Fray Marcos's narratives offers us a closer look at the production of cultural meaning in the making and a better understanding of the elements that formed it. It also explains how both documents became such powerful creators and transmitters of signs in their own right—catalysts of the new relationships between cultures and the new models of communication they demanded in the interior of North America, on new frontiers that lay beyond the maps.

ACKNOWLEDGMENTS

This paper incorporates segments of my unpublished paper "The Semiosis of Miracles and Mythmaking in *La Relación* of Alvar Núñez Cabeza de Vaca," read at the Latin American Studies Association meeting at Albuquerque on 19 May 1985. Preliminary versions of this essay were read as papers at the Symposium on Colonial Letters of the Kentucky Modern Languages Association at Lexington, Kentucky, in April 1988, and at the Planning Conference for the Columbus Quincentennary at the Southwest Center of the University of Arizona in Tucson on 17 November 1988. The research presented here was made possible through funding by and a sabbatical leave from the Arizona State University College of Liberal Arts and Sciences, during the 1985–86 academic year, a Columbian Quincentennial Grant at the Herbert Dunlap Smith Center for the History of Cartography at the Newberry Library in Chicago, and a supplementary grant from the American Philosophical Society during the summer of 1988, to which I extend my thanks for support of my work.

NOTES

1. Cabeza de Vaca's original narrative published in Zamora in 1542 was entitled *La relacion que dio Aluar nunez cabeca de vaca de lo acaescido en las Indias en la armada donde yua por gouernador panfhilo de narbaez . . .* Quotations in English from *La relación* are from Fanny Bandelier's translation of the 1542 edition (Cabeza de Vaca 1972). My analysis and the Spanish text used for it are based on the edition of 1555 prepared for publication in Valladolid with *privilegio* by the author, consulted in the copy owned by the New York Public Library, which I thank for permission to use this rare item. (It is also referred to as *Los Naufragios*.) For critical editions, see *La relación o Naufragios de Alvar Núñez Cabeca de Vaca,* ed. Martín A. Favata and José B. Fernández, and the annotated *Los Naufragios* prepared by Enrique Pupo-Walker, which compare the 1542 and 1555 editions. There is another narrative of the Narváez expedition, the "official" report submitted by Cabeza de Vaca with Dorantes and Castillo and called *The Joint Report,* that Gonzalo Fernández de Oviedo included in his *Historia general y natural de las Indias* (1547). The translation of it by Gerald Thiesen was published with the Bandelier translation in 1972 as *The Expedition of Pánfilo de Narváez.* The extent to which the report was edited or rewritten by Oviedo is not certain, but his references to the curing procedures are recorded as *miraglos* and are few in comparison with those Cabeza de Vaca himself narrated, a topic which bears further examination.

2. Space does not permit reproduction of the Spanish texts of the narratives cited herein. They are identified by chapter and page numbers from the Bandelier translation and, in brackets, the folio numbers from the 1555 edition of Cabeza de Vaca's *Relación* that I consulted at the New York Public Library. Bracketed items within the English translation by Fanny Bandelier are my own modifications of her at times inaccurate or incomplete renditions.

3. Most studies of the healing episodes in this *relación* have been viewed from the perspective of European or modern Latin American literary traditions. David Lagmanovich qualified them as part of a pilgrimage tale (1978), and Robert Lewis's incisive essay on the tensions between history and fiction included an analysis of Christian symbology (1982). More recently, Enrique Pupo-Walker discussed the text in terms of its sources in the Christian hagiographic tradition (1987). An exception is Sylvia Molloy's lucid discussion of "alterity and recognition," which shows how Cabeza de Vaca's "curative journey, with its progressive complication and ritual valorization, changes the relation between the I and the other" (1987, 187). While several points made by Molloy coincide with my own, my essay proposes an analysis of the ritual exchanges in Cabeza de Vaca's narrative in terms of the cross-cultural contacts that took place and their essential relationship with subsequent events that occurred during Fray Marcos de Niza and Esteban's journey, within the larger context of first contacts beyond the northern frontiers of New Spain. After my essay for this volume was submitted, Adorno's 1991 study posited her reading of ritual exchange and *La Mala Cosa* as a "negotiation of fear." While our ideas converge on certain points, our work has been conducted independently. Rabasa's analysis examines Cabeza de Vaca's *Naufragios* and the scarcely studied *Comentarios* in terms of allegory and ethnography. As this volume goes to press, Enrique Pupo-Walker has published an annotated critical edition of the *Relación* entitled *Los Naufragios* (1992), prefaced by an extensive critical study and bibliography, which includes a discussion of the evangelizing shaman (pp. 122–25).

4. On the obligation of giving, receiving, and repaying, see Mauss 1967, 37–45, and note 15 below on Taussig.

5. In the final eleven chapters of his narrative, particularly chapter 24, on Indian customs, and chapter 26, on Indian nations and languages, Cabeza de Vaca explicitly distinguishes the many distinct language groups, their mutual intelligibility or lack thereof, the names and relationships of these different ethnic groups, whether the tribes were warring or friendly, and how they passed the Spaniards from friendly to enemy tribes guided by the women. Campbell and Campbell observe that the "Maliacones, Avavares and Cutalchuches apparently spoke different languages. The Avavares are said to have spoken their own languages, as well as that of the Mariames" (1981, 32). For the most complete treatment of the location, languages, and cultures of the indigenous groups that the Cabeza de Vaca party met in what is now southern Texas, see Campbell and Campbell 1981, Krieger 1961, and Riley 1971

and 1987. Campbell and Campbell have identified these peoples as among those who occupied the inland region between the lower Guadalupe and the lower Nueces rivers in Texas, who regularly moved southward in the summer to the prickly pear region (1981, 37–40). Most are extinct, and their linguistic and ethnic groupings as Caddoan, Karakarawan, Tonkawa, or Coahuiltecan is speculative because the nature of the linguistic evidence is tenuous (Campbell and Campbell 1981, 33). "Most of the Indian groups of Area 2," the Campbells write, "have at times been referred to as 'Coahuiltecans.' Originally this name was used to refer only to certain groups that were believed to have spoken the language now known as Coahuilteca. In recent years the name *Coahuiltecan* has come to be rather loosely used to refer to nearly all of the hunting and gathering groups of southern Texas and northeastern Mexico, who are assumed to have had similar cultures" (Campbell and Campbell 1981, 36–37).

6. I am indebted to Stephen Nichols's analysis of these kinds of strategies in terms of narrative meaning for telling about miracles and miracle sites in medieval chronicles (1983, 157) and to Ronald Finucane's discussion of the Gospels as the established context for discussing miracles and faith healing in the Middle Ages (1973, 47–50) for the insights they have provided for Cabeza de Vaca's telling of healing events.

7. Cabeza de Vaca's account of the healing episodes and their qualification as *miraglos* by Oviedo in his reprint of the *Joint Report* sparked considerable controversy among readers across the centuries. Lafaye discussed them in the context of sixteenth-century Mexican evangelization. In 1621, Padre Honorio Philopono [Caspar Plautius] published his *Novo typis transacta navigatio* in Linz, which severely censured Cabeza de Vaca's accounts of miraculous healing. They were vigorously defended by Ardoino in 1736 in his *Examen apologético*.

8. For a recent discussion of the many interpretations of the route taken by the Cabeza de Vaca party, see Chipman 1987, including Chipman's estimate of the locations of the Isla de Mal Hado and of the prickly-pear region on the Texas coastal plain. Chipman's review is largely based on Campbell and Campbell's detailed analysis of the internal ethnographic evidence from Cabeza de Vaca's writings on the three rivers area of southern Texas, identifying the "river of nuts" as the lower Guadalupe River and the prickly pear harvesting grounds as being near the lower Nueces River west of Corpus Christi Bay in the vicinity of Alice, Texas, in Jim Wells County (Chipman 1987, 4–7). Chipman and the Campbells draw on Krieger's "alternative" route (1961), which took the travelers down into northeastern Mexico after their first crossing of the Río Grande.

9. "It was after leaving the Cuchendados that the Río Grande was crossed, and shortly thereafter the Spaniards saw their first mountains in what is now northern Nuevo León. . . . It was when the Spaniards were at the foot of the mountains that a change in travel plan was made: they decided to travel westward before turning southward to Spanish settlements in lower Mexico. When they proceeded northwest they reached the 'junta' or juncture of the Río Grande and the Río Concho" (Campbell and Campbell 1981, 37).

10. Riley points out that "the cultural situation at La Junta [in the sixteenth century] is confused by a welter of names of diverse peoples, and especially by the relationship of the settled agricultural folk to the group called Jumano, tattooed or painted, nomadic bison hunting Indians who wintered in the La Junta area" (1987, 295–96). After a careful review of the research, he concludes that "at present we cannot make a final linguistic answer to the linguistic situation in the La Junta area. From the data at hand, it is probable that the sedentary La Junta people were Uto-Aztecan speakers and with the strong possibility, at any rate, that the Jumano were early Apacheans" (1987, 298). See also Forbes 1959 and 1960, and Scholes 1940.

11. The specific textual comments on the authority the gourd rattles commanded and their use in distinct ethnic and geographical areas, found in chapters 28 through 31, supports the Campbells' conclusion that "shamans were probably universal in this area" of southern Texas, as well as Hallenbeck's statement for tribes in northeastern and central Mexico: "So it appears that each of the tribes he thereafter encountered—Sumas, Jumanos, Mansos, Opatas, Pimas and Cahitas—respected even alien religious symbols" (1987, 105n176). For the route of the Cabeza de Vaca party through north central and western Mexico, see the discussion and maps in Krieger 1961. It is important to remember that the areas occupied by these Uto-Aztecan peoples in the first half of the sixteenth century were more extensive than, and different from, their modern territories. See also the discussion and maps in Riley 1987, esp. chap. 4 and 5; Spicer 1962, 11; Bahr 1988, 197; and *Historia general de Sonora*, 1:268. For the larger context, see the map of indigenous languages and ethnic boundaries of North America as they existed when first encountered by European explorers in Coe et al. 1986, 44–45. In all probability, the Cabeza de Vaca party traversed the territory of the Opatas in the upper drainages of the Sonora and Yaqui rivers in eastern Sonora. Johnson's important monograph on their culture identifies them as a sophisticated people, "numbering some sixty thousand at the time of the Conquest, [who] have completely disappeared today as a cultural and ethnic entity" (1971, 170). Their two lan-

guage groups, the Opata proper and the Eudeve, were part of the Cáhita-Opata-Tarahumar group of the Uto-Aztecan linguistic family (Kroeber 1934). They became staunch allies of the Spanish and underwent rapid acculturation (Johnson 1970, 171, 192–98).

12. "And as soon as we would arrive those that went with us would sack the houses of the others; but as they knew of the custom before our coming, they hid some of their chattels, and, after receiving us with much rejoicing, they took out the things which they had concealed and presented them to us. These were beads and ochre, and several little bags of silver. We, following the custom, turned the gifts immediately over to the Indians who had come in our company, and after they had given these presents they began their dances and celebrations, and sent for others from another village nearby to come and look at us. In the afternoon they all came, and brought us beads, bows, and other little things, which we also distributed" (chap. 28, p. 110 [fol. 38v]).

13. Documented in the several *relaciones* of the expeditions of Guzmán and his troops published by García Icazbalceta in 1886. See, for example, the account by García del Pilar, p. 258. Also see the discussion in Riley 1987, esp. chap. 4.

14. See also Molloy's discussion of this same passage in terms of Cabeza de Vaca's changing concept of "otherness" and *ellos* and *nosotros* (1987, 448).

15. I am indebted to Michael Taussig's 1980 study for important insights into the role of the folk healer as a transmitter of knowledge and power in colonial society and to Regina Harrison for first bringing it to my attention. The Campbells point to the significance of Cabeza de Vaca's role as an ethnographer, based on participant observation: "No Spaniard of later times lived with Indians of the area and survived to write about his experiences. Cabeza de Vaca is the only Spaniard who gave names for most of the groups he encountered, who indicated where each group lived relative to other groups, and who described in some detail the sociocultural behavior of specific Indian groups. His Mariames and Avavares are still the best described Indians native to southern Texas. His cultural information quantitatively exceeds that of all his successors combined. Cabeza de Vaca should be regarded as the first and indeed the only true ethnographer of southern Texas who was a contemporary of the Indians that he described" (1981, 64–65).

16. For the analogy to a palimpsest I am indebted to Thérèse Bouysse-Cassagne's discussion of ritual practices and the coding of spatial and political dimensions in Aymara and colonial organization in the Andes (1986).

17. The English citations are from Hallenbeck's translation, *The Journey of Fray Marcos de Niza*. My analysis of his discourse is based on the Spanish text printed in the *Colección de documentos inéditos* (Madrid 1865), 3:325–51, from the *Colección de Muñoz*, vol. 81, and hereafter referred to as CDI 3.

18. Riley's discussion of the interpreters and informants of Fray Marcos and Esteban (1971, 289–94) concludes that they were "probably speakers of one or the other Lower Pima dialect. There must have been Cáhitan speakers as well" (293). When they reached the Gila–Salt River areas, they were in Pima Alto country, but Riley concluded that "it is extremely likely that Marcos's Pima could communicate fairly easily with northern Pima speakers" (294). Hallenbeck considers that Fray Marcos's interpreters must have been Cáhitas who had been purchased and freed from slavery by Mendoza (74). Spicer identifies the Indians that accompanied Fray Marcos as Opatas and Lower Pimas. Cáhita (now extinct), Opata (now extinct), and Pima are Uto-Aztecan languages. Zuni has no easily traceable relatives (Hale and Harris 1979, 170–73).

19. See Riley 1975 and 1987, 76–88, on trade in the Serrana Province, esp. his map, "Major Trade Routes in Sonora, A.D. 1500," in Riley 1987, 77.

20. See Finucane 1977 and also my study (1989) on how Fray Marcos de Niza's text certifies the reports of Esteban's visual sign, the cross, and the Indians' verbal sign.

21. The location of Vacapá and the route of Fray Marcos's journey have long been the subject of historical debate, in the course of which three routes have been reconstructed. Drawing on Wagner 1934 and Sauer 1932, Hallenbeck (1940) went to great lengths to show that Fray Marcos probably never got much beyond the Sonora Valley. The Wagner-Sauer-Hallenbeck position is that Fray Marcos never reached Cíbola or the Zuni town of Hawikuh, while other scholars, like Di Peso (1974), reconstructed a route far to the east. Undreimer (1947) argued that Fray Marcos got as far as he said he did, while Rodack (1985) assumed that Fray Marcos did see Cíbola and, asking simply which of the six Zuni villages it was, made a strong case for Kiakima instead of Hawikuh. Petersen's calculations place Cíbola at the confluence of the Salt and Gila rivers, 300 miles north of the Sonora Valley. For a recent discussion of this and other historical issues concerning the journey of Fray Marcos, see Weber 1987 and Reff 1991.

22. The first version of the telling is cast in indirect discourse in Hallenbeck, 29–30, and CDI 3:334.

23. See Riley 1975, 1976a, and 1976b.

24. Personal communication from Donald Bahr to Maureen Ahern, April 1987.

25. Both authors seemed to understand the significance of their appropriations, as they explicitly inscribed the symbolic objects and acts into the climactic segments of their texts. Like their Andean counterparts of the same decade, the narratives of Alvar Núñez Cabeza de Vaca and Fray Marcos represent "the incorporation of native life into the enterprise of colonial communication" (Cummins 1988, 284). Even though both Fray Marcos and Esteban brought many interpreters with them, their narratives confirm that they made extensive use of nonverbal native signs as well as Spanish ones in the critical contact moments.

BIBLIOGRAPHY

Adorno, Rolena. 1991. The Negotiation of Fear in Cabeza de Vaca's Naufragios. Representations 33:163–99.

Ahern, Maureen. 1985. The Semiosis of Miracles and Mythmaking in La Relación by Alvar Núñez Cabeza de Vaca. Unpublished paper read at the Latin American Studies Association meeting in Albuquerque, New Mexico, on May 19.

————. 1989. The Certification of Cíbola: Discursive Strategies in La Relación del descubrimiento de las siete ciudades by Fray Marcos de Niza (1539). Dispositio 14:1–11.

Alarcón, Fernando de. [1540; 1598–1600] 1903–5. The Relation of the Navigation and Discovery Which Captaine Fernando Alarchon made by the Order of the Right Honourable Lord Don Antonio de Mendoza Vizeroy of New Spaine, Dated in Colima an Haven of New Spaine. In The Principal Navigations, Voiages, Trafiques and Discoueries of the English nation . . . , ed. R. Hakluyt, 9:297–318. London: 1598–1600. Reprint. Glasgow: James MacLehose and Sons, 1903–5. Translated from the Italian in Ramusio, Navigationi et Viaggi, vol. 3, Venice: 1556.

Ardoino, Antonio. 1736. Examen apologético de la histórica narración de los naufragios, peregrinaciones, i milagros de Alvar Núñez Cabeza de Baca, en las tierras de la Florida i del Nuevo Mexico. Madrid: Imprenta de Juan de Zúñiga.

Bahr, Donald M., et al. 1974. Piman Shamanism and Staying Sickness (Ká:cim Múmkidag). Tucson: University of Arizona Press.

————. 1988. Pima-Papago Christianity. Journal of the Southwest 1:133–66.

Bouysse-Cassagne, Thérèse. 1986. Urco and Auma: Aymara Concepts of Space. In Anthropological History of Andean Polities, ed. John V. Murra, Nathan Wachtel, and Jacques Revell, 201–27. New York: Cambridge University Press and Editions de la Maison des Sciences de l'Homme.

Cabeza de Vaca, Alvar Núñez. *See* Núñez Cabeza de Vaca, Alvar

Campbell, T. N., and T. J. Campbell. 1981. *Historical Indian Groups of the Choke Canyon Reservoir and Surrounding Area, Southern Texas.* San Antonio: Center for Archeological Research, University of Texas at San Antonio.

Castañeda y Náçera, Pedro. [1563; 1596] 1896. *Relación de la jornada de Cíbola.* In *The Coronado Expedition, 1540–42,* ed. and trans. George Parker Winship, 108–85. Denver: Rio Grande Press.

Chipman, Donald E. 1987. In Search of Cabeza de Vaca's Route Across Texas: An Historiographical Survey. *Southwest Historical Quarterly* 91:127–48.

Coe, Michael, Dean Snow, and Elizabeth Benson, eds. 1986. *Atlas of Ancient America.* New York: Facts on File Publications.

Crampton, C. Gregory. 1977. *The Zunis of Cibola.* Salt Lake City: University of Utah Press.

Cummins, Thomas B. F. 1988. Abstraction to Narrative: Kero Imagery of Peru and the Colonial Alteration of Native Identity. Ph.D. diss., University of California at Los Angeles.

Cushing, Frank Hamilton. 1979. *Zuni: Selected Writings of Frank Hamilton Cushing.* Ed. Jesse Green. Lincoln: University of Nebraska Press.

Di Peso, Charles. 1974. *Casas Grandes: A Fallen Trading Center of the Gran Chichimeca.* 8 vols. Flagstaff, Ariz.: Northland Press.

Fernández de Oviedo, Gonzalo. [1547] 1959. *Historia general y natural de las Indias.* Ed. Juan Pérez de Tudela Bueso. Vol. 4. Madrid: Biblioteca de Autores Españoles.

Finucane, Ronald L. 1977. *Miracles and Pilgrims.* Totowa, N.J.: Rowman and Littlefield.

Forbes, Jack D. 1959. Unknown Athapaskans: The Identification of the Jano, Jocome, Jumano, Manso and Suma, and other Indian tribes of the Southwest. *Ethnohistory* 6:97–159.

———. 1960. *Apache, Navaho and Spaniard.* Norman: University of Oklahoma Press.

García Icazbalceta, Joaquín. 1886. *Colección de documentos para la historia de México.* Vol. 2. Mexico City: Antigua Librería.

Hale, Kenneth, and David Harris. 1979. Historical Linguistics and Archeology. In *Handbook of North American Indians,* ed. William C. Sturtevant, 9:170–77. Washington, D.C.: Smithsonian Institution.

Hallenbeck, Cleve. 1987. *The Journey of Fray Marcos de Niza.* Introduction by David J. Weber. Illustrations by José Cisneros. Dallas: Southern Methodist University Press.

Hammond, George P. 1940. *Narratives of the Coronado Expedition, 1540–42.* Ed. and trans. G. P. Hammond and Agapito Rey. Albuquerque: University of New Mexico Press.

Historia general de Sonora. 1985. Período Prehistórico y Prehispánico. Vol. 1. Hermosillo, Sonora, Mex.: Gobierno del Estado de Sonora.

Johnson, Jean B. 1971. The Opata: An Inland Tribe of Sonora. In *The Northern Mexican Frontier,* ed. Basil J. Hedrik, J. Charles Kelly, and Carrol L. Riley, 169–99. Carbondale: Southern Illinois University Press.

Krieger, Alex D. 1961. The Travels of Alvar Núñez Cabeza de Vaca in Texas and Mexico, 1534–36. In *Homenaje a Pablo Martínez del Río en el vigésimoquinto aniversario de la prima edición de Los Orígenes Americanos,* 459–74. Mexico City: Instituto Nacional de Antropología.

Kroeber, Alfred L. 1934. "Uto-Aztecan Languages of Mexico." *Ibero-Americana* (Berkeley) 8:1–27.

Lafaye, Jacques. 1962. Les miracles d'Alvar Núñez Cabeza de Vaca (1527–36). *Bulletin Hispanique* 64:137–53.

Lagmanovich, David. 1978. Los *Naufragios* de Alvar Núñez como construcción narrativa. *Kentucky Romance Quarterly* 25:27–37.

Lewis, Robert E. 1982. Los *Naufragios* de Alvar Núñez: Historia y ficción. *Revista Iberoamericana* 48:681–94.

Mauss, Marcel. 1967. *The Gift: Forms and Functions of Exchange in Archaic Societies.* Trans. Ian Cunnison. New York: W. W. Norton.

Molloy, Sylvia. 1987. Alteridad y reconocimiento en los *Naufragios* de Alvar Núñez Cabeza de Vaca. *Nueva Revista de Filología Hispánica* 35:425–49.

Nichols, Stephen, Jr. 1983. *Romanesque Signs: Early Medieval Narrative and Iconography.* New Haven: Yale University Press.

Niza, Fray Marcos de. [1539] 1865. Descubrimiento de las siete ciudades: Relación. In *Colección de documentos inéditos relativos al descubrimiento, conquista y colonización de las posesiones españolas en América y Oceanía,* 3:325–51. Madrid: Imprenta de Manuel B. de Quirós.

Núñez Cabeza de Vaca, Alvar. [1542] 1555. *La relación y comentarios del gouernador Aluar Nunez Cabeza de Vaca de lo acaescido en las dos jornadas que hizo a las Indias.* Valladolid, Spain.

———. 1972. *The Narrative of Alvar Núñez Cabeza de Vaca.* Trans. Fanny Bandelier.

Introduction by John Francis Bannon. Illustrations by Michael McCurdy. With Oviedo's version of the lost joint report, trans. Gerald Theisen. Barre, Mass.: Imprint Society.

———. 1986. *La Relación o naufragios de Alvar Núñez Cabeza de Vaca*. Ed. Martín A. Favata and José B. Fernández. Potomac, Md.: Scripta Humanística.

———. 1992. *Los Naufragios*. Ed. Enrique Pupo-Walker. Nueva Biblioteca de Erudición y Crítica, no 5. Madrid: Editorial Castalia.

Parsons, Elsie Clews. [1939] 1974. *Pueblo Indian Religion*. 4 vols. Parts I and II. Chicago: University of Chicago Press. Midway Reprint.

Pennington, Campbell W. 1980. *The Pima Bajo of Central Sonora Mexico*. Vol. 1: *The Material Culture*, ed. Campbell W. Pennington. Salt Lake City: University of Utah Press.

Petersen, Richard. 1985. *The Lost Cities of Cibola*. Phoenix, Ariz.: G. and H. Books.

Philopono, Honorio [Caspar Plautius]. 1621. *Novo typis transacta navigatio*. Linz.

Pupo-Walker, Enrique. 1987. Pesquisas para una nueva lectura de los *Naufragios* de Alvar Núñez Cabeza de Vaca. *Revista Iberoamericana* 141:517–39.

———. 1992. I: Sección introductoria; and II: Valoraciones del texto. In *Los Naufragios*, by Alvar Núñez Cabeza de Vaca. Madrid: Editorial Castalia.

Rabasa, José. Forthcoming. Allegory and Ethnography in Cabeza de Vaca's *Naufragios* and *Comentarios*. In *Violence, Resistance and Survival in the Americas: The Legacy of Conquest*, ed. William B. Taylor and Franklin Pease. Washington, D.C.: Smithsonian Institution Press.

Reff, Daniel T. 1991. Anthropological Analysis of Exploration Texts: Cultural Discourse and the Ethnological Import of Fray Marcos de Niza's Journey to Cibola. *American Anthropologist* 93:636–55.

Riley, Carroll L. 1971. Early Spanish-Indian Communication in the Greater Southwest. *New Mexico Historical Review* 46:285–314.

———. 1975. The Road to Hawikuh: Trade and Trade Routes to Cibola-Zuni During the Late Prehistoric and Early Historic Times. *The Kiva* 41 (4): 137–59.

———. 1976a. *Sixteenth Century Trade in the Greater Southwest*. Mesoamerican Studies, 10. Research Records of the University Museum. Carbondale: Southern Illinois University.

———. 1976b. Pecos and Trade. In *Across the Chichimec Sea: Papers in Honor of J. Charles Kelley*, ed. C. L. Riley and B. C. Hedrick, 53–64. Carbondale: Southern Illinois University Press.

———. 1987. *The Frontier People: The Greater Southwest in the Protohistoric Period*. Revised and expanded ed. Albuquerque: University of New Mexico Press.

Rodack, Madeleine Turrell. 1985. Cibola Revisited. *Southwest Cultural History* 10:163–82.

Sauer, Carl O. 1932. *The Road to Cíbola*. Berkeley: University of California Press.

Scholes, Frances V. 1940. Documentary Evidence Relating to the Jumanan Indians. *Contributions to American Anthropology and History* 6:271–89.

Simmons, Marc. 1979. History of Pueblo-Spanish Relations to 1821. In *Handbook of North American Indians*, ed. William C. Sturtevant, 9:178–93. Washington, D.C.: Smithsonian Institution.

Spicer, Edward H. 1962. *Cycles of Conquest*. Tucson: University of Arizona Press.

Taussig, Michael. 1980. Folk Healing and the Structure of Conquest in Southwest Colombia. *Journal of Latin American Lore* 6:217–78.

Tedlock, Dennis. 1979. Zuni Religion and World View. In *Handbook of North American Indians*, ed. William C. Sturtevant, 9:499–508. Washington, D.C.: Smithsonian Institution.

Undreimer, George J. 1947. Fray Marcos de Niza and His Journey to Cibola. *Americas* 3:415–86.

Uspensky, Boris. 1973. *The Poetics of Composition*. Trans. Valentine Zavarin and Susan Witting. Berkeley: University of California Press.

Wagner, Henry R. 1934. Fray Marcos de Niza. *New Mexico Historical Review* 9:184–227.

Weber, David. 1987. Cleve Hallenbeck, Fray Marcos and the Historians. Introduction to *The Journey of Fray Marcos de Niza*, by Cleve Hallenbeck, vii–xxxvii. Dallas: Southern Methodist University Press.

IV   The Seductive Power of Science

10

American Discoveries Noted on the Planisphere of Sancho Gutiérrez

Harry Kelsey

Among the great cartographical records in the Österreichische Nation-albibliothek in Vienna is a vellum planisphere made by Sancho Gutié-rrez in the middle of the sixteenth century. The son of Diego Gutiérrez, official cosmographer in the Casa de Contratación (the Spanish House of Trade in Seville), Sancho was himself a noted instrument and chart maker. At the time he completed his map, Sancho Gutiérrez was *cosmógrafo de honor* but had no official position in the Casa de Contratación. Within a few years, however, he received a royal appointment as cosmographer, the same position his father had held.[1]

Because of his positions, official and unofficial, it can be assumed that the Gutiérrez world map (see fig. 10.1) is a reasonably close copy of the *padrón general*, the official world map in the Casa de Contratación. Since nothing could be added to this map without consultation and verification, it can also be assumed that the Sancho Gutiérrez copy of the *padrón* is a reasonably accurate representation of the cartographic understanding of Spanish pilots and cosmographers of the time.

One interesting feature of the Gutiérrez map is a series of narrative legends scattered through the body of the work and also pasted along the righthand margin. The text describes recent discoveries, regional peculiarities, and stories from the early geographical commentaries. Some of these tales describe incredible men and beasts inhabiting various parts of the world, a fact that has puzzled many historians, who think the Spanish geographers should have known better.[2] But fanciful beasts and men were common features of Renais-

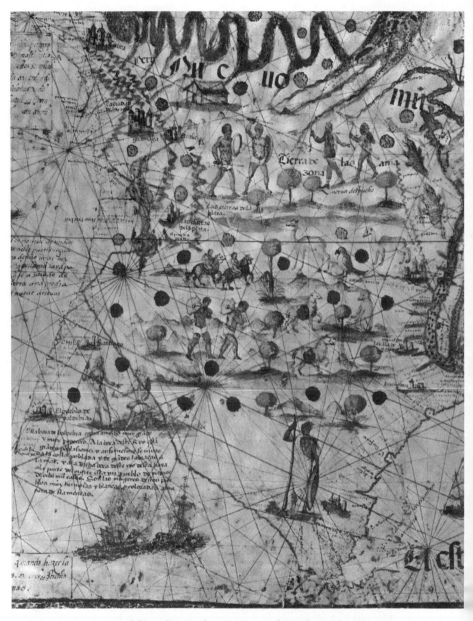

FIGURE 10.1. Detail from the Sancho Gutiérrez planisphere, showing two coastlines at the Strait of Magellan. Both are unsuccessful attempts to revise the manuscript to fit the results of coastal surveys. The basic problem is that this and other early maps showed the continent to be much wider than it actually was. (Courtesy the Österreichische Nationalbibliothek, Vienna.)

sance maps. Their inclusion does not mean that Gutiérrez believed these tales.[3] In a sense the stories were footnotes intended to show learned readers that Gutiérrez was familiar with all the standard classical works on geography. His accounts of more recent discoveries were quite different. These were based on eyewitness reports confirmed by persons of recognized ability or otherwise convincing to the officials of the Casa de Contratación.[4]

Perhaps the most interesting section of the text on the Gutiérrez map is the brief description of a voyage by John and Sebastian Cabot that has been a matter of dispute for nearly two centuries.[5] In describing the east coast of North America, the legend says: "This land was discovered by John Cabot, the Venetian, and Sebastian his son, in the year of the birth of Our Savior Jesus Christ 1494" ("Esta tierra fue descubierta por Joan Caboto Veneciano y Sebastian Caboto su hijo, año del nascimiento de ñro Salvador jesu christo de .m.cccc.xc.iiij.").

This is the same text that appeared on a map and in a booklet from the 1540s, both attributed to Sebastian Cabot.[6] Though he was probably not the author of the text, Cabot can be presumed to be the source of the story.[7] The full text claims that Cabot and his father reached the North American continent with their boatload of English sailors little more than a year after the return of Christopher Columbus from his voyage of discovery in the West Indies and several years before the Cabots' well-documented discovery of 1497.

While the account is probably true, it must be noted that neither the Cabots nor the English government made any effort to publicize their early discovery. Richard Henry Major, writing more than a century ago, considered the matter a problem in paleography, and his explanation has gained wide acceptance. In the view of Major, the date is a simple error on the part of the printer, who read the Roman numeral vii as iiii, seeing the two strokes of the letter v as two separate renderings of the letter i.[8] Other historians have looked at the statement and called Sebastian Cabot a liar.[9]

Despite Major's clever reasoning and the criticisms of the other historians, Sebastian Cabot's description of the 1494 discovery is almost certainly true, and his critics have simply misinterpreted the evidence. If the date arose from an error, as Major said, then Sebastian Cabot knew about the error and let it pass in silence. So did those who knew him well. At least two other large maps were made by or for Sebastian Cabot after 1544, and they were accompanied by similar explanatory texts. Though none of these maps is known to exist today, copies of the texts were made by people who saw the originals. In the copies some of the wording appears to have been changed extensively, but the date 1494 was left unchanged.

In 1565 or shortly thereafter, Nathan Chytraeus was at Oxford, where he saw a Cabot map printed in 1549. Carefully copying the descriptive texts, he wrote the date of discovery as 1494.[10] Richard Hakluyt, who saw a completely different Cabot map and text before 1589, also copied the date as 1494.[11] Sancho Gutiérrez, whose family was very close to the Cabot family in Seville, also copied the date as 1494, using the same manuscript copy (now missing) that was used in printing the text for Cabot's 1544 world map. Fully aware of the early voyages, Sancho Gutiérrez saw nothing wrong with this date and allowed it to adorn his map, just as Sebastian Cabot had done.[12]

Well before 1494, fishing ships from Bristol were going out in search of a mysterious island called Brazil, located somewhere to the west of Ireland. In a letter written in 1498, Pedro de Ayala briefly described the early involvement of a Genoese navigator in this exploration of the North Atlantic fishery. According to Ayala, several ships went out each year from Bristol, "following the route charted by this Genoese" mariner ("con la fantasía de este ginovés")[13] and searching for Brazil.

Born in Genoa, naturalized in Venice, resident in Spain and later in England, John Cabot has left only a shadowy record of his own exploits, and most of these have become hopelessly confused with the achievements of his son Sebastian. This probably accounts for the fact that both Ramusio and Martyr thought that Sebastian was born in Venice. Sebastian himself claimed to have come from Bristol, and Richard Hakluyt, among others, believed the story. In any case, it is clear that the *ginovés* in the letter was John Cabot, who was well known in Bristol years before 1493, which is the date usually given for his family's appearance there. It is equally clear that "fantasía" refers to a chart recording the route of an earlier voyage with men from Bristol, almost certainly the voyage made in 1494, as the son of John Cabot later claimed.[14]

Sebastian Cabot's claim draws added confirmation from another letter of 1498, by John Day, describing John Cabot's 1497 voyage to this northern Brazil, which Cabot had shown to be a continent, not an island. In the letter, Day refers to a "first voyage" (*viaje primero*) and an earlier discovery—"to have found and discovered in other times the cape of said land" ("averse hallado e descubierto en otros tiempos el cabo de la dicha tierra")[15]—that was itself followed by several failed attempts to rediscover the new land. On this first voyage John Cabot, accompanied by his young son Sebastian, caught sight of land for the first time and called it "first landfall" (*prima vista* in good Italian or *prima tierra vista*) in that curious mixture of Italian and Spanish that also appears on the map and in the text.[16]

Unable to land, for all of the usual reasons (contrary winds and currents, sick and starving crewmen, fear of hostile inhabitants, and the loneliness of command in a tiny ship on an unknown sea), he turned back. On the second trip, in 1497, the Cabots and their Bristol seamen landed near Cabot's "first landfall," as John Day reported, twice identifying it in Spanish by the name John Cabot had given it: "where the first sighting was" ("donde fue la primera vista") and "near where they had the first sighting" ("cercano adonde ovieron la primera vista").

To summarize the accomplishments of the voyage of 1494, John the Venetian, Sebastian Cabot the native of Bristol, and the other Bristol mariners saw the coastline but did not land or even get close enough to prepare a really accurate chart. The Cabots called the place prima vista, in good Italian, but the Bristol seamen called it Brazil for the mythical island they thought it was. No one was really sure of its exact location until the Cabots rediscovered it in 1497. The Cabot feat of 1494—discovering land without actually landing there—is confirmed by the letters of Pedro de Ayala and John Day and by the maps and texts of Sancho Gutiérrez and Sebastian Cabot, copied from the official map in the Casa de Contratación. It was a significant achievement but more modest than that of Columbus, who was still credited with having discovered "the islands and Tierra Firme of the Indies." [17]

The cartouche on the planisphere says the map was drawn in 1551 by Sancho Gutiérrez, "cosmographer of His Majesty." However, Sancho Gutiérrez did not become royal cosmographer until 1553. The apparent contradiction is resolved upon closer inspection of the map. The cartouche, along with most of the other explanatory text, was added after the map was finished. These legends are not written on the vellum itself but on thin sheets of paper carefully pasted to the vellum surface, where they overlap portions of the original geographical depictions. The date 1551 is the year in which the basic map was completed, but the cartouche, the legends, and the other features were added after Gutiérrez became royal cosmographer in 1553. Another discovery noted on the map allows us to verify the date of completion with reasonable certainty.

The depiction of the coast of Chile originally ended just south of Valdivia, which was founded in 1552. The Pueblo de Valdivia and all the decorative illustrations were then added to the vellum surface of the map, probably in 1553 or 1554 but certainly before the end of the decade, when information about the coastline from Valdivia to the Strait of Magellan became available in Seville. The coast south of Valdivia was explored in 1553–54 by Francisco de Ulloa, but his reports seem to have perished in the confusion surrounding the death of Pedro de Valdivia. Consequently, a new expedition under

Juan Fernández de Ladrillero was dispatched in 1557 to cover much the same area, returning about January 1559.[18] A brief legend reporting the second of the two expeditions was added on the vellum surface: "The pilot Ju[an] [Fernández] de Ladrillero discovered this coast in the year 1558. He went with two ships and a *bergantín* by order of Don G[arcí]a H[urtad]o [de] M[endoza] to the land in the Strait of Magellan, and he returned" ("Esta costa fue descubierta por el piloto Jū Ladrillero en el .a°. 1558. y fue con dos navios y un vergantin hasta la tierra en el estrecho de magallanes y volvio por mandado de don G^a H° M.").

By this time it was clear that the South American landmass had been drawn too broadly on the *padrón*, but the cosmographers in Seville were not certain what the true delineation should be. While they considered the matter, a copy of the report of García Hurtado de Mendoza reached the laboratory of Bartolomé Olives in Messina. On a map of the strait dated 1562 his cartographer solved the problem by simply drawing a diagonal coastline running southeast from Santiago to the strait, with no regard for the true geography of the region. A similar line was later added to the Gutiérrez planisphere, where an unknown hand gave this part of South America a strange double coastline, connecting the strait with the original coastline, which Gutiérrez had placed too far to the west.[19] It is not clear who made this addition. It was probably not done by Gutiérrez, for the new diagonal coastline contradicts all that was then known about the west coast of South America.

Even more curious is a line of tiny letters running across the Pacific Ocean and describing a voyage of discovery from the Mexican port of Navidad to the Philippines and back again. Long thought to mark the 1542 voyage of Ruy López de Villalobos, this thin line of text actually describes the supposed route of Alonso de Arellano across the Pacific Ocean in 1565: "This is the voyage and the route followed by Don Alonso de Arellano, who went as captain of a ship . . . in the year 1565" ("Este es el viage e derrotero que hizo don Al° de Arellano yendo por capitan de un navio . . . en el año de 65"; KI 99.416, ON, Vienna). Arellano began his trip as commander of a small vessel in the fleet that Miguel López de Legazpi took to the Philippines that year. Arellano either deliberately left the fleet or became separated in a storm a few hundred miles west of the Mexican coast, just where it was supposed the biblical islands of Tharsis and Ophir might be found. Although his ship did not reach the Philippines, he concocted a fanciful report claiming to have done so and submitted the report to the authorities when he returned to New Spain a few months later. However, his claim was contradicted by his own crewmen, one of whom later testified in Manila that he had never before been in the Philippines, "because he came in the frigate San Lucas that went back to New Spain" ("[no llego a esta ysla] por venir en el patax que se volvio a la Nueva España").[20] While not describing the Arellano voyage, the line of red dots on the map does give an approximation of the route followed by Andrés de Urdaneta and Felipe de Salcedo on their return voyage from Cebú to Acapulco from 1 June to late September 1565 (Kelsey 1986a, 162–63).

Added, again, by another hand, this fictitious route is a puzzling feature, for it was doubtless well known in the Casa de Contratación and in the Spanish court that Arellano did not reach the Philippines on this voyage. Perhaps the addition was made by a friend of the important Arellano family or by Arellano himself during one of his attempts to secure royal recognition for his supposed discovery (Kelsey 1986a, 162–63). No cosmographer in Seville could have made either addition to the Gutiérrez chart. Just as the second coastline of South America contradicts what was already known about the coast in this part of the world, the Arellano route as marked on the chart contradicts the facts as they were accepted in the Casa de Contratación. The purported route, as marked on the Gutiérrez chart, moves west across the Pacific in a fairly accurate representation of the route followed by Villalobos. But the return route is a perfect great circle that goes north to 44.5° and then heads south again. It is a route that could have been discussed by navigators as an ideal, but not one that could have been sailed, given the vagaries of winds and currents.

Interestingly enough, the two men who explored the coast of California are omitted entirely from the map and from the legends that accompany it. Francisco de Ulloa, who explored and doubtless mapped the coast of lower California for Cortés in 1539, is often said to be the same man who sailed from Valdivia to the Strait of Magellan and mapped that stretch of coast in 1554. Both of these expeditions are omitted from the map, the first in order to give credit to Hernán Cortés and the second because his detailed reports were seemingly lost in the confusion that followed the death of Pedro de Valdivia in Chile.[21]

Somewhat more puzzling is the omission of the discoveries made by Juan Rodríguez Cabrillo in upper California. There were probably two reasons for this omission. First, the area he explored was not much different from what had been expected all along, a long stretch of coastline running to the northwest, perhaps all the way to China. Second, the report of his exploits apparently did not get back to Spain until it was taken or sent there by Andrés de

Urdaneta in 1558 or 1559. In that year the Cabrillo discoveries appeared on the world map of Andrés Homem, which was also copied from the *padrón general* (Kelsey 1986a, 115).

Since the original maps are missing, the world map of Sancho Gutiérrez provides us with a good idea of the look of the *padrón general* in the middle of the sixteenth century. More than this, the Gutiérrez planisphere provides us with a look at the sources of information and the methods used in constructing maps. But its importance goes beyond the *padrón*. The Gutiérrez map legends serve as a record of what were then considered to be the most significant events in the long process of discovering the American coasts.

NOTES

Note: The following abbreviations are used in the notes:

AGI   Archivo General de Indias, Seville

ON   Österreichische Nationalbibliothek, Vienna

1. KI 99.416, ON, Vienna (item 3). Because of disputes arising from the cartographic projections used by his father and Sebastian Cabot, the *piloto mayor* in the Casa de Contratación, Sancho's official appointment as cosmographer was delayed for several years. The details of the dispute are described in Lamb 1969, a fascinating study of sixteenth-century cosmography. More about the checkered career of Sancho Gutiérrez appears in her more recent study (Lamb 1987). For other information about Sancho Gutiérrez, see Pulido Rubio 1950, 309–12 and Toribio Medina 1903, 1:555–57.

2. See Kohl 1869, 369–70, and Deane 1884, 3:24.

3. Maximilian of Transylvania (1523) said that neither he nor anyone else believed these things. Eden (1555, 216), in his free translation of the introduction to Maximilian's letter, remarked that the Spaniards had neither seen nor reported any such monstrous beings in their travels about the globe. Fernández de Enciso (1530, fols. 30, 60, and 68) while repeating other stories, sometimes with the cautionary phrase "they say," wrote that "it is unbelievable" that there were Amazon women who lived without men and trained themselves as warriors. Of course, many people did repeat these stories, and some believed them. Antonio Pigafetta insisted that the Patagonian giants were twice as tall as ordinary men. See his account in Robertson 1906, 1:49. Nonetheless, Gonzalo Fernández de Oviedo, official chronicler of the Indies,

said the Patagonians were no more than a dozen *palmos* in height, or about seven and one-half feet; see Oviedo [1547] 1959, 2:219.

4. For example, Hieronymo de Chaves in giving his opinion about the location of the Philippines, summed it all up by saying that the *padrón* and all his charts were "based on the authority of Ptolemy and the experience of navigators" ("se fundan en authoridad de Ptholemeo, y en experiencia de Navegantes"); see his Parecer (opinion) of 10 October 1566, AGI, Patronato 49, no. 4, fol. 6. Martín Fernández de Enciso (1530) noted in his colophon that while he had consulted the classical accounts, he made revisions in them based on "the experience of our time, which is the mother of everything." For a lengthier explanation of these curious illustrations, see Kelsey 1987.

5. Among the earliest combatants were Richard Biddle (1832) and Patrick F. Tytler (1833), but they had not seen the Cabot map. Following several decades of debate, Henry Harrisse (1896) wrote a comprehensive analysis of the available evidence, concluding that the date 1494 was wrong and in any case was not supplied by Cabot but by a Dr. Grajales, who was, Harrisse believed, the author of the texts. The Grajales matter was explained by José Toribio Medina (1908, 2:561–63). Toribio Medina also printed for the first time the contract Cabot signed for publication of his world map and concluded, rightly, that the printing was done in Nuremberg (1908 2:555–61).

6. *Declaratio chartae novae navigatoriae domini almirantis* (Nuremberg: Joannes Petreius, ca. 1548), Huntington Library 8953. See Wagner 1951, 47–49, and True 1956, 17.

7. Using the texts on the Cabot and Gutiérrez maps, the seventeenth-century manuscript in the Biblioteca Universitaria de Salamanca (Declaratio chartae novae navigatoriae Domini Almirantis, MS 2327), the text of the pamphlet printed to accompany the map (*Declaratio chartae novae navigatoriae domini almirantis* [Nuremberg: Joannes Petreius, c. 1548], Huntington Library 8953), the copy made at Oxford by Nathan Chytraeus (1594, 773–95) the portions quoted by Richard Hakluyt (1589, 511), and the portions quoted and paraphrased by Eden (1551, 315–24), I made a word-by-word comparison and concluded that the original text was written in decently idiomatic Spanish and was therefore by someone other than Sebastian Cabot. I also concluded that the Gutiérrez and Salamanca texts, as well as the now-missing manuscript from which the Cabot versions were set in type, were copied directly from this now-missing original and that the portions quoted by Eden, Hakluyt, and Chytraeus were made later from a copy Cabot took with him to England and revised there.

8. See Major 1870, 17–18.

9. One of the most virulent early historians to attack Sebastian Cabot was Sir Clements R. Markham (1893, xli–xliv). The man who became the leading critic of Cabot, Henry Harrisse, said that Sebastian Cabot had a way of "disguising the truth whenever it was to his interest to do so" (1896, 115). See also Quinn 1974, 135–37, and Williamson 1962, 25–26.

10. See Chytraeus 1589, 773–95. The date of his visit to England is explained in the introduction, fol. 3v.

11. See Hakluyt 1859, 511. Although the sense is exactly the same, the Latin text of this map is entirely different from that seen by Chytraeus, which seems to argue for a separate translation of the text by Richard Eden, who "cut" or engraved the map in England for Cabot.

12. See the legend written above the northeast part of North America in KI 99.416, ON, Vienna.

13. See his letter of 15 July 1498 in Ayala 1894, 2:218.

14. Robert H. Fuson (1988, 36–46) reviews the confusing Cabot family history. While reprinting the accounts from Ramusio and Peter Martyr, Richard Hakluyt himself thought that Sebastian Cabot was an Englishman, "borne in the citie of Bristol" (1589, table of contents, fifth page). There has been a lot of discussion about the term *fantasía*, with most historians thinking that it meant only that the voyage was an idea or "fancy" of Cabot. David B. Quinn (1974, 9–10) continues to translate the word as *fancy*, although he explains in a note that "reckoning" is "the most likely meaning." Actually, *fantasía* refers to a course recorded on a sailing chart, based on estimates of distance and direction but not confirmed by the observation of known landmarks. This is the meaning ascribed by Pedro de Medina (1545, bk. 3, chap. 12, fol. 32). His text describes a method of computing location "when the chart is marked by *esquadria* or *fantasía*, that is, by counting the distance which the ship has sailed and in what direction" ("Este auiso se terna quando se echa punto por esquadria o fantasia, q̃ es contando las singladuras que el nauio a hecho, y arbitrar quanto pudo ser el camino, q̃ en cada una anduuo, y porq̃ rūbo"). The phrase *echa punto* means to mark the route on the map. The same phrase was used in the 10 February 1493 entry of the Columbus diary: "*carteavan [y] echavan punto*" (Varela 1982, 124). This is also what Hieronymo de Chaves had in mind in 1565 when he described courses computed on charts as "calculations by *Phantasia*, as the navigators say, and mental computations" ("*cuentas de Phantasia, como dizen los navegantes, y echadas de cabeça*"; Parecer, 10 October 1566, AGI, Patronato 49, no. 4, fol. 5v). A similar usage is found in Medina 1563, bk. 3, chap. 7, fol. 42, where he explains that *fantasia* applies to a course recorded on a sailing

chart when conditions do not allow position to be computed by other means. Diego García de Palacio (1587, fol. 113) uses the term in the same context. It is impossible to explain why historians are so reluctant to credit Cabot's claim. One recent writer, McGrath (1978, 82–84), refuses to accept either Ayala's letter or the John Day letter as valid evidence of any discovery prior to 1497.

15. The letter is printed with editorial comments and bibliographical notes in Gil and Varela 1984, 266–69. The John Day letter was first discussed in print in Vigneras 1956. See also Vigneras 1961. Ruddock (1966) showed that John Day was known in England as Hugh Say. Additional information about John Day appeared in Varela 1986.

16. The name is written as *prima vista* and *prima tierra vista* on the Cabot map. Of course, the phrase is Italian, except for the word *tierra*, which is Spanish. According to the *Oxford English Dictionary*, the phrase *prima vista* became accepted English usage some years later as another way of saying landfall.

17. Item number 1 in the legends on the right margin of KI 99.416, ON, Vienna.

18. Juan Fernández de Ladrillero charted the coast from Valdivia to the strait and navigated the strait from south to north during a voyage that lasted from November 1557 to January 1559; see Jaudenes García 1959. See also the "Relación de las derrotas y navegación que hizo el Capitán Francisco Cortés Ogea con el navío nombrado San Sebastián, uno de las dos con que salió del Puerto de Valparaíso el Capitán Juan Ladrillero en 17 de noviembre de 1557 al descubrimiento del estrecho de Magallanes," Colección de documentos de Fernández Navarrete, vol. 20, fols. 38–70, Museo Naval, Madrid.

19. In his letter to the Council of the Indies dated 30 August 1559, García Hurtado de Mendoza reminded the council that he had already reported the results of the Ladrillero expedition; see Barros Arana 1884, 2:205. The pilots and cosmographers in the Casa de Contratación did not change the *padrón* immediately, doubtless because of the coastline discrepancies. The report of García Hurtado de Mendoza was first used on the 1562 map of the strait found in an atlas attributed to Bartolomé Olives, (Biblioteca Vaticana, Urb. Lat. 283, pl. 10; microfilm copies of the Urbinates Latini manuscripts are available in the Vatican Film Library, St. Louis University, St. Louis, Mo.). There is a description of the atlas and a brief review of the work of Olives in Almagià 1944–55, 1:72–75 and pl. 41. The Gutiérrez depiction of the Strait of Magellan is described and reproduced photographically in Wallis 1965, 201, 204 (N.B., the maps and legends in figs. 20 and 22 are transposed).

20. Testimony of Antonio Cavallero, Patronato 52, sec. 2, fol. 22v, AGI.

21. See the legend near the western tip of South America on KI 99.416, ON, Vienna. An early mistaken assertion by Bernal Díaz del Castillo led many later writers to assume that Francisco de Ulloa died on the 1539 voyage to California, but this error was corrected by Wagner (1940). Other writers had suspected as much, including Diego Barros Arana (1884, 1:417–19). For his comments on Ladrillero and his explorations in California, see Arana 1884, 2:208–9.

BIBLIOGRAPHY

Almagià, Roberto. 1944–55. *Monumenta cartographica vaticana iussu Pii XII P. M.* 4 vols. Vatican City: Biblioteca Apostolica Vaticana.

Ayala, Pedro de. 1894. Letter of 15 July 1498, in *Raccolta di documenti e studi pubblicati dalla R. Commissione Colombiana del Quarto Centenario dalla Scoperta dell' America*, pt. 5, 2:218. Rome: Ministero della Pubblica Istruzione.

Barros Arana, Diego. 1884. *Historia Jeneral de Chile.* 2 vols. Santiago: Rafael Jover.

Biddle, Richard. 1832. *A Memoir of Sebastian Cabot; with a Review of the History of Maritime Discovery, Illustrated by Documents from the Rolls, Now First Published.* 2d ed. London: Sherwood, Gilbert, and Piper.

Chytraeus, Nathan. 1594. *Variorum in Europa itinerum deliciae.* Herbornae Nassouiorum.

Day, John. 1978. Bristol and America, 1480–1631. In *The Westward Enterprise: English Activities in Ireland, the Atlantic, and America, 1480–1650*, ed. K. R. Andrews, N. P. Canny, and P.E.H. Hair, 82–84. Liverpool: Liverpool University Press.

Deane, Charles. 1884. The Voyages of the Cabots. In *Narrative and Critical History of America*, ed. Justin Winsor, 3:1–58. Boston: Houghton Mifflin.

Eden, Richard. 1551. *The Decades of the Newe Worlde or West India.* London: Guilhelmi Powell.

——. 1555. *The Decades of the Newe Worlde.* London: Guilhelmi Powell.

Fernández de Enciso, Martín. 1530. *Suma de geografia.* Seville: Juan Cromberger.

Fuson, Robert H. 1988. The John Cabot Mystique. In *Essays on the History of North American Discovery and Exploration*, ed. Stanley Palmer and Dennis Reinhartz, 36–46. College Station: Texas A&M University Press.

García de Palacio, Diego. 1587. *Instrucción nautica para navegar.* Mexico City: Pedro Ocharte.

Gil, Juan, and Consuelo Varela, eds. 1984. *Cartas de particulares a Colón y relaciones coetáneas.* Madrid: Alianza Editorial.

Hakluyt, Richard. 1589. *The Principall Navigations, Voiages and Discoveries of the English Nation.* London: George Bishop and Ralph Newberie.

Harrisse, Henry. 1896. *John Cabot, the Discoverer of North-America and Sebastian His Son; A Chapter of the Maritime History of England Under the Tudors, 1496–1557.* London: Benjamin Franklin Stevens.

Jaudenes García, José. 1959. El Piloto Juan Fernández de Ladrillero. *Revista General de Marina* (Madrid) 47 (July): 90–91.

Kelsey, Harry. 1986a. Finding the Way Home: Spanish Exploration of the Round-Trip Route Across the Pacific Ocean. *Western Historical Quarterly* 17:145–64.

———. 1986b. *Juan Rodriguez Cabrillo.* San Marino, Calif.: Huntington Library.

———. 1987. The Planispheres of Sebastian Cabot and Sancho Gutiérrez. *Terrae Incognitae* 19:44–47.

Kohl, Johann Georg. 1869. *History of the Discovery of Maine.* Portland: Bailey and Noyes.

Lamb, Ursula. 1969. Science by Litigation: A Cosmographic Feud. *Terrae Incognitae* 1:40–58.

———. 1987. The Sevillian Lodestone: Science and Circumstance. *Terrae Incognitae* 19:29–39.

McGrath, Patrick. 1978. Bristol and America, 1480–1631. In *The Westward Enterprise: English Activities in Ireland, the Atlantic, and America, 1480–1650*, ed. K. R. Andrews, N. P. Canny, and P.E.H. Hair, 81–102. Liverpool: Liverpool University Press.

Major, Richard Henry. 1870. *The True Date of the English Discovery of the American Continent Under John and Sebastian Cabot.* London: J. B. Nichols & Son.

Markham, Sir Clements R. 1893. *The Journal of Christopher Columbus (During his First Voyage, 1492–93), and Documents Relating to the Voyages of John Cabot and Gaspar Corte Real.* London: Hakluyt Society.

Maximilian of Transylvania. 1523. *De Molucci Insulis, itemq̃; Aliis pluribus miradis, quae nouissima castellanorum nauigatio Serenis. Imperatoris Caroli .V. auspicio suscepto, nuper inuenit.* Cologne: Eucharius Cerviornus.

Medina, Pedro de. 1545. *Arte de Nauegar, en que se contienen todas las reglas, declaraciones, secretos, y auisos, q̃ la buena nauegacão son necessarios, y se deue saber.* Valladolid: Francisco Fernández de Cordova.

Oviedo, Gonzalo Fernández de. [1547] 1959. Historia general y natural de las Indias. Ed. Juan Pérez de Tudela Bueso. 5 vols. Biblioteca de autores españoles, 117–21. Madrid: Ediciones Atlas.

———. 1563. Regimiento de Navegación. Seville: Simon Carpintero.

Pulido Rubio, José. 1950. El piloto mayor de la Casa de Contratación de Sevilla, pilotos mayores, catedráticos de cosmografía y cosmógrafos. Seville: Escuela de Estudios Hispano-Americanos.

Quinn, David B. 1974. England and the Discovery of America, 1481–1620; From the Bristol Voyages of the Fifteenth Century to the Pilgrim Settlement at Plymouth; The Exploration, Exploitation, and Trial-and-Error Colonization of North America by the English. New York: Alfred A. Knopf.

Robertson, James Alexander, ed. 1906. Magellan's Voyage Around the World. 2 vols. Cleveland: Arthur H. Clark.

Ruddock, Alwyn A. 1966. John Day of Bristol and the English Voyages Across the Atlantic Before 1497. Geographical Journal 132:225–33.

Toribio Medina, José. 1908. El Veneciano, Sebastián Caboto al servicio de España y especialmente de su proyectado viaje á las Molucas por el Estrecho de Magallanes y al reconocimiento de la costa del continente hasta la gobernación de Pedrarias Dávila. 2 vols. Santiago, Chile: Imprenta y Encuadernación Universitaria.

True, David O. 1956. Cabot Explorations in North America. Imago Mundi 13: 11–25.

Tytler, Patrick F. 1833. Historical View of the Progress of Discovery on the Northern Coasts of America, from the Earliest Period to the Present Time. New York: J. & J. Harper.

Varela, Consuelo. 1982. Cristóbal Colón: Textos y documentos completos. Madrid: Alianza Editorial.

———. 1986. John Day, los Genoveses y Colón. In Scritti in Onore del Prof. Paolo Emiliano Taviani, ed. Achille Agnati et al., 3:363–71. Genoa: Università degli Studi di Genova.

Vigneras, Louis-André. 1956. New Light on the Cabot Voyage to America. Hispanic American Historical Review 36:503–9.

———. 1961. Etat présent des études sur Jean Cabot. Congreso Internacional de Historia dos Descobrimentos, Actas, 3:3–15.

Wagner, Henry R. 1940. Francisco de Ulloa Returned. California Historical Society Quarterly 19:240–44.

———. 1951. A Map of Sancho Gutiérrez of 1551. Imago Mundi 8:47–49.

Wallis, Helen. 1965. English Enterprise in the Region of the Strait of Magellan. In *Merchants and Scholars: Essays in the History of Exploration and Trade*, ed. John Parker, 193–220. Minneapolis: University of Minnesota Press.

Williamson, James A. 1962. *The Cabot Voyages and Bristol Discovery under Henry VII.* Cambridge: Cambridge University Press.

Ptolemy's *Geography* and the New World

Oswald A. W. Dilke and Margaret S. Dilke

"In Renaissance cartography the Ptolemaic map was both the starting-point and the model against which subsequent change could be measured." The object of the present study is to show how this remark by Norman J. W. Thrower (1976, 660) may be illustrated by the most famous events affecting Renaissance cartography: the American explorations of Christopher Columbus and others.

The question of how maps based on Ptolemy's coordinates compiled thirteen centuries earlier can affect the cartography of American exploration deserves more explanation than it is sometimes given. When Claudius Ptolemy was writing his *Geographike hyphegesis* (Manual of geography) in Alexandria in the middle of the second century A.D., the usual concept of the "inhabited earth" (*oikumene*) was of all those parts of Europe, Asia, and Africa not considered too hot or too cold to explore, let alone inhabit. The only cartographic attempt to portray other landmasses known from classical antiquity was the Orb of Crates, ca. 160 to 150 B.C. (fig. 11.1). In emending the Homeric text Crates of Pergamon (or of Mallos) tried to explain Homer's idea of eastern and western Ethiopians, i.e., blacks, by assuming a wide water channel between what he took to be the northern and southern Ethiopians. To him there were two other landmasses symmetrically arranged. Those west of the Atlantic Ocean (it is not known whether he named it so) were inhabited by Perioikoi ("dwellers round") in the north and Antipodes in the south. One could therefore claim that Crates put forward the idea that there were continents in the approximate location of America, and thus American cartography

FIGURE 11.1. Reconstruction of the Orb of Crates. (Dilke 1985, 36); reprinted from O.A.W. Dilke, *Greek and Roman Maps,* © 1985 Thames & Hudson Ltd., London, used by permission of the publishers, Cornell University Press and Thames & Hudson Ltd.)

might be said to go back to him. It is perhaps more appropriate, however, to think of the orb as a philosopher's theoretical model.

The first scholar known to have made some attempt at plotting settlements on a map by degrees of latitude and longitude, though not very systematically, was Marinus of Tyre, who may have been working about A.D. 100 to 110. Our knowledge of his work comes from Ptolemy, who criticizes his figures for the *oikumene* of 225° from east to west and more than 112° from north to south as excessive. A journey to the Far East either by land or sea, Ptolemy claimed, might take far more time than the straight-line distance would suggest. He also disapproved of Marinus's rectilinear projection for a world map, built as it was around the latitude of Rhodes. Finally, he criticized Marinus for often quoting either the latitude or the longitude of a place but not both.

Ptolemy approached terrestrial cartography from the standpoint of celestial cartography. In his *Almagest* he improved appreciably on Hipparchus's coordinates for constellations and stars (Toomer 1984). For terrestrial cartography he adopted different projection systems for world mapping and for regional mapping. For world maps he advocated one of three systems:

1. Divergent straight meridians at 20 minutes of time, or 5°, on the equator, contracting south of the equator by what at the east and west extremities are angles of about 113°.

2. Meridians, curved except for the central one.
3. A theoretical projection, whereby an observer well outside the armillary sphere would be able to see a horizontal plane passing through Syene and have his vision unimpeded by the armillary rings. (Harley and Woodward 1987, 1:185–89)

Ptolemy's regional map grids are based on representative fractions appropriate to latitudes, from 11:20 longitude:latitude for the British Isles to 1:1 for equatorial areas. All lines in these are straight.

His coordinates (like those of Marinus, we may presume) worked for latitudes just as they do today, but longitude 0° started at the western point of the Fortunate Islands (the Canaries). They were expressed in Milesian notation in degrees and fractions of degrees, e.g., 1/3 for 20′, 1/3 + 1/12 for 25′ (Dilke 1989, 14). This system was perpetuated in the Renaissance but with Arabic rather than Roman numerals in the Latin translations. We also find, in the margins of some Ptolemaic maps, "latitude bands" (*climata*) and/or maximum daylight hours.

The question of whether Ptolemy had maps made for his geographical treatise has been disputed by scholars. It has often been wrongly held that he wrote, "we shall have maps made," whereas this is a Renaissance mistranslation of "we have had maps made" (Polaschek 1959). At some point,[1] a world map was drawn from his work by one Agathodaimon or Agathos Daimon, a technician in Alexandria, and ninth-century Arab geographers knew of maps attached to his work. Some of them could not read the place names in Greek, but others were able to adapt Ptolemaic coordinates to towns in north Africa and elsewhere founded after Ptolemy's time. Arabic manuscripts of Ptolemy's *Geography* exist in Istanbul (Constantinopolitanus Arabicus 2610, Aya Sofia), and there is one manuscript of al-Khwarizmi's revision in Strasbourg (Bibliothèque Universitaire et Régionale, L. arab. cod. Spitta 18).

In 1295 the monk Maximus Planudes, a famous Greek and Latin scholar at the monastery of Chora in Constantinople, was rewarded in his search for manuscripts of Ptolemy's *Geography*, known to be very rare (Dilke 1985, 157–60; Harley and Woodward 1987, 268). When he finally found one, almost certainly the Codex Vaticanus Graecus 177 from the late thirteenth century (which indicates that he was its owner), he was disappointed that it no longer contained any maps. He studied the text carefully and set about producing, with the help of the retired patriarch of Alexandria, Athanasius, a fine new copy, which he presented to the emperor, Andronicus II Palaeologus, who had acted as patron of the scheme. From that time onward the fifty extant[2]

Greek manuscripts of the *Geography* and many more were produced, though to what extent they go back to the same archetype is disputed. Most Greek manuscripts had twenty-six or twenty-seven maps, but we also find a group from the fourteenth century with sixty-five maps.

The next major step came a century later in Italy. The Byzantine scholar Manuel Chrysoloras taught Greek in Florence, and after first intending to translate Ptolemy's *Geography* into Latin himself, handed the task over to his pupil Jacopo d'Angelo, who completed his translation in 1406. It is no exaggeration to say that this Latin version, produced in one of the greatest cultural centers, revolutionized the progress not only of cartography but also of maritime exploration (Dilke, 1991). When, some years later, all the place names had been Latinized, monarchs and patrons were keen to acquire lavishly produced and illustrated manuscripts of the *Geography*. One was Federico, duke of Urbino (the Codex Urbinas Graecus 82, now in the Vatican Library, is known to have been in the library of Duke Federico's son).

Not long after, from about 1425, a feature of particular interest for the history of American exploration occurred when manuscript maps of Scandinavia and Greenland began to appear. Apart from Denmark, Ptolemy had hardly treated Scandinavia at all. The Danish cartographer Claudius Clavus (Clausson) had clearly read of the Norsemen's exploratory sea journeys to Greenland and Vinland (Cumming et al. 1971, 37; Fischer 1903, 69ff.; Nordenskiöld 1897, 85, 87). A simple map of Scandinavia and Greenland by him exists in the Nancy public library in France, while maps proved to be his or based on his map and dating from about 1466–68 onward are to be found in the Ptolemy Latin manuscripts at Warsaw, Florence, and elsewhere. Curiously enough, the chronological sequence resulted in a deterioration. The first tradition that features these northern regions makes Greenland a very long, thin promontory or sometimes an island stretching far westward from northern Scandinavia. The second tradition shows it within Scandinavia; thus in the Strasbourg 1513 Ptolemy, Engroneland is the immediate northwest neighbor of Norbegia.

It seems to have been only after the voyages of John Cabot in 1497 and 1498 that the cartographic position and shape of Greenland came to be better understood, as is seen below, where it becomes clear that Clavus maps played an important part in the early printed editions of Ptolemy's *Geography*.

In 1466 a manuscript of that work which deserves special mention (Paris, Bibliothèque Nationale, MS lat. 4801) was dedicated to Duke Borso of Este. From its distinctive features we know that the author was Donnus Nicolaus Germanus.[3] In the first place, he invented the trapezoidal projection, not used by Ptolemy or earlier Renaissance editors. It proved popular, being at least as good as either of the Ptolemaic projections used in Greek manuscripts, which were concerned, like Ptolemy himself, with the Old World. Nicolaus Germanus placed the numbers for degrees of latitude and longitude between parallels or meridians, not opposite them, and he originated, both in manuscripts and in printed editions, the idea of adding "new" maps to the Ptolemaic regional ones. The intention was to supplement Ptolemy in areas where he was known to be incorrect and to add areas that he had not covered. As a result, Latin manuscripts (Fischer's L20–L23) and printed texts associated with Donnus Nicolaus Germanus contain not only the map of the North based on Clavus (Fischer 1932, 1:355ff.) but "new" maps of France, Spain, and Italy, as well as the map of Palestine mentioned below, without the trapezoidal projection, though sometimes with *climata*, a concept originally favored by Marinus rather than Ptolemy (Honigmann 1929).

So Ptolemy's *Geography* was developing into an "atlas of the world" and was not rendered outmoded as a result of the age of discovery. In fact, with the invention of printing, the circulation of this work, mainly in Latin, was greatly extended. Although its *editio princeps* (Vicenza, 1475) had no maps, Bologna and Rome were soon competing to produce the first edition with them, at first usually the world, ten of Europe, four of Africa, and twelve of Asia, as well as the text (bks. 2–6, mainly coordinates). The Bologna edition, published in 1477,[4] contains the first maps to be printed from copper plates and the first examples in print of Donnus Nicolaus Germanus's trapezoidal projection. The earliest edition printed outside Italy, the Ulm edition of 1482, has this same projection and the first Tabulae Novae found in a Ptolemy printed edition. Both are described as novelties in the editor's preface. The Tabulae Novae include not only the updated maps of some European countries mentioned above but also one much earlier map. This closely follows that of the Holy Land drawn for Marin Sanudo's *Liber secretorum fidelium crucis*, presented to the Pope in 1321 (Dilke and Dilke 1987 and 1989). The crusade never materialized, but the cartography lived on. This was especially true of the map of the Holy Land, which was accompanied by grid references and biblical allusions to tribes or cities.

Such was the situation when Paolo dal Pozzo Toscanelli (1397–1482), the Florentine doctor, astronomer and polymath who had already written to Afonso V of Portugal urging an expedition westward to the Indies, encouraged Columbus in his plan and sent him a map, unfortunately lost.[5] Columbus himself had a copy of a printed edition of Ptolemy's *Geography*, the Rome 1478 edition, now in the Real Academia de la Historia in Madrid, bearing his signature Χρο (=Christo) ferens (Sanz López 1959b, 73, 77). Although Ptolemy considered the east–west extent of the Old World to be 177°, his predecessor Marinus of Tyre had reckoned it as 225°. If we think of eastern Vietnam as the farthest point likely to have been reached by Graeco-Roman sailors, the actual distance from La Palma in the Canaries to that area is only 127°, but such a figure was not known in the Renaissance. If Marinus was right, it was thought, Columbus would have to navigate for only 135°, not 183° as he would if Ptolemy was right. But maps based on Marinus were not extant,[6] and theories of the circumference of the earth had to be taken into consideration. Columbus is said to have scaled down the distance by following an estimate by the Arabic geographer al-Farghani (Alfragan), but he reckoned in Roman miles, not realizing that al-Farghani had reckoned in Arabic miles.[7] He also eagerly studied a chorus in Seneca's *Medea*, 375–79, which seemed to him prophetic of his own age:

> A generation shall come in the later years, when Ocean shall unloose the chains of nature, and a vast land shall be revealed, and Tethys shall uncover new worlds, and Thule shall not be the last place on earth.[8]

> Venient annis saecula seris,
> quibus Oceanus vincula rerum
> laxet et ingens pateat tellus
> Tethysque[9] novos detegat orbes
> nec sit terris ultima Thule.

The natural reaction when it was established that a substantial landmass had been reached at about 58° west of the Canaries was to conclude that both Marinus and Ptolemy had been wrong and that Columbus had reached parts of eastern Asia. Columbus believed firmly that Cuba was part of eastern Asia, so it is not surprising that many Ptolemaic and non-Ptolemaic maps followed suit. The regional name "upper India" (India superior) is found on some Ptolemaic maps issued after Columbus's expedition, placed toward the center of the east coast of Asia.

With this topographical uncertainty, it is not surprising that there were delays in adding to or correcting existing world maps. But another factor was also circumscribing the work of cartographers—namely, the secrecy imposed by the Spanish and Portuguese authorities (Harley 1989). In particular, the Padrón Real, the Spanish record office for discoveries, established in 1508, was unwilling to share discoveries made by Spain with other countries.

From about 1500 onward, a number of portolan maps with directional navigation lines but no latitude or longitude included parts of America explored by Columbus and his successors. The first seems to have been that of Juan de La Cosa (ca. 1500), followed by that of Alberto Cantino (1502). Some of these can be shown to have influenced the coastal delineation of place names of Ptolemaic Tabulae Novae, though on the latter there are latitude and longitude coordinates. Among them is a map perhaps not sufficiently recognized: the Pesaro World Map (ca. 1505, parchment, 1.22 m x 2.06 m, in the Biblioteca Oliveriana in Pesaro, Italy).[10]

On this map the principal regional heading over South America is MVNDVS NOVVS, so it may justly be claimed as the first map to recognize a continent that is not Asia but a new one. This phrase in the Pesaro Map may go back to the Mundus Novus letter of 1504, attributed to Amerigo Vespucci (Pohl 1944, 147ff.; Quinn 1976, 2:639–47). The first Ptolemy map to contain the phrase is the Ruysch edition, mentioned below. The 1508 Rome edition of Ptolemy's *Geography*, edited by Johann Ruysch, has no information in the text on the western explorations, but it has a world map[11] that includes the areas explored. The east coast of Asia is made to swing eastward as far as Newfoundland (terra nova) and then to link up with Greenland (Gruenlant) around the Gulf of Greenland. On the map are a number of Latin explanations. The most significant of these, inserted at the point where the delineation of the north coast of South America fades out, reads:

> The Spanish sailors reached this point, and called this land, because of its size, the New World. But since they did not see the country as a whole and have not up to now traveled beyond this boundary, he (the mapmaker) is leaving it incomplete, especially as it is not known in which direction it extends.

> Hucusque naut(a)e Hispani ve(ne)ru(n)t et hanc terram propter eius magnitudinem Mundum Novum appellarunt. Quia vero eam totaliter non viderunt nec usque in tempore hoc longius qua(m) ad hu(n)c ter-minu(m) perlustrarunt, ideo hic i(m)perfecta reli(n)quit, p(rae)serti(m) cu(m) nesciatur quo vergitur.

Similarly, the land that corresponds to Cuba is given named features but is purposely left as either an island or part of the mainland, with the inscription: "The ships of Ferdinand King of Spain reached this point" ("Huc usq(ue) naves Ferdina(n)di regis Hispani(a)e p(er)veneru(n)t"). In addition to these Latin captions, the original wording on a reused block of the Ruysch edition has recently been partially deciphered.[12] It refers to the northern bounds, "where the extreme [cardinal] points of the world are" ("ubi sunt extremi cardines mundi"), with the Hyperboreans and the tribes occupying the north-ernmost islands of Europe and Asia.

The name for the New World that eventually prevailed arose out of re-search that resulted, though only after a long delay, in the Strasbourg editions of Ptolemy's *Geography*.[13] In the early years of the sixteenth century, Saint-Dié in Alsace was a center of learning and had its own academy. Research into ancient and contemporary geography was carried out by Martin Waldsee-müller (who also used Ilacomylus as a learned name) and the humanist Mat-thias Ringmann. From their Latin correspondence and their *Cosmographiae introductio* we gather that at first they thought that Amerigo Vespucci had dis-covered South America and deserved to have it named after him. A feminine form seemed appropriate, since Europe and Asia, as they point out, had been named after demigoddesses. One suggestion was Amerige, telescoped from *Amerig-* and *gê* (earth or land), but the name approved by Waldseemüller and Ringmann was America, which the former placed on a woodcut map of 1507 now at the John Carter Brown Library in Providence, Rhode Island, and on his map of globe gores.[14] Waldseemüller did not want the name America to appear in the 1513 Strasbourg edition of Ptolemy, however, as he no longer considered Amerigo Vespucci to be its discoverer. But the idea appealed to Lorenz Fries, the editor, and after Waldseemüller's death the name made its way into Strasbourg editions of Ptolemy and thence into works of wider dis-tribution. At first it was limited to South America, but Mercator changed the usage by having AME inserted on North America and RICA on South America in the gore immediately east of the former. As for Brazil,[15] it varied on maps between the whole of South America, as in Sebastian Münster's edition (Basel, 1552), and a small island west of Ireland, with numerous variations (see Cor-tesão 1969–71, 2:522–73; and Campbell 1987b, 1:410–11).

The Venice edition of 1511 was based on an experiment that was not after-ward repeated. Since Ptolemy had lived so many centuries earlier and since there had been so many changes since his time, it was argued, why not change the coordinates of latitude and longitude in his text to correct any known errors? Then, the preface continued, particularly if any important new places were plotted,[16] there would be no need of two maps for each region, one old and one new. The editor, Bernardus Sylvanus of Eboli, foresaw the reaction of classicists, and in his Latin preface wrote that he could envisage most readers frowning with amazement on seeing maps so different from those of his predecessors.

Mention of the exploratory voyages to America is also made in this preface, part of which may be rendered:

> We have also decided to add from our own resources a map [*figuram*]
> of the habitable world, together with all the features that have been
> discovered through the sea voyages of contemporaries and passed on
> to us. All the same, how little would you feel that they differ from Ptol-
> emy's general description, provided that everything unknown to Ptol-
> emy is removed? (Sylvanus 1511, 7–8)

The projection used by the 1511 edition for its world map is heart-shaped.
The east coast of Asia ends well before the limit of the map, with Iava minor,
Zampagu ins. (Japan), and other islands. To the north are Catai regio (China)
and farther north, somewhat as in the Ruysch edition, GRVENLANT (Greenland) with the *e* partly deleted. Some distance west of Ireland we find *terra
laboratorum* (Labrador) as an island, then to the west *regalis domus* (king's house),
referring to one of the lands discovered by Gaspar and Miguel Corte-Real in
1500–1502.[17] Well to the south are *terra cu[ ]s* (Cuba), *ispania ins.* (Hispaniola),
and an unnamed Caribbean island. South America is described as Terra
Sanctae Crucis, with a further mention of cannibalism.

The Strasbourg Ptolemy of 1513[18] shows evidence that Lorenz Fries, who
was also a physician and astronomer, collected material on America from
various sources, including maps compiled by Waldseemüller at Saint-Dié. It
breaks the Ptolemaic tradition by including a portolan chart said to have originated with the admiral, "formerly of His Majesty King Ferdinand of Portugal
[sic]" ("quondam serenissimi Portugaliae regis Ferdinandi"). Either *Portugaliae*
is a mistake for *Hispaniae* or, more likely, there is a lacuna, in which case the
admiral in question is not Columbus but Vespucci.[19] This map is entitled "Image of the Whole World in Portolan Chart Makers' Tradition" (*Orbis typus universalis iuxta hydrographorum traditionem*). Attached to Scandinavia and absurdly
corresponding in the margin to a latitude of 90° is a long, thin peninsula
marked GRONLAND. West of it is an unnamed coastal area corresponding to
the coast of Labrador. South of it are only rough sketches of Spagnolla and
Isabella (Hispaniola and Cuba) and of South America as detailed on the
next map. The only names on the coast of South America on this map are
batoia; binsil (= insula) gigantum (giants' island); Canibales; Caput S(an)ct(a)e
Crucis; and alte (= alter?) pagus de S. paulo (? second village of St. Paul).

The other map, entitled *Tabula nova: Tabula terre nove* (see fig. 11.2), may be
called the first regional map of the New World. It includes the western parts
of the Old World for reference. In America, the eastern seaboard (with nineteen names), the Caribbean, and South America are shown. This last is labeled
in its central area *terra incognita*, with an inscription that may be rendered: "This

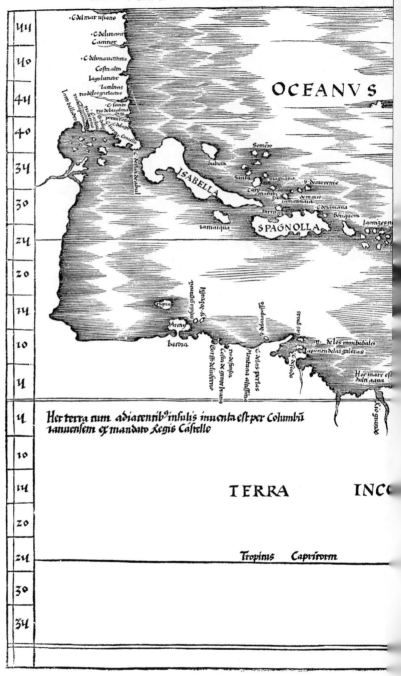

TABVLA   TER

OCEANVS

Her terra num adiatentib'infulis inuenta est per Columbū ianuensem ex mandato Regis Castello

TERRA   INCO

Tropinus   Capritorm

FIGURE 11.2. *Tabula nova: Tabula terre nove,* the first regional map of the New World. (From Ptolemy, *Geography* [Strasbourg, 1513]; reproduced in Nordenskiöld [1889] 1973, p. 36.)

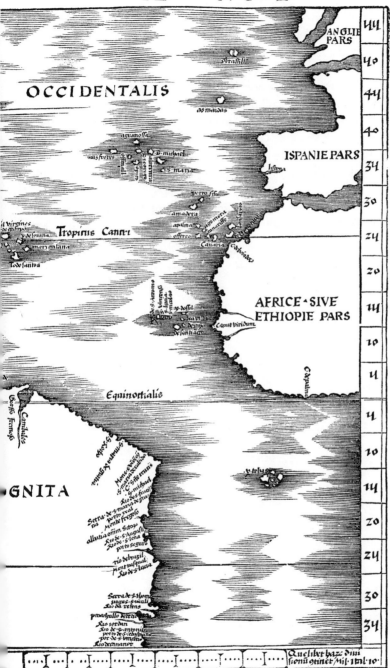

OCCIDENTALIS

ANGLIE PARS

Brasill

as maidas

aguanossa

ISPANIE PARS

dos fruos

S. michael

listona

S. maria

porro sso

amadera
apalma
offerto

Canaria

Tropirus Cancri

ij virgines
y.de ona
marigalana

Todos santos

S. Antonio

AFRICE · SIVE
ETHIOPIE PARS

S. iacobo
S. villa

Caput Viridum

Equinottialis

Corsis sermos
Canibales

GNITA

v. trinas

Monte
C. sste trinis

Serra de s. maria de gut

allanta omin S. doye
Rio de S. Augusti
Rio de S. lena
porto seguro

rio de brazil
Mont salmal
Rio de S. luna

Serra de S. then
pagus casali
Rio de reserus

p maryallo
Rio jordan
Rio de S. antonia
porto de S. sebastian
por de S. vincen
Rio de innano

land with the adjacent islands was discovered by Christopher Columbus on instructions from the King of Castile."

If we compare places on the coast of South America in the Strasbourg 1513 atlas with those on the Pesaro world map, ca. 1505, and the Ptolemy Rome 1508 (Ruysch) map, we find that those eastward and southward from S. Maria de Gratia correspond with each other much more closely than those on the north coast west of S. Maria de Gratia[20] (see Table 11.1). It is clear from the above concordance that anyone wanting to trace the sources of place names in that period will need to distinguish between sections A and B in Table 11.1.

TABLE 11.1 Early Features on the North and East Coasts of South America Marked on the Pesaro World Map and the Two Subsequent Editions of Ptolemy's *Geography*

Pesaro	Rome 1508[a]	Strasbourg 1513
A. NORTH COAST, WEST TO EAST		
16 named features, none corresponding to those in the other columns	LIX LEO TERRA SECA	Arcay
	GOLFO DE VERICIDA MONS ROTVNDVS	bacoia
	GOLFO DEL INFERNO	Gorffo del inferno Costa de gente brana rio de fonsoa
hic piscantur perle montana[b]		Montana altissima
	8 named features, none corresponding to those in the other columns, and CANIBALOS IN(sula), cf. col. 3 below.	C. de las perlas las gaias C. deseado[c]
punta de la galea		La punta de las galeras Hoc mare est de dulci aqua[d]
(Two large estuaries)	RIO GRANDO	Rio grande Gorffo fremoso[e]
	CANIBALOS IN (insula)	Canibales[f]
cauo de san domenego		S. Rocho
Santa maria de gratia		S. Maria de gratia
monte de san uicenso	MŌS. S. VINCENTI	Mons S. vicetii (= Vincentii)
santa ma(ria) de rabida		S. Maria de rabida
cano (= cauo) s. croxe	CAPVT S. CRVCIS	C. S(an)ct(a)e crucis

TABLE 11.1 (*continued*)

Pesaro	Rome 1508[a]	Strasbourg 1513
B. EAST COAST, NORTH TO SOUTH		
san michel		S. michael
riuo de s. fransesco		Rio de s. fracis (= Francisco)
porto real		Serra de S. maria de gracia porto real
riuo de san ieronimo	R. DE S. IERONIMO	
		Monte fregoso
	ABATIA O(M)NIV(M) SA(N)CTORV(M)	abbatia o(m)ni(u)m S(an)ctorum
riuo de s. agostino		Rio de S. Augustino
riuo de san iacomo		Rio de s. lena
		porto seguro[g]
riuo de brazir	R. DE BRAZI.LI	rio de brazil
mont passqual	MO(N)TE PASQVALE	Mont pasqual
[ends]	R. DE S. LVCIA	Rio de s. lucia
	SERRA DE S. ANTONIO	Serra de s. Thome
		pagus s. pauli
	R. DE OREFERIS	Rio da refens[h]
	BAIA DE REIS	pinachullo deretio
	R. IORDAN	Rio iordan
	R. DE S. ANTONIO	Rio de s. antonio
		Porto de s. sebastiano
	R. DE S. VI(N)CENT	Por(to) de s. vince(n)tio
	R. DE CANANOR	Rio de cananor

NOTES:

[a] This is the edition by Johann Ruysch.

[b] "Mountain" and "very high mountain" are interchanged with allusions to pearl fishing.

[c] "Cape desired."

[d] "This sea is of fresh water."

[e] Cf. Gorffo Spemoso in Joannes de Stobnicza's map, *Introductio in Phtholomei Cosmographiam* (Cracow, 1512); wrongly spelled "Spemosa" in Nordenskiöld 1973, 69a.

[f] See D. B. Quinn 1976, esp. 638, 640, 643–6 and his index under Cannibalism.

[g] "Safe harbor."

[h] This, rather than *referis*, seems to be what is printed; if so, it must be a corruption but from a manuscript map, not directly from the clear capitals of the Ruysch map.

The 1525 Strasbourg edition, also by Lorenz Fries, included Greenland (called Engroneland) as part of Scandinavia, an area where men "practice free love: none recognize regular marriage" ("utuntur foeminis vulgo: certum matrimonium nullis"). The editor's preface includes a substantial section on Columbus and his discovery of six islands, of which the two largest were Hispania and Ioanna.

What may be called the last of the Strasbourg maps was not printed there nor by an editor working there. Michael Servetus has come down to history as one who was burned at the stake as a heretic. Among his heresies were denying the Trinity and maintaining that the Holy Land had never been a land of milk and honey. His edition of Ptolemy (1541) came out as edited by Michael Villanovanus, this pseudonym being derived from his hometown, Villanueva, Spain, and it was said, perhaps as a disguise, to have been published at Lyon. The debt to Strasbourg maps is evident, and it seems to be acknowledged. Thus the portolan map (see fig. 11.3) includes in its heading across the full map the words "most carefully drawn in 1522" ("exactissime depicta 1522"). Greenland is attached to Europe but has become an island. Of islands in America, only Spagnola and Ijsabella [sic] are shown, and the only mainland shown is a large part of South America, called America. Apart from Caput S. cru(cis), the only names given are Batoia and Cambales, a misreading of Canibales.

On the "Tabula moderna" of America (see fig. 11.4), the Atlantic is carelessly called OCEANVNVS (changed to OCEANVNVS, i.e., Oceanus) OCCIDENTALIS. The North American mainland is called Parias, a name more often attached to part of South America. The latter is named Terra Nova. It not only has the usual text about Columbus's discovery but also includes a drawing of an indigenous family and an unknown animal, with the words "here are cannibals" ("Antropophagi hic sunt"). The caption on Hispaniola may be rendered: "The inhabitants, instead of bread, eat very large snakes and sweet roots that taste like chestnuts."

To follow the tradition, the navigator's chart, Charta marina nova tabula, in the Gastaldi Ptolemy atlas (Venice, 1548) combines East Asia with North America somewhat in the manner of the 1508 Ruysch map, except that here, among the regional names, India and India Superior appear in the same landmass with Florida (Shirley 1984, 99–100). This map was copied by Ruscelli in his 1561 Venice edition despite the fact that the Basel 1552 Ptolemy (fig. 11.5) had shown North and South America as an island. Editions of Ptolemy continued to be turned out long after the more prolific period. The reading public had

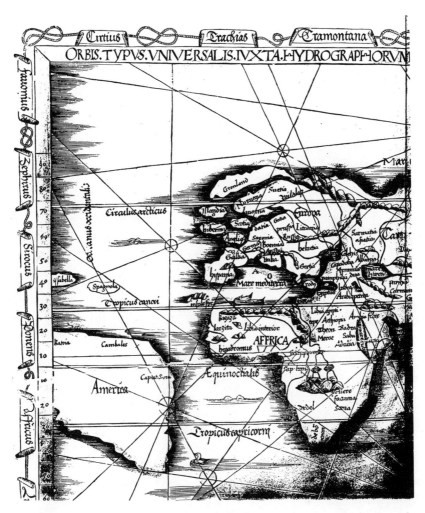

FIGURE 11.3. Detail of the *Orbis typus universalis* showing a portion of America and two of its islands. (From Ptolemy, *Geography* [Lyon, 1541].)

for many years become so used to thinking of the name Ptolemy as the most scientific worker in the field, not only in antiquity but long after, that it had survived two shocks. The first was that the southern regions of the Old World came to be changed. All extant Greek manuscripts of Ptolemy's *Geography* show that Africa could not be circumnavigated. Whether this was Ptolemy's intention is not certain, especially as it had already been circumnavigated in

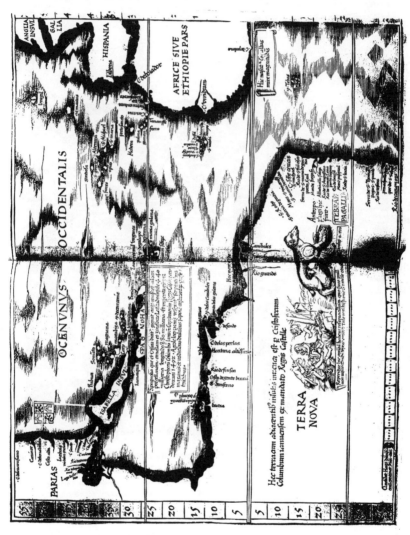

FIGURE 11.4. Illustrations adorn the Tabula moderna, which refers to cannibalism and to Columbus's landfall, and recasts the name of North America. (From Ptolemy, Geography [Lyon, 1541].)

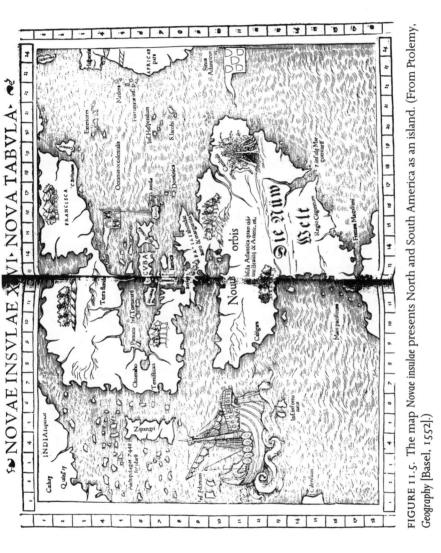

FIGURE 11.5. The map *Novae insulae* presents North and South America as an island. (From Ptolemy, *Geography* [Basel, 1552].)

antiquity.[21] When, however, the Portuguese proved that it could be, and Venetian maps from about 1415 onward portrayed Africa as surrounded by sea on the south, informed opinion changed. Fra Mauro, maker of the 1459 world map, was not afraid of contradicting Ptolemy. Aeneas Silvius Piccolomini (Pope Pius II, d. 1464), a copy of whose *Historia rerum ubique gestarum* (1477) was in Christopher Columbus's library, suggested that the traditional Ptolemaic understanding of the shape of southern Africa and the Indian Ocean should be abandoned. Finally, the fourth map of Africa in the Wilczek-Brown codex of Ptolemy maps,[22] perhaps to be dated about 1480, shows alterations to include a south coast of Africa.

The second shock was the discovery of Central and South America. In the north, Greenland had at first been regarded as an appendage of Europe, and even Cabot's voyages did not identify continental areas. For a long time after Columbus's expedition there was an obsession with proving attachment to Asia, certainly for the more southerly regions. The above-mentioned Basel Ptolemy places Cat(t)igara, from Ptolemy's eleventh map of Asia, in a coastal area of South America that may correspond to Ecuador. D. E. Ibarra Grasso (1970, 199) argued that Ptolemy's eastern Great Gulf was really the Pacific and that, by a misunderstanding of scale, his Cattigara, Rhabana, and Promontory of Satyrs correspond to Trujillo, Tumbes, and Aguja Point in Peru.

The significant fact is that Ptolemy's *Geography* continued, despite all the new knowledge, to be the collecting point for the many changes. The continuation of this series of what we would call atlases established a scientific basis for the development of American cartography. Eventually it was a Ptolemaic scholar who led the way in maintaining that there should be a dichotomy between maps of the Old World as Ptolemy knew it and maps of the whole known world as the people of the Renaissance had come to know it. Gerardus Mercator, who devoted his mature years to atlases (and gave us the word *atlas* in this sense with his *Atlas sive Cosmographiae meditationes*), first, in 1578, produced his beautifully illustrated Ptolemaic atlas of the classical world, *Tabulae Geographicae Claudii Ptolemaei ad mentem autoris restitutae et emendatae* (Maps of Claudius Ptolemy restored and emended to fit the author's intention). Then, from 1585 to 1589 and in a posthumous publication by his son Rumold in 1595, he produced maps of the known world that did not in the least attempt to imitate or accommodate Ptolemy. Only one cartographer, Cornelius Wytfliet (Louvain, 1597), contrived to produce original maps of America and still call his work "a supplement to Ptolemy's *Geography*" (*Descriptionis Ptolemaicae augmentum*). After him, Ptolemy as a continuous atlas maker was allowed to take his rest.

NOTES

1. Bagrow (1945) wrote that the date could have been after the sixth century A.D. This is virtually impossible, since the name is Greek and no Greek cartographers operated in Alexandria after that period.

2. Of the fifty-one entries in Harley and Woodward 1987, 1:272–74, London MS Add. 19391 is, as there indicated, part of Mount Athos, Vatopedi 9.

3. See Babicz forthcoming. *Donnus* is a Late Latin contraction for *dominus* (master). The projection invented by Nicolaus Germanus used to be called the Donis projection, but this is simply a corruption of *Donnus*.

4. It has been shown that the date given, 1462, is incorrect. See Skelton's 1963 preface to his facsimile of the edition *Cosmographia*, Bologna, 1477 (1963), and Campbell 1987a, 129–30.

5. But the longitudinal distances attributed to Toscanelli have been shown to correspond to those on the Behaim globe of 1492.

6. They seem at least to have been still extant during the caliphate of Baghdad.

7. See Morison 1942, 1:103. From the table on that page it will be seen that Alfragan's length of a degree is the lowest only if it is interpreted, as Columbus did, in Roman miles (45.2). If interpreted correctly in Arabic miles, it is the equivalent of 66.2 nautical miles, the highest, as opposed to the modern length of 60 nautical miles. See Mercier 1992.

8. For Graeco-Roman writers on the West, see Sanz López 1958.

9. Tethys, goddess of the ocean, is a better manuscript reading than Tiphys, helmsman of the Argo.

10. See Dilke and Brancati 1979. Unsigned and undated, this map is thought to have been made in Italy. The right margin, near which the coast of eastern Asia is shown, is enigmatically left without a border. Was it torn, or was it perhaps left open for possible additions? North America is given three green ridges, thought to represent Greenland, Labrador, and Nova Scotia, with named physical features. Florida is labeled "beautiful coast" (*costa fermoza*). The coastline of Central America is not shown, but the representation of the South American coast is remarkably good, right down to what may be the estuary of the Río de la Plata. *C. de san domenego* refers to the cape named after Saint Dominic by Amerigo Vespucci on his landfall on 4 August 1499.

11. See the facsimile in Nordenskiöld [1889] 1973, pl. 32.

12. The block was discovered by Donald L. McGuirk of Denver, Colo-

rado, and deciphered by him with the help of Oswald Dilke. See McGuirk 1989 on the Ruysch map, though some of the Latin quotes and some of his translations from the Latin in the essay are incorrect. See also Dilke 1988.

13. Argentin(a)e (Strasbourg) 1513, 1520, 1522, and 1525. See also Sanz López 1959a.

14. *The Martin Waldseemüller 1507 Hauslab-Liechtenstein Globular Map of the World* (auction catalogue, New York, 1950); now in the James Ford Bell Collection, University of Minnesota.

15. See Cortesão 1969–71, 2:522–73; and criticism by Tony Campbell (1987b) in Harley and Woodward 1987, 1:410–11.

16. Thus in the ninth century al-Khwarizmi added new places like Kairouan, Tunisia, by adapting Ptolemaic coordinates in North Africa.

17. See Nordenskiöld [1889] 1973, 68. In a Wolfenbüttel parchment, the name Labrador is said to have been derived from one of the Azores laborers, taken on a Bristol expedition (i.e., by Cabot), who first reported land.

18. See facsimile with introduction by Skelton (1966).

19. For the text, see Nordenskiöld [1889] 1973, 69b, and Skelton 1966, n. 32.

20. For concordances, see Bellio 1892, 2.

21. Herodotus's account of the circumnavigation carried out under the order of Pharaoh Necho, ca. 600 B.C., is discussed well in Thomson 1948, 71–72.

22. The map is at the John Carter Brown Library, Providence, R.I.; see Dilke and Dilke 1988.

BIBLIOGRAPHY

Babicz, J. Forthcoming. The Reception of Ptolemy's *Geography*. In *The History of Cartography*, ed. J. B. Harley and David Woodward, vol. 3. Chicago: University of Chicago Press.

Bagrow, L. 1945. The Origin of Ptolemy's *Geographia*. *Geografiska Annaler* 27: 318–87.

Bellio, V. 1892. Notizie delle più antiche carte geografiche. In *Raccolta Colombiana* (Rome) 4:2.

Campbell, Tony. 1987a. *The Earliest Printed Maps, 1472–1500*. Berkeley: University of California Press.

———. 1987b. Portolan Charts from the Late Thirteenth Century to 1500. In

The History of Cartography, ed. J. B. Harley and David Woodward, 1:371–463. Chicago: University of Chicago Press.

Cortesão, Armando. 1969–71. *History of Portuguese Cartography*. 2 vols. Lisbon and Coimbra: Junta de Investigacões de Ultramar.

Cumming, William P., R. A. Skelton, and D. B. Quinn. 1971. *The Discovery of North America*. London: Elek.

Dilke, Margaret S., and A. Brancati. 1979. The New World in the Pesaro World Map. *Imago Mundi* 31:78–83.

Dilke, Margaret, and Oswald Dilke. 1987. Marin Sanudo: Was He a Great Cartographer? *Map Collector* 39:229–32.

———. 1988. The Wilczek-Brown Codex of Ptolemy Maps. *Imago Mundi* 40: 119–24.

———. 1989. Mapping a Crusade: Propaganda and War in Fourteenth-Century Palestine. *History Today* 39 (August): 31–35.

Dilke, Oswald A. W. 1985. *Greek and Roman Maps*. Ithaca, N.Y.: Cornell University Press.

———. 1988. Note on the Ruysch Palimpsest. *Imago Mundi* 40:132.

———. 1989. *Mathematics and Measurement*. 2d ed. London: British Museum.

———. 1991. Latin Interpretations of Ptolemy's *Geographia*. In *Acta conventus neo-Latini Torontonensis*, ed. Alexander Dalzell, Charles Fantazzi, and Richard J. Schoeck, 293–300. Proceedings of the Seventh International Congress of Neo-Latin Studies, Toronto 1988. Binghamton, N.Y.: International Association for Neo-Latin Studies,

Fischer, Joseph. 1903. *The Discoveries of the Norsemen in America*. Trans. Basil Stanley Soulsby. London: H. Stevens, Sons and Stiles.

———. 1932. *Claudii Ptolemaei Geographiae codex Vaticanus Urbinas graecus 82, phototypice depictus consilio et opera curatorum Bibliothecae Vaticanae.* . . . Leiden: Apud E. J. Brill; and Leipzig: Apud Ottonem Harrassowitz.

Harley, J. B. 1989. Maps, Knowledge and Power. In *The Iconography of Landscape*, ed. Denis Cosgrove and Stephen Daniels, 277–312. Cambridge: Cambridge University Press.

Harley, John Brian, and David Woodward, eds. 1987–. *The History of Cartography*. 2 vols. to date. Chicago: University of Chicago Press.

Honigmann, Ernst. 1929. *Die sieben Klimata und die 'poleis episemoi': Eine Untersuchung zur Geschichte der Geographie und Astrologie im Altertum und Mittelalter*. Heidelberg: C. Winter.

Ibarra Grasso, Dick E. 1970. *La representación de América en mapas romanos de tiempos de Cristo*. Buenos Aires: Ibarra Grasso.

————. 1979. *La representación de América en mapas romanos de tiempos de Cristo.* Buenos Aires: Ediciones Ibarra Grasso.

McGuirk, Donald L., Jr. 1989. Ruysch World Map: Census and Commentary. *Imago Mundi* 41:133–41.

Mercier, Raymond P. 1992. Arabic Scientific Geodesy. In *The History of Cartography,* ed. J. B. Harley and David Woodward, 2:175–88. Chicago: University of Chicago Press.

Morison, Samuel Eliot. 1942. *Admiral of the Ocean Sea.* 2 vols. Boston: Little, Brown and Company.

Nordenskiöld, Adolf Erik. [1889] 1973. *Facsimile Atlas to the Early History of Cartography, with Reproductions of the Most Important Maps Printed in the XV and XVI Centuries.* Trans. Johan Adolf Ekelöf and Clements R. Markham. Introduction by J. B. Post. New York: Dover Publications.

————. 1897. *Periplus: An Essay on the Early History of Charts and Sailing Directions.* Trans. Francis A. Bather. Stockholm: P. A. Norstedt.

Pohl, Frederick J. 1944. *Amerigo Vespucci: Pilot Major.* New York: Columbia University Press.

Polaschek, E. 1959. Ptolemy's *Geography* in a New Light. *Imago Mundi* 14:317–37.

Quinn, D. B. 1976. New Geographical Horizons: Literature. In *First Images of America,* ed. F. Chiappelli, 2:635–58. Berkeley: University of California Press.

Sanz López, Carlos, ed. 1958. *Nociones de los escritores antiguos sobre la existencia de tierras occidentales.* Madrid: Artes Gráficas.

————. 1959a. *El nombre América: Libros y mapas que lo impusieron.* Madrid: Suárez.

————. 1959b. *La Geographia de Ptolomeo ampliada con los primeros mapas impresos de América (desde 1507).* Madrid: Suárez.

Shirley, Rodney W. 1984. *The Mapping of the World: Early Printed World Maps.* London: Holland Press.

Skelton, Raleigh Ashlin L. 1963. *Cosmographia, Bologna, 1477.* Amsterdam: N. Israel.

————. 1966. *Geographia, Florence, 1482.* Amsterdam: N. Israel.

Sylvanus, Bernardus, ed. 1511. *Ptolemaei 'Geographia.'* Venice.

Thomson, James Oliver. 1948. *History of Ancient Geography.* Cambridge: Cambridge University Press.

Thrower, Norman J. W. 1976. New Geographical Horizons: Maps. In *First Im-*

ages of America, ed. F. Chiappelli, 2:659–74. Berkeley: University of California Press.

Toomer, G. J., trans. 1984. *Ptolemy's 'Almagest.'* London and New York: Springer-Verlag.

English Motifs in Mexican Books

A Case of Sixteenth-Century Information Transfer

Antonio Rodríguez-Buckingham

Intellectual content and physical characteristics are the main components of books. Studies of the first are the realm of most disciplines, whereas those of the second are generally associated with descriptive bibliography. The physical format of the early printed page includes printing equipment such as type and wood blocks, ink, and the press itself; the paper on which these devices leave their mark; and the binding that holds the whole together. However, a study of the physical components of books may transcend the limits of strict description by approaching the book as an artifact that synthesizes Western thought better than any other. This essay is an interpretation of the similarities and an analysis of the motifs—or themes in the illustrations—noted in eighteen initial letters and engravings found in twenty-one Mexican and European books from the sixteenth century. The evidence reinforces my previous research suggesting a need to reevaluate widely accepted beliefs about early bookmaking in the Spanish colonies of America.

To study the book as an artifact, we must view it as an object whose time and place of origin are often revealed as much by physical format as by intellectual content. Most studies of the physical format of printed books are stylistic analyses of the vast array of images imprinted on the paper. The staggering difficulty of such analyses becomes clear if one considers the distinction between the equipment that produced an image and the actual image seen on a printed page. Type and metal or wood engravings of decorative initials, illustrations, and vignettes are tangible equipment that leave their images on paper in the process of printing. The term *engraving* is applied in this essay to both the metal plate or wood block and the figure printed on the page. We must keep in mind at all times, however, that the element analyzed is the image, not the metal plate or wood block itself. Since most of the early printing equipment has disappeared, the evidence is largely the letters—known as typefaces—and the other images printed in books. Thus, while such evidence is analogous to a footprint left in mud at the scene of a crime, the typographic historian's detective work is compounded by having to identify thousands of "footprints" made by shoes that, for the most part, no longer exist.

Because more than a third of all fifteenth-century printed works contain no information as to where and when they were produced, incunabulists like Konrad Haebler, Curt F. Buehler, Stanley Morison, and Daniel Berkeley Updike soon recognized the value of analyzing illustrations and typefaces for the study of bookmaking.[1] The great diversity of manuscript letters available as models for fifteenth-century printers resulted in the production of a vast array of printed letterforms. Thus the main task of early incunabulists was the painstaking identification of all the existing families of typefaces. Decorative initials, illustrations, binding styles, and the composition of the paper and ink used in incunabula were also studied.[2] Consequently, knowledge about fifteenth-century books is considerable. More recently, scholars have applied some principles of the study of incunabula to the analysis of books from the sixteenth century on, though with some methodological differences.

The first task of historians of sixteenth-century typography was to classify all available typefaces as either gothic, roman, or italic—the three families of letters that have prevailed since about 1500. By studying the general presentation of a printed page and the decorative initials, illustrations, typefaces, and vignettes employed, particular solutions for logistical, design, and aesthetic problems could be identified. The next task was to trace the origin of fonts across space and time and to fit them into a broad and meaningful historical framework (Carter 1969, 4). Letters with an identical design or illustrations with the same motifs enabled researchers to clarify business relations between printing houses and to chart the trade routes of the book industry.

The value of using illustrations or decorative initial letters as tools for historical research requires clarification. The fact that books from different locations or periods of time—here referred to as the books' provenance—exhibit similar initial letters does not necessarily imply a direct connection between the printing houses that produced them. The high level of skill of sixteenth-century engravers coupled with the considerable efficiency of the distribution networks make it possible for books of diverse provenance to exhibit identical initials. In such instances, initials may be used to support other kinds of evidence of direct interactions, such as documentary evidence. On the other hand, slight differences in motifs among initials in books of different provenance are more important for historical research than the obvious similarities. In comparing such initials for both similarities and differences, scholars should consider two points. First, the printers may have acquired their equipment from a common source, such as a book fair, and second, the means necessary to do engraving may have existed near or within the printing shop. The production of new engraving plates would have required samples of the copied book—which were probably at hand—and skilled individuals either directly or indirectly associated with the press. These collaborative associations, which in Europe were very complex, were further complicated in America by the environment and the geographic isolation in which the printers operated. For example, the printers had no book fairs to act as important distribution networks.

Typographic History and the New World

The first printer in the Americas was Juan Pablos, an Italian from Brescia who had worked in the Cromberger printing shop in Seville. He signed a contract on 12 June 1539 to represent the firm and print books under its name in Mexico City (Carlo and Calvo 1953). Pablos's earliest imprint—whose location is presently unknown—dates from 1539, and his latest from 1560. Another printer, Estéban Martín, lived in Mexico before Pablos, but if he worked there, his imprints are unknown. Antonio de Espinosa, a Spaniard from Jaen who moved to Mexico to work for Pablos, began to print on his own in 1559, becoming the second printer in the Western Hemisphere. Three other printers began work in Mexico before 1580: Pedro Ocharte (1563–92), a Frenchman from Rouen; Pedro Balli (1574–1600), also a Frenchman; and Antonio Ricardo (1576–79), an Italian from Turin who moved to Peru in 1580, becoming the first printer in South America.[3]

While early bibliographers have recorded the production of these presses in monumental scholarly works (e.g., Valton 1935), the history of their typography has remained largely unstudied, particularly in the English-speaking world. This lack of attention is due to at least four misconceptions. The first is that bookmaking in the New World during the colonial period was a mere replica of the work then being done in Spain. This view implies that Spain was the exclusive source of the labor, printing ideas, and equipment for the early presses of Spanish America. Scholars seem to assume that since the relationship between the colonies and the mother country was one of absolute dependency—as indeed it was in many respects—the Spanish colonial administration could control the huge body of ideas flowing, often inconspicuously, to America from Renaissance Europe. The fact that four of the first five printers in the Western Hemisphere were non-Spaniards strongly contradicts this point. These individuals had direct exposure to the milieu of sixteenth-century Italy and France, which is often reflected in the books they produced while in the colonies.[4]

A second misconception is that early printing in America had little or no effect on printing in Europe at the time. Historians have confined their studies to a particular country or continent, assuming that an exported information technology, superimposed on an alien culture, would reveal nothing of the place from which that technology originated. In his world history of typefaces, Daniel Berkeley Updike excludes Latin American books because, he says, "they had so little influence on typographical usage in general that they are beyond the boundaries of the subject of this book" (Updike 1966, 2:60). J. H. Elliott, one of the foremost scholars in New World studies, objects that the literature from early periods of European colonization, while enormous, is often presented as "fragmentary and disconnected, as if it formed a special field of historical study of its own" (Elliott 1970, 6).

A third scholarly misconception is that Latin American books—often octavos printed with old fonts used by the Cromberger press of Seville and, after 1550, with a mixed typography of gothic and roman fonts—were "generally inferior" in quality to those printed in Europe (Haring 1963, 229). Historians have assumed that the combined use of different type families, particularly roman and gothic, in some Mexican books was not up to the standards of good printing. Since printing aesthetics is a somatic issue requiring the actual examination of texts, it is not discussed here. However, to appreciate the quality of these early imprints, one must recognize the printers' effective use of the resources available in the surrounding area. Economy is the essence of all good printing; it characterizes the works of even the great masters. The combination of different typefaces noted in many Mexican books should be viewed as the printers' response to the scarcity of materials coupled with a demand for printing. As may be seen in many of Espinosa's and Ocharte's imprints, this combination often makes a positive impression on the reader. The works of Ricardo in both Mexico and Peru, which always exhibit roman typefaces, are often examples of fine printing (Rodríguez-Buckingham 1977).

Finally, a fourth misconception is that the presses of Mexico and Peru were not very active, the sole reason for their existence being to print religious books in native tongues for the friars to use to teach the Indians (see Elliot 1984, 1:336; Escolar Sobrino 1984, 354–58; Leonard 1964, 198; and Steinberg 1974, 98). But it is erroneous to assume that sale of religious books in native tongues to agencies of the Church or the Crown gave printers sufficient business. Recent studies show that a fair diversity of subjects existed among the printed books of the early colonies, and that the production of broadsides for legal and administrative purposes, the printing of religious images for quick sale, and the making of playing cards probably constituted the main portion of printers' incomes (Rodríguez-Buckingham 1979).

My research strongly suggests that printing technology in America acquired distinctive characteristics relatively early in its history. It is true that the gothic type and decorative initials used by Juan Pablos in his earliest imprints had been used by the Cromberger firm of Seville, but from 1554 on, his books and those of his successors exhibit a variety of roman typefaces and decorative initials whose motifs and designs are found in books originally printed in England, Belgium, and of course, Spain (Rodríguez-Buckingham 1989). Their appearance coincides with the arrival in Mexico in 1550 of the type designer, engraver, and later printer Antonio de Espinosa (Rodríguez-Buckingham 1984a, 1984b). A contract between Juan Pablos and Antonio de Espinosa signed in Spain on 24 September 1550 required Espinosa to move to Mexico with an assistant to "cut and cast type" for Pablos (McMurtrie 1927). Espinosa probably brought equipment from Spain, but his typography needs to be more thoroughly studied.[5]

After Pablos's death, Ocharte, who was a friend of the printer's family, rented the press from his widow and proceeded to solidify the relationship by marrying the couple's daughter. Not only did Ocharte himself print with his father-in-law's equipment, he also commissioned Espinosa and Juan Ortiz, a French engraver, to do special work for the press (Stols 1962, 7). The appearance in Mexican books of a new set of roman characters in the mid-1570s coincides with the arrival of Antonio Ricardo, another Ocharte associate. Ricardo took his own and part of Ocharte's equipment with him to Peru. Some of the decorative initials he used in Lima have motifs identical to those used in Venetian and Lyonnaise books, while others have been traced to specific Spanish printing establishments (Rodríguez-Buckingham 1984a, 72).

Printing in Europe and America

By the year 1539, when printing was introduced to America, the European enterprise had attained the features of a "big business." Some printing establishments were large enough to require the division of labor as a managerial solution to the demand for greater production. The printing process had evolved into an elaborate sequence of techniques and procedures that later ushered in the distinction between the printing shop and the publishing house. Printers were located mainly in large cities, and the urban milieu fostered the necessary professional interactions among them. Similarities in the motifs and designs of initials are a common occurrence in sixteenth-century European books, though they have not been thoroughly studied. Printers bought their equipment mainly at book fairs, either in person or through contacts they had with people in the trade. In addition, the urban environment provided the printing shops with an ample supply of skilled laborers, who often worked as freelancers under contract. All this suggests that European printers obtained both their equipment and their knowledge of book technology through a complex network of sources, which often crossed the geographic and even religious boundaries that normally separated sixteenth-century Europe.

The American environment presented a special set of challenges to printers. Technical and managerial adjustments were necessary in the face of the New World's isolation. Perhaps the most serious obstacles were a lack of peer evaluation and an absence of the creative spark often ignited by intellectual exchange and professional discussion. While documents state that skilled laborers moved to the New World to work for the printers there, the documents also stress the specific need for people with engraving, punch-cutting, matrix-justifying, and typefounding skills (Carlo and Calvo 1953).

American printers overcame these obstacles in at least three ways. The first was by returning to a broad array of procedures that by that time in Europe belonged solely to skilled, specialized technicians working in segmented operations. This more general approach had been used by the European printers in earlier years. In the fifteenth century, when bookmaking was in *cunae*—from which the term *incunabula* is derived—printers did a great deal of the work that was later executed by specialists. The second way the printers overcame the obstacle of isolation was by using the European books in the monastic libraries of the New World as models of book design (Rodríguez-Buckingham 1989). Finally, American printers saw the advantage of utilizing the unique labor resources and raw materials available in the new environment.

In the absence of a support system analogous to the professional networks in Europe, the pioneer printers of America probably filled the demand for production by using local labor. This labor force undoubtedly included Native Americans, carefully trained in certain aspects of the printing process by Spanish supervisors. After all, the printers of Mexico and Peru were surrounded by native artisans whose cultures included rich traditions of sophisticated metallurgy and stone and wood engraving. One of the foremost scholars of colonial Mexico, Charles Gibson, indicates that a large number of crafts were being practiced by Indian artisans by the middle of the sixteenth century. Documents confirm "the statement of a Spaniard of 1569 that there was then no trade in the city that Indians had not learned" (Gibson 1964, 397–98). A similar situation is noted in colonial Peru. James Lockhart, an authority in colonial Peru, states that during the first half of the 1550s some Peruvian Indians began to appear in the shops of Spanish artisans. Indian boys "also began to enter formal apprenticeship under Spanish artisans, so that by 1560 it appears that Peruvian Indians were finally preparing to take a place in Spanish artisanry alongside the Spaniards and the Negroes" (Lockhart 1968, 218). Peruvian documents specifically mention Indians working under contract to Antonio Ricardo and natives allocated by the Crown to help him in his shop (see Márquez Abanto 1955, 295; and Medina [1904] 1965a, 1:438–39). While it is reasonable to conclude that Amerindians worked in the early printing shops, their influence on the books they helped to produce is barely noticeable. However, there do seem to be subtle elements in some illustrations that suggest parallels between images from sixteenth-century Mexican printed books and contemporary native manuscripts.

The Decorative Initials of Mexican and European Books

For approximately twenty-five years I have been compiling copies of decorative initials, illustrations, typefaces, and other physical evidence of sixteenth-century books from Mexico and Peru. In the process I have also collected samples from Spanish, English, Flemish, Italian, and French books that include some 5,000 initial letters alone.[6] This body of information, while far from complete, has enabled me to characterize Spanish-American printed images and their possible origin in the printing establishments of Europe. As noted above, the evidence has sometimes supported and at other times contradicted the observations and conclusions scholars have made about the book industry in the New World.[7]

A complete list of the twenty-one books examined for this essay is given in the Appendix. Two of these books were printed in Antwerp, four in London, fourteen in Mexico City, and one in Valladolid, Spain. The figures show

FIGURE 12.1. Initials showing the Elephant Man from (a) London, (b) Mexico, and (c) Mexico (variant).

the initials and engravings discussed here, accompanied by references to the books in which they are found. The initials in figures 12.1 to 12.5 appear in books printed by Edward Whitchurch, Richard Grafton, Guihelmi Powell, and William Bohan in London, by Juan Pablos and Pedro Ocharte in Mexico City, and by Christophe Plantin in Antwerp.

When comparing European and New World specimens, the variations of execution shown in figures 12.1, "Elephant Man," and 12.2, "Castaway," deserve special consideration. Though the "Elephant Man" initials are not identical, the London version and the Mexican "variant" are similar in detail, including the headdress of the anthropomorphic elephant. The other Mexican initial (fig. 12.1, Mexico) shows the elephant wearing a robe that resembles the one seen in the variant and a crown rather than a headdress. Stephen

FIGURE 12.2. Versions of the Castaway from (a) London, (b) Mexico, and (c) Antwerp.

Harvard, an authority on book illustration, reports that an initial—also with a crown—similar to the Mexican example was used in two books printed in Antwerp by Christophe Plantin in 1571 and 1589.[8] It is noteworthy that the dates would place the initial as appearing in Antwerp after it was used in either London or Mexico.

Figure 12.2, "Castaway," shows initials from London, Mexico City, and Antwerp. The Antwerp specimen, which was located in the Plantin books examined by Harvard, is almost identical to the initial from London, particularly with reference to the masts and sails on the ships. The Mexican initial, on the other hand, differs from the two European examples in that the ship lacks the rudder at the stern of the ship. Since the Mexican initial appears unchanged in a number of books, it seems safe to assume that the engraving was originally without these features.

A   B

FIGURE 12.3. Depictions of "Man and Woman" from (a) London and (b) Mexico.

An understanding of various engraving processes enhances the comparison of some of these decorative initials. Figure 12.3, "Man and Woman," shows English and Mexican initials with the same motif but made using different techniques. The Mexican initial was probably cut in wood, while the specimen from London was engraved in metal, possibly in relief.[9] The English and Mexican initials shown in figures 12.4, "E Arabesque," and 12.5, "I Arabesque," are almost indistinguishable from one another. The technique used to make them, known as the *manière criblée*, is characterized by groups of dots produced by sieve-like punches on either metal or wood (Hind [1935] 1963, 1:20). Because the technique leaves random marks in the background of the figure, images of initials with an identical distribution of dots were assuredly

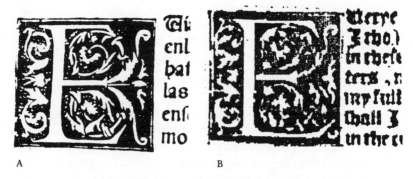

A   B

FIGURE 12.4. Designs of E Arabesque from (a) Mexico and (b) London.

made with the same woodblock or metal engraving. Note, however, that the initials shown in both figures, while almost identical in other respects, differ in the distribution of dots.

Further evidence of engraving activity in the New World is provided by some of the illustrations used in books. For example, figures 12.6a and 12.6b, "Doctors," from Valladolid and Mexico City, portray a common motif of the Middle Ages and the Renaissance: two physicians inspecting a bottle and noting their observations on a tablet. A closer inspection of the illustrations reveals that the figures are drawn in mirror image to each other. The position of the figures, especially the manner in which the robes fold, when reversed (see fig. 12.7, which shows the figures from Mexico reversed with the aid of a computer) corresponds to such an extent that the similarity can hardly be thought of as coincidental. The person who worked on the Mexican engraving probably had the illustration from Valladolid very near at hand.

A   B

FIGURE 12.5. Designs of I Arabesque from (a) Mexico and (b) London.

A   B

FIGURE 12.6. Two scenes of doctors examining the contents of a bottle, from
(a) Valladolid (Aberacin 1516) and (b) Mexico (López de Hinojosos 1578).

The "Head of Christ" in figure 12.8a appeared for the first time in 1565 in
Espinosa's printing of Alonso de Molina's *Confesionario mayor*, one of the printer's greatest achievements. Copies of the illustration are also seen in books
printed by Ocharte and Ricardo. It is unknown whether Pablos or Espinosa
brought the woodblock or a book from Spain, but it is unlikely to have been
the original work of a local artist. However, the variants of the figure used in
books by Ocharte and Ricardo probably were produced from woodblocks
made in America (see fig. 12.8b and c). More important, the angels around

A   B

FIGURE 12.7. The doctors from figure 12.6, with those from the Mexican
engraving reversed.

A

B

FIGURE 12.8. Three engravings of
the head of Christ from Mexico by (a)
Espinosa (Molina 1565), (b) Ocharte and
Ricardo (Cordova 1578), and (c) Ocharte
(Molina 1578).

C

FIGURE 12.9. A circle from the *Florentine Codex*, from Mexico.

the head of the figure are similar to those adorning Book VII of the native Mexican manuscript known as the *Florentine Codex* (fig. 12.9, from Robertson 1959, pl. 64). The codex is the final and complete version of an ethnographic manuscript from early Mexico entitled *Historia general de las cosas de la Nueva España*. Composed by carefully trained Mexican natives under the direction of Fray Bernardino de Sahagún, the main text of the book is in Nahuatl, with a parallel Spanish text. In addition, the codex contains 1,846 drawings and an assortment of decorative tailpieces and ornamental designs (Glass and Robertson 1976, 14:190). According to Donald Robertson, an authority on early Mexican manuscripts, the major part of the work was made between 1566 and 1577, and the last of its twelve books was finished in 1586. The codex was made as a "clean copy" to be brought to Spain by Fray Rodrigo de Sequera (Robertson 1959, 173).[10] Upon examining the manuscript, Robertson noticed that, for the early parts of the work, Sahagún depended on this text of written Nahuatl and the pictures made and explained by his native informants when he prepared the Spanish translation. Robertson states: "The original vehicle of the idea then was the pictorial content with a verbal explanation. This is the old native tradition as we have described it from sixteenth century Spanish sources" (1959, 174). Sahagún depended on the 1529 Toledo edition of *De proprietatibus rerum*, by the thirteenth-century author Bartholomaeus Anglicus, for his own contribution to the *Historia general*. Robertson notes the similarity between a woodcut used in that book and the illustration from the codex shown in figure 12.9.

Considering the far-reaching impact of Sahagún's influence on the culture of early colonial Mexico, it is reasonable to argue that the apprentices to the presses and some of the pupils of Sahagún had similar backgrounds and were probably trained in similar fashion. Some of them, in fact, may have been both students and apprentices. This argument is supported by the similarity in physical format and time of manufacture between the image from the codex and the "Head of Christ," and by the fact that later in the century Ocharte's widow moved the press to the college founded by Sahagún at Tlatelolco in Mexico City (Mathes 1982, 36).

Conclusion

The early Mexican books studied here contain illustrations and decorative initials whose motifs and designs are similar to those used by several printers in London and by at least one Flemish printer. Though there are great similarities between these European and New World initials, the details that differentiate them strongly support documentary evidence of a local professional network very early in the history of Mexican printing. This diversity of motifs and designs negates the notion held by many scholars that early Mexican printing was no more than a replica of printing in contemporary Spain. Although there is little doubt that colonial printers used the labor of Native Americans, the question of their influence on the design of books remains unanswered. The repetition of images in printed books and early manuscripts from colonial Mexico suggests that the training of apprentices was similar to that received by the informants of Fray Bernardino de Sahagún. Finally, similarities exist among initials used by various printers in London, and some of the initials have motifs identical to those used in Antwerp. Likewise, earlier studies have found motifs in Mexican and Peruvian books that are similar to those in Venetian and Lyonnaise books, and also to several Flemish books. The temporal overlap and design similarities found in New World printing support the argument that American typography had a definite impact on its European counterpart.

APPENDIX

Books Whose Initial Letters Were Examined in This Essay

Antwerp:

    Baronius. 1589. *Martryologium romanum.* 2 vols. Christophe Plantin.

    Garibay y Zamalloa, Estéban de. 1589. *Compendio historial de las crónicas y universal historia de todos los reynos de España.* 4 vols. Christophe Plantin.

London:

Chaucer, Geoffrey. 1542. *The Works of Geffray Chaucer*. William Boham.

Church of England. 1549. *The Booke of Common Prayer*. Richard Grafton.

———. 1554. *The Booke of Common Prayer*. Edward Whitchurch.

Martyr, Peter, of Anglería. 1555. *The Decades of the Newe World of West Indies*. Guihelmi Powell.

Mexico City:

Bravo, Francisco. 1570. *Opera medicinalia*. Pedro Ocharte.

Catholic Church. Archbishopric of Mexico. 1556. *Constituciones del Arzobispado de México*. Juan Pablos.

Catholic Church. Order of St. Augustine. 1556. *Constituciones fratum haeremitarum*. Juan Pablos.

Cordova, Juan de. 1578. *Vocabulario en lengua zapoteca*. Pedro Ocharte and Antonio Ricardo.

Gilberti, Maturino. 1559. *Vocabulario en lengua de Michoacán*. Juan Pablos.

Gutiérrez de la Vera Cruz, Alonso. 1554. *Recognitio summularum*. Juan Pablos.

———. 1556. *Speculum coniugiorum*. Juan Pablos.

———. 1557. *Phisica speculatio*. Juan Pablos.

Hernández, Benito. 1568. *Doctrina christiana en lengua mixteca*. Pedro Ocharte.

López de Hinojosos, Alonso. 1578. *Suma y recopilación de chirugía*. Antonio Ricardo.

Molina, Alonso de. 1555. *Aquí comienza un vocabulario en la lengua castellana y mexicana*. Juan Pablos.

———. 1565. *Confesionario mayor*. Antonio de Espinosa.

Sahagún, Bernardino de. 1577? *Historia general de las cosas de la Nueva España* [Florentine Codex]. Book VII, pt. 1. Mexico City.

Vasco de Puga. 1563. *Provisiones, cédulas, instrucciones*. Pedro Ocharte.

Valladolid:

Ben Aberacin, Albuchasis. 1516. *Servidor de Albuchasis*. Arnaldo Guillén de Brocar.

NOTES

1. Incunabula are books printed before 1501. For some recent works by outstanding incunabulists, see Buehler 1973; Haebler 1968; Morison 1963; and Updike 1966.

2. Recent examples of the product of such study include Needham 1985 and Schwab et al. 1985.

3. The best biographical information about the first printers of the New World is provided in García Icazbalceta 1954; Medina [1904] 1965a, [1912] 1965b; Valton 1935; and Wagner 1940.

4. See Rodríguez-Buckingham 1984a and the expanded Spanish version of the article (Rodríguez-Buckingham 1984b).

5. For excellent studies of Espinosa and Ocharte, see Stols 1962a and 1962b.

6. This body of information was considerably increased during the summer of 1991 thanks to a four-month research trip to Spain, mainly Seville, sponsored by the National Endowment for the Humanities and monitored by the Center for Latin American Studies at Ohio State University and the Centro de Estudios Hispano-Americanos in Seville.

7. With the help of an Abaton 300 AB scanner; a Macintosh SE computer; and C-Scan Plus, Hypercard, and Superpaint programs, I am presently developing an electronic database of images and texts of sixteenth-century books. This hardware and software have been used for nearly all of the illustrations in this chapter.

8. I was unable to locate the initial in the copies housed at the British Library, perhaps because it appears only in variants of those books. Harvard (1974, no. 46) indicates that this initial appears in Garibay y Zamalloa 1571 and Baronius 1589.

9. For an explanation of the techniques involved in this type of illustration, see Hind [1935] 1963, 1:175–97.

10. The manuscript is now housed at the Laurentian Library in Florence.

BIBLIOGRAPHY

Baronius. 1589. *Martyrologium romanum*. 2 vols. Antwerp: Christophe Plantin.

Buehler, Curt F. 1973. *Early Books and Manuscripts: Forty Years of Research*. New York: Grolier Club and the Pierpont Morgan Library.

Carlo, Agustín Millarres, and Julian Calvo. 1953. *Juan Pablos: Primer impresor que a esta tierra vino*. Mexico City: Librería de Manuel Porrúa.

Carter, Harry. 1969. *A View of Early Typography*. Oxford: Clarendon Press.

Elliott, J. H. 1970. *The Old World and the New, 1492–1650*. Cambridge: Cambridge University Press.

———. 1984. Spain and America in the Sixteenth and Seventeenth Centuries. In *The Cambridge History of Latin America*, ed. Leslie Bethell, 1:287–339. Cambridge: Cambridge University Press.

Escolar Sobrino, Hipólito. 1984. *Historia del libro*. Madrid: Fundación Germán Sánchez Ruipérez.

García Icazbalceta, Joaquín. 1954. *Bibliografía mexicana del siglo XVI*. Mexico City: Fondo de Cultura Económica.

Garibay y Zamalloa, Estéban de. 1571. *Compendio historial de las crónicas y historia universal de todos los reynos de España*. 4 vols. Antwerp: Christophe Plantin.

Gibson, Charles. 1964. *The Aztecs Under Spanish Rule: A History of the Indians of the Valley of Mexico, 1519–1810*. Stanford, Calif.: Stanford University Press.

Glass, John B., and Donald Robertson. 1976. A Census of Native Middle American Pictorial Manuscripts. In *Handbook of Middle American Indians*, ed. Robert Wauchope, vol. 14, pt. 3: *Guide to Ethnohistorical Sources*, ed. Howard F. Cline, 81–252. Austin: University of Texas Press.

Haebler, Konrad. 1968. *Typenrepertorium de Wiegendrucke*. 5 vols. Netherlands and Liechtenstein: Kraus.

Haring, Kenneth H. 1963. *The Spanish Empire in America*. New York: Harcourt, Brace and World.

Harvard, Stephen. 1974. *Ornamental Initials: The Woodcut Initials of Christophe Plantin; A Complete Catalogue by Stephen Harvard*. New York: American Friends of the Plantin-Moretus Museum.

Hind, Arthur M. [1935] 1963. *An Introduction to the History of Woodcut with Detailed Survey Work Done in the Fifteenth Century*. 2 vols. New York: Dover.

Leonard, Irving A. 1964. *Books of the Brave: Being an Account of Books and of Men in the Spanish Conquest and Settlement of the Sixteenth Century New World*. New York: Gordian Press.

Lockhart, James. 1968. *Spanish Peru, 1532–60: A Colonial Society*. Madison: University of Wisconsin Press.

McMurtrie, Douglas C. 1927. The First Type-Founding in Mexico. *The Library: A Quarterly Review of Bibliography* 8 (June): 119–22.

Márquez Abanto, Alberto. 1955. Don Antonio Ricardo: Introductor de la imprenta en Lima; Su testamento y codicilio. *Revista del Archivo Nacional del Perú* 19:295.

Mathes, Miguel. 1982. *Santa Cruz de Tlatelolco: La primera biblioteca académica de las Américas*. Mexico City: Secretaria de Relaciones Exteriores.

Medina, José Toribio. [1904] 1965b. *La imprenta en Lima, 1584–1824*. Vol. 1. Reprint. Amsterdam: N. Israel.

———. [1912] 1965a. *La imprenta en México, 1539–1821*. Vol. 1. Reprint. Amsterdam: N. Israel.

Morison, Stanley. 1963. Preface: On the Classification of Typographical Variations. In *Type Specimen Facsimiles: Reproductions of Fifteen Type Specimen Sheets Issued Between the Sixteenth and the Eighteenth Centuries*, ed. J. Dreyfus. London: Bowse and Bowse.

Needham, Paul. 1985. The Paper Supply of the Gutenberg Bible. *Papers of the Bibliographical Society of America* 79:303–74.

Robertson, Donald. 1959. *Mexican Manuscript Painting of the Early Colonial Period: The Metropolitan Schools*. New Haven, Conn.: Yale University Press.

Rodríguez-Buckingham, Antonio. 1977. Colonial Peru and the Printing Press of Antonio Ricardo. Ph.D. diss., University of Michigan, Ann Arbor.

———. 1979. The Arm of Spain: Content Analysis of the Materials Printed in Mexico and Peru in the Sixteenth Century. In *Latin American Studies in Europe*, ed. Anne H. Jordan, 249–80. Austin: University of Texas Press.

———. 1984a. The Renaissance in the New World: Printing in Colonial South America. *Explorations in Renaissance Culture* 10:67–79.

———. 1984b. Antonio Ricardo: Impresor renacentista. *Revista de la Universidad Católica* (Lima), new ser., 15–16:129–48.

———. 1989. Monastic Libraries and Early Printing in Sixteenth-Century Spanish America. *Libraries and Culture* 24 (Winter): 35–40.

Schwab, Richard N., et al. 1985. New Evidence on the Printing of the Gutenberg Bible: The Inks in the Doheny Copy. *Papers of the Bibliographical Society of America* 79:375–410.

Steinberg, S. H. 1974. *Five Hundred Years of Printing*. Harmondsworth, U.K.: Penguin Books.

Stols, Alexander A. M. 1962a. *Antonio de Espinosa: El segundo impresor mexicano*. Biblioteca Nacional, Instituto Bibliográfico Mexicano, No. 7. Mexico City: Universidad Nacional Autónoma de México.

———. 1962b. *Pedro Ocharte: El tercer impresor mexicano*. Mexico City: Imprenta Año Nuevo.

Updike, Daniel B. 1966. *Printing Types: Their History, Forms and Use; A Study of Survivals*. 2 vols. Cambridge, Mass.: Harvard University Press.

Valton, Emilio. 1935. *Biblioteca Nacional de México: Impresos mexicanos del siglo XVI; Incunables americanos, Estudio bibliográfico con una introducción sobre el origen de la imprenta en América*. Mexico City: Imprenta Universitaria.

Wagner, Enrique R. 1940. *Nueva bibliografía mexicana del siglo XVI: Suplemento a las bibliografías de Don Joaquín García Icazbalceta, Don José Toribio Medina y Don Nicolás León*. Trans. Joaquín García Pimentel and Federico Gómez de Orozco. Mexico City: Editorial Polis.

Index